FERTILE GROUND

Fertile Ground

Exploring Reproduction in Canada

EDITED BY

Stephanie Paterson, Francesca Scala,
and Marlene K. Sokolon

McGill-Queen's University Press
Montreal & Kingston · London · Ithaca

© McGill-Queen's University Press 2014

ISBN 978-0-7735-4368-3 (cloth)
ISBN 978-0-7735-4369-0 (paper)
ISBN 978-0-7735-9212-4 (ePUB)
ISBN 978-0-7735-9213-1 (ePDF)

Legal deposit second quarter 2014
Bibliothèque nationale du Québec

Printed in Canada on acid-free paper that is 100% ancient forest free
(100% post-consumer recycled), processed chlorine free

This book has been published with the help of a grant from the Canadian
Federation for the Humanities and Social Sciences, through the Awards to
Scholarly Publications Program, using funds provided by the Social Sciences
and Humanities Research Council of Canada.

McGill-Queen's University Press acknowledges the support of the Canada
Council for the Arts for our publishing program. We also acknowledge the
financial support of the Government of Canada through the Canada Book
Fund for our publishing activities.

Library and Archives Canada Cataloguing in Publication

Fertile ground (2014)
    Fertile ground: exploring reproduction in Canada / edited by
Stephanie Paterson, Francesca Scala, and Marlene K. Sokolon.

    Includes bibliographical references and index.
    Issued in print and electronic formats.
    ISBN 978-0-7735-4368-3 (bound). – ISBN 978-0-7735-4369-0 (pbk.). –
ISBN 978-0-7735-9212-4 (ePDF). – ISBN 978-0-7735-9213-1 (ePUB)

    1. Human reproduction – Political aspects – Canada. 2. Human
reproduction – Social aspects – Canada. 3. Fertility, Human – Political
aspects – Canada. 4. Fertility, Human – Social aspects – Canada.
5. Women – Health and hygiene – Canada. 6. Women's rights – Canada.
7. Feminism – Canada. I. Paterson, Stephanie, 1972– , author, editor
of compilation II. Scala, Francesca, author, editor of compilation
III. Sokolon, Marlene K., 1967– , author, editor of compilation IV. Title.

HQ766.5.C3F47 2014   363.9'60971   C2014-901230-6
                                                    C2014-901231-4

This book was typeset by Interscript in 10.5/13 Sabon.

Contents

Tables and Figures   vii

Abbreviations   ix

Acknowledgments   xi

Foreword   xiii

Introduction   3

PART ONE   THE POLITICS OF EXPERIENCE

1   Exploring How Women Think About and Make Their
Reproductive Choices: A Generational Approach
Diana L. Gustafson and Marilyn Porter   19

2   IVF Policy and the Stratification of Reproduction in Canada
Francesca Scala   48

3   Stratified Reproduction: Making the Case for Butch Lesbians',
Transmen's, and Genderqueer Individuals' Experiences in British
Columbia
Michelle Walks   74

4   Reproducing Inequality and Identity: An Intersectional Analysis
of Maternal Health Preferences
Candace Johnson   94

PART TWO   THE STATE OF REPRODUCTION

5   Quebec's Constitutional Challenge to the Assisted Human
Reproduction Act: Overlooking Women's Reproductive Autonomy?
Vanessa Gruben and Angela Cameron   125

6 On Reproductive Citizenship: Thinking about Social Rights and
   Assisted Reproduction in Canada
   Alana Cattapan   152

7 Deinstitutionalizing Pregnancy and Birth: Alternative Childbirth
   and the New Scalar Politics of Reproduction
   Stephanie Paterson   178

8 With Breast Intentions: Breastfeeding Policy in Canada
   Marlene K. Sokolon   205

9 Doctor Knows Best: The Illusion of Reproductive Freedom
   in Canada
   Julia Thomson-Philbrook   230

   PART THREE   THE DISCURSIVE POLITICS OF
   REPRODUCTION: SUBJECTIVITY, DISCOURSE, AND POWER

10 Girl Power and the Pill: Unpacking Web-based Marketing for
    Alesse and Yasmin
    Lisa Smith   257

11 Promoting Breastfeeding, Solving Social Problems: Exploring State
    Involvement in Breastfeeding
    Tasnim Nathoo and Aleck Ostry   280

12 Care of the Self: An Alternative Way to Understand Breastfeeding
    Robyn Lee   300

13 Indigenous Body as Contaminated Site? Examining Struggles
    for Reproductive Justice in Aamjiwnaang
    Sarah Marie Wiebe and Erin Marie Konsmo   325

    Conclusion   359

    Contributors   369

    Index   373

Tables and Figures

TABLES

11.1 Strategies to promote breastfeeding undertaken by the federal government, 1920–2000   291

13.1 Total live births, proportion of live male births (male live births/total births), χ2, and ρ-value for Aamjiwnaang. First Nation 1984–2003 arranged in 5- and 10-year periods. Reproduced with permission from Environmental Health Perspectives   342

FIGURES

11.1 Advertisement for Glaxo the Super-milk, an alternative to breastfeeding (*Globe*, 8 July 1921)   283

13.1 Artwork by Erin Marie Konsmo   326

13.2 Proportion of live male births (male live births/total live births) for Aamjiwnaang First Nation 1984–2003. Reproduced with permission from Environmental Health Perspectives   341

13.3 A body map. Image used with permission from the Aamjiwnaang Environment Department   344

Abbreviations

AHRA   Assisted Human Reproduction Act

AI   assisted insemination

ARTS   assisted reproductive technologies

CHA   Canada Health Act

IVF   in vitro fertilization

RCAP   Royal Commission on Aboriginal Peoples

RCNRT   Royal Commission on New Reproductive Technologies

SI   self-insemination

Acknowledgments

Many people have been instrumental in bringing this book to fruition. First and foremost we are grateful to the contributors of this volume for their insightful research on reproduction in Canada and their steadfast commitment to this project. We are also thankful to Abby Lippman for writing an inspiring "call to arms" foreword for our book. We extend our gratitude to Daniel Mastine and Jenna Germaine for their research and editorial assistance on this project and to Mary Newberry for her work on the book's index. The development of this project and the publication of this book benefitted from the financial and institutional support of Concordia University's Department of Political Science and Faculty of Arts and Science, as well as the Workshop grant from the Social Sciences and Humanities Research Council of Canada. Finally, we wish to thank the editorial team at McGill-Queen's University Press, in particular Kyla Madden and Jessica Howarth, along with the anonymous reviewers, whose guidance and advice significantly contributed to the quality of the volume.

Foreword

Fertile Ground: Exploring Reproduction in Canada takes readers on visits to the past and the future. What is striking in these voyages is the reminder that many issues related to reproduction and mother-hood in Canada have been of concern to women for decades – if not longer – and that many of them will remain of concern in years to come.

These chapters also illustrate the extent to which issues that are framed as ethical issues are actually reflections of social policies and societal structures that involve questions of power, privilege, and control over women's bodies and childbearing/child raising activi-ties. As a result, they highlight the need to attend to how the changes in women's concerns over time are shaped as well as to their sub-stance. And importantly, they remind us of the need to avoid di-chotomies in understanding these issues.

Women's bodies have always been, and continue to be, sites for struggles of control. But to grasp fully the nature of this control, we need to think beyond issues of reproductive health and reproductive rights and consider the larger, more inclusive, and more complex concept, first developed by women of colour in the United States, of reproductive justice.

In fact, seeing the issues addressed in this book through reproduc-tive justice lenses actually enriches our understanding of how and why women's bodies are such contested sites for struggles over con-trol. These lenses, too, may clarify how it is possible to begin writing about women and reproduction without starting with the word "choice."

Choice has been a clarion call of the women's health movement. But choice is in many ways a downstream issue – important but not primary, a necessary but not a sufficient condition for women. To focus on choice will, at best, lead to considering reproductive rights and the kinds of reproductive health care obtained by and accessible to women. But at worst, a focus on choice can lead to consumerist thinking, commercializing women's bodies, victim blaming, and making individuals responsible for creating and dealing with problems of reproduction, motherhood, and sexuality. Moreover, what we think of as a choice changes over time.

For too many women who lack resources and power, choice is non-existent because of how others (and their oppressive policies) limit or control their options. Yet for these women, for all women, thinking about concerns and needs as issues of reproductive justice reveals the critical roles of power and privilege: who has these and who does not.

If choice is a social construction that changes over time, place, and space (the latter referring to where and how we are each located because of our multiple identities), then we are forced to look upstream to what choices are available to different women and how and why these are their options. Similarly, we must confront not only the degree to which various technologies and other interventions related to reproduction, motherhood, and sexuality are double-edged (e.g., contraceptive drugs may help some women avoid pregnancies they don't want but can also be used to keep some women from having pregnancies they do want in population control programs aimed at racialized women and women with disabilities) but also how some women are valued as mothers while others (e.g., women in prisons or immigrant women) are not.

Reproductive justice is a reminder that what seems to empower some women may disempower or harm others: "either/or" won't do when women need both (e.g., physician obstetricians and midwives). Even the standard oppositions of pro-choice and pro-life need questioning: one can welcome and cherish a developing fetus while still accepting the need for abortion.

Reproductive justice is also a reminder of the harms of individualizing solutions to social problems, harms that too often result in blaming the victims and not the circumstances and determinants that have shaped their lives. Yet here, too, we need to be wary of simple dichotomies: the same processes of medicalization that bring too much under professional scrutiny for women of privilege can be just what marginalized women who lack the resources for and access to health care truly need. Likewise, the travelling by some women to obtain high-tech services not available to all must be distinguished from the travelling by other women to find basic care (e.g., abortion) not made available where they live.

We live in a highly stratified, increasingly inequitable society in Canada – a context that affects how women experience their bodies and their agency. But each of us also helps shape these strata and inequities; after all, if choice is socially constructed, we are among the social actors helping to construct it. This means that individual decisions and actions that appear private have public consequences. To the extent that in vitro fertilization is seen as the "proper" response for women seeking to become pregnant in their forties, will there still be the political will to change employment and childcare policies that constrain women from having children at younger ages? To the extent that prenatal testing is seen as the "proper" response to risks about having children with some disorders, will there still be public commitment to offer educational and other services for these children and their mothers?

Just as we know that colonial and racial policies are played out in women's bodies, we also need to acknowledge how policies that reinforce privilege play out and sustain, if not increase, inequities. When it comes to reproduction, motherhood, and sexuality, the playing field is far from level. *Fertile Ground* reminds us of where the "bumps" are and how they were created, but it is up to readers to engage with and remove these bumps to ensure reproductive justice for all.

Abby Lippman, McGill University

FERTILE GROUND

Introduction

STEPHANIE PATERSON, FRANCESCA SCALA,
AND MARLENE K. SOKOLON

Reproduction is rarely removed from government and public agendas. In recent years, Canadian politics has been marked by bitter controversies surrounding reproduction. In the fall of 2012, for example, a private member's bill calling for a study on when human life begins was defeated in the House of Commons, despite support from the minister responsible for the status of women, Conservative Rona Ambrose. The bill once again brought to the fore the precarious position in which abortion services are situated and prompted widespread public discussion about reproductive rights in Canada.

Similarly, in the spring of 2010, reproduction and motherhood became a focal point of political and media discussion. The controversy, sparked by the Muskoka Initiative on Maternal, Newborn, and Child Health, focused on abortion funding abroad and prompted debate about what constitutes "maternal health" and the services it might require, as well as about how it might differ from "women's health" more generally (see Cawthorne 2010). Although the initiative was designed for women in developing nations and focused specifically on health, the ensuing conversation prompted several points for reflection in the Canadian context. In particular, it revealed the complexities surrounding the politics of reproduction, exposing the ways in which concepts such as gender, race, and nation shape contemporary discourses on reproduction and motherhood and stratify subjects therein. Moreover, it illuminated the limits of rights-based frameworks, shifting the dialogue to questions of access and service provision even within Canada.

Perhaps most important, the discussion revealed a certain continuity between "reproductive moments," such as fertility, abortion, and conception; pregnancy and childbirth; breastfeeding; and motherhood. In this volume, we seek to build on this idea, interrogating and integrating the various aspects of women's reproductive lives to investigate and expose the political dimensions of reproduction. In so doing, we situate ourselves within a long tradition of feminist policy studies that demonstrates how women's experiences and well-being are directly, and often negatively, affected by the state and public policy (Burt 1996; Phillips 1996; Bacchi 1999).

Since Confederation, all levels of the Canadian state have played a pivotal role in shaping women's experiences with reproduction. During the nineteenth century, state interventions linked reproduction to nationalist goals, promoting population growth as key to national development. Although population growth has served to be an enduring theme running through reproductive politics in Canada – one that was especially pronounced in post–Quiet Revolution Quebec (see Maroney 1992; Milligan 2002), during the early twentieth century – public discourse shifted to emphasize quality over previously privileged concerns about quantity. For example, policies aimed at improving reproductive outcomes – such as family allowances, eugenics policies, state-supported monopoly of medical science in the area of obstetric care, and recent early childhood development initiatives – often shaped and were shaped by ideas about race, class, and heteronormativity (Valverde 1992; McLaren 1999).

By the 1970s, however, Canadian feminists began to frame reproductive policy much differently. Rather than state-centred policies, which aimed to monitor and improve populations, feminist movements in Canada began to expose the connections between reproduction and gender oppression and made calls for abortion on demand, alternative childbirth, and universal childcare. Today, in the early twenty-first century, feminists continue in these struggles, claiming new reproductive technologies, midwifery services, and reproductive justice as key to gender equality.

The link between reproduction and gender inequality has presented several challenges to state action and inaction in the area of reproductive politics. The complex and unique character of Canadian federalism has served to both facilitate and constrain advocacy in various areas of reproductive politics. On the one hand, the federal state has enabled multiple access points for feminist activists, prompting action at federal, provincial, and, in some cases, municipal levels of government (Mahon 2009; for a discussion on abortion politics and federalism, see Haussman 2005). On the other hand, federalism and jurisdictional wrangling have frustrated attempts to prioritize women's reproductive rights, resulting in provincial disparities in the areas of abortion access, fertility services, midwifery services, breastfeeding, and child-care.

Federalism is not the only challenge for activists and scholars attempting to explore and accurately represent the state's engagement with reproductive health. Policy discourses, particularly those of neo-liberalism and medicalization, have been comprehensively integrated into the government's approaches to reproductive health, an occurrence that has both fostered and stymied feminist activism.[1] Where neo-liberal discourse resulted in individualist approaches to reproduction and motherhood at the expense of collective approaches (see, for example, McKeen 2009), medicalization privileged expertise at the expense of experiential knowledge (Mitchinson 1991, 2002; Code 1991; Multerud et al. 2004). While the former tends to render women's reproductive lives invisible, the latter tends to reify them. Paradoxically, while both perpetuate gender domination and reproductive injustice, they have also offered points for reflection and state engagement among feminist activists.

However, much like other issues targeted by feminist activism, the field of reproductive politics is complicated not only by internal debates, but also by multiple and often competing frames and points of reference. For example, although the ascendance of neo-liberalism enabled some feminists to secure a number of gains in the area of reproduction, including abortion, assisted reproductive technologies (ARTs), and midwifery, by deploying choice- and rights-based discourses, such framings have been points of contestation themselves (Kallianes and Rubenfeld 1997; Ruhl 2002; Weir 1994). Specifically, the radical left and marginalized women have troubled these paradigms, exposing the ways in which they construct the reproductive subject and obstruct access to reproductive justice for particular groups (see, for example, Smith 2005; Silliman et al. 2004; Ruhl 2002; Weir 1994; Granzow 2007; Bacchi 1999).[2] Medicalization has been similarly acknowledged as liberating in areas such as abortion and fertility, but oppressive in areas such as pregnancy and childbirth. Moreover, global representations of medicine and progress shape how women perceive biomedicine.

For example, women in the North are more likely to view medical expertise with suspicion, whereas women in the South are more likely to view medical knowledge as a sign of development and prosperity (Johnson 2009). Such divisions can also be observed between racialized groups. For example, one of the fault lines in the abortion movement emerged between white women, who largely supported medicalized abortions and sterilizations on demand, and women of colour, who were more critical of such practices due to their colonial past (Wattleton 2003; Ross 1998; Siliman et al. 2004). Thus, within the more general investigation of reproductive policy, it is important to investigate how the issues contained within such an overarching theme are represented and negotiated among various groups, particularly those based on age, ability, race, nation, sexuality, and gender expression.

The current political climate in Canada necessitates a broader understanding of the links between the politics of reproduction, the state, and gender oppression. We thus require analyses devoted to the ways in which various dimensions of reproduction are connected to each other and to how these dimensions undergird or disrupt broader state objectives. At present, the literature on reproduction, both in Canada and abroad, has tended to "stove-pipe" reproductive events, examining issues such as abortion (e.g., Brodie et al. 1992; Haussman 2001, 2005; Kellough 1996; Lovenduski and Outshoorn 1986; McBride Stetson 2001; Nossiff 1998; Scheppelle 1996; Solinger 1998; Weir 1994), contraception (e.g., Haussman 2013; Sethna 2006), HPV vaccines (e.g., Aronowitz et al. 2010; Haussman 2013), fertility and ARTS (e.g., Scala 2005; Smith 2006; Basen et al. 1993; Farquhar 1996), pregnancy and childbirth (e.g., Johnson 2009; Bourgeault 2004; Harrison 2010; Nestel 2006; MacDonald 2004; Twine 2012; Paterson 2010, 2011; Weir 2006), and breastfeeding (e.g., Arneil 2000; Kedrowski and Lipscomb 2008; Knaak 2006; Nathoo and Ostry 2009) in isolation. While such analyses have garnered important insights into the ways in which states structure reproductive lives, little attention has been paid to the ways in which the intersection of these areas might contribute to or challenge contemporary gender politics. For example, what discourses are common to each of these policy areas, and how are reproductive subjects constituted? How are these discourses racialized, class-based, ableist, and/or heteronormative, sustaining power relations and marginality through their outlooks and vocabularies?

What discursive and non-discursive strategies have social movements and other coalitions employed to bring attention and action to these issues? How do these subject areas collectively and individually contribute to or challenge the current gender order and social marginalization of particular groups?

In this volume, we bring together scholars working in diverse disciplines, including political science, legal studies, sociology, and anthropology, to address these broad questions by challenging the current conceptualization of reproduction as a series of events, such as fertility choice and abortion, pregnancy, childbirth, and breastfeeding (see O'Brien 1981). Rather, we aim to engage in multidisciplinary discussion to illuminate points of continuity, demonstrating the ways in which these reproductive moments are embedded in broader socio-political discourses that give shape and meaning to lived experiences. In particular, we explore three transversal themes that link reproductive politics to marginalization, women's lived experiences, and the role of the state (see also O'Brien 1981; Ginsberg and Rapp 1995). These themes offer interesting organizational tools that enable us to explore connections and points of tension between reproductive moments, such as fertility, conception and abortion, pregnancy and childbirth, breastfeeding, and motherhood.

THEMES IN THIS BOOK

The Politics of Experience

A starting point of feminist political research is the recognition of diversity in women's interests and experiences across race, ethnicity, sexuality, class, and other social statuses. The term *intersectionality* is often used to theorize and explain how women's political and social experiences are informed by their social locations, thus requiring an analysis that moves beyond the male-female oppositional, hierarchical division that characterized earlier feminist projects (Williams 2004, 56). By adopting an intersectional lens, feminist research strives to uncover the interlocking processes and practices that produce and reproduce existing social hierarchies that disadvantage women in general and some women in particular.

In recent years, diversity and social location have become key themes in the empirical study of women's experiences with reproduction and motherhood (e.g., Ginsberg and Rapp 1995; Arnup 1990). Mothering and reproduction is associated with women because, universally, it is women who perform mothering and reproductive duties. However, the cultural meaning, significance, and practices of reproduction are not universal; rather, political and social contexts mediate women's relationships to reproduction and motherhood. The term *stratified reproduction* has been used to explain how state policy, cultural norms, and social and economic forces directly or indirectly privilege and valorize the reproductive work of certain groups while vilifying the capabilities of others (Colen 1986; Ginsburg and Rapp 1995). For example, in the North American context, the reproductive choices among women who are poor, racialized, queer, disabled, or single are often restricted via government policy, and by particular representations of the "good mother." In examining the intersection between reproduction, race, sexual orientation, and class, we aim to uncover how reproduction both constitutes and reproduces existing social inequalities and hierarchies.

The themes of reproductive autonomy and choice have dominated research and activism about the politics of reproduction. The legal struggle for reproductive rights, in particular abortion rights, has dominated the research agendas of political scientists and policy scholars (for a classic example, see Brodie, Jenson, and Gavigan 1992; see also Baer 1999; Haussman 2001, 2005, 2013; Kedrowski and Lipscomb 2008; Kellough 1996; Lovenduski and Outshoorn 1986; McBride Stetson 2001; Scheppelle 1996; Weir 1994). In recent years, however, the preoccupation with reproductive rights, while not displaced, has been accompanied by a greater interest in exploring how women negotiate their reproductive lives within a system that maintains interlocking oppressions and social hierarchies (Smith 2005; Silliman et al. 2004; Ruhl 2002). Working within the framework of reproductive justice, this expanded research agenda pays greater attention to broader issues that affect women's reproductive health, such as racism, poverty, and domestic violence. In this context, reproductive rights include not only the right to birth control and abortion, but also the right to "economic resources, and the multitude of supports needed to control fertility, activate fertility, raise children, select birthing options, and live in fundamentally good housing, among other concerns" (Davis 2009, 112).

The importance of social location to understanding reproductive politics and practices is underscored in a number of chapters in this volume. In chapter 1, Diana L. Gustafson and Marilyn Porter conduct a generational case study of women's reproductive choices, in particular the choice of motherhood, in Newfoundland families. They portray women's reproductive choices not as isolated medical events but rather as relational moments "integrated within the social, emotional, familial, and cultural contexts of their lives." Using the biographic-narrative interpretive method, the authors uncover how family relationships, especially those among women across generations, mediate the cultural, religious, social, and medical discourses that inform women's experiences and reproductive choices.

Chapter 2 by Francesca Scala and chapter 3 by Michelle Walks both use the framework of stratified reproduction in their analysis of reproductive technologies in Canada. Scala explores how policies that govern the funding of infertility treatments and eligibility requirements "can simultaneously challenge prevailing notions of motherhood, parenthood, and the family and contribute to the stratification of reproduction by reinforcing divisions along class, gender, race, and sexual orientation." Due to the characterization of infertility as a social or health concern rather than a disease or illness, in vitro fertilization (IVF) treatments in most provinces are not publicly funded because they are not deemed a "medical necessity." IVF is therefore only accessible to middle- and upper-class women, often white, who have the resources to pay for it; underprivileged women, who experience infertility at a higher rate, are excluded from becoming mothers through this avenue. By relegating IVF to the private market, the federal government is contributing to the stratification of reproduction by perpetuating social hierarchies based on class and race. Moreover, although Canada's Assisted Human Reproduction Act (AHRA) prohibits biomedical agents from restricting access to fertility treatments based on sexual orientation and marital status, it remains silent on other discriminatory practices based on age, disability, and health status. The recent listing of IVF as a publicly funded medical service in Quebec seems to extend benefits to all women regardless of income. However, the setting of age limits by government for prospective patients perpetuates another way in which women are unequally situated with respect to reproduction.

The concept of stratified reproduction once again takes centre stage in Walks's exploration of the reproductive choices and experiences of butch lesbians, transmen, and genderqueer individuals in British Columbia. Walks argues that these individuals face several institutional and cultural obstacles when pursuing assisted conception services, including financial constraints, heterosexist standard practice of care in medicine, and cultural representations of the "good parent." Moreover, the association of fertility with femininity also has a stratifying effect on reproduction, because it marginalizes individuals on the basis of non/normative gender practices. The author stresses the importance of breaking down such stereotypes by investigating "the diverse challenges, choices, and experiences of pregnancy and parenting by female-bodied, masculine-, and androgynous-identified individuals."

In chapter 4, Candace Johnson builds on earlier work (Johnson 2009) to study the impact of social location on women's relationships to reproduction through an examination of maternal health preferences among immigrant women in Guelph, Ontario. In comparing the preferences in maternal health and birthing options of Canadian-born and immigrant women, Johnson identifies significant differences in perspectives on "medical" and "natural" births. Canadian-born women prefer midwife-assisted births outside of a hospital setting while the majority of immigrant women prefer hospital births attended by an obstetrician. To explain these differences, Johnson suggests that the intersection of inequality and identity and how these shape women's relationship to the health care system and to society as a whole need to be examined. She argues that "a transversal discursive approach might be one that encourages full expression of diversity and difference, and considers matters that span or cross borders." Only by examining the diversity of experiences and preferences of women vis-à-vis birthing options and related health services can effective maternal health policies be put in place, both domestically and internationally.

The State of Reproduction

The role of the state, which figures prominently in the literature on women's reproductive health, is a central concern in this section's readings. The state, via its bureaucratic and legal arrangements, is actively involved in shaping gender relations and regulating women's reproductive work and choices. General family and labour market policy, as well as more targeted policies that govern access to abortion and contraceptives, shape all aspects of women's reproductive lives. The state is thus directly implicated in the construction of motherhood and gender roles, and in delineating who is included or excluded from these cultural representations. On the issue of reproductive health, contemporary feminists (Wajcman 1991; Apple 1987; Mitchinson 1991, 2002) have examined the gendered implications of institutional medical knowledge in reproductive activities. In its privileging of the biomedical model of reproduction, the state contributes to the prevailing view of reproduction as a series of disassociated events, rather than as part of a woman's life story. Institutional arrangements, such as federalism, also affect gender relations in general and reproductive rights in particular. As noted above, the jurisdictional division of powers embedded in the Canadian constitution can generate inequalities among women because of regional disparities in the provision and availability of abortion services, contraceptives, daycare, and maternal health services, such as access to midwifery (e.g., Haussman 2005; Schroff 1997).

In chapter 5, Vanessa Gruben and Angela Cameron explore the effect of federalism on women's reproductive autonomy through a discussion of federal–provincial squabbling in the area of reproductive technologies. Challenged by the Quebec government on the ground that certain sections of the Assisted Human Reproduction Act violated federal–provincial division of powers, on 22 December 2010 the Supreme Court upheld the right of the provinces to regulate health care, including fertility treatments. Cameron and Gruben argue, "in the absence of bright dividing lines [of constitutional jurisdiction] those ambiguities must be resolved with women's reproductive autonomy in mind." They further argue that this ruling will lead to fragmented and absent policy on the use of reproductive technologies; such fragmentation will affect the well-being of women, since they are most directly affected by the application of this technology. By upholding the supremacy of provincial concerns, the ruling undermines women's reproductive autonomy, which is crucial for equality and full constitutional membership in the Canadian state.

Alana Cattapan also examines the issue of reproductive technology, but in the context of reproductive citizenship. In chapter 6, she focuses not on the legal arguments but on the rights and entitlements that those seeking the use of reproductive technologies can claim

from the Canadian state. Citizenship, she argues, is a matter of belonging, and recognition has traditionally been found through the
roles of worker, soldier, and parents. Cattapan argues that this duty-
based view has evolved in Canada to broader social citizenship
rights through claims on the welfare state. This approach to reproductive technologies locates ARTS within the medical model and
thus in the provincial medicare system with a neo-liberal, market-
oriented, and individualist choice-based model of service. Such a
medical model of reproductive citizenship, Cattapan maintains,
"privileges certain actors and supports choice in reproductive services without making provisions for universal access."

In chapter 7, Stephanie Paterson emphasizes the "state" of reproduction in her analysis of the scalar politics of reproduction in
Ontario. Tracing the emergence of the "new midwifery" in Ontario
from the Alternative Birth Movement in the 1960s in Canada and
the United States, Paterson argues that midwifery debates extend
beyond questions of how and where to give birth, instead centring
on questions about contemporary governance arrangements in the
arena of reproduction. Using the theoretical construct of scale, she
demonstrates the ways in which advocates used and constructed
scale to negotiate a new spatial politics of reproduction. In so doing,
the politics of scale in Ontario became a process of identity formation that both fractured and continued biomedical discourses in reproductive politics.

The role of the state in regulating women's reproductive lives is
again uncovered in Marlene K. Sokolon's analysis of Health Canada's
breastfeeding guidelines in chapter 8. She argues that in its policy
statement supporting six months of exclusive breastfeeding, the
federal government adheres to the medical model of breastfeeding,
which characterizes it primarily in terms of infant care and health
benefits rather than as a sociocultural practice. Since the policy gives
primacy to this medical model, it reduces breastfeeding to a "medical
event" that exists alongside other medical events such as birth control, infertility, and childbirth, thus splintering the larger sociocultural perspective of women's reproductive lives. Sokolon also explores
how the policy statement advances classist and racist conceptions of
the "good mother" by targeting the behaviour of individual mothers
rather than addressing the social and economic realities that expand
or limit women's choices vis-à-vis breastfeeding.

Perhaps the most contested field in the arena of reproductive politics is abortion. In chapter 9, Julia Thomson-Philbrook challenges the common misperception that abortion policy is a constitutional right in Canada. On the contrary, by way of comparison with US policy, which has moved from a medicalized to a constitutional and rights-based discourse, she argues that abortion policy in Canada remains firmly entrenched within a medicalized tradition that privileges the right of doctors to practise as they see fit over the right of Canadian woman to choose.

The Discursive Politics of Reproduction: Subjectivity, Discourse, and Power

Discourse is "an ensemble of ideas, concepts, and categories through which meaning is given to social and physical phenomena, and which is produced and reproduced through an identifiable set of practices" (Hajer 2006, 67). Discourse analysis begins with the assumption that language does not merely reflect the social world, but also shapes it. Moreover, discourses are the medium through which power works, assigning meanings to phenomena and positioning actors therein. Discourse, however, is not deterministic. Indeed, actors can create change by exploiting contradictions and tensions arising within discursive fields, which comprise the multiple overlapping and often contradictory discourses that define a given phenomenon. The authors in this book who explore this theme work to expose these tensions and potential openings for change within the arena of reproduction.

The discursive field in which reproduction is constituted, negotiated, and performed is complex, including multiple discourses operating at various levels of specificity. Such complexity has both fostered and constrained efforts for change and social justice in reproductive politics. Historically, reproduction in Canada has been implicated in broader discourses such as state, nation, citizenship, and family, which assign the particular roles and responsibilities of individuals within reproductive processes. Women, specifically white women, have been charged with both generational and social reproduction (although the literature here is extensive, for recent discussions see Bezanson and Luxton 2006). Such "private" duties provided leverage for early maternalist feminists to secure a role in "public" life (e.g., Valverde 1992): building on their assumed nurturing capabilities, women sought the right to participate in formal political life while also reforming society by protecting it from the ills (such as alcohol) that would potentially destroy it.

Maternalist discourses were both premised on and reproduced by a particular social order that was not only gendered, but also heteronormative, racialized, and classed. This order, undergirded by a male breadwinner and a female caregiver, provided the foundation on which the post-war welfare state was erected (for a classic Canadian example, see Little 1998). Reproduction and its associated responsibilities were interwoven with the post-war citizenship regime, as (white) males were offered "universal entitlements" based on a standardized employment relationship and females were offered means-tested benefits based on their family relationships and the often-precarious employment that followed (Vosko 2000).

The neo-liberal era brought with it its own set of challenges, basing policies on seemingly degendered, sexless, autonomous agents (Cossman 2002). As noted above, with its emphasis on choice, rights, and responsibilities, neo-liberal discourse has enabled some gains for feminists in the area of reproduction, while at the same time obscuring the discursive and structural contexts in which choices are made and responsibilities are assigned, negated, or performed. While (white) feminists have secured gains in the areas of abortion, midwifery, and assisted reproductive technologies by deploying choice and rights discourses, the discursive positioning of agents therein has often been problematic, rendering social location invisible (Basen et al. 1993; Rothman 1989, 2004; Simonds et al. 2007; Lippman 1999; Colen 1995; Ginsberg and Rapp 1995; see also Weir 2006; Smith 2005; Paterson 2010; Thaychuk 2006). Thus, reproductive discourses extend far beyond biology to include nationalism, citizenship, and social location. How individuals are positioned within this complex field is the subject of inquiry for many of the papers presented in this volume.

In chapter 10, Lisa Smith's analysis of the birth control products Alesse and Yasmin reveals the ways in which identities are bound up in reproductive discourses. Exploring the marketing campaigns for the pill, Smith offers a critique of the choice and empowerment discourses surrounding birth control and reproduction. She notes that, while marketing campaigns often "portray the pill user as a powerful and independent subject ... the websites equally construct her, and young women more generally, as fundamentally problematic and thus in need of the control offered by the pill." The "out of control" nature of contemporary young femininity necessitates interventions such as the pill as a way through which to gain control over one's life. Contemporary usage of the pill, then, is not just a mode of birth control, but rather a constitutive element of modern young womanhood. Thus, for the author, the concepts of choice and empowerment must be considered within wider systems of social meaning.

Complementing Smith's work, Tasnim Nathoo and Aleck Ostry in chapter 11 and Robyn Lee in chapter 12 on breastfeeding illuminate the complexity of identities and expose the contradictions and tensions arising from maternalist discourses for contemporary motherhood. Both of these chapters seek to decentre the discourses shaping breastfeeding in contemporary society, albeit in very different ways. For Nathoo and Ostry, this requires a woman-centred approach to breastfeeding that focuses on women's experiences, with the emphasis on exclusivity and duration rather than education and initiation. Their analysis traces the historical evolution of the discourse used by state intervention in breastfeeding in Canada from the late nineteenth century, illuminating the ways in which moral judgment and notions of "the good mother" became intertwined with breastfeeding policy and practice. Despite high and constant rates of breastfeeding initiation, policy interventions continue to focus on the less-effective educational program about the benefits of breast milk, rather than on women's experiences as a way to foster exclusive six-month breastfeeding recommendations. From this perspective, a multi-sectoral policy approach is necessary to harness enabling factors such as community and employer support.

Lee also seeks to shift the focus of discourse away from infants and maternalism to women and their experiences. She writes, "although maternalism values women's caring roles, like western medicine, it has also focused primarily on the benefits breastfeeding provides for infants ... Breastfeeding advocates often overlook the enormous challenges that breastfeeding poses to women's autonomy: an activity stretching out over many months or even years, it requires time-consuming labour, is inadequately accommodated in the workplace, and is often still viewed as obscene when performed outside the home." Using Foucault's ethic of the self to expose the ways in which breastfeeding might be reconceptualized, Lee demonstrates the arbitrary underpinnings of contemporary breast-feeding discourses and suggests that women problematize current discourses as they work toward understanding their individual and relational experiences.

In chapter 13, Sarah Marie Wiebe and Erin Marie Konsmo extend these discussions of discourse and power to link the reproductive body to environmental politics. Examining concerns regarding the skewed birth ratio favouring girls in the indigenous community of Aamjiwnaang, near Sarnia, Ontario, downstream from Canada's "Chemical Valley," Wiebe and Konsmo expose systemic colonial dimensions inscribed through the reproductive body's pollution exposures, and argue that through the discourse of "lost boys," the body has become the site for the persistence of colonization. In so doing, the authors claim that the Indigenous reproductive body on reserve is at the frontlines for toxic exposure, and consequently experiences pollution harm in different ways than the wider population of Lambton County. Thus, the authors argue, the Indigenous reproductive body is marked by pollution in distinct ways.

In sum, in *Fertile Ground*, we seek to decentre the discreteness of reproductive moments, as well as liberal and medical paradigms. Instead, linking reproduction to marginalization and the state, we illuminate the continuity of reproductive moments and their implications for identity, activism, policy formation, and further scholarship.

NOTES

1 *Neo-liberalism* is a term often used to describe a modern form of liberal thought and practice, entailing extreme individualism and state retrenchment from all areas of private life. *Medicalization* is a term used to describe the ascendance of modern biomedicine, beginning in the late nineteenth century, in which bodies were increasingly objectified and subject to allopathic treatment.

2 This is not to suggest that feminists have accepted these discourses uncritically until now (e.g., Lippman 1999). However, the reproductive justice movement brings these issues to the fore (see Smith 2005; Silliman et al. 2004).

PART ONE

The Politics of Experience

1

Exploring How Women Think About and Make Their Reproductive Choices: A Generational Approach

DIANA L. GUSTAFSON AND MARILYN PORTER

In this chapter, we discuss the complex operation of choice, specifically how choosing to mother (or not) is reproduced in the context of family and revealed in women's life stories.[1] We draw on Canadian data collected as part of an international comparative study that explored the narratives of three generations of women. Their stories illustrate how dominant discourses about chastity, conception, contraception, abortion, and becoming a mother are conveyed by society, including the health care system, the Church, and the state – sometimes directly, sometimes indirectly – and mediated by women within the family and transmitted across generations. We intend to convey several key messages.

First, women experience their reproductive lives not as discrete medicalized events, but as part of their entire life story. Decisions about becoming a mother are an integral part of these stories and are responses to life events as much as, or more than, the medical issues women manage. As we theorize the politics of reproduction for this chapter, we incorporate lessons learned from the women we interviewed about how they have integrated reproductive decisions within the social, emotional, familial, and cultural contexts of their lives. Sometimes the links between the social, political, and familial context and the choices that women have made are explicit and sometimes they are implicit.

Second, we understand the family both as a social and ideological institution and as a particularized social environment that operates within pre-existing and mutually constitutive medicalizing, religious, and state discourses that become materialized in women's reproductive experiences. A generational case study approach to exploring women's reproductive lives tells us much about how ideas and practices change over time; that dominant discourses about conception, contraception, abortion, and becoming a mother echo in the life stories told within families; and that such longitudinal data offer us valuable insights into how information and values are transmitted, given authority, acted upon, and resisted across generations.

Third, reproductive choice is relational. This means that we acknowledge the power of individuals to exercise agency and the power of social structures and discursive environments to inform how women think, feel, interpret, and perform the choices they make. Like the relational moments in women's reproductive lives, choice is a process that evolves over time. Choosing to be or not to be a mother is not a one-time event, but a continuing part of women's construction of their reproductive lives. Thus, such choice is a relational process of decision-making that happens over time within families as an integral part of how women construct their reproductive lives.

These key messages are framed by our understanding of the concept of meaningful choice. All choices are framed by the social, economic, political, and cultural context in which women live. Meaningful choice is constructed from the resources available to each woman at a particular point in her life. We present narrative data in some detail so that the reader can see how women think about and make reproductive choices, first by looking across several families and later in the chapter, by focusing on the "H" family. In these families, choices were informed by the health care system, the Church, and the state, and were integrated into the broader context of their lives. Before we enter these narratives, we examine the theoretical context in which we have developed our interpretive framework.

REPRODUCTIVE LIVES AND RELATIONAL MOMENTS

Mary O'Brien (1981) argues that women's embodied experience of reproduction was, and is, inseparable from their reproductive consciousness of the event. Medical language, she writes, strips context and consciousness from women's embodied experience, instead reinforcing the notion that women's reproductive capacity is a series of isolated, time-dependent, bodily events from menarche to meno-pause. She advances the concept of *relational moments* as an alternative to the medicalization of these events, stressing their momentous emotional and social significance in women's lives (O'Brien 1981). We apply this concept to examining the range of reproductive moments in women's lives from menarche to menopause and beyond (Porter and Gustafson 2012) but in this chapter focus our attention on the decision to become a mother. Also within this volume, both Lee (chapter 12) and Sokolon (chapter 8) emphasize this concept with relation to breastfeeding, while Johnson (chapter 4) highlights how women's childbirth preferences are intertwined with their social and cultural backgrounds.

The social aspects of women's reproductive lives are much more all-encompassing than the biological aspects, and affect women before, during, and after their procreative periods. Consider, for instance, that the opening and closing markers of menarche and menopause are typically used to bracket a woman's reproductive life. As many women in Canada may live until their eighties or nineties, these markers mean that for approximately half her life, a woman is not considered reproductive in the biological sense. But this runs counter to our research, which revealed that women did not see their reproductive role as limited to their childbearing years. They saw themselves as actively reproductive, not only in reproducing children but also in reproducing family, community, and cultural values and traditions – a role that continued long past menopause. Kate Bezanson and Meg Luxton (2006, 3) define social reproduction as "the processes involved in maintaining and reproducing people, specifically the labouring population, and their labour power on a daily and generational basis ... It involves the provision of food, clothing, shelter, basic safety and health care, along with the development and transmission of knowledge, social values and cultural practices and the construction of individual and collective identities."

We do not, nor did our participants, ignore biological events and changes in their bodies and lives, but we do insist that these events, or relational moments, are always located within their social and cultural contexts, especially that of the family. For this reason, we coined the term *reproductive lives* to better reflect women's accounts of how they interpret and put together their lives as continuous, interrelated, locally constituted, and embodied moments rather than as a series of discrete biological (and medicalized) procreative events (Porter and Gustafson 2012). This concept of reproductive lives merges with the relational model of choice.

REPRODUCTIVE LIVES AND THE RELATIONAL MODEL OF CHOICE

As a girl grows into womanhood she is faced with many embodied social experiences that call for her to make decisions that shape her reproductive life: if and when to have sex and with whom; if and when to become pregnant; who might support her through pregnancy, birthing, and beyond as she rears her children; whether to accept medical intervention and the use of biotechnologies for fertility or pharmaceuticals for contraception and childbirth; managing the size of her family; and so on. She also has to make decisions about her children's health – what and how they eat, how much television they watch – while participating in their health care by making decisions such as whether to immunize them against Human papillomavirus (HPV). Many women will also have to make choices about the health of their partner and their aging parents. The role of choice in the wider context of women's reproductive lives is, therefore, complex and persistent over time.

Erin Nelson (2004, 598) notes that the feminist debate has, in the past, focused largely on "whether women have choices, which ones they have, or which ones they ought to have but do not." Similarly, Mullin (2005) and Kaposy and Downie (2008) have also commented on how the fixated gaze on the quantity and quality of choices available to women at one moment of their reproductive lives (exemplified by the prominence of the abortion debate in academic, political, and public spheres) diverts attention away from a woman's choices in her pregnancy, her pre- and post-pregnancy body, and at many other moments in her reproductive life. While we agree with Johnstone (2010) and others that the abortion debate is an important one, in this chapter we explore the concept and operation of choice because it informs a range of issues that relate to becoming a mother.

Most discussions about the concept of choice have developed in the realms of psychology or economics. Both these starting points tend to detach the act of choosing from its social context. For example, Ball (2005) conceives of choice based on the presumption that a woman is free to make independent decisions that are in keeping with her life goals. This way of thinking about choice as "rational action in relation to commensurable goods" has intuitive appeal in liberal society where individualism, autonomy, independence, and self-sufficiency are valued (Nelson 2004, 617). Under the law, the conception of autonomous choice is a powerful one that protects the fundamental individual right to self-determination or self-governance.

When we think about the issue of choice for women in the context of their reproductive lives, we are challenged by the arbitrary distinction between private and public spheres and the privacy versus equality claims in reproductive choice. On the one hand, neo-liberal expectations dictate that women should have the right to make autonomous decisions and expect that the state will not interfere in personal and private relationships. On the other hand, there is the widespread social expectation that the state will act as a guarantor of women's equality in the public sphere (Ball 2005; Johnstone 2010). Therefore, at the same time that the state has an obligation not to interfere in private relationships, society expects the state to intervene where women's rights are being infringed.

We agree with feminists and others (e.g., Ball 2005; Hanigsberg 1995, 2002; Johnstone 2010; Nelson 2004) who argue in favour of safeguarding equality (the state recognition of the same rights, benefits, and privileges among groups) as well as individuals' rights and authority to make decisions about their own bodies, both under the law and in everyday practice. At the same time, we are persuaded by the argument that the concept of autonomous choice is flawed (Anderson 1993).

Autonomous choice assumes an atomistic individual disconnected from all other external influences and relationships (Friedman 2003), to say nothing of their social location. Autonomous choice also presumes that decision-making is without moral conflict and can be freely undertaken, ignoring influences from multiple powerful sources. We believe instead that individuals are socially embedded beings whose fluid identities are constituted by gender, race, class, ethnicity, religious affiliation, and other social dimensions. At any moment in time, an individual (or group) may have differing degrees of access to power, information, and material resources. Moreover, the important reproductive choices women face (such as preventing or promoting conception or maintaining or terminating a pregnancy) can be fraught with moral uncertainty and constrained by strong religious beliefs or other institutionalized pressures to conform to normative practices (Sherwin 1998). Depending on the individual woman or group of women, access to accurate and timely health information and confidential counselling or money for travel to a women's health centre, for example, may affect the ability to make a meaningful reproductive choice.

For these reasons, we prefer the concept of *meaningful choice*. Meaningful choice operates when women are self-aware and well informed, have a set of realistically available options from which to choose, and are able to communicate a decision. Not all women enjoy the same range of options from which to choose and the same degree of power to exercise a choice. This perspective acknowledges those relational factors that may at any given historical or political moment be construed as oppressive or limiting agency or free choice.

Consider a woman who learns that she is ten weeks pregnant. Deciding whether to continue a pregnancy in such circumstances is a relational choice that takes place in a particular space and at a particular historical and political moment. This moment of decision may come after consultation with family, friends, a religious leader, or a health care provider. To make a meaningful choice about whether to continue the pregnancy or to mother the newborn, she needs information about the day-to-day issues of caring for a child, the support she can reasonably expect to access for herself and the fetus during and after pregnancy, and information about and access to health care options. She must locate this information in her own situation – she may be unemployed, she may be single, she may have chronic health issues, she may have other children or caregiving responsibilities to other family members. To make an informed decision, she also needs support in determining the fit between the information and available options, and her needs and that of the prospective child, her hopes and dreams for herself, her career, her family, and the expectations that others, including the Church, the state, or her community, have of her.

The choice (in this case, to terminate or continue the pregnancy) is expressed by the action (such as obtaining an abortion or consulting a midwife) that, in turn, may express the valuation of becoming a mother in a given set of circumstances. Thus, choice-making must be considered in light of a woman's desires, values, concerns, commitments, social context, relationship to family and others, and resources (Friedman 2003). However, as we argue in this chapter, to focus solely on this particular choice (to proceed with a pregnancy or to terminate it) ignores how women interpret and put together their lives as continuous, interrelated, locally constituted, and embodied moments rather than as a series of discrete and often medicalized events. Thus meaningful choices are those that are consistent with and consider the complex intersections that make up a reproductive life.

Relationships with people, places, things, and events are valued and valuable if we regard them as having some intrinsic or extrinsic value. These valuations do not exist in a vacuum but have meaning that can be deeply rooted in social institutions, including the health care system, the family, and, possibly, a religious institution. These valuations are socially embedded, and so it seems reasonable to assert that making a choice expresses regard for these relationships, for the social connectedness and attachments of the decision-maker (Furlong 2003). Additionally, to assert that decision-making occurs in the context of social relationships suggests that choice is relational and interdependent. Therefore, our assertion is that women have varying power to exercise agency and that power operates in the context of relationships, social structures, and discursive environments that shape or inform how they think, feel, interpret, and act on the choices they make. Moreover, the quality of relationships with family and others affects decision-making and ultimately the character and quality of women's reproductive lives.

Our findings suggest that choice, like other relational moments in women's reproductive lives, evolves over time and is not a one-time event. Therefore we use choice, and especially choice about becoming a mother, as an example of the complexity and relational aspects of an evolving process: in other words, the continuity (or not), congruence (or not), and contingency of choice-making occurs in the context of family as both particularized space and social institution.

THE CONTEXT OF CHOICE IN WOMEN'S LIVES

This chapter draws from our study, *Women's Experience of their Reproductive Lives*, a comparative s s h r c (Social Sciences and Humanities Research Council)- and i d r c (International Development Research Centre)-funded project that gathered qualitative data about the reproductive lives of three generations of women. For our contribution to the study we collected stories from fifty-two women in twenty-four families from a variety of social, geographic, economic, and ethnic backgrounds in Newfoundland and Labrador. The oldest participant was born in 1912 and the youngest in 1987, providing a rich historical perspective. We interviewed one female member of each generation and aimed to secure life stories from grandmothers, mothers, and granddaughters in each family. For clarity, we refer to the grandmother as Generation A, to the daughter as Generation B, and to the granddaughter as Generation C. We gave each participant a pseudonym, and kept the initials the same in each family. We deliberately focused on generations of women in the same family so we could uncover the ways in which women's experience is rooted in the family, and especially in the relationships between generations of women. This, in turn, exposed the cultural context in which women live their lives, and the ways in which religious, biomedical, and other social discourses are mediated by the family, influencing individual decisions about becoming a mother and simultaneously influencing the reproduction of family, community life, and cultural traditions.

THE POSSIBILITY OF MEANINGFUL REPRODUCTIVE CHOICE

In this section we illustrate the complex workings of choice in women's reproductive lives, first by looking at some of the ways women decide whether to have children. We then take examples from women's narratives to illustrate how the limits of autonomy are mediated across generations. We start by looking at the changes in the range of reproductive choices across families and between each generation, starting with the P family.

In the 1920s and 1930s, when there was little information about or access to reliable contraception, raising the issue of mothering as if it were a choice assumed a degree of reproductive autonomy that did not exist for women of Peggy's generation (born 1914) (Purdy 2006). Her daughter Patricia (Generation B, born 1956) expressed difficulty in understanding how women like her mother negotiated a narrower range of reproductive options than she had herself: "So she [Peggy] had five children right away. I'm sure that must have been a big shock to her. I think sometimes my mother woke up one morning and said, 'How the hell did I get here?' I'm sure she must have. That's the way I feel sometimes – that she must have, you know. Not that she ... She was loving and everything like that you know ... Sometimes you feel like she was, I don't know, like wondered how the hell she got there."

Even if Patricia did not quite understand it, Peggy's reproductive life was typical of a particular historical moment in Newfoundland, when having children (and how many) was seen as being in God's hands. Having large families was also an economic necessity (or proof of prosperity), and offset higher rates of infant mortality (Schenker 2005). That Peggy may have awakened one morning, as Patricia said, and asked herself, "How the hell did I get here?" is plausible. However, when Peggy was a young woman there were few acceptable options: most women became wives, and usually mothers. The only alternatives were convents (for Catholics), school teaching (one of the few paid jobs available to women), or remaining a single woman dependent on other members of her natal family (Cavanagh 2006). Therefore, for women of Peggy's generation, deciding to mother came earlier in their reproductive life and was implicitly tied to the decision about whether to marry.

Peggy's decision to marry, and by extension to have children, can be understood in the context of the value of the family as a social institution. The family, and especially the function of reproducing the next generation, was incorporated into both Catholic and Protestant teachings, which emphasize the religious duty to "be fruitful and multiply." The high value given to the family as an institution was deeply rooted in Peggy's Catholic upbringing, the family lives she witnessed around her, and the discursive environment of that historical moment. That she and other Generation A women conformed to the normative practice of marrying and having a large family is understandable given the lack of reliable information and the means to prevent conception. Women exercised agency within the bounds of available options, while at the same time subject to Church doctrine that informed how they felt about, interpreted, and performed their choices.

For Patricia and other women of Generation B, the introduction of reliable contraception, women's expanded opportunities for fulfillment beyond the family, and the diminishing power of the Church increased the range of choices available. Patricia responded both to her mother's experience and these changing social and political conditions by firmly controlling both the timing of her conceptions and limiting the number of her children to two. For her, making a meaningful and informed decision about when to have children was central to defining the kind of life she wanted for herself – a life that was different from her mother's.

In the following exchange, Patricia's daughter, Paula (Generation C, born 1987), describes the tension between living an independent single life and the social pressure to marry, have children, and reproduce family. For Generation C, the lure of romantic love rather than the Church appears to be the powerful voice that informs the social desirability and obligation to choose motherhood. Paula's account illustrates well the preoccupation of her peers with choosing whether to have children, and if so, when. She was – for the moment – choosing not to have children although she (and at least one of her peers) was not shutting out the possibility that she may make a different choice sometime in the future:

> Paula: They all get married. But one of my friends don't want to have kids. But I don't believe it because I know. I can tell. She says it but I know she'll meet a man and fall in love with him and have kids.
> Natalie (interviewer): So why does she say she doesn't want to have them?
> Paula: She thinks they are too much trouble.
> Natalie: But you think she will change her mind?
> Paula: I think she will. She has a very – her and her mother are close, they are. Her mom is very interesting and I think she'll want that. She'll want that relationship [with a child] when she gets older. I know I do. I think she will just because she doesn't talk about her feelings as much as the rest of us do. She has a lot, she hides a lot but I can tell. I know.

Paula's musings suggest that choosing motherhood (or not) is not a one-time event but an evolving and integral part of women's construction of their reproductive lives as continuous, interrelated, and locally constituted. What is also interesting in this passage is that Paula thinks, possibly because of her own close relationship with her mother (Patricia), that a decision to mother is closely connected with reproducing a strong (adult) mother-daughter bond, especially when the adult mother becomes a grandmother. Thus, choosing motherhood is also about reproducing family over time.

Women live their lives against a background of personal and cultural assumptions that all females are or want to be mothers (Gustafson 1998; Letherby 1994). The generational case study approach shows how the relational process of negotiating that choice operates, even if the choice or outcome itself differs across generations. The P family accounts illustrate that limits of choice were different for each generation of women and were deeply informed by the shifting power of religious and other social discourses to structure attitudes about women's autonomy over their bodies and their relationship to family, work, and caregiving responsibilities.

Women's biological capacity to procreate has, in past and present, tended to define their identity and position within the family as responsible for parenting children and reproducing the family. Like Peggy, Winifred (born 1937) was typical of the Generation A women we interviewed. She had six children, but health issues thwarted her desire to have even more: "I never done anything [contraception] because I had six children. I had five boys and one girl and only for I had surgery I think I would have had six more. Mom loved children and I think the same thing would have happened to me."

For women in Generations B and C, the biological capacity to have children was increasingly connected to medical interventions – either to assist in conception or to warn against or prevent further conceptions. Yet, several women like Winifred who wanted but were unable to have more children because of other health issues accepted both their physiological limitations and their doctors' advice in the same way that their mothers accepted the Church's limits to their reproductive autonomy. Mary (Generation B, born 1950) came from a remote northern community with few medical or social services. She had had many difficulties in her life, including a history of abuse and failed pregnancies. The health care she had received was less than ideal. When she learned that she was unable to have more than one child she said she "felt bad" while conveying a resigned acceptance of her situation: "I wanted six. Yes. But then again, I was lucky to have one, you know, instead of having none at all."

Similarly, Irene's (Generation B, born 1952) reproductive life was also limited by a complex health history that made it more difficult for her to conceive Ilya (Generation C, born 1974), her first and only child:

Irene: I was in the hospital a lot when I was pregnant with Ilya and when I mentioned about, you know, ever having another child, and the doctor said, "You'll be lucky to get one."
Natalie (Interviewer): Why is that?
Irene: Because I was a diabetic. She was born six weeks early.
Natalie: Oh, so because of the diabetes?
Irene: Yeah.
Ilya: Is that why it was six years after you got married you had me. Was it the diabetes that was um ... because you were having trouble getting pregnant? Is that why?
Irene: I guess it probably ... I mean, I just wasn't getting pregnant, and I wasn't trying to stop it either.

Although it took six years for Irene to carry a pregnancy to full term, she did not question why she was having difficulty. Nor did she challenge her doctor's apparently heartless remark about being "lucky to get one [child]." Her recollection of that time in her life suggests that she had not received sufficient health information to be both aware of her reproductive body and how diabetes may affect her ability to conceive. Without such information, she was unable to name her difficulty conceiving as a problem or communicate her need for appropriate medical support and intervention.

On the surface, lack of medical information and support seems to be a key factor affecting Irene's ability to make a meaningful decision about when and how many children to have. A deeper examination of Irene's account shows how choice-making was integrated within the emotional and familial context of her life and that of her daughter's. The following exchange illustrates how Irene's health concerns affected the information she shared with her daughter and consequently how Ilya interpreted her reproductive options.

Irene: I always told Ilya never have children because they say that the second generation has ... Okay, so Ilya doesn't have diabetes but her children probably will.
Ilya: It skips a generation.
Irene: That's what I've always heard but you know. I know what a diabetic child can go through and I wouldn't wish that on my worst enemy, let alone a grandchild.

Although Ilya did not have diabetes this did not diminish either woman's fears or perception of genetic risk. Irene spoke of her embodied experience of being a child with diabetes while Ilya referred to diabetes skipping a generation. Irene's expressed fear of passing along a chronic illness to a potential grandchild is echoed in Ilya's decision not to become a mother. Whether the risk was perceived or actual, mother and daughter drew on this information when referring to Ilya's choice. This excerpt illustrates two points: first, decision-making is relational, occurs in the context of particularized familial relationships, and draws on medicalized discourses to frame specific reproductive choices; and second, choice-making involves balancing a woman's desire to mother with available information and the obligation to ensure a good quality of life for a prospective child.

This second point that choice-making is about balancing desires, values, and relationships in a specific local context is also evident in Ruth's story. When Ruth (Generation B, born 1967) became pregnant at the age of twenty-three, she chose to continue the pregnancy but end her relationship with the biological father: "A big part of my decision back then had to do with the father being irresponsible and I didn't figure we'd end up being together for a long, long time." Her decision to become a lone parent rested on her desire for the child coupled with her lack of faith in her relationship with the father. Worth noting is that having a child outside a legally sanctioned union was a more reasonable option (Farrar 2005; Petrie 1998). At an earlier historical moment, Ruth's choice-making may have been fraught with moral uncertainty and constrained by religious or other institutionalized pressures to surrender her child for adoption or marry a person she described as "irresponsible."

Ruth recounted a similar situation years later when, as a woman with a young child in another uncertain relationship, she carefully considered having a second child:

I started going out with Johnny about a year or so after I moved home. And I really wanted to have children and he wasn't ready. And it turns out he wasn't ready now. And I'm thirty-six now and when I was thirty-two I wanted a baby. But I haven't been pregnant since Tyler. And then I just felt like okay ... I have a feeling that this feeling isn't going to stay with me. Like physically, I don't think I'll want to do it in another couple of years. My body is changing, I don't have the energy. I watch people who are forty-five bringing their kids to kindergarten and I think oh my God, I can't imagine being there again.

She went on to say: "And I thought about it really carefully because I thought well ... maybe this is just something to do with my relationship. But it wasn't, clearly. And I thought about [artificial insemination], researched it and me having done everything naturally. I can't take hormones. I've tried it different times to be on the pill again."

Ruth's account shows us a woman in full command of her own reproductive life, if not all the personal relationships that go with it. As a young woman, she chose to continue the pregnancy and as a more mature woman, she opted not to conceive. Ruth understood her body, its responses to hormones, her physical limits, the embodied experience of carrying a pregnancy, and the burden of motherwork. She was articulate in expressing her desire to have a child and her need for a stable and supportive relationship in which to raise that child. She had access to information and, in the second instance, reproductive technologies that were not available to earlier generations.

While Ruth's choices differed, both decision-making processes illuminate well the complex interplay of multiple factors that affect women's ability to make meaningful choices: life goals and aspirations; a particular range of values, concerns, and commitments; the local and broader social context; relationships with family and others; and access to resources, including medical information and interventions. This story also illustrates a point to which Sara Goering (2009) alluded. The complexity of decision-making as a prospective parent does not end with birth. A relational understanding of choice and its operation acknowledges that choosing to mother (or not) is made in the context of the imagined or actual experience of mothering.

CHOICE IN THE H FAMILY

At the beginning of this chapter, we outlined key messages we wanted to convey: reproduction is an integral and continuous part of women's entire lives; the family is both a particularized social environment and also a social and ideological institution; reproductive choice is not a discrete one-time event but a relational and interconnected process; and these messages can be framed by the concept of meaningful choice. To try to link these messages and anchor them in the data, we trace the concept of choice in the reproductive lives of women in one family, demonstrating our understanding of the concept of meaningful choice. We begin by providing something of the context in which one particular family made the choices they did.

Hilda (Generation A) was born in 1921 in Belfast, Ireland. Her early life was characterized by significant life-defining events, such as the death of her mother, the outbreak of the Second World War, a whirlwind marriage, the death of a newborn son, and immigration to Canada. After the death of her parents, she and her two brothers were sent to live with her grandmother. Hilda was taken out of school to help look after her younger brothers. This early experience did not encourage her to expect to exercise agency or have many options for her life. Rather, she expected a destiny of good fortune balanced by a sense of responsibility to and the protection of her extended family. She says: "I was seventeen and my youngest brother was six. So we were very fortunate that my grandmother and all my mother's sisters, they wouldn't let nothing happen to us, so that was that, they looked after us."

In the absence of her mother, Hilda's grandmother was a powerful and omnipresent figure in the family. She orchestrated a traditional family life with a gendered division of domestic labour typical of that place and moment in history. Hilda remembered being responsible for the household chores while her brothers played. By their actions, Hilda's grandmother and aunts taught her that there were women's roles and responsibilities, which included the arduous and unavoidable tasks of scrubbing and cleaning for a large family with few household aids.

In Hilda's accounts of her early life, the concept of choice and with it the possibility of exercising agency did not appear. Her narrative exemplifies the social imperative to mother, to reproduce family, and, in the case of her grandmother, to continue that emotional and instrumental labour after the death of her daughter. To paraphrase Bertaux and Delcroix (2000), it is through such concrete everyday actions that ordinary women reproduce the family as a social and ideological institution. Thus, Hilda's recollection of these familial relations helps us understand how the H family continued those traditions of women's roles and responsibilities.

Hilda, like many women of her age, entered marriage having learned very little from other women in the family about any aspect of her reproductive life and options, including sexual relations and contraception. She had little preparation for pregnancy and childbirth, even though she was present at the time of her brother's birth.

> Hilda: Oh yes, I can remember [when my brother was born] the midwife going upstairs to my mother. But I didn't ... You weren't that far advanced that you even knew your mother was pregnant.
> Kim (interviewer): Yeah, you didn't really know what was happening ...
> Hilda: You were sort of stupid when you think of it now. And all I can remember when I went in to see my mother after everything was all over. And the nurse went down the stairs would stop and tell me not to look at it [the post-birth scene] so that still stays with me. But that's all I can remember about that part of it.

Hilda married a Newfoundland serviceman stationed in Belfast in one of the whirlwind romances typical of the time. She did not tell us whether she made a conscious decision to have children, or even if she discussed it with her new husband. She had two children: Hazel, and a boy who died shortly after he was born. Hilda took for granted that the midwife would provide her and her son with appropriate care. Much later on, when she became more informed about childbirth and medical options, she came to believe that her newborn's life might have been saved if hospital treatment had been available and she had had a C-section. Hilda said, "When Hazel was born I had problems and then I had a little boy. I should have had a C-section. He was too big for me to have and he didn't live. So I only had the two. I never had no more."

Some years after the war, Hilda left Ireland with her husband and their daughter Hazel, and moved to his home community in rural Newfoundland. It is not clear whether Hilda took an active part in the decision to move. Many young women followed their wartime sweethearts or husbands to their countries of origin. Over 500 came to Newfoundland, and while some quickly returned to Britain, many more remained and settled into their new lives (Barrett 1996; Jarratt 2009). Initially, Hilda was lonely and bitterly unhappy in her husband's rural community. After the family moved to St John's, where they were still living at the time of the interviews, Hilda raised her own family and her adjustment was reflected in the more positive tone in which she recounted her later life. Hilda's account makes

clear the social and familial expectations and the limits of choice-
making for women of her generation. Stories about her early life as
well as her everyday actions clearly influenced her daughter and her
granddaughters or, to paraphrase Bonnie Fox (2001; 2009), created
gendered adults, gendered identities, and gendered practices on an
ongoing basis.

Hazel (Generation B) was born in 1947 in Belfast and lived there
until she was twelve, when her family immigrated to Newfoundland.
As the only living child, Hazel was determined to have more than
one child herself, although her own preparation with regard to sex,
conception, and pregnancy was almost as minimal as her mother's.

> Hazel: Well again, my poor mother. You know you didn't discuss
> stuff like that [sex] with your mother. You just didn't ask because
> you knew you weren't going to be given an answer anyway.
> Phyllis (interviewer): She never told you anything?
> Hazel: Never told me.
> Phyllis: Nothing about … What about your first period?
> Hazel: Oh no. I remember standing up in our bathroom and cry-
> ing, "I'm dying. There's something wrong with me." Right and …
> Phyllis: And you never talked to any of your girlfriends about it?
> Hazel: I did after … That's when Mom found out about it and I
> said, "What's going on?" and then she told me "You started your
> period." That was it.
> Phyllis: That was it. What did she do? Did she supply you with
> some napkins?
> Hazel: That was basically it.

By providing Hazel with so little information, Hilda not only left
her daughter ill-prepared for menarche and subsequent reproductive
events, but perpetuated the association between the lack of knowledge and lack of meaningful choice that she had experienced herself.
Hazel's story is a clear example of how not having appropriate information to understand normal reproductive moments limited her
ability to make meaningful choices about conception, pregnancy,
and birthing.

In her first pregnancy, Hazel tried to equip herself with the knowledge she needed to make more informed choices about pregnancy
and birthing by attending prenatal classes. Despite this, she still had
a "terrible" labour because the baby was breached. Although her

doctors told her about the breach presentation, Hazel was too in-
timidated to ask them what this meant for her and the birthing. She
recounted the story this way:

Hazel: Oh, I had a terrible labour ... You know it's so funny because she was completely breached, and they knew that when
I was about five or six months pregnant, and you talk about not
knowing very much, I mean I really was a sheltered child when
you think about it. I goes to the doctor and coming home and
I was really upset. I remember crying on the way home. And he
was saying, "We're really gonna have to watch you, may put you
in the hospital." I said, "Why?" He said, "Because your baby is
breached." Now I did not have a clue what a breached baby was.
I really didn't have a clue.
Phyllis: And did you ask him?
Hazel: I didn't ask him. I was too stupid to ask him. He caught
me so off guard and I just didn't ask. Well, I came home to mom
and I said, "Mom, he said I'm having a breached birth." I said,
"What is that?" "Well now," she said ...
Phyllis: She said what?
Hazel: "Oh you dear child," I said, "Ok, what is it?" She said, "It
means," she said, "that the baby's head is not going to come out
first. It will be some other part of the baby." Okay. I'll do that,
right. So it was after the fact that I heard tell of a breached birth.
Phyllis: After you got the baby?
Hazel: No, no, after I asked. And I said to mom, "Is it a big
deal?" and she said, "Well, they'll watch you and sometimes it
turns and sometimes it doesn't. And she said, "You were
breached on me." Now if I was breached on mom and here's
Heidi was going to be breached, doesn't that make you wonder
if there is something there?
Phyllis: It does, it really does.
Hazel: I'm convinced that there is something [genetic or familial].
Why would I have a breach baby, I mean why?

This poignant account charts the historical dimension of the experience of pregnancy and childbirth within one family, highlighting
the significance of when information is shared between mother and
daughter as a factor in choice-making. It also shows the difficulty
some women experience in finding the language and motivation to

share with their daughters their own embodied experience in a social and familial environment where the language to engage in body talk was undeveloped. In this case, Hilda was jolted out of her silence by the realization that her daughter was going to go through the same experience in childbirth that she had had. The case shows that women live and make choices within a familial environment with a specific history. Hilda's history of growing up in a family where she did not exercise agency echoes in Hazel's interactions with her physician and her difficulty seeking the information she needed so she could make meaningful decisions about her first pregnancy.

Hazel's second pregnancy was against medical advice, but she was determined to have more than one child. This desire was understandable given her family history and her experience as an only child. By that time, Hazel was more knowledgeable about her body and the possible health consequences of another pregnancy, and was able to make a more informed, if problematic, choice.

> Hazel: Well, he [my husband] wasn't fussy on having any more [children], and I just said no, actually I was … The doctor didn't recommend that I even get pregnant again right, but I said no, I'm having another one. I just didn't want Heidi to grow up on her own. I made sure I wasn't going through that torture anymore and they were … When I did go in labour on Helen … there was no fuss, nothing. They scheduled [a] section for that day and that was it. They tried to talk me into an epidural when I got there. I said, "No, forget it. I don't want it. No more chances."

This account illustrates the difference in outcome when a woman is better informed and able to make a meaningful choice. Hazel was determined to have a second child and expressed her desire to her husband. This power to exercise her agency extended beyond the family to her medical team. It is clear that she saw her physicians as partners in her care, rather than as unquestioned authorities, and was able to override their advice. Hazel's ability to make decisions about her body is noteworthy given the medicalizing discourse of women's reproductive bodies emerging at the time, but is, at the same time, consistent with women's emerging political voice in the wider social arena.

Perhaps because of Hazel's ultimate success in negotiating the birth of her second child, coupled with her own history of having limited knowledge and control over menarche and her first pregnancy, she was determined to be more forthright in addressing these topics with her daughters. Hazel wanted to ensure that her daughters would be much better equipped than she and able to make meaningful choices in their lives. Clearly, this process of decision-making evolved over time and makes sense in the context of this family story. However, Hazel's decision was made more possible because the H family lived in an urban centre more informed by the growing liberalization of society in the 1970s than their counterparts in rural Newfoundland. Hazel talked to her daughters about sex, offered to get them contraceptives, and would have advised in favour of abortion if they had become pregnant as teenagers. In other words, Hazel worked actively to provide her daughters with the maximum degree of choice in their reproductive lives. She reports:

> I took my two to the doctor when they were in university and that last year of high school and that. I told them all about contraception and everything, warned them what to do and what not to do ... They knew more than I did but I mean to feel that I was giving them my little motherly speech, not like my mother didn't give me I wanted to give to my girls. Not knowing it would make me feel less guilt if something did happen to them, I don't know but I mean, I was open enough about it and told them everything that I knew to the best of my ability. I'm sure they knew a lot more than I do, and I told them, "I got no bones about taking you girls into the doctor getting contraceptives right." It was either that or you know. I don't know maybe I was wrong in doing that, but I don't feel like I was.

Hazel had thought carefully about sexuality, values, and choice, and how these related to her moral framework and upbringing. She described how far she would be prepared to take this line of thinking:

> My idea on it was: they were my children, my responsibility. I taught them right from wrong, to the best of my ability and I knew they knew right from wrong. But I mean there's nobody perfect and it [getting pregnant outside marriage] could happen

to anyone, right? So the way I looked at it, it had nothing to do with religion. Religion wasn't a factor into it at all. I just wanted them to know that maybe they were too embarrassed to say, "Mom, would you come with me to get pills?" Maybe they wouldn't ask it, but I wanted to make sure that they knew that I would go with them and taking them, and I wasn't against them getting them because if you got a future for your kids in mind, even though it isn't your future, you know the children and you know basically what they want.

She went on to say: "So even a child is factored into that, when they're only children themselves, you know, I don't know what I'm trying to say because ... it wasn't the fact that, I didn't really want them to have, it wouldn't be a sin to me. I wouldn't look at it as a sin if they had come home pregnant. But when you want something better for them and I knew they wanted something better themselves, why? Why, when they're not ready for it? That's the way I looks at it."

CHOICE AND THE TRANSMISSION OF VALUES

In their accounts, the H family illustrates how three women exercised choice in their reproductive lives. In this section we explore how values are transmitted from mother to daughter to granddaughter, and how this transmission also goes up the generations. While some key values remained firm, especially those of the importance of family and commitment to a life partner, some changed as the values in their social context changed. We heard the women in this family having to work through in detail the relationship between the social and religious values they grew up learning and the increasing range of options available to them, especially in the area of reproductive choice. Like most women we interviewed, the women in the H family expressed a strong sense of an autonomous self, an understanding of the choices available to them given the social context of their eras, and a commitment to making responsible decisions.

In this family as in the others, mothers were, to varying degrees, a source of information about sexual health and reproduction, whether spoken clearly, in code, or silently revealed and remembered through everyday actions. When Hilda got her first period, her mother provided her with both practical guidance and one cryptic piece of advice that Hilda rightly took as an explanation of sorts about both menstruation and sexual relations between women and men:

> Kim (interviewer): So you didn't know really why you got your period?
> Hilda: Not really, but I suppose, in a way, when she said, "don't tell no wee boys," that was one way of her thinking that she had told me ... And where we were living with my grandmother and my mother's sisters, they weren't ones for talking about it either. What you picked up, you picked up on your own, really.

Hilda's suspicions that sex was fraught with difficulty and danger were confirmed by an incident in the family. She says: "I can remember my cousin; well there was no talk of anybody getting pregnant then; that was an awful thing if you weren't married ... that's what happened to my cousin. My cousin got his girlfriend pregnant. And they were all in tears; his people were in tears ... And there was nothing for them but to get married. Although it worked out for them, but lots of times they get married for that reason and it doesn't work out."

This incident highlights a point previously made about the expectation that women who became pregnant were expected to choose marriage over shaming their family. Choosing to marry reconfigured women's lives, not always in positive ways. Yet, despite the risk of an unintended pregnancy in a social and religious context that frowned upon premarital sex, Hilda did not feel able to protect her daughter by equipping her with the accurate information she needed to make informed decisions. In contrast, Hazel took her responsibility toward her own daughters very seriously, not only providing them with all the sexual education they needed, but also ensuring they had effective contraceptives.

In this family, there is a marked difference across the generations about what they thought had changed for women. Hilda, born just after the Second World War, believed emphatically that contemporary women have greater control over all aspects of their lives, but especially over their reproductive lives:

> Kim (interviewer): What about things that are different now for girls?

Hilda: It's all different sure. I think it's wonderful now because
there's no need of any wee girl of getting herself in trouble.
There's no need, is there?
Kim: What kind of things, though?
Hilda: Well, sure, there's everything to keep yourself from getting
pregnant. And sure the fellows know what to do to keep you
from getting diseases, don't they? So that's all different. It's very
up to date.

A little later in the interview, she continued:

Hilda: That's what [Heidi] says when she gets her PhD. She'll be
the one making the most money so she says [her partner] is going
to have to look after the youngsters when they come. So that's,
I think that's great. There was none of that in my day. That's why
I think it's wonderful for girls. They don't have to depend on a
man anymore. They're independent and I think that's wonderful.
You're not dependent on any man and, if they don't like what
he's doing, you can chuck him out, get rid of him [*laughter*] you
know what I mean? You don't have to put up with any nonsense.
That's a good thing.

In sharp contrast, Helen (Generation C) seems to ache to go back
to the more traditional ways of doing things reminiscent of her
grandmother's story.

Helen: Okay. Well I don't know where it came from because my
mom and my dad they worked my entire lives, my mom is still
working. Somewhere along the way I picked up this traditional
sense of things, I don't know where it came from – maybe my
grandma. My ideal world would be like even though I am still in
university and this is my second degree, but my ideal world
would be to be a stay at home mom and let the man be the supporter, monetary supporter and that's what I would love to do
and it's not going to happen I know that.
    It changed in the past few years. I know that because when
I was still at [university]. All I was thinking was well this is what
I am going to university for. I want to be independent; I want
to be self-sufficient. I don't want to rely on anybody and then
I don't know when it changed. Perhaps when I could see that
[boyfriend] was actually making a lot of money. And it was

really good money. And I guess I could see that and he would always say, "You can stop school whenever you want to and you move here and I'll take care of everything." ... I guess at first I was like, you're so stupid. I don't want to do that. I want to have my own job and support myself. But I guess somewhere along the way I started thinking that would be so great. I'd love to stay at home and be a normal typical housewife and raise children. I don't want to leave my children with nannies if I ever have them. I want a family. I want to have kids.

Kim (interviewer): How many kids do you want to have?

Helen: I want to have two or three. Like I know it was just me and my sister. I'd never want to have just one.

We cannot know whether Helen would ultimately pursue her ambition to be a "typical housewife and raise children," and, in many ways replicate the ideal pattern her grandmother subscribed to. But this young woman, who had a much wider range of choices than either her mother or grandmother and the power to exercise her agency was imagining her reproductive life according to values and preferences that she had learned and that were expressed in her family. Helen's experience reminds us both of how much has changed for women since her grandmother was her age in Belfast and that the concept of choice, like other social constructions, is complex.

Somewhat diffidently, Helen presents a romanticized version of traditional life. She seems to yearn for the clarity of strict gendered rules about who does what in the so-called traditional family, perhaps in response to the arrangements that became the norm in her family as she was growing up. She expresses the ambivalence many young women feel about their success on the roller coaster of education and career and the pressures to succeed in the public world that are expressed all around her. This ambivalence is also part of the current political shift toward embracing so-called traditional family values in the face of the reality of more diverse family constellations.

All three generations of women in this family saw themselves as being a little behind the times in terms of their sexual experience, and spoke wonderingly about how innocent they were. At the same time, all three generations were open in terms of their views on sexual freedoms. For example, Hazel (Generation B) discussed the possibility of her daughters getting an abortion: "Seven or eight years ago, I'd have said no, not an option to have the baby, you should have an abortion, because at that point they just started university and we wanted the best for them. And ... the way I look at it then, well, her life, well not ruined, but certainly wouldn't be where we wanted her to be and where she wanted to be herself."

Helen's account confirms her mother's openness and her own conviction that her children should have information and that she, as a mother, needed to be active in declaring support for a wider range of options for her children to consider in making possible choices about whether to choose motherhood. Helen (Generation C) states: "I remember my sister's friend having an abortion when my sister was in grade twelve and that's when my mom really talked to me and my sister a lot about abortion. My mom would never tell us what to do and I don't know where she stands on certain topics because she would never influence us in that way. So, I'm very pro-choice, like it's up to the person."

Hazel's activist response to the lack of information she had received about sex and reproduction, and her positive approach to preparing her daughters alters the course of this family narrative. It also resists the Church position, reflecting a wider range of legal–medical options that are now available to many women in Canada.

CONCLUSION

In this chapter we have focused on the boundaries and operation of choices at one relational moment in a woman's reproductive life – that of becoming a mother. At the same time, our exploration has been mindful of critiques of this approach (Kaposy and Downie 2008; Mullin 2005; Nelson 2004) in that we have shown that choice in one moment is integrated within and inseparable from the social, emotional, familial, and cultural contexts of women's entire lives. This means that we reject the medicalized notion – as have others – that the operation of choice can be reduced to discrete decisions about, for instance, whether to use contraception, continue a pregnancy, or have two instead of one child (Purdy 2006; Sherwin 1998).

Our generational approach to exploring the operation of choice provided us with valuable insights into how information and values are transmitted, given authority, acted upon, and resisted by women across generations and within the same family. We treat the family as a social and ideological institution that mediates what and how a girl learns to be a woman, mother, and grandmother, and shapes how she chooses to reproduce herself, her family and its legacy, and the cultural values and traditions of the broader society in which she lives. At the same time, we acknowledge that the family also operates as a particularized social environment with a unique history that informs how individual women's reproductive lives play out. Using the experience of particular women in the same family, we have shown how the cultural and social discourses such as those expressed by churches and the medical establishment were mediated by the family as both social institution and particularized social environment.

All the women we interviewed made choices – even if they were only to conform to, rather than resist, normative expectations; none had the complete informed freedom of choice that Sherwin (1998) would characterize as autonomy. By tracing the operation of choice-making within families, we have highlighted the complex and ever-changing ways in which women negotiate between their ideals and values, their personal preferences, the needs of their families, their gendered location in society, and the economic, social, and religious constraints within which they live and interpret their lives.

Our analysis shows that choice operates at the problematic nexus of many issues that concern feminists (and others), such as the medicalization of women's bodies (Purdy 2006; Sherwin 1998), women's autonomy over the integrity of their bodies (Hanigsberg 1995; Johnstone 2010; Sethna and Doull 2007), and the gendering of work and caregiving responsibilities (Friedman 2003; Mullin 2005). At different historical moments, family planning, contraception, and abortion have been forbidden, making these acts unspeakable in public and, as our study shows, sometimes unspeakable within the family. Therefore, how reproductive choice is defined, interpreted, and concretized in institutional practice affects the operation of choice as everyday practice and, in turn, the construction of women's lives. The factors that facilitate meaningful choice such as access to contraception, health care, and reliable and timely information, increase the range of options available to women. A broader range of socially acceptable options increases opportunities to engage in body talk within (and beyond) the family in ways that enable women to interpret, resist, and perform their reproductive choices.

NOTE

1 In this chapter, we report on some of the Canadian data collected as part of a SSHRC and IDRC-funded three-country study, *Women's Experience of Reproductive Health in the Family in Canada, Indonesia and Pakistan: A Comparative-Intergenerational Life Story Project*. The project was led by Marilyn Porter with a Canadian research team that included Natalie Beausoleil, Phyllis Artiss, and research assistants Carla Barton and Kim Bonia; a Pakistani team lead by Tahera Aftab that included the late Zareen Ilyas and the late Shakila Rehman; and an Indonesian team lead by Anita Rahman that included Tita Marlita and Kristi Poerwandari. Additionally, our sincere thanks to the editors and to Chris Kaposy for their comments on earlier versions of this chapter.

BIBLIOGRAPHY

Anderson, Elizabeth. 1993. *Value in Ethics and Economics*. Cambridge: Harvard University Press.

Ball, Carlos A. 2005. "This Is Not Your Father's Autonomy: Lesbian and Gay Rights from a Feminist and Relational Perspective." *Harvard Journal of Law & Gender* 28(2): 345–79.

Barrett, Barbara B. c.m., Eileen Dicks, Isobel Brown, Hilda Chaulk Murray, and Helen Fogwill Porter, eds. 1996. *We Came From over The Sea: British War Brides in Newfoundland*. Portugal Cove: ESPress.

Bertaux, Daniel, and Catherine Delcroix. 2000. "Case Histories of Families and Social Processes: Enriching Sociology." In *The Turn to Biographical Methods in Social Science: Comparative Issues and Examples*, P. Chamberlayne, J. Bornat, and T. Wengraf, eds., 71–89. London: Routledge.

Bezanson, Kate, and Meg Luxton, eds. 2006. *Social Reproduction: Feminist Political Economy Challenges Neo-Liberalism*. Montreal & Kingston: McGill-Queen's University Press.

Cavanagh, Sheila L. 2006. "Spinsters, Schoolmarms, and Queers: Female Teacher Gender and Sexuality in Medicine and Psychoanalytic Theory and History." *Discourse: Studies in the Cultural Politics of Education* 27(4): 421–40.

Farrar, Patricia D. 2005. "Abject Mothers: Women Separated from Their Babies Lost to Adoption." In *Unbecoming Mothers: The Social Production of Maternal Absence*, Diana L. Gustafson, ed. New York: Routledge.

Fox, Bonnie. 2009. *When Couples Become Parents: The Creation of Gender in the Transition to Parenthood*. Toronto: University of Toronto Press.

– 2001. "The Formative Years: How Parenthood Creates Gender." *Canadian Review of Sociology & Anthropology* 38(4): 373–90.

Friedman, Marilyn. 2003. *Autonomy, Gender, Politics*. New York: Oxford University Press.

Furlong, Mark. 2003. "Critiquing the Goal of Autonomy: Towards Strengthening the 'Relational Self' and the Quality of Belonging in Casework Practice." *European Journal of Social Work* 6(1): 5–18.

Goering, Sara. 2009. "Postnatal Reproductive Autonomy: Promoting Relational. Autonomy and Self-Trust in New Parents." *Bioethics* 23(1): 9–19.

Gustafson, Diana L. 1998. "Learning to Wear Mother Clothes to Cover Woman Dreams." *Canadian Woman Studies Journal* 18(2/3): 105–8.

Hanigsberg, Julia E. 2002. "Mother Troubles: Rethinking Contemporary Maternal Dilemmas." *NWSA Journal* 14(2): 221–5.

– 1995. "Homologizing Pregnancy and Motherhood: A Consideration of Abortion." *Michigan Law Review* 94(2): 371–418.

Jarratt, Melinda. 2009. *War Brides: The Stories of the Women Who Left Everything Behind to Follow the Men They Loved*. Fredericton: Dundurn Press.

Johnstone Rachael. 2010. "Framing Reproductive Rights: The Politics of Abortion Access and Citizenship in a Post-Morgentaler Era." Accessed 1 December 2011. http://www.cpsa-acsp.ca.

Kaposy, Chris, and Jocelyn Downie. 2008. "Judicial Reasoning about Pregnancy and Choice." *Health Law Journal* 16: 281–304.

Letherby, Gayle. 1994. "Mother or Not, Mother or What: Problems of Definition and Identity." *Women's Studies International Forum* 17(5): 525–32.

Mullin, Amy. 2005. *Reconceiving Pregnancy and Childcare: Ethics, Experience and Reproductive Labour*. New York: Cambridge University Press.

Nelson, Erin. 2004. "Choice and Legal Reasoning." *McGill Law Journal* 49: 593–634.

O'Brien, Mary. 1981. *The Politics of Reproduction*. London: Routledge.

Petrie, Ann. 1998. *Gone to an Aunt's: Remembering Canada's Homes for Unwed Mothers*. Toronto: McClelland Stewart.

Porter, Marilyn, and Diana L. Gustafson. 2012. *Reproducing Women: Family and Health Work across Three Generations*. Black Point, NS: Fernwood Books.

Purdy, L. 2006. "Women's Reproductive Autonomy: Medicalisation and Beyond." *Journal of Medical Ethics* 32: 287–91.

Schenker, Joseph G. 2005. "Assisted Reproductive Practice: Religious Perspectives." *Reproductive Biomedicine* 10(3): 310–19.

Sethna, Christabelle, and Marion Doull. 2007. "Far From Home? A Pilot Study Tracking Women's Journeys to a Canadian Abortion Clinic." *Journal of the Society for Obstetricians and Gynaecologists* 29(8): 640–7.

Sherwin, Susan. 1998. "A Relational Approach to Autonomy in Health Care." In *The Politics of Women's Health: Exploring Agency and Autonomy*, S. Sherwin et al., eds. Philadelphia: Temple University Press.

2

IVF Policy and the Stratification of Reproduction in Canada[1]

FRANCESCA SCALA

The provision of in vitro fertilization and other related infertility treatments has been a subject of much debate among researchers and commentators. For some, infertility is regarded as a legitimate health issue deserving of medical and state intervention. Among feminist critics, assisted human reproduction is regarded as a new site for the medical exploitation of women. While acknowledging the inequalities engendered by reproductive technologies on a social scale, this chapter's main focus is the politics of the public provision of infertility treatments, in particular the consequences of distinguishing "legitimate" versus "illegitimate" users of these services. Through public policy, decisions surrounding accessibility, eligibility requirements, and funding of IVF treatment can simultaneously challenge prevailing notions of motherhood, parenthood, and the family while contributing to the stratification of reproduction by reinforcing divisions along class, gender, race, and sexual orientation. As Michelle (2006, 111) explains, "the potential of ART to transgress and re-inscribe these conventional meanings is determined not by the technologies themselves but by various implicit and explicit constraints placed on their use within the broader social, political, medical, legal and representational realms, constraints which can and do change over time."

In this chapter, I examine the intended and unintended consequences of assisted reproduction policies for women, especially policies governing funding arrangements and eligibility requirements as they relate to IVF policies. With the notable exception of Quebec,

IV F treatments in Canada are not covered by provincial health care programs. Conceptualizing I V F as a reproductive benefit, I examine how the use of evidence-based analysis and biomedical definitions of infertility has contributed to the stratification of reproduction in Canada. I uncover how fiscal concerns and the provision of I V F by the market have commodified infertility treatments in Canada and have, in turn, led to the unequal distribution of reproductive benefits among women. In the first section, I situate I V F provision in the theoretical context of stratified reproduction and explore the various ways the medical community and the state are implicated in the distribution of reproductive benefits. In the second section, I examine the medicalization of infertility and discuss how state policy in Canada has limited and/or expanded the gatekeeping function of physicians in determining the legitimate users of I V F treatments. In the third section, I examine how Evidence-Based Medicine (E B M) and policy analysis have governed Canada's official discourse on reproductive technologies, leading to the commodification of I V F in Canada. Finally, I discuss the implications of provincial flexibility in determining "medical necessity" and the recent decommodification of I V F in Quebec.

STRATIFIED REPRODUCTION AND ASSISTED HUMAN REPRODUCTION

The term *new reproductive technologies* is used to identify a category of biomedical practices and procedures used to assist conception and pregnancy. New reproductive technologies include in vitro fertilization, surrogacy, egg donation, therapeutic donor insemination, and embryo freezing and transfer. As a group, these practices provide means to insemination and fertilization other than heterosexual intercourse. Individually, these technologies differ significantly in terms of their technological sophistication and level of medical intervention. For example, assisted insemination (A I)[2] entails a lower level of technology and medical intervention than sperm and egg micromanipulation do. Moreover, each of these technologies has their own unique history and development. Several of the so-called new technologies, in particular surrogacy and artificial insemination, have been around for a long time. For instance, the earliest recorded artificial insemination of a woman by a physician took place in 1884 in Britain (Eichler 1988). However, it was not until the 1978 birth of the first I V F [3] baby in England that the once-futuristic, sci-fi tale of "test-tube" babies became a scientific reality and, soon thereafter, a widely accepted treatment for infertility.

While the medical and scientific literature on assisted human reproduction regards these technologies as inherently value-neutral, feminist research on infertility treatments and surrogacy arrangements has focused on the "detrimental" effect of these technologies on the health and well-being of women. For the most part, feminist scholarship has been highly critical of these technologies, arguing that they further contribute to the medical control of conception, gestation, and birth, and reinforce the gendered social roles of women as mothers. Moreover, feminist research also highlights how A R T S work to reinforce existing *structural* inequalities among women, with white, middle-class women availing themselves of costly, fertility-enhancing treatments while low-income and minority women struggle to access basic medical services. In the United States and Canada (with the exception of Quebec) infertility treatments, like I V F, are delivered by private clinics as fee-for-service, effectively restricting access to white, elite couples while disadvantaging poor women who cannot afford to pay for the services. In several countries where infertility treatments are covered by national health insurance programs, such as France, Germany, and Switzerland, relationship status, sexual orientation, and the notions of the "best interests of the child," are often used to determine eligibility to treatments. In many countries, lesbian and unmarried women who are attempting to produce biological offspring are often restricted from accessing these services. By choosing I V F's funding arrangements and eligibility requirements, the state is once again actively engaged in what some refer to as "stratified reproduction."

Stratified reproduction is a term first coined by Colen (1995) to describe power relations that empower or disempower certain groups of people to nurture and reproduce. Societal inequalities based on class, race, ethnicity, sexual orientation, and gender are both reflected and reproduced by a stratified system of reproduction. These power relations are reflected and reinforced by cultural and political representations of motherhood, which advance certain images of "the good mother" and "the natural family." For example, in the United States, images of "welfare mothers" are often depicted in racialized terms, with African-American mothers represented as highly fertile and a drain to the welfare system (Bell 2009).

Government policy plays an important part in contributing to this stratified system of reproduction, politicizing issues such as fertility and infertility, pregnancy, contraception, abortion, and maternal health. According to Ginsburg and Rapp (1995, 3), the state contributes to inequalities in reproduction, oftentimes adopting a strategy of "discursive exclusion of women (and others) from cultural representations and social practices." Cultural images and social practices are reinforced by government policy, which structure the benefits and costs of reproduction and motherhood along existing societal cleavages (McCormack 2005).

One of the areas where stratified reproduction is being played out is reproductive technologies. Infertility treatments like in vitro fertilization and assisted insemination, gamete donations, and surrogacy arrangements are all challenging conventional notions of motherhood, parenthood, kinship, and the family. Many of these developments and their consequences are being played out both at the national and international levels. While government programs and international initiatives in developing countries have focused on controlling women's fertility as a solution to the poverty of those regions, discourses of reproduction in advanced industrialized countries have advanced pronatalist programs to address the "problem" of low birth rates and infertility. These pronatalist programs, however, often target a certain group of women. For example, in the United States, poor and minority women are often encouraged through government policy to control their fertility while white, middle-, and upper-class women's reproductive choices are enhanced through the availability and use of expensive treatments. In countries where infertility treatments are not covered by national health care programs, reproduction is stratified along economic lines and insurance status. For many feminists, the advent of reproductive technologies further solidifies a reproductive hierarchy based on class and race that already exists among women. As Roberts (2009, 784) explains, "the multi-billion-dollar apparatus devoted to technologically facilitating affluent couples' procreative decisions stands in glaring contrast to the high rate of infant death among black people, which remains more than twice the rate for whites."

Along with the state, the medical community is also implicated in the distribution of reproductive benefits. The construction of infertility as a biomedical condition and/or a disease has assigned physicians a great deal of authority over who can claim to be infertile and, therefore, who should have access to treatment (Greil and McQuillan 2010). State policy mediates the authority of physicians in defining and interpreting infertility as a medical condition, devising treatment options, and controlling access to these treatments. For example, in Sweden, government regulation allows only one embryo (two in older women) to be transferred per IVF cycle. In other countries, medical associations, individual physicians, and clinics retain a greater degree of authority in determining guidelines on the number of embryos transferred. IVF policy is therefore an important site for uncovering the involvement of the state and the medical community in the distribution and protection of reproductive benefits in Canada and elsewhere As King and Meyer (1997, 9) explain, "If the state does not guarantee all women the right to a full range of reproductive treatments, regardless of social and economic class, the state may be implicitly endorsing a de facto fertility policy that encourages births among working and middle-class women and discourages births among the poor and welfare recipients."

In the case of Canada, there is no single, unilateral program or policy that governs IVF and related treatments. Different aspects of infertility treatments are governed by the 2004 Assisted Human Reproduction Act (AHRA), the Canada Health Act (CHA), and provincial health care regulations. The AHRA governs research and clinical activities related to assisted human reproduction and outlines those that are prohibited or regulated, such as the prohibition on commercial surrogacy and the sale of human gametes. As a health service, infertility treatments fall under the exclusive jurisdiction of provinces while their funding or lack of funding is guided by provisions of the Canada Health Act. Together, these pieces of legislation and regulations determine the funding arrangements, insurance coverage, and eligibility requirements for infertility treatments and, in turn, outline the state's role in the distribution of reproductive benefits in Canada. In the following sections, I explore the manner in which IVF policy in Canada stratifies reproduction.

THE MEDICALIZATION OF INFERTILITY AND PHYSICIANS AS GATEKEEPERS

Issues of coverage and access to IVF and related treatments emerged as infertility became increasingly medicalized. *Medicalization* refers to a process by which social and biological conditions and developments that were once perceived to be "normal" or "natural" are transformed into medical conditions requiring medical treatment or intervention. Simply defined, it is the "process whereby more and more of everyday life has come under medical dominion, influence and supervision" (Zola 1983, 295). Some view the process of medicalization as inherently neutral, but as having effects that can negatively or positively affect certain individuals and groups. Others conceptualize medicalization as a social institution and ideology that contributes to and is embedded in patriarchal and classist processes and practices (Bell 2009).

According to Conrad (1992), medicalization is a broad process that occurs on three different fronts: conceptual, institutional, and physician–patient interactions. At the conceptual level, biomedical models can be used to characterize a problem or condition without necessarily involving the medical profession or the use of medical remedies. Medicalization also occurs at the institutional level when organizations specializing in a particular field adopt a medical approach to addressing a problem that falls under their purview. Finally, medicalization takes place at the individual patient–doctor level, where physicians provide a medical diagnosis and offer medical treatments to problems previously deemed as social in nature. At each level, medicalization can be accepted, negotiated, or rejected by individuals, groups, and societies (Conrad 1992). A pivotal actor that is implicated in the process of medicalization is the state. The transformation of social problems into medical problems and the ability of the medical profession to influence the process of medicalization are also shaped by state policies and agendas. More precisely, how a problem is defined and what types of interventions are deemed appropriate is mediated by government policies, especially in countries that have state sponsored or publicly funded health care systems.

Since the advent of reproductive technologies in the 1970s and 1980s, infertility has been constructed as a disease or medical condition requiring medical intervention. In the past, physicians often dismissed these ailments as emotional rather than physical problems, telling patients "to relax, accept God's will, or adopt" (King and Meyer 1997, 10). Today, infertility is regarded as a medical condition or disease that can be treated with biomedical treatments. As an illness, the category "infertility" subsumes a broad range of biological conditions and clinical criteria for childlessness. The label "infertile," which had traditionally been used to refer to individuals who were sterile, is now a medical diagnosis for individuals who remain childless after a one-year period of unprotected intercourse. The development and proliferation of reproductive technologies has redefined infertility as a broad diagnostic category for all unexplained incidences of childlessness. Critics argue that the lack of consistency and clarity in delineating the origins of childlessness ultimately works to validate the broad application of reproductive techniques. For instance, the term infertility does not distinguish between infertility cases resulting from environmental factors as opposed to innate, biological conditions. As Steinberg (1997, 44) explains: "Environmentally induced and iatrogenic 'infertility' clearly constitute (often preventable) problems which do not originate in the individual affected. However, when infertility is strictly a diagnostic/treatment question, the power relations surrounding the relationship between infertility, environmental pollution and adverse effects of medical treatment become begged."

Moreover, the medicalization of infertility often works to obfuscate the social or cultural reasons for "involuntary childlessness." For example, age has become an important contributing factor to infertility as a result of women delaying childbirth due to professional and other work-related commitments. The lack of social and state support available to lone parents, such as affordable daycare, as well as the social stigma still attached to being a single mother often prevents women from having children in their twenties, a time when they are at their most fertile. Moreover, the medicalization of infertility does not address the obstacles to biological parenthood experienced by lesbian and gay individuals and couples. When infertility becomes medicalized, the individual becomes the focus of attention and the target of intervention, rather than the underlying social and material conditions that contribute to the phenomenon. As Chang and Christakis (2002, 152) explain, "Structural conditions such as sociocultural, environmental, and material context are often obscured or ignored in favour of isolated individual factors such as lifestyle and personal behaviours. Social problems thus become individualised."

With infertility regarded as a medical condition, physicians have assumed the role of gatekeepers to treatment. Often, social, rather than medical, criteria are used to determine who should have access to IVF and other treatments and who should not. According to

Heitman and Schlachtenhaufen (1996), physicians often make decisions regarding who has access to fertility treatments on the basis of social rather than medical considerations. Physicians working in both privately and publicly funded clinics often rule out patients who do not fit the stereotypical, heterosexual middle-to-upper-class married couple. Moreover, as is the case with adoption requirements, the "well-being of the offspring" often plays a part in determining the ideal patient for IVF and related services. As the authors explain, clinics "typically have treatment criteria for IVF that include such socioeconomic factors as a 'stable' marriage, sufficient education to comply with treatment regimens, and often sufficient financial resources to provide 'adequately' for a child if conception and birth should occur" (243). These socio-economic criteria work to exclude poorer women and couples, as well as lesbian and unmarried women.

In many countries, physicians and expert panels have excluded prospective patients from receiving treatment on the basis of sexual orientation and marital status. Early on, state policy would uphold these social criteria as legitimate grounds to deny access to individuals and couples. In the 1980s and early 1990s, government inquiries and professional bodies in Canada gave doctors a great deal of discretion on this matter and oftentimes explicitly came out in favour of restricting access to assisted reproductive technologies on "moral" or social grounds. For example, Canadian inquiries appointed by provincial governments and law commissions during the 1980s and early 1990s reinforced the role of physicians as gatekeepers to reproductive benefits. Inquiries, such as the 1985 Ontario Law Reform Commission, left decisions regarding admittance to IVF clinics and sperm banks to the sole discretion of the attending physician and upheld non-medical criteria as legitimate means for screening suitable patients. Many of the inquiries either explicitly recommended that access to reproductive technologies be restricted to heterosexual couples, especially married couples, or they made reference to the importance of prospective patients being "stable men and stable women in stable relationships" (Ontario Law Reform Commission 1985, 120). Single and lesbian women were therefore denied access to the treatments because they were regarded as less suitable parents. Moreover, married women were restricted from using reproductive treatments if they did not have their husband's consent. The importance of male consent and the legitimacy of the children born from in vitro fertilization and artificial insemination were recurring themes in the majority of the Canadian and international inquiries. For example, the *Ontario Law Reform Commission Report* recommended that the male partner's consent be obtained to avert any questions regarding the fidelity of the woman and the "legitimacy" of the child. Ultimately, the inquiries upheld the notion of the traditional, two-parent, heterosexual family and reinforced the importance of ensuring a child's legal and legitimate status through male consent.

The use of non-medical criteria to screen prospective patients would once again come up during the deliberations of the 1993 Royal Commission on New Reproductive Technologies (RCNRT). The Commission's review of the admission policies of individual IVF clinics found that they varied significantly across the country. The lack of enforceable universal guidelines or regulations in the area of reproductive technologies allowed fertility clinics and practitioners to use socially biased and non-medical criteria to determine the ability of an individual or couple to parent a child. The Commission reported that physicians were guided by their own personal biases when deciding on whether to treat a prospective patient. For example, prospective patients were sometimes refused access to treatment because of "doubtful parenting ability," or because they were lesbian or unmarried women. Couples that conformed to the traditional, heterosexual family unit were considered more appropriate candidates for these procedures. In contrast, single males or females, as well as lesbian or gay couples, were usually denied access because they were considered unfit parents. This type of discrimination against individuals or couples because of their marital status or sexual orientation was said to be a common practice at individual fertility clinics despite the existence of equality provisions in the Canadian Charter of Rights and Freedoms (RCNRT 1993).

During the Commission's hearings, the discretionary authority of physicians in determining who should have access to the assisted reproductive technologies was challenged by several lesbian and gay rights groups that appeared before the RCNRT. The briefs presented by these groups centred on the issue of access to reproductive technologies and the protection of their reproductive choices. A major problem confronting lesbians and gays seeking fertility treatments was the discriminatory elements of existing clinic regulations that determined an individual's or couple's suitability for parenthood.

Fertility clinics often used selection criteria that inevitably favoured heterosexual couples in a stable (i.e., married) relationship. The brief presented by the Halifax Lesbian Committee on Reproductive Technologies – a lesbian-rights organization – challenged the prevailing social understanding of the notion of a "stable relationship" and its marginalization of alternative family arrangements. Appealing to the Charter and human rights laws, lesbian rights organizations called for an end to discriminating criteria that prevented lesbians and gays from gaining access to fertility treatments. The group stated, "Single women, whether they are heterosexual or lesbian, find themselves denied access to fertility treatment and to artificial insemination. We are here to suggest that it is critical that these technologies not be limited to a select population. We believe that access to AI should not be influenced by race, class, physical disability, marital status, or sexual orientation" (Halifax Lesbian Committee on New Reproductive Technologies 1990). Appealing to the notion of "family values," gay and lesbian rights activists argued that assisted reproductive technologies could offer people not in traditional heterosexual relationships the opportunity to be parents. These technologies would "promote family life by extending the joys of parenting to infertile or homosexual couples and single people" (RCNRT 1993, 552). In the end, the Royal Commission on New Reproductive Technologies recommended that access to IVF treatment be based on legitimate medical criteria and that admission policies set up by IVF treatment facilities should not discriminate on the basis of marital status, economic status, or sexual orientation.

Lesbian and gay individuals and couples would also look to the courts to challenge discriminating admission practices. In British Columbia, a lesbian couple brought a complaint to the College of Physicians and Surgeons against a specialist who had refused them as patients for artificial insemination. The College sided with the physician, arguing that it was not unethical for him to refuse the respondents as patients "as long as there was no emergency or urgent need for services" (*Korn v. Potter* [1996] B.C.J. No. 692 (B.C.S.C.)). The lesbian couple then filed a complaint with the BC Human Rights Council alleging that they were being discriminated against because of their sexual orientation. The decision of the Human Rights Tribunal, which was later upheld by a BC Supreme Court decision, Korn v. Potter, stated that refusing a lesbian couple access to assisted insemination constituted discrimination on the basis of sexual orientation.

The *Korn v. Potter* ruling stated that all women who meet the medical standards should have access to available fertility treatments. In 2005, the discretionary authority of physicians was once again challenged when a fertility clinic in Quebec was told by the Quebec Human Rights Commission to pay compensation to a lesbian woman who had been refused I V F treatments due to her sexual orientation and/or single status. As she stated to a news reporter: "One of the doctors said if I had shown up with a man, they would have treated me" (C T V News, 30 September 2005).

In 2004, the introduction of the Assisted Human Reproduction Act in Canada significantly curtailed the ability of physicians to limit access to reproductive technologies on the basis of marital status and sexual orientation. The Act states that: "Persons who seek to undergo assisted reproduction procedures must not be discriminated against, including on the basis of their sexual orientation or marital status" (Assisted Human Reproduction Act [S.C. 2004, c. 2]). While the Act effectively extended reproductive benefits to lesbian and single women, it also provided an opening for the use of other nonmedical criteria with its adoption of the "welfare principle." In its preliminary provisions, the Act (c. 2) states: "The health and well-being of children born as a result of the performance of an assisted reproductive procedure or an established procedure should be an important consideration in all decisions about that procedure." Drawing from family law and social work, the "welfare principle" or the "best interest of the child" principle is meant to guide legislation and practice in child and family welfare policy. Critics, however, argue that this principle is highly subjective and therefore susceptible to cultural and professional bias (Ralph 1998). In Canada's legislation on assisted human reproduction, physicians and other biomedical agents are not provided any instructions beyond considering the "health" and "welfare" of the child in their decision-making, thus leaving open the use of non-medical criteria in determining access to these treatments. Thus, as Walks's chapter in this volume demonstrates, significant obstacles to parenthood remain for members of the gay, lesbian, bisexual, and transgender community. The welfare principle also discriminates against heterosexual infertile individuals and couples, since similar controls on the reproductive decisions of fertile couples do not exist. The bodily integrity of the fertile individual and his or her right to have children overrides any concerns for the welfare of his or her future offspring.

In Canada and elsewhere, the welfare of the child principle has informed discussions surrounding I V F treatments for post-menopausal women. Whereas in the past, age-related infertility was considered to be a "natural" stage of women's reproductive lives, it has been transformed into a condition that can be "fixed" by medical intervention. Post-menopausal women seeking treatment often have to rely on egg donation to achieve pregnancy. While media accounts of older women giving birth via I V F have risen in the past few years, physicians and fertility experts are often reluctant to treat post-menopausal women. Professional guidelines often recommend that post-menopausal women be denied access to treatment for a number of reasons, including: the well-being of the child; the scarcity of eggs available for donation; and in general, the inappropriateness of older women being mothers. Older women are viewed as lacking the emotional and physical capabilities to raise children and of being at higher risk for leaving their children orphaned. Professional guidelines and state policies tend to prioritize younger women over older women when allocating I V F treatments with donor eggs and embryos. In Canada, the Royal Commission on New Reproductive Technologies recommended that younger women be given priority in accessing donor eggs and embryos, characterizing the use of donor eggs by those who are post-menopausal as "invasive, expensive and an inappropriate use of resources" (1993, 499). It cited the principle of fairness as a reason for limiting the use of I V F by older women, arguing that younger women should have priority, given they had not yet had the opportunity to be mothers, unlike older women who could have been mothers at an earlier time in their reproductive lives. As Parks (1999, 80) explains, "It might be felt that older women, who 'selfishly' choose a career path over motherhood in a timely fashion, should not have the right to change their minds when it is too late to reproduce without aid." Moreover, infertility among post-menopausal women is viewed as a normal process of the female body. As mentioned in the Royal Commission report, since infertility among post-menopausal women is natural, given the "normal" diminishment of fertility as a woman ages, intervention is not medically justifiable (Parks 1999). While the 2004 legislation is silent on the issue of age and access to treatment, its welfare principle, which preserves a role for cultural and professional biases, allows physicians to allocate reproductive benefits on the basis of age.

More recently, health status has become a basis for stratification. In the United Kingdom, for example, the UK association of fertility experts, the British Fertility Society, recently recommended that fertility specialists in both private clinics and clinics funded by the country's National Health System (N H S) deny treatment to obese women. Citing evidence showing that the success of I V F decreases for women whose B M I score is higher than thirty-five, the Society urged fertility experts to offer treatment only once the B M I scores fell below thirty. Obesity rather than I V F was said to lead to complications during treatment and pregnancy: "It [obesity] also increases the risk of complications during fertility treatment and pregnancy and endangers the health and welfare of both mother and child." (B B C News 2007). The advice put forward by the Society depicted the obese woman's body as a "troubled" female body not easily malleable to medical intervention. "Complications" cited by the report included the difficulty of monitoring obese women's ovaries with ultrasounds and the difficulty of administering anaesthesia to obese women during treatment (B B C News 2007). The British Fertility Society's Canadian counterpart, the Canadian Fertility and Andrology Society, is also considering introducing guidelines that would restrict obese women's access to I V F. Individual clinics have already put in place policies to withhold I V F to women whose body mass index (B M I) is over thirty-five, a number indicating obesity. While recognizing that this policy is explicitly discriminatory, the increased medical risks of an I V F pregnancy for obese women are cited as a legitimate reason for putting this ban in place. As one doctor stated in defence of this ban, "We've had many angry patients say to us, 'This is discriminatory' and I say, 'Yes, it is. But I still won't do it,'" he continued. "A patient doesn't have the right to make a choice that's going to be harmful to them" (Kay 2011).

EVIDENCE-BASED MEDICINE AND THE COMMODIFICATION OF "MEDICALIZED INFERTILITY" IN CANADA

The decision to fund I V F treatments under insurance plans is contingent on whether they are deemed to be a "medical necessity." Under the Canada Health Act, comprehensive coverage only extends to those services that are deemed "medically necessary." While at first glance the term "medical necessity" seems to provide a neutral and objective criterion for making health decisions, the term is in fact highly subjective and open to interpretation. As Baker and Bhabha (2004) explain: "Disputes about medical necessity can arise when services that had previously been listed are de-listed, whether based on 'evidence-based' analysis, physician–government negotiations designed to respond to financial constraints or the political viewpoint of the government of the day."

With the notable exception of Quebec, IVF treatments are not covered under provincial health care programs. While basic fertility services such as diagnostic testing are provided through public funding, IVF coverage is absent or limited, as is the case in Ontario. IVF treatments are purchased privately by patients at a cost of $3,000 to $5,000 per treatment cycle. The cost-effectiveness of IVF as a treatment for infertility is often cited as a justification for its exclusion from public coverage. From early on, the policy discourse on IVF in Canada has been shaped by Evidence-Based Medicine (EBM), a set of principles and practices that seeks to achieve efficiency, transparency, and "value-neutrality" in clinical practice and health policy decision-making. Developed by a group of biostatisticians and medical information experts in the 1990s, EBM was touted as the best approach to ensuring cost efficiency and effectiveness in patient care and treatment options because of its use of statistical and therefore "objective" evidence: "Since its first conceptualization, EBM has gained and retained considerable power, becoming incorporated into medical curricula worldwide, colonizing other fields of practice, such as nursing, complementary medicine and public health, and spawning journals, research centres, websites and the like" (Kerridge 2010, 366). In many ways, EBM shifted decision-making authority away from individual physicians and toward health care managers. It significantly challenges the discretion and authority of physicians when making medical decisions by reducing the importance of medical expertise and clinical training in medical practice. As Rodwin (2001, 441) explains, "Traditionally doctors defined the standard of care. Now, armed with more and better information about medical practices, payers and purchasers can deny payment for medical services that they deem medically unnecessary or ineffective. In so doing, they redefine standards for appropriate medical practice."

EBM provided the ideological and political backdrop for official deliberations on IVF in Canada. Declining economic growth, rising health care costs, and the expanding definition of health services made the cost-effectiveness of ARTS an important area of study, for both the Canadian government and the RCNRT. The issue of health care funding of reproductive technologies, as well as their effectiveness and safety as medical treatments, would become a central theme in the Commission's work. Cognizant of fiscal pressures on the health care system, the Commissioners adopted an EBM approach to assess the cost-effectiveness of fertility treatments and, on this basis, to determine whether they should be provided within the health care system. Historically, decisions about which services are publicly supported through provincial health insurance coverage were said to be influenced not by evaluation results but by lobbying, media coverage, and emotional appeals. Commissioners regarded EBM as a "rational and equitable way of allocating public health dollars by suggesting which treatments are beneficial to people at what cost to the system and which are ineffective or overly costly given their likely benefits" (RCNRT Research Volume 11, 1993, 72).

The positions taken by many groups that participated in the public consultations were also informed by concerns over the allocation of diminishing health care resources. The majority of exchanges between Commissioners and interveners during the hearings focused on the issue of funding. Several groups argued that reproductive technologies should not be offered as a medical treatment through the publicly funded health care system because they would divert funds from more pressing health care needs. For example, Aboriginal communities argued that the funding of expensive fertility treatments constituted an inappropriate allocation of resources given the difficulties they encountered in accessing basic medical services. Feminist groups and public health organizations argued that more funding should be made available for the prevention of infertility rather than for the provision of costly technologies to achieve a pregnancy.

Most medical organizations, with the notable exception of physicians aligned with anti-abortion groups, defined infertility as a reproductive disease amenable to medical treatment. These groups claimed that infertility should be both regarded and treated as any other medical condition covered by the Canada Health Act. However, while the notion of reproductive choice was supported in principle by most medical professional organizations, there was a lack of consensus on a number of issues, including the extent to which procreation is an inherent and socially guaranteed right. Two distinct positions emerged within the medical discourse on the rights of individuals to procreate and the state's obligation in safeguarding or indeed enhancing reproductive choices. The medical community was largely divided between fertility specialists, who depicted biological parenthood as an inherent right, and broad-based professional organizations that stressed the need to balance equal access to fertility treatments against current fiscal constraints in health care. The theme of fiscal restraint coupled with the demand for equal access to fertility treatments within the medical discourse favoured a two-tier, public–private mixed system for fertility treatments.

This stance was reiterated numerous times by several professional organizations. The largest medical organization to favour equal access to reproductive treatments was the Canadian Medical Association (CMA). As the primary voice of organized medicine in Canada, the CMA was an important and frequent participant in the Commission's hearings across the country. The association argued that biological parenthood is a "socially" guaranteed right and that infertility should be considered a health problem. However, the CMA also argued that this right is not an inherent one but rather is subject to certain conditions, including the availability of financial and human resources. Moreover, while it argued that fertility treatments should be made available to all members of society in an equitable fashion, it established a medical criterion for determining whether or not the services would be privately or publicly funded, stating "access to publicly funded assisted reproduction services be only on the condition that it is a health service and not a matter of private choice (Canadian Medical Association 1990). Essentially, the CMA advocated a two-tier system in the area of reproductive health services, in which only individuals with a "medical condition" could gain access to publicly funded services. Consequently, individuals who are childless for social rather than medical reasons, such as single women and lesbian or gay couples, could only make use of private fertility clinics at their own expense. Ultimately, the association advanced an interpretation of equality that was based on rectifying physical or biological impairments to fertility rather than the childlessness caused by social or economic conditions. As the CMA (1990) explains: "Access to socially funded programs of assisted reproduction should be determined solely by equitable criteria that find their basis in health reasons rooted in the health status of the individual; and that socially funded access should not become an instrument of furthering economic plans or privately held values but should be in keeping with the rationale underlying access to existing health care services."

This emphasis on the medical rather than the social dimension of infertility informed the Commission's recommendations as well as subsequent federal legislation on reproductive technologies. While the Commission recommended that admission policies set up by IVF treatment facilities not discriminate on the basis of marital status, economic status, or sexual orientation, it did call for access to IVF treatment to be based on legitimate medical criteria. Medical standards were said to provide a neutral and objective criterion for determining access to fertility treatments. Moreover, fiscal concerns and notions of "cost-effectiveness" would shape the Commission's recommendation regarding access to IVF treatments. The final report made this clear early on when it stated, "If new reproductive technologies are to be made available, it will be in the context of a health care system that is already under considerable pressure" (RCNRT 1993, 72).

The evidence-based medicine approach adopted by the Commission influenced a number of recommendations on IVF treatments and AI. The Commission's research found that IVF has only been proven effective in treating infertility due to fallopian tube blockage – the condition the treatment was originally developed to rectify. The Commission's survey of treatment facilities found that IVF services were being used to treat conditions that they were ineffective in treating. The report stated that this trend "gives rise to risk, uncertainty, misinformation, and unfairness" (RCNRT 1993, 499).

The Commission's research also examined the relative cost-effectiveness of IVF from the perspective of the health care system. The success of IVF as an infertility treatment has been difficult to ascertain, given the lack of consensus on an appropriate measurement criterion. Fertility clinics have traditionally defined effectiveness or success in terms of the rate of pregnancy rather than actual live births.[4] This, not surprisingly, discredits the data of fertility clinics, which characterized IVF treatments as highly effective. The Commission conducted a comparative study of couples undergoing IVF treatments, on the one hand, and on the other hand couples undergoing other less expensive fertility treatments or no treatments at all. The study found no difference in the rate of live births (Goeree et al. 1993).[5] Given these research findings, and the criticism launched against IVF by women's groups and public health organizations, the Commission recommended that IVF be offered as an insured treatment only to women suffering from fallopian tube blockage. IVF treatments that have not been proven effective, such as the creation of embryos for surrogacy arrangements, "unexplained infertility," and the transfer of donor embryos to postmenopausal women, would be classed as experimental research, and therefore subject to professional research guidelines. As the Commission stated: "It is misleading to patients, and costly to the health care system to offer unproven treatments, except in the context of research studies designed to assess their safety and effectiveness, in which participants are fully informed about its experimental nature before consenting to treatment and have the other protections inherent in medical research involving human subjects" (RCNRT 1993, 449).

By not insuring IVF, governments have relegated it to a private-exchange market, turning it into a private commodity rather than a medical service. In this context, money often determines who has access to reproductive treatments and who does not. Individuals seeking ARTS are not only regarded as patients in need of medical treatment, but as clients or consumers of a badly needed commodity. More often than not, these "consumers" tend to be white middle- or upper-class couples who can afford the expensive treatments. Economically disadvantaged groups are essentially excluded from accessing these services.

Infertility patients therefore represent only a subset of infertile women who have the social and material resources to have a child. The dominant image of the "infertile woman" as an economically privileged woman who attends infertility clinics renders invisible the high rate of infertility that plagues economically disadvantaged women. As Ryan (2001, 23) explains in the case of the United States: "There is a marked disparity between the epidemiological profile of infertile women in the United States (who are likely to be under thirty, African-American and with a high school education and a low income) and the profile of those receiving infertility services (who are typically over thirty, white, middle-class, with an average of two and one-half years of college)."

DE-COMMODIFYING IVF IN QUEBEC

As discussed earlier, IVF funding varies across provinces in Canada. In the 1980s and 1990s, Ontario was the only province to provide public coverage for up to three cycles of IVF treatment. In 1994, the

Ontario government de-listed IVF treatments from the province's Health Insurance Schedule of Benefits, except for complete fallopian tube blockage. As was the case with RCNRT, fiscal concerns and the cost-effectiveness of IVF motivated the decision to restrict public coverage of IVF in Ontario. In 2010, Quebec became the only province to pay for infertility treatments, including in vitro fertilization, pre-implant genetic testing, embryo transfer, and sperm sample collection. Under this new system, Quebec residents are covered for up to three stimulated cycles of IVF or up to six natural or modified natural IVF cycles. The province would also cover sperm donations for lesbian couples and single women. Prior to 2010, the province offered a 50 per cent refundable tax credit for artificial insemination and/or IVF expenses, for a maximum credit of $10,000 a year.[6] The new policy, however, does limit the number of transferable embryos to one per treatment cycle, a clear change from past practice when the fertility specialist decided on the number of transferable embryos. The new regulations do not include age restrictions for accessing infertility treatments except to state that they were available until menopause. Fertility specialists and clinics are therefore free to set their own age restrictions when accepting prospective patients.

Quebec's decision to provide public coverage for infertility treatments has effectively "decommodified" IVF as a reproductive benefit in that province. In the area of social policy, decommodification "permit[s] actions and choices by citizens – to get married, have children, seek higher education, engage in political activity – that are, in principle, unconstrained by market considerations" (Messner and Rosenfeld 1997; 1394). To a large degree, Quebec's policy has removed economic status as a precondition for accessing IVF treatments in that province. Money, or the lack thereof, no longer determines who can avail themselves of infertility treatments. Regardless of whether treatments were sought in private or public clinics, patients do not pay from their own pockets. Recently, the Quebec government has reduced the amount paid to cover fees at private clinics and is opening additional public clinics in Montreal and in other major cities, including Sherbrooke and Quebec City.

The decision to provide public coverage for IVF was motivated by two factors: economic concerns and a commitment to family-friendly policies. While Canada is traditionally characterized as a liberal welfare regime, Quebec is said to be closer to a more social democratic model of welfare provision and social policies (Baker 2006).

Moreover, in terms of social policy, Quebec has distinguished itself from its provincial counterparts, with its more generous, pronatalist polices, many of them prompted by concerns over the province's low fertility rates and aging population. For example, in 1988, the Quebec government introduced the Allowance for Newborn Children, which gave bonuses of up to $8,000 for an offspring. In 1997, it introduced universal, low fee child care in an effort to boost fertility rates and to encourage women to enter and stay in the labour market. More recently, in 2006, the Quebec government replaced the federal parental program with its own, more generous program, which includes five-week leave benefits for fathers. Quebec's IVF policy is consistent with these pronatalist and pro-family policies, and according to Quebec Health Minister Yves Bolduc, the province's new policy "demonstrate [s] the willingness of our government to maintain Quebec's status as a (so-called) paradise for families" (*Montreal Gazette*, 22 December 2011).

A more important consideration, however, was the economic benefits of decommodifying IVF treatments for the province's health care program. While cost-effectiveness and fiscal concerns have informed decisions to de-list or exclude IVF from insurable health services in other provinces and federal levels, the high costs related to multiple births, a common occurrence with IVF, were cited by the Quebec government as a central reason for moving infertility treatments away from the market and placing it under public purview. The expenses associated with IVF created incentives for patients and clinics to transfer two or more embryos during an IVF cycle, to increase the chances of achieving a pregnancy. This practice increases the possibility of multiple births, and these babies require longer hospitalization and higher post-natal health care than single deliveries do. Moreover, multiple births are typically premature, and therefore at greater risk for short- and long-term complications. In an effort to mitigate the high medical costs related to multiple births, the new Quebec policy requires clinics to transfer only one embryo during each cycle (two for older women).

The new policy in Quebec, while beneficial for infertile individuals and couples in that province, has certain implications for the stratification of reproduction in Canada in general. As with other policies, federalism oftentimes leads to a patchwork of social policies and programs, increasing variation across regions. In the case of health care, Canada's system assigns a great deal of leeway to provinces in allocating resources and setting priorities. While provinces must adhere to the Canada Health Act's five principles (universality, public administration, comprehensiveness, accessibility, and portability), they are free to shape health policy and delivery systems and define which "medically necessary" services are covered by their insurance program (Banting and Corbett 2002). The right of provinces to regulate fertility clinics and infertility treatments was recently upheld by the Supreme Court of Canada. In 2008, Quebec had challenged the federal government's Assisted Human Reproduction Act, arguing that it infringed on the right of provinces to regulate health care. In December 2010, the Supreme Court released its decision and upheld the right of provinces to regulate health care, including fertility clinics, a ruling that Cameron and Gruben discuss in more detail in this volume. This decision has several consequences: first, the delivery of infertility services will continue to vary across regions, given the flexibility afforded to provinces in defining "medical necessity," and regional inequities in access will continue to characterize IVF treatment in Canada. Second, in some provinces IVF will continue to be a privilege for those who can afford it, while in others, in particular Quebec, IVF treatments will, over time, be regarded as an entitlement or social right. Third, wealthier infertile individuals and couples can continue to engage in reproductive tourism, that is, cross provincial lines to receive infertility treatments in other jurisdictions.

CONCLUSION

The provision of IVF in Canada offers a rich site for investigating how government and biomedical policies and discourses contribute to the stratification of reproduction along lines of class, race, and sexual orientation. In Canada, the federal government's ideological commitment to evidence-based medicine and policy analysis has greatly informed the decision not to include IVF among its list of insurable medical treatments. While the federal government recognizes infertility as a medical condition or disease, fiscal concerns and limited health resources took centre stage during its decision-making process. Consequently, IVF provision was relegated to the market, effectively excluding low-income earners from accessing treatment. Policy governing eligibility, however, would remove marital status and sexual orientation as barriers to accessing IVF treatment.

The 2004 Assisted Human Reproduction Act significantly curtailed a physician's or clinic's autonomy to determine the "suitability" of prospective patients. As discussed by this chapter and others in this volume, clinics often discriminated against individuals and couples who did conform to the traditional, heterosexual family. The Act prohibited this practice and required clinics to consider prospective patients solely on the basis of "medical criteria."

While the Act significantly limited the gatekeeping function of clinics and physicians, it did not eliminate it altogether. The Act's reference to upholding the "best interest" or "well-being" of the offspring conceived via IVF left room for physicians to exercise some discretionary authority when choosing prospective patients. For example, many physicians and professional associations use this discretionary authority to limit or deny treatment to older women whose infertility is perceived to be a normal consequence of aging. Concerns over the higher than normal risk of children born to older women being orphaned have provided the basis for denying older women access to IVF. The welfare of the child conceived via IVF may also be used to deny access, on the basis of poor health status and disability.

Not surprisingly, Canadian federalism also contributed to the stratification of reproduction. Access to IVF and other reproductive benefits (such as abortion, discussed in this volume by Thompson-Philbrook) varies across regions. Quebec's decision to cover the costs of up to three IVF cycles has essentially removed income as a point of stratification in that province. In the rest of Canada, provinces continue to exclude IVF from their health care systems because such procedures are not deemed medically necessary. As a result, income continues to distinguish whose infertility is medicalized and whose is not. The Quebec example, however, may change the landscape of IVF policy in the rest of the country as infertility-rights advocates and fertility specialists lobby for similar policies in their own provinces.

In conclusion, Canadian policy on assisted reproductive technologies offers important insights into how biomedical agents and policy-makers control and define social norms accompanying the medicalization of infertility. Decisions regarding who will provide IVF and who will be selected to receive the treatment mitigate, perpetuate, or produce inequalities among women. Classism, heteronormativity, ageism, and racism inscribe discourses and polices that govern I V F and related infertility treatments. However, policies can also provide an avenue for changing societal norms about motherhood, parenthood, and biological capacity and, in turn, for reshaping women's reproductive lives. These opportunities for change provide a fruitful area for interdisciplinary research.

NOTES

1 The author would like to thank Stephanie Paterson, Marlene Sokolon, and the anonymous reviewers for their helpful comments.
2 Assisted insemination (A I) refers to all forms of insemination without intercourse using donor or partner's sperm. The sperm can be placed inside the vagina or in the uterus. The procedure can take place in fertility clinics or can be performed without medical assistance by the parties involved. The latter scenario is usually referred to as self-insemination (S I).
3 I V F is a procedure in which mature eggs are removed from a woman's ovary and fertilized with sperm in the laboratory. After fertilization, the egg is placed in the woman's uterus. The resulting embryos can also be donated to another woman.
4 Moreover, many of the studies relied solely on statistical data on the number of births following I V F treatment, which is an unreliable measurement of effectiveness given the absence of a control group.
5 The study found that in 1990 the average cost to society for a live birth following I V F treatments was $3,827.44, compared with $1,345.40 for a live birth without I V F treatment.
6 In 2010, Manitoba became the second province to offer a refundable tax credit for I V F treatments of up to $8,000 a year (40 per cent of $20,000 in expenses).

BIBLIOGRAPHY

Baker, David, and Faisal Bhabha. 2004. "Universality and Medical Necessity: Statutory and Charter Remedies to Individual Claims to Ontario Health Insurance Funding." *Health Law Review* 13(1): 25–35.

Baker, Maureen. 2001. *Families, Labour and Love: Family Diversity in a Changing World*. Vancouver: U B C Press.

Banting, Keith G., and Stanley M. Corbett. 2002. *Health Policy and Federalism: A Comparative Perspective on Multi-Level Governance*. Kingston: Queen's University Institute of Intergovernmental Relations.

B B C News. 2007. "Obese Should be Barred from I V F," 13 November.

Bell, Ann V. 2009. "'It's Way Out of My League': Low-Income Women's Experiences of Medicalized Infertility." *Gender & Society* 23(5).

Canada. Health Canada. 2004. Assisted Human Reproduction Act (S.C. 2004, c. 2).

Canada. Royal Commission on New Reproductive Technologies. 1993. *Proceed with Care: Final Report of the Royal Commission on New Reproductive Technologies, Volume 1*. Ottawa: Minister of Government Services Canada.

– 1993. *New Reproductive Technologies and the Health Care System: The Case for Evidence-Based Medicine, Research Volume 11 of the Royal Commission on New Reproductive Technologies*. Ottawa: Minister of Government Services.

Canadian Medical Association. 1990. *Brief to the Royal Commission on New Reproductive Technologies*. 1 November.

Chang, Virginia W., and Nicholas A. Christakis. 2002. "Medical Modeling of Obesity: A Transition from Action to Experience in a 20th Century American Medical Textbook." *Sociology of Health & Illness* 24(2): 151–77.

Colen, Shellee. 1995. "'Like a Mother to Them': Stratified Reproduction and West Indian Childcare Workers and Employers in New York." In *Conceiving the New World Order: The Global Politics of Reprodcution*, Faye Ginsberg and Rayna Rapp, eds. Berkeley: University of California Press.

Conrad, Peter. 1992. "Medicalization and Social Control." *Annual Review of Sociology* 18: 209–32.

Eichler, Margrit. 1988. "New Reproductive Technologies: Their Implications for Women." In *Feminist Research: Prospect and Retrospect*, Peta Tancred-Sheriff, ed. Montreal & Kingston: McGill-Queen's University Press.

Farquhar, Dion. 1996. *The Other Machine: Discourse and Reproductive Technologies*. New York: Routledge.

Ginsburg, Faye D., and Rayna Rapp, eds. 1995 *Conceiving the New World Order*. Berkeley: University of California Press.

Goeree, R., R. Labelle, and J.F. Jarrell. 1993. *Cost-Effectiveness of an In-vitro Fertilisation Program and the Costs of Associated Hospitalisations and Other Infertility Treatments*. Prepared for the Royal Commission on New Reproductive Technologies. Ministry of Supply and Services, 569–99. Ottawa: Minister of Government Services.

Greil, Arthur L., and Julia McQuillan. 2004. "Help-Seeking Patterns Among Infertile Women." *Journal of Reproductive and Infant Psychology* 22: 305–19.

– 2010. "'Trying' Times: Medicalization, Intent, and Ambiguity in the Definition of Infertility." *Medical Anthropology Quarterly* 24: 137–56.

Halifax Lesbian Committee on New Reproductive Technologies. 1990. Public Hearings of the Royal Commission on New Reproductive Technologies. Transcripts, Halifax, Nova Scotia, 17 October.

Heitman, Elizabeth, and Mary Schlachtenhaufen. 1996. "The Differential Effects of Race, Ethnicity, and Socioeconomic Status on Infertility and its Treatment: Ethical and Policy Issues for Oocyte Donation." In *New Ways of Making Babies: The Case of Egg Donation*, Cynthia B. Cohen, ed. Bloomington: Indiana University Press.

Kay, Victoria. 2011. "Obese Women May Be Denied I V F Treatment by Canadian Clinic." *BioNews*, 26 September.

Kerridge, Ian. 2010. "Ethics and E B M : Acknowledging Bias, Accepting Difference and Embracing Politics." *Journal of Evaluation in Clinical Practice* 16(2): 365–73.

King, Leslie, and Madonna Harrington Meyer. 1997. "The Politics of Reproductive Benefits: U.S. Insurance Coverage of Contraceptive and Infertility Treatments." *Gender & Society* 11: 8–30.

Korn v. Potter, [1996] B.C.J. No. 692 (B.C.S.C.).

McCormack, Karen. 2005. "Stratified Reproduction and Poor Women's Resistance." *Gender and Society* 19(5): 660–79.

Messner, Stephen F., and Richard Rosenfeld. 1997. "Political Restraint of the Market and Levels of Criminal Homicide: A Cross-National Application of Institutional-Anomie Theory." *Social Forces* 75(4): 1393–1416.

Michelle, Carolyn. 2006. "Transgressive Technologies? Strategies of Discursive Containment in the Representation and Regulation of Assisted Reproductive Technologies in Aotearoa / New Zealand." *Women's Studies International Forum* 29(2): 109–24.

Montreal Gazette. "Quebec Inaugurates Second Public In-Vitro Clinic." 22 December 2011. *www.ideaslab.ca/media/supportingMaterial119_2.docx*.

Ontario Law Reform Commission. 1985. *Report on Human Artificial Reproduction and Related Matters*. Toronto: Ministry of the Attorney General.

Parks, Jennifer. 1999. "On the Use of I V F by Post-Menopausal Women." *Hypatia* 14(1).

Pfeffer, Naomi, and Ann Woollett. 1983. *The Experience of Infertility*. London: Virago.

Ralph, Stephen. 1998. "The Best Interests of the Aboriginal Child in Family Law Proceedings." *Australian Journal of Family Law* 12: 140–9.

Raymond, Janice. 1993. *Women as Wombs: Reproductive Technologies and the Battle Over Women's Freedom.* New York: HarperCollins Publishers.

Roberts, Dorothy E. 2009. "Race, Gender, and Genetic Technologies: A New Reproductive Dystopia?" *Signs: Journal of Women in Culture and Society* 34(4): 783–804.

Rodwin, Marc A. 2001. "The Politics of Evidence-Based Medicine." *Suffolk University Health & Biomedical Law* 26(2): 441

Ryan, Maura A. 2001. *Ethics and Economics of Assisted Reproduction: The Cost of Longing.* Washington, D C: Georgetown University Press.

Scala, Francesca. 2002. *Experts, Non-experts, and Policy Discourse: A Case Study of the Royal Commission on New Reproductive Technologies.* Ottawa: Carleton University.

Steinberg, Deborah Lynn. 1997. *Bodies in Glass: Genetics, Eugenics, Embryo Ethics.* Manchester: Manchester University Press.

Zola, Irving Kenneth. 1983. *Socio-Medical Inquiries.* Philadelphia: Temple University Press.

3

Stratified Reproduction: Making the Case for Butch Lesbians', Transmen's, and Genderqueer Individuals' Experiences in British Columbia

MICHELLE WALKS

Since the mid-1990s, the legal rights relating to queer reproduction and family rights have been revised a number of times in British Columbia. Three particular policy updates exemplify these changes. The first of these occurred in 1995, when a Human Rights Tribunal decision made it illegal for physicians and clinics to deny lesbians access to fertility services in BC. The second change happened the following year, when it became legal in BC for any one or two adults – regardless of sexual orientation or marital status – to adopt children. Third, in 2001, a BC Human Rights Tribunal ruled that it was discriminatory to not allow the naming of two women on their child's Registration of Live Birth or birth certificate, if their child was conceived using the sperm of an anonymous donor. These changes have brought about legal equality, fostering both an increase in access and also a reduction in discrimination for queer families.

A closer investigation, however, reveals that these acts have not necessarily brought about equality, nor have they resulted in a universal change of practice on the micro level. As an example, the right of two women to be named as parents on the birth certificate of their (anonymous) donor-conceived child may seem a fait accompli since the Human Rights Tribunal decision in 2001. The last ten years, however, have demonstrated problems with two women's ability to do so. The procedures involved in putting this change into practice have proven to be bureaucratically complex and dysfunctional in several ways, including the lack of availability of the new forms, in addition to three sets of revisions relating to definitions and the practices the forms recognize.[1] Further, the six-year delay in creating a unified and accessible form is not simply an issue of procedural bureaucracy. New forms regarding lesbian mothers were readily available in Quebec within weeks of their legislative update. Rather, it exemplifies the continuing social, political, and practical obstacles that queer parents and queers trying to become parents in B C face. Moreover, along with some later examples, it demonstrates that while considerations and policies have changed for *queer* sexuality, people of non-normative gender identities continue to face misunderstandings and barriers in the guise of policy with respect to their reproductive choices and experiences.

In particular, the needs and experiences of butch lesbians,[2] transmen,[3] and genderqueer individuals[4] who experience pregnancy, breastfeeding, and biological parenthood have been neglected within the legal and procedural changes of the last twenty-five years. To be clear, while headway has been made for the rights, visibility, and social acceptance of lesbians and gays, there remains a general misunderstanding and confusion in Canadian culture about those who embody non-normative genders (such as tomboys, butch lesbians, genderqueer individuals, and effeminate men). Just as heterocentrism influences our cultural ideas of who should partner together (i.e., people of different sexes), it also limits how people perform their gender (specifically, men must appear and behave in ways that society deems "masculine," while women must be "feminine").[5] Thus, more work in research and policy change is needed in relation to the needs and experiences of people who embody non-normative genders. This chapter begins such work through an investigation of the reproductive choices and experiences of butch lesbians, transmen, and genderqueer individuals in British Columbia.

While the public and media reaction to Thomas Beatie's three pregnancies (in 2008, 2009, and 2010)[6] demonstrated some of the social hostility that gender non-conforming individuals may face with respect to biological reproduction, an in-depth Canadian perspective on such experiences has thus far been lacking. Further, consideration of the diverse challenges, choices, and experiences of pregnancy and parenting by female-bodied, masculine-, and androgynous-identified individuals is important.[7] A Canadian perspective on this phenomenon is fundamental, as the structural access to fertility services, legislative policies regarding fertility and reproduction, and perceptions and treatment of "queer" individuals and bodies in Canada are all innately different from those in the United States and elsewhere. In other words, the ways in which the Western medical model – which strips patients of their individuality and compares them with a socially constructed "medical norm"; further perpetuates a heteronormative status quo; and has a deep-seated history of othering female bodies, queers, and individuals who do not meet normative ideals of gender – engages with its patients differs across national borders (Goldberg, Harbin, and Campbell 2011; Kuehn 2011; Obedin-Maliver et al. 2011; Craven 2010; Bauer et al. 2009; Cattapan 2009; Goldberg, Ryan, and Sawchyn 2009; Chan and Turner 2005; Agigian 2004; Davis-Floyd 2004; Lupton 2000). In fact, within Canada, policies regarding reproduction and access to fertility services differ even across provincial and territorial jurisdictions. Considering these factors, and using data from my P h D research,[8] in this chapter I address the legal, political, and social effects of existing legislation for butch lesbians, transmen, and genderqueer individuals who choose pregnancy in B C. In other words, using the narratives of butch lesbians, transmen, and genderqueer individuals who have experienced pregnancy in B C, I focus on how the policies and practices related to health care and well-being affect these individuals' reproductive experiences and choices. In so doing, I will show that the concept of stratified reproduction – "the power relations by which some categories of people are empowered to nurture and reproduce, while others are disempowered" (Ginsburg and Rapp 1995, 3) – is well-suited to serve as the foundation of such a discussion.

STRATIFIED REPRODUCTION

Womanhood is almost universally defined through one's status as a mother (Walks 2011; Liamputtong 2007b; Letherby and Williams 1999). The pressures females face with respect to social and biological reproduction, however, differ considerably depending on their demographics and culture. Jamileh Abu-Duhou, for example, notes that in Palestinian culture "women['s] identity and passage to women hood [sic] is bond [sic] by their ability to reproduce and become mothers, however, their claim to motherhood maybe [sic] denied once they fail to reproduce sons" (2007, 215). In Canada women's identities are often not as tied to motherhood as in Palestinian or some other cultures, however women in Canada are still subject to pressures and expectations regarding motherhood, albeit pressures and expectations that range considerably depending on demographics and subcultures. The disparity among social pressures to reproduce (and not) is the essence of stratified reproduction. Shellee Colen coined the term stratified reproduction in an effort to call attention to the way that different types of reproduction/reproductive work are valued among particular populations, as well as to how specific acts of reproduction are generally devalued.

Colen's chapter "'Like a Mother to Them': Stratified Reproduction and West Indian Childcare Workers and Employers in New York" (1995) serves as the ovarian text of stratified reproduction. Colen (1995, 78) explains:

> By *stratified reproduction* I mean that physical and social reproductive tasks are accomplished differently according to inequalities that are based on hierarchies of class, race, ethnicity, gender, place in a global economy, and migration status and that are structured by social, economic, and political forces. The reproductive labor – physical, mental, and emotional – of bearing, raising, and socializing children and of creating and maintaining households and people (from infancy to old age) is differently experienced, valued, and rewarded according to inequalities of access to material and social resources in particular historical and cultural contexts.

Colen recognizes how childcare and household work are naturalized and trivialized based on sex, race, and class: "Devalued when passed from men to women in the society at large and within the same households, the work is further devalued when passed from one woman who chooses not to do it and can pay for it, to another woman who performs it in someone else's household for the wages she needs to maintain her own household" (1986, 54). Thus she explained that the concept of stratified reproduction refers not only to the stratified expectations and respect related to *biological* reproduction, but also to the physical, emotional, and mental labour of raising or enculturing children.

Various scholars have built off Colen's work and demonstrated how stratified reproduction can relate not only to sex, race, and class, but also to sexuality (Letherby and William 1999; Lewin 1995, 1993); and both infertility and disability (Letherby and Williams 1999); as well as how stratified reproduction is often supported by institutions and social policy (McCormack 2005). As Johnson and Paterson point out in this volume, women and mothers can each be categorized through a multitude of demographics (including, but not limited to, age, race, religion/spirituality, ethnic background(s), dis/ability, education level, class, sexuality, gender identity, and geographic location) and can face opposing pressures regarding their (potential) reproductive practices. Individual diversity is not considered, however, in stereotypes or policies. On the other hand, consideration of individual diversity figured prominently in my research.

METHODOLOGY

The P h D research project from which this chapter is derived used mixed ethnographic research methods. With the aim of being a descriptive and exploratory project, its purpose was to get a better understanding of the fertility and infertility experiences of people labelled "female" at birth who now, as adults, present or identify as "queer" and "masculine" or "androgynous." I approached this project using feminist, queer, and Pagan epistemologies. These three epistemologies worked well together, sharing the purpose of identifying and challenging structural power. More specifically, feminist epistemologies aim to dispel stereotypes regarding gender and sexual orientation (Lewin 1993); see women as having agency and take their experiences into account (Luce 2010; Liamputtong 2007a; Mamo 2007; Lewin 2006, 1995, 1993); and lessen the "objective" distance between the research and the researched, privileging the subjective (Liamputtong 2007a; Mamo 2007; Lewin 1995). Queer epistemologies recognize fluidity and change, and "[aim] to destabilize the overall discursive legitimacy of modern sexual classifications, and the power relations they sustain and protect" (Watney 1994, 23). Last, Pagan epistemologies necessarily have a holistic approach, and, like queer epistemologies, recognize both social and individual fluidity/flux (Agigian 2004). Considering the views of these epistemologies, I decided to make use of multiple methods and involve multiple populations to best achieve a holistic, deep understanding of not only people's experiences but also the structural relations that influence these experiences.

Specifically, I have used participant observation, questionnaires, and face-to-face interviews. The interviews and questionnaires both involve two populations: (1) health care professionals; and (2) butch lesbians, transmen, and genderqueer individuals. While the face-to-face interviews revealed deep knowledge regarding personal experiences, the questionnaires provide more "surface-level" information about a larger number of people, in addition to some deeper knowledge when anonymous participants used the opportunity to expand on their ideas, experiences, knowledge, and opinions. Moreover, because social contexts are key to not just anthropology, but to a holistic view, I engaged in participant observation at Pride and queer-focused events (such as special queer film and queer coffee events) in different locations around BC, as well as by spending time within the communities in which the research participants live and work. By the end of the research period, I had conducted interviews with twenty-one individuals and had fifty-nine surveys returned.[9]

Despite the perhaps seemingly low numbers of research participants, their experiences represent a fair amount of diversity. In fact, I interviewed four individuals who had either experienced or been diagnosed with a condition linked to infertility, and seven individuals who had experienced a successful pregnancy. I also interviewed eleven health care professionals (including four midwives, three physicians who specialize in trans health, and two nurses who work with birthing and new parents). Twenty questionnaires were returned from health care professionals and forty-six returned from butch lesbians, transmen, or genderqueer-identified individuals (including nine who have either been diagnosed with or otherwise experienced a condition linked to infertility and five who are parents via their own pregnancy). Ethnically, the participants are mainly white, with the exception of one interviewee identifying as a person of colour, and twelve questionnaire respondents stating they are of mixed or non-white ethnicity (i.e., Arab, Asian, First Nations). Respondents ranged from nineteen to sixty-seven years old. Of the eleven butch lesbians, transmen, and genderqueer individuals I interviewed, two have no children, five have one child, and four have two children; these children ranged from two to eleven years of age. Moreover, six interview participants expressed their desire to conceive a child within the next two years (one was already trying to conceive). Last, in terms of their geographic location, research participants were from Vancouver (n=45), the Southern Interior (n=25),

Vancouver's suburbs (n=12), Vancouver Island (n=9), and Other/no response (n=2). Because the research was designed to be exploratory and descriptive, seeking out diverse experiences for what they are, the sample size effectively revealed some of the diversity that exists, and described and explored current practices. Due to the fact that my main population of interest is part of a marginalized population that has a history of being misrepresented, abused, and neglected in research, it is not surprising that the number of (questionnaire) respondents has remained low, regardless of the fact that I am queer myself. Furthermore, it is impossible to know just how many people in British Columbia currently identify as butch lesbians, transmen, and genderqueer,[10] or to estimate how many of those individuals have experienced either a pregnancy or a condition linked to infertility. As I plan to continue exploring this area, future studies will lead to a larger and more diverse sample in terms of demographics and experiences.

STRATIFIED REPRODUCTION IN EVERYDAY EXPERIENCES

Stratified reproduction occurs both explicitly as part of policy, and just as a part of maintaining the status quo. My research shows that stratified reproduction is implicitly made visible through the inability of friends, family, and the general public to recognize masculine pregnancy or breastfeeding, or anything other than feminine desire for pregnancy and breastfeeding. This is because feminine pregnancy and breastfeeding is what is valued and socially recognized. In this light, I want to draw attention to some of the effects of the everyday social experiences that butch lesbians, transmen, and genderqueer individuals face in a culture where they and their reproductive choices and stories are ignored and misunderstood, even by their friends, family, and communities.

To counter the status quo, individual agency and the ability to construct new parental/familial roles is important in how butch lesbians, transmen, and genderqueer individuals live their lives. Bryn, Cathy, Lou, Imogen, Joy, Quinn, Tash, Tracy, and Vanessa each embody a masculinity that leads them to at least occasionally be perceived as male in public. Lou (an androgynous parent in their thirties, who had experienced infertility) mentioned that in public they sometimes use the men's washroom with their son when the lineup for the women's is long, and Cathy (a butch/dyke mom in her forties) noted that when asked by her son's friends, "'Are you Josh's daddy?' I say, 'Uh, yeah, sometimes.'" Moreover, when Bryn was breastfeeding her child at the mall, a boy excitedly urged his mother to, "Look at him – look what he's doing!" Upon hearing this, Bryn felt a sense of contentment at having her masculinity recognized. In summary, Lou, Cathy, and Bryn engage their individual agency to carve out a parenthood that they can comfortably partake in. This, however, does not mean that their experiences have gone without any misunderstandings.

In my interviews with the butch lesbians and genderqueer individuals who had experienced a pregnancy, it was often noted that their friends, family, and communities struggled to see the realities of those I interviewed. This is not difficult to understand, considering the only clothes that are sold for pregnant individuals are overtly feminine (by our culture's standards), meaning that even not-so-feminine women appear more feminine when pregnant due to the frills, florals, and colours of the maternity clothes they wear. Given this context, Bryn provided examples relating to how friends, family, and strangers could not fathom pregnancy and breastfeeding as anything other than feminine. She commented on how people made inaccurate assumptions about her pregnancy and breastfeeding experience and her gender identity, revealing that her parents believed her pregnancy meant she was *finally* embracing femininity. Similarly, she noted how her friends were sometimes unable to see beyond the status quo and thus imagine pregnancy as something someone butch could do: "We were at a friend's dinner party – I even said, 'oh I am pregnant,' and she said, 'oh that's great,' and later she offered me a drink. When I said 'no,' she said, 'So big of you not drinking when your partner is pregnant.'" Bryn further explained, "Like over and over again with my friends, they just wouldn't get it ... 'What, you're pregnant? Oh there must be something wrong with Sheila.' And I felt awkward about it too ... 'Cause then, when they realized there is nothing wrong with Sheila – that I fought for this – I felt like I had to get into the details of the relationship that I wasn't even comfortable talking about ... But no, thank you very much, Sheila is okay. They just assumed there [are] fertility issues there." Bryn, Cathy, Joy, Quinn, Tracy, and Vanessa did not see pregnancy as something innately feminine, but rather as something they really wanted to experience, despite their butch/gender non-conformist identity.

Cathy and Tanya discussed the discordance expressed by others regarding their gender identity and pregnancy/breastfeeding. Cathy, a butch/dyke parent in her forties, noted: "I felt that people just couldn't wrap their head around it [a butch/masculine-presenting person being pregnant]. These two things do not go together. You know like that *Sesame Street* thing, [*singing*] 'One of these things is not like the other, one of these things just doesn't belong.'" Tanya (a butch-identified questionnaire respondent) noted that when she was pregnant, friends responded by saying, "You aren't going to breastfeed are you? 'Cause that would be too weird!" The strength of this social perception – that masculinity/androgyny and pregnancy/ breastfeeding are paradoxical, in both straight and queer contexts, caused inner struggles for both Bryn and Vanessa.

For Bryn, the major struggle was with perceptions from within the queer community, while for Vanessa it was with perceptions from mainstream/heteronormative culture. Before conceiving Sage, Bryn weighed her desire to experience a pregnancy against her need to be recognized and accepted as a butch by fellow queers: "It's not acceptable in the queer community to have trans people, butch people, all these people who are not feminine to be pregnant – I have to feel people ... think weird of me, I mean if we are supposed to be a community that is about accepting ... and yeah, I do this thing, and it is like, 'Why would you do that?'" Overall, these narratives bring attention to the stratified nature of reproduction in Canada. While these examples do not explicitly link to potential policy changes, the next section gives such examples.

POLICY AND PRACTICE

Due to different social pressures on various individuals regarding the expectation for them to be mothers, and despite increased legislation giving rights to queer populations, "heterosexism permeates virtually every aspect of Canadian culture: language, guiding practices of all gatekeeping institutions, and social interactions" (Shroff 1997, 287). Unfortunately, the combined effects of these attitudes, policies, and institutional practices mean that particular families and reproductive practices are more valued and acknowledged than others. For example, when Prime Minister Stephen Harper speaks of "family values," the Canadian public recognizes that he is not referring to the values of all families, and in particular not likely those of queer parents. In this way, experiences that do not fit the norm (such as those of queer parented families) are erased from public discourse and the popular imagination, just as they are erased from the status quo (Bauer et al. 2009; Agigian 2004).

Part of this erasure is what Bill C-389 and Bill M-207 aim to address, by fostering a more respectful and understanding society with regard to non-normative gender identities.[11] Bill C-389 is a federal private member's bill that seeks to add "gender identity" and "gender expression" to the Canadian Human Rights Act and the Criminal Code of Canada. Provincial Bill M-207, in British Columbia, also a private member's bill, focuses on explicitly recognizing that the term "sex" in human rights discourse includes "gender identity" and "gender expression." Both bills are usually touted for their ability to foster the identification and prosecution of acts of violence toward trans and gender-variant individuals as official "hate crimes," acknowledging the added seriousness of such offences. These bills are also recognized as tools to reduce discrimination against similarly identifying/presenting individuals when applying for jobs or seeking housing. The bills would, however, also be useful in providing people of non-normative genders increased access to relevant and respectful health care services.

With regard to reproduction, Bill C-389 and Bill M-207 would go a step further than the 1995 ruling that prohibits discrimination in the provision of fertility services based on sexual orientation. These bills would officially make it also illegal to deny (access to) fertility services due to gender identity and gender expression – this would apply to the very people who, because of their gender, would most likely have difficulty convincing a physician or fertility clinic nurse of their capacity to be a "good" parent, or even of their real desire to become a parent. Imogen and Deidre[12] each informed me about incidents occurring after 1995 when a butch lesbian presented herself for intended pregnancy and was subsequently denied access to fertility services.

First, in 1999 when Imogen and her wife Jacq sought fertility services at one of the fertility clinics in Vancouver, they were explicitly told, "we [at the clinic] do not serve lesbians." Shocked and disappointed at this response, Imogen and Jacq subsequently approached and were welcomed at a different fertility clinic in Vancouver. Focused on their goal of having children, and not even considering pursuing legal action against the clinic they first approached, Imogen and Jacq went on with their lives, almost forgetting the original dismissal until Imogen was reminded of it during her interview with me.

Second, Deidre (a registered nurse) told me of a lesbian couple who had, only days before our interview in the summer of 2011, left their family physician's office without a signature on their referral to a fertility clinic. Deidre explained that in this instance it was her butch friend who sought to get pregnant, and thus it was this friend's physician who was "not comfortable" signing the referral. Instead of signing it, he suggested that his patient use "a more traditional method of achieving pregnancy," not specifying exactly what he meant. It is possible that this physician does not sign anyone's referrals to fertility clinics. It is also possible that despite the 1995 decision, the women in both instances (i.e., both Imogen and Deidre's friend) were denied as a result of their sexual orientation. What is also likely is that the denial of access to fertility services was a result of the women's butch gender expression. While it cannot be unambiguously concluded that the responses these butch lesbians received were due solely to their gender identity/presentation, that possibility also cannot be neglected. At this point in time, the physician and clinic could legally be supported in making the claim that it was not due to the fact that they were lesbians – as this would be considered an illegal decision – but instead that the women were "too masculine" to receive services, thus underscoring the necessity of Bills C-389 and M-207.

CONCLUSION:
A POLITICS OF TRANSGENDER REPRODUCTION

Although few have recognized an explicit "transgender politics of reproduction," Gerodetti and Mottier (2009) are among those who have. They noted that "thirty years after the birth of the first test tube baby in Manchester (UK) in 1978, media debates are still raging after another first, that is, the first birth by a transman; signalling, perhaps, the need for future feminist theory to develop in-depth analyses of the transgender politics of reproduction" (151). I urge us to go further than just theorizing and analyzing, by truly investigating the reproductive choices, needs, and experiences of various transgender and gender variant/non-conforming individuals. Understanding the reproductive experiences and choices of butch lesbians, transmen, and genderqueer individuals in Canada has immense linkages and consequences for many different areas – not limited to identifying and challenging social norms and expectations related to gender, sexuality, and mothering.

In fact, using the politics of reproduction, and particularly stratified reproduction, which "helps us to see the arrangements by which some reproductive futures are valued while others are despised" (Ginsburg and Rapp 1995, 3), fosters a critical view that highlights otherwise less visible, "erased," and taken for granted "normalized" practices. Identifying or seeing through a lens focused on stratified reproduction helps us to see discrepancies in the treatment of people, and helps bring light to the different barriers various populations and individuals face, so we can begin to critique the inequalities, contradictions, and hypocrisies within our society. The politics of reproduction serves as a magnifying glass and a science experiment of sorts, in that it assists us in identifying the discrepancies that exist in our culture. Further, when changes are made (through policy or the practice of a particular marginalized group), it is possible to see the influences they can have on society as a whole.

Thus, while research related to the reproductive health and experiences of butch lesbians, transmen, and genderqueer individuals most explicitly relates to such populations, it also facilitates a flipping, so to speak, of cultural norms. Instead of viewing practices, identities, and experiences through a typical/hegemonic lens, of those maintaining the status quo, highlighting a particular marginalized perspective offers new insights about what barriers and injustices exist within our culture. Moreover, while gay and lesbian studies of reproduction have, in the past, leaned toward proving the worthiness of parenthood and sameness between "gay parents" and "heterosexual parents" (Luce 2010; Peel 2010; Epstein 2009; Spector 2009; Mamo 2007; Agigian 2004; Owen 2001; Nelson 1996; Lewin 1995, 1993), a politics of transgender reproduction moves beyond these narratives and demonstrates how difference and marginality can highlight otherwise invisible or neglected injustices, such as the cultural pressure placed on cis-women to be feminine, heterosexual, and mothers.

As Jacquelyne Luce (2010, 211) notes, "Perhaps it is now time to re-emphasize the importance of analyzing the politics of reproduction and queer reproductive politics beyond clinic access, beyond donor insemination, and beyond the narratives of becoming a mother." While lesbian conception, pregnancy, and parenting has gained visibility and credibility over the last thirty years, the lack of research focused on butch lesbians, transmen, and genderqueer individuals is striking. If "butch is *the* recognizable form of lesbianism" (Munt 2001, 95), then why has no research been explicitly focused on butches' relationships to issues of fertility? Instead, while the focus of "lesbian parenting" has remained on the "issue of sexuality," gender has maintained its undeniable role in our cultural perceptions of appropriate reproduction and parenting. It thus presents itself as an important point of inquiry – how does gender (identity) relate to issues of infertility, fertility, pregnancy, and mothering? On a theoretical level, this information can also help to critique/challenge the assumed relationship between femininity, heterosexuality, and fertility, because if respectful space can be made to consider masculine fertility/pregnancy/motherhood then space can also be made for reduced pressure on feminine women – queer and heterosexual alike – to reproduce and mother.

NOTES

1 From 2001 to 2007, two Registration of Live Birth forms existed: the old (mother/father) form that was readily available, and the new (two-mother/co-parent) form that was only accessible through direct communication with the Vital Statistics Agency in Victoria. The new form explicitly noted that a second mother could only be listed when the sperm donor was anonymous. In 2007, a unified form was made available with a space to name a "Mother/Parent 1" and a "Father/Co-Parent/Parent 2." This form lacked an explicit reference to sperm donors. Instead, the 2007 form and the more recent (2010) version clearly note that if a "co-parent" is listed (instead of a "father"), the mother is to check a box officially claiming that, "the father is incapable or not present in the country or the father is unacknowledged by the mother or the father is unknown by the mother or the father refused to acknowledge the child" (BC Vital Statistics Agency). Moreover, unlike the first two revised forms, the 2011 edition specifies that the co-parent is to be "in a spousal relationship with the mother of the child at the time of the child's birth" (BC Vital Statistics Agency). Despite this specificity – and a definition of co-parent as "not the father, but someone who has an agreement with the mother to raise the child" – there is no definition of "father." The lack of such a definition assumes a universal understanding, and simultaneously leaves room for

transmen, butch lesbians, and genderqueer individuals who so desire to be named as fathers. This was likely not the government's intent.

2 Butch lesbians are one of the two main stereotypes of lesbians (with femmes being the other stereotype). Historically, butches were recognized as "the lesbian" seen as "not a woman but rather an 'invert,' or the embodiment of some third and anomalous gender category (Caunceу 1989; Davis and Kennedy 1986; Newton 1984)" (Lewin 1995, 106–7). I generally define butches as women who are sexually attracted to other women and who often identify or express themselves in a more androgynous or masculine manner – though there are many exceptions, as Bergman (2010) and Coyote and Sharman (2011) note. For the purposes of this research project, I let people self-define. Popular-culture examples of butch lesbians include Rachel Maddow (a US political commentator, radio personality, and T V show host), as well as actresses Rosie O'Donnell and Ellen DeGeneres.

3 Transmen (also known as female-to-male trans folks or F T M s) identify and present as male despite being categorized as female at birth. (*Trans* refers to people with gender / sex identities different from those assigned at birth. By contrast, *cis* refers to people with gender / sex identities that are the same as those assigned at birth) Transmen often, but do not always, inject testosterone (either through prescription or illegal means), have one or more surgeries to alter their chest, and / or have a hysterectomy. Transmen may or may not pursue genital altering surgery. Three examples of transmen who have been the focus of popular culture over the last few years are Thomas Beatie ("the pregnant man"), Chaz Bono (grown child of Cher and Sonny Bono), and Lucas Silveira (the lead singer of the Canadian band The Cliks).

4 *Genderqueer* is a term and identity less familiar to many people. Genderqueer individuals explicitly challenge gender norms, and thus sometimes consider what they do as "genderfucking." Using politically correct language, they may otherwise identify as "gender variant" or "gender non-conforming." Genderqueer individuals may simply present as androgynous, or may also purposefully mix stereotypical masculine and feminine signifiers. As an example, they might wear a beard with a pink dress or skirt. Their identity and embodiment typically goes beyond the type of gender / boundary pushing that Lady Gaga is currently known for – although her drag performance at the M T V Music Awards in August 2011 can certainly be considered genderqueer. Genesis P-Orridge (of the bands Throbbing Gristle and Psychic T v, and of the performance art duo [now solo] Breyer-P-Orridge), Peaches (a Canadian musician and

performer), and Andrej Pejic (a Serbian-Australian model, known for his modelling of female clothing) are public figures that more explicitly and on an ongoing basis exemplify genderqueer identities.

5 For more on gender and gender performance, see Judith Halberstam's *Female Masculinity* (1998) and Judith Butler's *Gender Trouble* (1990). For examples of how gender is performed in non-normative and fluid ways, see Ivan Coyote and Zena Sharman's co-edited anthology *Persistence: All Ways Butch and Femme* (2011).

6 Thomas Beatie is a transman from Bend, Oregon, who became known as "the pregnant man" in the spring of 2008 when he was pregnant with his eldest child. He and his pregnancy were featured on Oprah and 20/20, in the *Advocate*, and in other popular culture media (Ryan 2009; Ware 2009; Beatie 2008).

7 I use the terms *female-assigned, masculine-, and androgynous-identified* to refer to people who were identified as female at birth and who now identify or present within a spectrum of gender that includes butch women, transmen, and/or genderqueer individuals. While others use terms like *biologically female*, I acknowledge that biology is a cultural/medical category fixated on genitalia and hormones. Moreover, many such individuals feel their identity is innate and therefore understood as biological.

8 As part of my ongoing PhD research– partially funded by the Social Sciences and Humanities Research Council of Canada – I am researching "Gender Identity and In/Fertility" in British Columbia. The narratives presented in this chapter are taken from the one-on-one interviews that are part of this research.

9 In an effort to make it easier to reach this hidden and marginalized population, the questionnaires were designed to be available online. The feasibility of this decreased, however, upon experiencing numerous technical challenges with the online questionnaire software.

Participants were recruited via purposive and snowball sampling, through my attendance at queer events in various places throughout the province, as well as through the use of Internet listservs, facebook, and word of mouth. The individuals who participated in face-to-face interviews stemmed from one of two populations. The first population included butch lesbians, transmen, and genderqueer individuals who had experienced a successful pregnancy and/or experienced or been diagnosed with a condition linked to infertility. These interviews took place at their home, office, or at a conveniently located park. After a brief discussion of the ethics forms and format, the semi-structured interviews were recorded, lasted about one to two hours in length, and included questions such as,

"What did you think about potentially becoming a parent or mother when you grew up?," and when applicable: "Can you tell me about how you came to find out about your condition [linked to infertility]?" and "What was your initial reaction to being diagnosed with this condition?," or "At what point did you seriously consider getting pregnant, and start to consider how or when it might happen?" and "Tell me about your experience of being pregnant, of feeling and looking pregnant. What was your experience of being pregnant generally like?"

The second population that engaged in face-to-face interviews was health care and social service providers whose work explicitly relates to fertility/pregnancy/birthing or trans/queer populations. These interviews took place either at the interviewee's workplace, home, or a local coffee shop. The interviews were recorded, and lasted about thirty to ninety minutes. Interviews with health care professionals included questions such as: "Who are some of the main populations of patients/clients that you see in your profession?," "What interests you with respect to butch lesbians, transmen, and genderqueer individuals' fertility and infertility?," and, "Are there any recommendations that you can think of, that you would like to see happen, with respect to queer/trans reproductive health?."

There were two versions of the questionnaires, with one for all butch lesbians, transmen, and genderqueer individuals who are residents of British Columbia. This questionnaire was a total of eight pages (forty-one questions), but only respondents who had experienced both infertility and pregnancy were eligible to respond to all of the questions. Respondents who had experienced neither pregnancy nor infertility were only eligible for five of the pages (twenty-five questions), and individuals who had experienced pregnancy but not infertility or infertility but not pregnancy were eligible for between thirty and thirty-six questions. Questions varied in the types of answers that were solicited, from multiple-choice to fill-in-the-blank to having seven lines (plus available margins and backs of pages) to respond. Questions related to the respondents' demographics and identities, childhood expectations regarding their future parenting/mothering, as well as current opinions and experiences regarding queer/masculine reproduction. Both this questionnaire and the one for health care and social service providers were given to potential participants with a postage-paid addressed envelope in which the questionnaire could be returned to me (at the university).

Health care and social service practitioners were eligible to respond to a one-page (double-sided) questionnaire comprising sixteen questions. These questions were mostly demographic (i.e., position in the health care profession, length of time in the health care profession, age, geographic location), or about their experience with and attitudes about butch lesbian, transmen, and genderqueer individuals (as patients/clients).

   The total of fifty-nine returned questionnaires includes two that were returned but that were completed by individuals not eligible for the questionnaire. (For example, one listed their residency as being outside of B C and self-identified as a transwoman.)

10 While impossible to know an exact number, the closest figure for comparison that is available is from an online survey for "trans" individuals, conducted in 2007. It had about 230 respondents. These included people at any stage of their transition, and both those who were identified as "female" and "male" (as well as those identified as intersex) at birth (Marria Townsend, presentation on the Community-Based Trans Health Survey, at the Trans Health Forum in Vancouver, B C , 25 July 2010).

11 Bill C-389 was introduced twice to the fortieth Parliament (in the second and third sessions), by M P Bill Siksay (B C : Burnaby-Douglas). At neither time did it have the opportunity to complete the process of becoming law, due to Parliament being dissolved – through prorogation and an election. On 19 September 2011 it was re-introduced (now to the forty-first Parliament) by Liberal Hedy Fry (B C : Vancouver Centre). Bill M-207 was introduced to B C legislature on 26 May 2011 by N D P M L A Spencer Chandra Herbert (Vancouver-West End). At the time of writing, it is uncertain when it will come up for debate in the legislature.

12 All names of research participants are pseudonyms. Bryn, Cathy, Lou, Imogen, Joy, Quinn, Tracy, and Vanessa all loosely identify as butch lesbian parents, although individually they might also use terms such as *androgynous*, *gender non-conforming*, and *tomboy*. Deidre is a labour and delivery nurse.

BIBLIOGRAPHY

Abu-Duhou, Jamileh. 2007. "Motherhood as a Script for Nationhood." *In Reproduction, Childbearing and Motherhood: A Cross-Cultural Perspective*, Pranee Liamputtong, ed., 211–38. New York: N O V A .

Agigian, Amy. 2004. *Baby Steps: How Lesbian Insemination Is Changing the World*. Middletown, C T : Wesleyan University Press.

Bauer, G.R., R. Hammond, R. Travers, M. Kaay, K.M. Hohenadel, and M. Boyce. 2009. "'I Don't Think This Is Theoretical; This Is Our Lives': How Erasure Impacts Health Care for Transgender People." *Journal of the Association of Nurses in A I D S Care* 20(5): 348–61.

Beatie, Thomas. 2008. *Labor of Love: The Story of One Man's Extraordinary Pregnancy.* Berkeley: Seal Press.

Bergman, S. Bear. 2010. *Butch is a Noun.* 2nd ed. Vancouver: Arsenal Pulp Press.

British Columbia Vital Statistics Agency. "Registration of Live Birth." Last modified 1 November 2010. http://www.vs.gov.bc.ca/forms/index.html.

Butler, Judith. 1990. *Gender Trouble.* New York: Routledge.

Cattapan, Alana. 2009. "Theorizing Transgender Citizenship in Canada." Presented at the Annual Meeting of the Canadian Political Science Association, Carleton University, Ottawa, 27 May 2009. Accessed 20 August 2011. http://www.cpsa-acsp.ca/papers-2009/cattapan.pdf.

Chan, L., and S. Turner. 2005. "The Marginalization of Some Medical Students. (Letter to the Editor)." *Canadian Medical Association Journal* 173(8): 849–50.

Colen, Shellee. 1995. "'Like a Mother To Them': Stratified Reproduction and West Indian Childcare Workers and Employers in New York." In *Conceiving the New World Order: The Global Politics of Reproduction,* Faye D. Ginsburg and Rayna Rapp, eds., 78–102. Berkeley: University of California Press.

– 1986. "'With Respect and Feelings': Voices of West Indian Child Care and Domestic Workers in New York City." In *All American Women: Lines that Divide, Ties that Bind,* Johnetta Cole, ed., 46–70. New York: The Free Press.

Coyote, Ivan E., and Zena Sharman, eds. 2011 *Persistence: All Ways Butch and Femme.* Vancouver: Arsenal Pulp Press.

Craven, Christa. 2010. *Pushing for Midwives: Homebirth Mothers and the Reproductive Rights Movement.* Philadelpha: Temple University Press.

Davis-Floyd, Robbie. 2004. *Birth as an American Right of Passage.* 2nd ed. Berkeley: University of California Press.

Epstein, Rachel. 2009. "Introduction." In *Who's Your Daddy? And Other Writings On Queer Parenting,* Rachel Epstein, ed. 13–32. Toronto: Sumach Press.

Fleming, Anne. 2011. "A Dad Called Mom." In *Persistence: All Ways Butch and Femme,* Ivan E. Coyote and Zena Sharman, eds., 43–52. Vancouver: Arsenal Pulp Press.

Gerodetti, N. and V. Mottier. 2009. "Feminism(s) and the Politics of Reproduction: Introduction to Special Issue on 'Feminist Politics of Reproduction.'" *Feminist Theory* 10(2): 147–52.

Gilman, Sander. 1985. "Black Bodies, White Bodies: Toward an Iconography of Female Sexuality in late Nineteenth Century Art, Medicine, and Literature." *Critical Inquiry* 12(1): 204–42.

Ginsburg, Faye D., and Rayna Rapp. 1995. "Introduction: Conceiving the New World Order." In *Conceiving the New World Order: The Global Politics of Reproduction*, Faye D. Ginsburg and Rayna Rapp, eds., 1–17. Berkeley: University of California Press.

Goldberg, L., A. Harbin, and S. Campbell. 2011. "Queering the Birthing Space: Phenomenological Interpretations of the Relationships between Lesbian Couples and Perinatal Nurses in the Context of Birthing Care." *Sexualities* 14(2): 173–92.

Goldberg, L., A. Ryan, and Jody Sawchyn. 2009. "Feminist and Queer Phenomenology: A Framework for Perinatal Nursing Practice, Research, and Education for Advancing Lesbian Health." *Health Care for Women International* 30: 536–49.

Halberstam, Judith. 1999. *Female Masculinity*. Durham: Duke University Press.

Kuehn, Bridget M. 2011. "IOM: Data on Health of Lesbian, Gay, Bisexual, and Transgender Persons Needed." *Journal of the American Medical Association* 305(19): 1950–1.

Letherby, Gayle, and C. Williams. 1999. "Non-Motherhood: Ambivalent Auto-biographies." *Feminist Studies* 25(3): 719–28.

Lewin, Ellen. 2006. "Introduction." In *Feminist Anthropology: A Reader*, Ellen Lewin, ed., 1–25. Malden, MA: Blackwell Press.

– 1995. "On the Outside Looking In: The Politics of Lesbian Motherhood." In *Conceiving the New World Order*, Faye Ginsburg and Rayna Rapp, eds., 103–21. Berkeley: University of California Press.

– 1993. *Lesbian Mothers: Accounts of Gender in American Culture*. Ithaca, NY: Cornell University Press.

Liamputtong, Pranee. 2007a. *Researching the Vulnerable*. Thousand Oaks: Sage.

– 2007b. "Situating Reproduction, Procreation and Motherhood within a Cross-Cultural Context: An Introduction." In *Reproduction, Childbearing and Motherhood: A Cross-Cultural Perspective*, Pranee Liamputtong, ed., 3–34. New York: NOVA.

Luce, Jacquelyne. 2010. *Beyond Expectation: Lesbian/Bi/Queer Women and Assisted Conception*. Toronto: University of Toronto Press.

Lupton, Deborah. 2000. "The Social Construction of Medicine and the Body." In *The Handbook of Social Studies in Health and Medicine*, G.L. Albrecht, R. Fitzpatrick, and S.C. Scrimshaw, eds., 50–63. London, UK: Sage.

Mamo, Laura. 2007. *Queering Reproduction: Achieving Pregnancy in the Age of Technoscience*. Durham: Duke University Press.

McCormack, Karen. 2005. "Stratified Reproduction and Poor Women's Resistance." *Gender and Society* 19(5): 660–79.

Munt, Sally. 2001. "The Butch Body." In *Contested Bodies*, Ruth Holliday and John Hassard, eds., 95. New York: Routledge.

Nelson, Fiona. 1996. *Lesbian Motherhood: An Exploration of Canadian Lesbian Families*. Toronto: University of Toronto Press.

Obedin-Maliver, Juno, Elizabeth S. Goldsmith, Leslie Stewart, William White, Eric Tran, Stephanie Brenman, Maggie Wells, David M. Fetterman, Gabriel Garcia, and Mitchell R. Lunn. 2011. "Lesbian, Gay, Bisexual, and Transgender-Related Content in Undergraduate Medical Education." *Journal of the American Medical Association* 306(9): 971–7.

Owen, M.K. 2001. "'Family' as a Site of Contestation: Queering the Normal or Normalizing the Queer?" In *In A Queer Country: Gay and Lesbian Studies in the Canadian Context*, Terry Goldie, ed., 86–102. Vancouver: Arsenal Pulp Press.

Peel, Elizabeth. 2010. "Pregnancy Loss in Lesbian and Bisexual Women: An Online Survey of Experiences." *Human Reproduction* 25(3): 721–7.

Ryan, Maura. 2009. "Beyond Thomas Beatie: Trans Men and the New Parenthood." In *Who's Your Daddy? And Other Writings On Queer Parenting*, Rachel Epstein, ed., 139–50. Toronto: Sumach Press.

Shroff, Farah. 1997. "All Petals of the Flower: Celebrating the Diversity of Ontario's Birthing Women within First-Year Midwifery Curriculum." In *The New Midwifery*, Farah Shroff, ed., 261–310. Toronto: Women's Press.

Spector, Shira. 2009. "Red Rock Baby Candy: Infertile Homosexual Speaks!" In *Who's Your Daddy? And Other Writings On Queer Parenting*, Rachel Epstein, ed., 73–80. Toronto: Sumach Press.

Walks, Michelle. 2011. "Introduction: Identifying an Anthropology of Mothering." In *An Anthropology of Mothering*, Michelle Walks and Naomi McPherson, eds., 1–47. Toronto: Demeter Press.

Ware, Syrus Marcus. 2009. "Boldly Going Where Few Men Have Gone Before: One Trans Man's Experience." In *Who's Your Daddy? And Other Writings On Queer Parenting*, Rachel Epstein, ed., 65–72. Toronto: Sumach Press.

Watney, S. 1994. "Queer Epistemology: Activism, 'Outing,' and the Politics of Sexual Identities." *Critical Quarterly*, 36(1), 13–27.

4

Reproducing Inequality and Identity: An Intersectional Analysis of Maternal Health Preferences

CANDACE JOHNSON

Interest in the conceptual innovation of intersectionality has increased steadily over the past three decades. Initially the contribution of critical race theory and feminist analysis, intersectionality has grown to include a wide range of philosophical and political approaches. The focus of intersectional research is the multiple ways in which systems of oppression combine to produce marginalizing effects. According to Laurel Weldon (2008, 195–6), intersectionality "is a social-theoretical contribution of feminist theory to efforts to understand and conceptualize social relations. It refers to a form of relationship between social structures, specifically one in which social structures combine to create social categories to which certain experiences and forms of oppression are unique." For example, while it might be reasonable to conclude, through gender analysis, that access to new reproductive technologies such as IVF and genetic screening is a central concern for women seeking to promote and secure gender equality, by further expanding their range of reproductive choices, a different picture emerges when race is included in the analysis.[1] For example, in the United States, the primary reproductive rights struggle for African-American women is not to gain access to a virtually unlimited range of technological advancements, but to win the right to bear children, to be free from policies of state coercion that have included forced sterilization and mandatory contraception. Dorothy E. Roberts (2009, 784) explains, "at a time when wealthy white women have access to technologies that assist them in having children who not only are genetically related to them or their partners but have also been genetically screened, various laws and policies discourage women of colour from having children at all." Similarly, in Canada, access to new reproductive technologies and abortion have been important political goals for many women, but for Aboriginal women, the struggle to maintain traditional medicine and healing and at the same time expand access to biomedical services has been primary. The dynamics and oppressions of "stratified reproduction" (Rapp 2000) are revealed through analysis that explicitly examines gender in addition to other vectors of social disadvantage. Intersectional analysis, then, can illuminate competing and complex realities that are often rendered invisible in single-unit analyses (such as gender only) where dominant perspectives prevail. Scholars of intersectionality often attempt the difficult task of explaining why certain social structures (such as race, class, and gender) interact to produce marginalizing effects. However, the task of illuminating and telling a different story is often ambitious enough, and can lead to fruitful discussions in many areas of policy, politics, and philosophy.

Most intersectional analysis, whether focused on illuminating (to reveal oppression) or on explaining *why* the intersection produces its effects, suffers from the same shortcoming: it has been treated first and foremost as a normative-theoretical matter and has rarely been empirically tested. Even the path-breaking work of Ange-Marie Hancock (2007a; 2007b), which makes a convincing case for intersectionality as a research paradigm and methodological approach, has not been applied to an empirical study.[2] Therefore, much work remains to be done in applying intersectionality, as both research design and conceptual innovation, beyond the simple provision of interesting examples. Further, there has been no application of intersectionality across the North-South axis, either by comparing developed and developing countries, or by considering the complexity and richness of North-South experiences within immigrant communities in developed countries. In this chapter, I seek to do the latter to illuminate marginalizing effects and divergent narratives, and also to explain, with reference to both global inequality and the dynamics of private/public distinctions, why the intersection of gender and immigrant status produces unique patterns of birth preferences.[3]

METHODS

In this chapter, I address the topic of maternal health preferences in Canada in regional and global contexts. These broader regional and global contexts are of critical importance for two main reasons. The first is that the reality for virtually every policy sector is that local phenomena are affected by global dynamics, and vice versa. This reality is reflected in the narratives and experiences of the Canadian immigrant women who are the primary focus of this study. The second is that data in the Canadian context are often much more limited and incomplete than they are elsewhere. Therefore, to provide fuller evidence for arguments concerning disparities, well-documented and relevant disparities from the United States are used to make inferences about the relationship between culture and health disparities in Canada. Expressed preferences for care during pregnancy and childbirth reveal a great deal about complex inequality and identity. The investigation focuses on relatively privileged and marginalized/vulnerable women, Canadian-born and immigrant, in the context of available health services for pregnant and parturient women. As such, the research addresses the intersection of gender and immigrant status in the context of global maternal health initiatives and inequality. The research advances normative/theoretical as well as empirical analyses. The theoretical terrain includes contributions from feminist political theory, notably competing conceptualizations of intersectionality, as well as contributions from health policy scholars on matters of inequality and health disparities. Various dimensions of these theoretical debates are employed to construct theoretical and discursive analysis of the data. For this chapter, and the larger comparative study of which it is a part, the data come from in-depth, semi-structured interviews. The larger project is a comparative study of maternal health preferences and complex inequality in Canada, the United States, Cuba, and Honduras. The Canadian site of the study was developed in partnership with Immigrant Services of Guelph-Wellington. Through this agency, which provides settlement services to New Canadians, six community researchers were recruited. Two additional researchers (graduate students) were recruited through the University of Guelph. In total, eight researchers conducted interviews (digitally recorded) with 120 women, immigrant and Canadian-born. I have analyzed transcripts of these interviews and conducted latent discourse analysis (that is, I have read transcripts and searched for recurring themes, issues, and the meanings of these themes and issues). Data collection is also complete for the Cuban and Honduran sites,[4] although this data and analysis will be presented elsewhere. This research tests intersectionality as a research strategy, and employs intersectionality as an analytical framework for understanding complex inequality and identity through the investigation and interpretation of birth preferences.

INEQUALITY AND INTERSECTIONALITY

Women's relative lack of decision-making power and their unequal access to employment, finances, education, basic health care and other resources are considered to be the root causes of their ill-health and that of their children.

WHO 2005, 4

These days, whenever someone says the word "women" to me, my mind goes blank. What "women"? What is this "women" thing you are talking about? Does that mean me? Does that mean my mother, my roommates, the white woman next door, the checkout clerk at the supermarket, my aunts in Korea, half the world's population?

Jeeyeun Lee, quoted in Farmer 1999, 59

The first quotation above directly links gender equality to health outcomes. Greater inequality between women and men means poorer health status for women, and concomitantly, diminished capacity for social, economic, and political participation. The importance of a continued focus on means to improve gender equality, therefore, cannot be overstated. There are many recent examples of continued dedication to this end (see McClain and Grossman 2009; Jackson 2009; Lombardo, Meier, and Verloo 2009; Brodie 2008; Jenson 2008; Kershaw 2008). Many of these contributions focus on legal and constitutional rights, particularly as they affect women's capacity to participate fully and equally in the labour force, and on the consequences of these rights (and their limitations) for citizenship. The conclusion drawn by most scholars, in American, Canadian, and European contexts alike, is that laws and policies do not go far enough in protecting and promoting gender equality, and in some cases they serve to undermine progress toward that end. For example, Joanna Grossman (2009) argues that pregnant women continue to be discriminated against in the United States despite legal changes that ostensibly promote equality. Pregnancy discrimination law has taken a formal equality approach, partially in response to "equal treatment feminists [who] were adamant that women could not receive special treatment because of pregnancy, for fear of emphasizing and essentializing gender differences and sacrificing the real needs of other workers" (Grossman 2009, 248). However, Grossman argues, this approach fails to recognize the requirements of social citizenship and the requisite development of capacities for full political membership and inclusion.

Within the context of the workforce, it is entirely appropriate to focus on the relation of women and men and their capacity to earn, which in itself is an important pillar of American citizenship (see Shklar 1991). However, the temporary leave provisions in the United States, under both the Pregnancy Discrimination Act (PDA) and the Family and Medical Leave Act (FMLA), leave aside any substantive matters related to difference and identity. Presumably, other programs address some elements of socio-economic inequality, and the formality and neutrality of the PDA and FMLA are preserved as a means to secure negative rights, rather than construct positive rights. But the problem for social citizenship, as Grossman makes clear, is that the formal provisions violate T.H. Marshall's formulation of citizenship as including at least some universally shared experiences (1964), such as access to uniform maternity leave.[5]

Another problem, well-known and well-documented by now, is that the traditional gender equality approach (which entails the consideration of the relational experiences of women and men) treats women as if they constituted a single social category. One important theoretical corrective to this problem comes from the literature on intersectionality. Approaches to intersectionality are varied and complex, and include philosophical, political, and methodological analyses (see for instance Bedolla 2007; Hancock 2007a; 2007b; McCall 2005; Nash 2008). Generally, they are considered to have originated in the domain of critical race (legal) theory (Crenshaw 1991; 1998; Collins 1997; 1998; 2000), although their roots go far deeper than that. To some extent, all approaches and analyses address the difficulty that is expressed in the Jeeyeun Lee quotation above. Who are "the women," and which differences among them are salient, relevant, or significant? How can women, as a single social category, be deconstructed or dissected in meaningful ways? In the analysis presented in this chapter, it is argued that sex/gender is a primary vector of inequality, which intersects with immigrant status (a composite indicator that includes socio-economic status (S E S), race, and nationality), to produce: (a) maternal health preferences; (b) maternal health outcomes; and (c) identities that either resist or reinforce the vectors of advantage/disadvantage that are the foundations of the analysis. For example, it appears that many affluent white women in Canada increasingly prefer "non-medicalized" childbirth, and therefore opt for the services of midwives (rather than obstetricians) in growing numbers (C I H I 2004, 12). There is no indication that this choice has any effect on maternal health outcomes (i.e., the risk of maternal or infant death). However, by resisting the medical regulation of a "natural" event, many Canadian-born women seem to have constructed identities that integrate the experience of pregnancy and childbirth into a social context that tends to separate them from other women, and in so doing have reinforced their privileged positions as persons in full control of their reproductive destinies. Immigrant women, by way of contrast, direct their efforts at gaining access to medical services. For many, the highest levels of medical service are only available to the most privileged in their countries of origin. Midwives are not a choice but a last or only resort for women with no access to hospitals or medical practitioners. For many, from countries like Afghanistan, for example, the difference between an obstetrician and a midwife at time of delivery is the difference between life and death. Therefore, many immigrant women view "medicalized" birth as a means to resist marginalization and risk. Moreover, for a large number of these women there is no need to construct meaning or to integrate the birthing experience into their fragmented lives, as their own cultures (of origin) tend to embody these social goals.

Intersectional analyses and approaches can thus help to understand and interrogate complex inequality within the social (and biological) category of women. However, contributions to the literature to date seem to focus on a single national or sub-national context. In fact, most scholarly work on intersectionality has been applied only to women in the United States.[6] It appears that within this family of scholars, little thought has been given to the meanings of particular experiences with inequality in a global context. While it is important to understand how intersections of gender, S E S , and nationality affect preferences for maternal health care, and how inequality and identity intersect to produce various social and political effects, it is also revealing and worthwhile to examine these understandings and findings in a larger regional, or global, context. What is the political significance of increased preferences for non-medicalized childbirth in Canada in the context of global health protocols (established, primarily, by the W H O) that insist on institutional births (attended by licensed practitioners) as the only way to ensure maternal and infant health? How can (should?) identity be balanced with health imperatives? How does culture interact with medicine in different contexts, and what does this mean for the construction (and feasibility) of a global health agenda? These questions are critical to understanding maternal health, and cannot be answered with evidence and analysis from a single country (or from only the perspective of developed countries). One of the main points of the research is to show that the experiences of immigrant women serve as philosophical and policy-relevant bridges between the local and the global. Through the experiences of immigrant women we are able to get a sense of the global diversity of birthing preferences, and by comparing these preferences with those of Canadian-born women, there are clear implications for both national and global maternal health policy. The juxtaposition of global protocols and country-specific preferences and trends indicates the political nature of maternal health care; women of different social classes, ethnic and national backgrounds, and so on, are affected in widely varying ways by the same recommendations. Some women increase their status through their ability to access the maximum amount of medical care and technology; some women are protected through compliance with medical protocols; and others derive status, empowerment, and identity by resisting those same protocols.

Unfortunately, there are few theoretical approaches that provide analytical and methodological frameworks for North-South or global gender analysis. One possibility for filling this gap is "transversal politics" (see Yuval-Davis 2006), which captures the global dimension, because its orientation is internationalist. But in resisting essentialisms, it makes it more difficult to identify intersecting sources of disadvantage, such as those relevant to gender, ethnicity, and socio-economic status. Nira Yuval-Davis explains, "transversal politics has developed as an alternative to the assimilationist 'universalistic' politics of the Left, on the one hand, and to identity politics, on the other hand" (281). The focus of transversal politics seems to be dialogue and activism on international and global scales, organizing, and value-balancing, whereas one of the primary goals of intersectionality is the interpretation and identification of those vectors that contribute to complex inequality. Transversalism is a model of advocacy, mostly in pursuit of broad political goals like human rights recognition and gender equality promotion (with particularistic needs and approaches). Its macro-level approach is well suited to the global political arena, and its attention to individualistic detail serves as an important corrective to the group-based essentialisms and exclusions of identity politics. However, it does not seem well equipped to deal on its own with specific problems, such as the ways in which the complexities of unequal social positions conspire to threaten maternal health. Widening the dialogue is essential to the global imperative of improving maternal health, but, in the absence of other approaches, will not result in material change.

Perhaps the most significant contribution of transversalism is a conceptual framework that could incorporate and facilitate North-South dialogue and comparison. While there has been excellent scholarship concerning transnational and North-South feminist activism and networking (see for example Tripp 2006; Joachim 2003), there remains limited theoretical exploration of the nexus. One of the main difficulties is that transnational, and particularly North-South, comparisons defy the theoretical contexts provided by citizenship, democracy, and rights. The first, citizenship, does not adequately lend itself to North-South comparative analysis because it is, by its very definition, exclusive to members of a national community, and the last two are insufficient because they are also exclusive to particular regimes or they mean very different things in different countries. Gender equity is a similarly problematic concept because its meaning and consequences are inseparable from innumerable localized legal and customary details.

One of the ways in which these details can be provided is through policy-specific problems and approaches. For this study, such details come from the health disparities literature (or social determinants of health: s d h). Contributors to this approach investigate disparities within societies (see for example Marmot and Wilkinson 2006; Levy and Sidel 2006; Heymann, Hertzman, Barer, and Evans 2006), and recent scholarship pays particular attention to the body-culture interface (Aronowitz 2008). For example, in the United States, the maternal mortality ratio (M M R) is 12.1, which is quite high in comparison with other developed countries, but low by global standards. When this figure is disaggregated, another picture emerges. The M M R for white women is 8.1, for Hispanic women 10.1, and for African-American women 31.2 (Hoyert 2007, 10). Why is the M M R for African-American women almost four times higher than the M M R for white women? What accounts for the disparity, even among women of the same socio-economic status (Nazroo and Williams 2006; Hoyert et al. 2000)? In Canada, it is likely the case that similar disparities exist for Aboriginal and immigrant women, although there are no disaggregated M M R data.[7] The social patterning of disease attempts to recognize and understand the "*contextual* factors 'above' the level of the individual" (Aronowitz 2008, 1–2). The health indicators and their disaggregated components provide the empirical starting points for the health disparities/S D H analyses, and a multidisciplinary effort is required to conduct the analysis. The research presented in this chapter attempts to explain what maternal health preferences reveal about complex inequality. Such inquiry also attends to contextual factors above the level of the individual. To better understand the relationship between inequality, identity, and maternal health, it makes sense to consider the global dimensions of the matter, and to create opportunities for North-South comparative analysis.

WIDENING THE DIALOGUE: BIRTH PREFERENCES IN CANADIAN-BORN AND IMMIGRANT POPULATIONS

The principal methodological claim of this chapter is that intersectionality is a theoretical contribution that requires robust empirical testing. The conceptual contribution of intersectionality, namely its insistence on examining multiple vectors of disadvantage or marginality to understand complex inequality, centres on acknowledging difference and diversity within populations or social categories. Therefore, it becomes critically important to accurately identify relevant differences or vectors in intersectional examinations. In this study of birth preferences among Canadian-born and immigrant women, the relevant intersections, or vectors, are gender and immigrant (or citizenship) status. The former indicates differences in biological sex and/or the performance of or resistance to culturally determined biological sex roles, while the latter is a composite indicator that implicates socio-economic status, race, nationality, and marginality or exclusion. Gender and immigrant status are descriptors that signify membership in particular social groups, but they also operate as systems that produce unique patterns of inequality or oppression (Weldon 2008). Further, this investigation considers those systems along the North-South axis in recognition of the larger global context for social systems and the policies and politics that interact with the domestic characteristics of gender and immigrant status.

As explained in the methods section, in the Canadian research site 120 interviews were conducted with a diverse range of women, both immigrant and Canadian-born (most of whom had given birth within the past five years). Many of the immigrant women had experienced pregnancy and childbirth in another country, often their country of origin, as well as in Canada. The community researchers who conducted the interviews had also had the unique experience of navigating maternal health services and patterns of care in at least two distinct contexts; their interpretations of some of the data shed important light on the political dimensions of maternal health preferences as well as the challenges of social position (i.e., immigrant with limited English-language skills). A transversal discursive approach might be one that encourages full expression of diversity and difference, and considers matters that span or cross borders; it seeks to widen the discussion to increase opportunities for understanding of problems and, ultimately, policy development. It also includes pregnant and parturient women themselves, speaking in their own voices, providing their own interpretations of the data.

As noted, in Canada there is no documented disparity in MMR, although there is clear evidence that other maternal health disparities do exist. For instance, the increasing trend in the use of midwifery services includes mostly white, affluent women. Racialized, Aboriginal, and immigrant women tend to access and/or prefer medical care during pregnancy and childbirth (despite the assumption that these groups of women are particularly vulnerable to the negative effects of medicalization). Therefore, marked differences are apparent in maternal health care preferences and patterns of use among different populations of women. In addition, many of the participants who had immigrated to Canada had difficulties accessing available services and navigating the larger health system, and many had trouble finding culturally appropriate care, or incorporating important cultural elements into the services available. As midwifery becomes increasingly popular and well-integrated into provincial health systems (illustrated in this volume by Paterson's contribution), and as governments continue to (a) respond to increasingly complex reproductive and maternal health environments (with the growing popularity of assisted reproductive technologies, for example); and (b) develop and respond to international health goals, it is imperative to understand the full range of preferences and experiences across diverse populations (on community, national, regional, and global scales).

The immigrant women who participated in the study overwhelmingly preferred to give birth in a hospital and to be attended by an obstetrician during childbirth. Participant P1 explains:

I'm not sure about home delivery. I know that this is a new trend, a new idea, a new attitude about childbirth at home, but it's not dominant in Iran. Because of the accessibility. Because if some complication arises at home it is not easy to commute to hospital because, for example, in Tehran it's not possible because of the traffic jam. If something happens at home it's not possible to go to the hospital, and it's dangerous and it's not recommended to deliver at home. And people are already medicalized in Iran. They just want to just go to different doctors, because if the system is different they can choose their doctor, they can go to several doctors for consultation and choose among them. So, it's not easy to cope with the situation here [in Canada]. I know that some people are not comfortable with their doctor but they do not have a chance to just choose among them.

Participant C1, also originally from Iran, elaborates:

I had both my kids here in Canada; I had professional care, like specialist, gynecologist, and I had a painless childbirth. I chose to have that. I went to the general hospital here almost with a bit of a pain. I said I have a lot of pain and I want epidural. I was very adamant. Epidural now. But of course they wait (for a period?) then they gave me epidural and that was it, and I slept through it. Literally. The reason I chose that was that "why not?" basically. It's easier. I don't need pain to experience affection toward my child. Was not sentimental about childbirth in any way shape or form. It was a technical matter. Get over with it. And maybe culturally in our culture, Iran is presumably a traditional society but mostly educated women were not into breastfeeding or natural childbirth. Or anything like that. Bada bing bada boom get the baby out. That's it. Especially I think in the educated level it was a kind of a too much of a sentimentality towards childbirth. Maybe it was some sort of some anti-feminist approach.

Participant M2, originally from Laos, states unequivocally that she prefers (and considers to be ideal) hospital birth attended by medical doctors. She explains that this preference is typical of other women in her community/country of origin: "they all dream of hospitals. Back home they don't tell you when the baby's going to be born. Here they tell you the date that your baby is going to be born and you have to prepare. The day, the week. But back home they don't even tell you within a month – so a woman sometimes they just have the baby at home because they have no choice. So of course here is better, much better."

Some prefer caesarean sections (due to complications during labour in previous pregnancies, fear of pain, concern about impairment of sexual abilities, and superstitions about lucky birth days). Participant E12, after losing a baby during her first pregnancy in Nigeria, chose to deliver her second through caesarean section: "I believe, for what I have gone through, the caesarean operation really helped me when I had my second baby. I wanted to make it, try it, but it was like, don't try it, so I think that's what God wants me to have. Not to have a normal delivery, not to waste time, not to danger the life of the baby, so I believe it's okay for me." Participant E7, originally from Pakistan, expressed the same preference: "When I lost my one child, I learned there are lots of options, so it's not necessary, if my mother and grandmother say the normal delivery was good, but it was not good for me. I was not feeling the natural labour pain, then I decided it would be better for me to have a caesarean."

In many developing countries, midwives are traditional birth attendants (TBAs), and have little if any formal training. Obstetricians are available only to affluent women, and are only accessible in urban settings. Therefore, obstetrical services become a marker of privilege in societies where there is an opportunity to acquire those services. However, in communities (mostly poor, rural, and remote) where there is no possibility of accessing medical services, women prefer to be attended by T B A S, whom they have learned to trust. Most services related to pregnancy and delivery require payment, and the services of nurses or midwives are much cheaper than those of medical doctors or obstetricians.

Participant E1, from Ghana, explains:

> I come from a family, or a background, where most women or most families would prefer to have normal, would prefer to have children born naturally by vagina birth in the hospitals or even at home, you know, attended by traditional birth attendant.
>
> There are various options of delivery, pregnancy, management of pregnancy, and deliveries where I come from or where I had or experienced my pregnancy and delivery. And there are those, most, when I say most, there are quite a number of people like to go through ante-natal care during pregnancy and then have the babies delivered in the hospital, ok? There are quite a number too, especially in the rural areas, who would also go through pregnancy without ante-natal care and have normal deliveries at home and there are also those who go through, or who may not go through ante-natal care but would have deliveries at home or with a traditional birth attendant, you know, taking care of them. We have women who have been trained, the traditional birth attendants, their knowledge and skills in delivery have been upgraded so that they can give the woman, rural, especially rural women, who do not want to come to the hospital, better care during delivery at home.

Other immigrant women who preferred midwives claimed to have had negative experiences with medical doctors, were unable to access medical services, or preferred the care of women (there is only one female obstetrician in the Guelph rotation and there is no guarantee that she will be available for the delivery).

One woman (P9), who had experienced complications related to a forceps delivery, reflects on her experiences in Canada in relation to her family (Sri Lankan) traditions:

> Actually I think here (in Canada) it will be better to use some of the traditional knowledge in medical services. In my nineteen years of stay in Canada I have different medical experiences

(apart from the pregnancy and childbirth). It is my view that doctors rely a lot on machines.

My thinking now is exactly the opposite of the thinking that I had when I first came to Canada nineteen years back. The reason is that, I thought it will be so good because everything is advanced but now our traditional knowledge seems much better. We nowadays rely so much on machines and not on our thinking. We have to undergo unnecessary tests and it disturbs our mind, develops a negative thinking and we become sicker because of all this. There has to be some change brought about not to rely so much on tests and machines. Even if we cannot go back to traditional ways completely, the traditional knowledge should be used compulsorily and it should be incorporated in our present medical services. I am saying all this because I have undergone unnecessary surgeries "only" because of the advanced medical system.

Similarly, participant P3, originally from Sudan, reveals:

Yeah I chose to have a midwife because I read a lot about that, and I also spoke with the midwife, and I found that their services are same like the doctor. Except that they don't have a lot scans, they do normal things, they just trying to, by using the traditional methods, and it was good. It wasn't bad at all. But you know, if I pregnant again I will choose a midwife, because I feel it is more, I was comfortable with the midwife, she was a woman and she can understand me, and she also give birth to kids to she has kids, and she can understand – I feel comfortable speaking with her. And I feel comfortable not doing a lot of scans, not a lot of blood test and urines, if I'm healthy and my baby is healthy. So why?

Participant D4 explains that she would have preferred to receive care from an obstetrician, but because she did not have access to public health insurance (she was in Canada on a visitor's visa from Mexico), the midwives were her only option (they provided services free of charge):

During the pregnancy I was under the care of the midwives, it was not with a doctor. It was all the time with a midwife and the service was very good, indeed. I am really happy with it and if I decide to have another child, it will be again with them.

[I chose the midwives] because when I came ... and, I was pregnant, I didn't have medical services here in Canada. Then, it was very expensive for me to go to the doctor and we didn't have the means to pay for it. And with the midwives it was for free and, then, we decided to go that way. Also everyone told us that once the child was born if I didn't have the medical service yet, it was going to be very expensive to go to the hospital. Then, the midwives offer you the service where the baby can be born in your house.

Although some expressed a preference for midwives or more "traditional" approaches to pregnancy and birth, the vast majority of immigrant women in the study preferred hospital births attended by an obstetrician. The justifications for the preference of obstetrical care focused on diminution of risk, and several had had poor outcomes (including perinatal infant deaths) in developing countries, where most women "dream of hospitals." Those women who expressed preference for midwifery care justified their inclination with reference to traditions, and the integration of those traditions with medical practices. There is also some evidence, as demonstrated by D4, that some migrant women who do not have access to publicly funded health care (either because they are in the country on temporary visas or because they need care for pregnancy and/or childbirth in the first three months – the mandatory waiting period – of their arrival as immigrants) go to midwives as an alternative. In accordance with provincial funding arrangements and practice guidelines, midwives are able to offer prenatal and birthing care free of charge to any Ontario resident, although any corresponding medical or hospital costs will be charged to the birthing mother. It is ironic that midwifery care is often a last and best resort for uninsured or undocumented immigrant women. As demonstrated, immigrant women tend to strongly prefer medical care, because midwifery in their countries of origin is practised by traditional birth attendants and signifies marginalization and risk.

Many of the Canadian-born women who participated in the study preferred and had accessed midwifery care. The justifications that they provided were different from those provided by immigrant women. The Canadian-born women spoke of personal attention and support (whereas the immigrant women mentioned the importance of family). They also emphasized the importance of autonomy in decision-making, and of resisting medical mandates. There was also a tendency for Canadian-born women to speak of "natural" childbirth (in contrast to "traditional" childbirth, which was emphasized by immigrant women) (see Johnson 2008).

According to participant N1 (Canadian-born): "The best, the ideal was the midwives. I think it was, the ideal pregnancy is having a midwife. It's not having a doctor because a doctor doesn't come to your home, whereas a midwife, you go see her but after the birth they come to your home, they help you get settled into bed, they help the baby get settled, if I needed her to come if I was concerned, she came to us. She came to our home to do the needle in his heel. I got to nurse him and hold him and then I stopped she did the needle and then I could nurse him again and comfort him, it was way, far more personal. So I think that's the ideal." Participant N3 (Canadian-born) elaborates:

I have had all three children in the hospital and I used a midwife each time. Unfortunately with all three births I had to transfer care to a doctor. So in that sense I'm glad I was at the hospital because giving birth was not easy for me. Having the midwife was very comforting. I felt midwives give you more information, let you make your own choices, whereas sometimes I felt the doctor were very, they told you how it was going to be and that's how it was going to be. I had a very difficult birth with my last one. So much so that she was born not breathing, and blue. And the midwives' support even though everything was transferred to a doctor was amazing and I don't know how I would have got through it without it. Because they were able to keep me informed, tell me how she was going to do, what it meant, um, because she didn't breathe on her own until five minutes of life. So all that was really good. I always, I tell any woman that I meet that a midwife is the way to go. Even if you want the traditional painkillers and all that, even if you want to have a doctor there, to have a midwife or a doula, a woman with you, the support! I mean because even though your husband is there maybe to hold your hand I mean, he doesn't get it. You know, he doesn't understand the emotion, the pain, the, I don't know. I think it was really great.

I think in keeping women informed. I think that sometimes women don't realize that you don't have to have a doctor for pre-natal as long as you have a healthy pregnancy, and even if you want a midwife that doesn't mean that you have to have this home birth with no painkillers... I think women believe that it's one way or the other. But I do think it's changing that you can have the best of both.

I think it's great in the way it's going, in that it's going back to more natural – and the way it used to be! My great grandmother was a midwife! Women helping women I think makes a difference. I've always said that, you know, like someone's who's had a baby, helping someone who's having a baby makes more sense. You understand it more, right?

Sheryl Nestel (2006) has documented, in her study of the development of the profession of midwifery in Ontario, the romanticization and idealization of the "natural" Third World woman, which often has not translated into positive outcomes for the actual women that are iconicized for the benefit of the privileged. Although there is no mention of Third World women in the above quotations, the participants' explanations suggest sentimentality and reverence for an imaginary "natural." This tendency is reflected in the words of participant N5 (Canadian-born):

Oh, to, prefer a natural birth and midwife [is the ideal]. And to learn how to take care of your body and listen to your body, exercise, eat healthy when you're pregnant. Definitely eat healthy and exercise, and your, a natural birth is best for everybody, but you have to prepare your body for that, you know, and really take care of yourself.

And support around it! Women need support around it, other women friends and support in eating healthy. People supporting you with meals and helping you around the house so you're not exhausted so when you have the baby you're not exhausted. And help for two months after I had [my child] – the midwives came to my house and helped me! They were supposed to, the hospital the doctors in McMaster were supposed to organize home care from when I came home after the hospital but nothing was set in place, they just kind of ignored it. But if I didn't have my midwife with me it would have been really difficult. You know, and uh, yeah. Lots of support. Lots and lots of support.

Some women, both immigrant and Canadian-born, identified the importance of combining obstetrical and midwifery services in a manner that would invite true collaboration, as opposed to opting for midwifery services in hospital so that the obstetrician on duty and other members of the medical staff serve as a back-up plan. Participant N6, who immigrated from Serbia, proposes the following:

I believe that women, have, generally, we all have to advocate for better collaboration between the midwives and the doctors. Because I believe that in this country, in Canada, there is kind of sort of tension between midwives and like the medical facilities and the doctors, so I feel like it's almost like if you choose to go to midwife you cannot have access to a hospital. There is that kind of sort of tension. But I believe that if we allow for both, if there is a good cooperation and collaboration because not all childbirth could happen at home, safely, and not all childbirth has to happen in the hospital to be safe and enjoyable. So if we kind of, advocate for better collaboration among these professionals there is no tension and they could work together. And in the case that you know, there is a need, for example if the childbirth starts at home and it needs to be transferred to the hospital, that this can be recognized and done safely without any tension.

When asked about her vision of the ideal health care arrangement for pregnancy and childbirth, N7 (who immigrated from Iran) responded as follows:

Actually, a combination. I wish everybody could have their family around to support them. I love the idea of midwife because I see how these nurses, these midwives are attached to these women who are here, doesn't matter if they are Canadian or from diverse community, they don't have their families and as much care and love, but they give enough care and love and they are visiting, they are in touch, and they are giving them the sense of security and safety that anytime you need help – just page us! And

they are going, they are there to answer your questions, they are
following up with them, they are going to hospital with them,
they are staying through the childbirth, they are following up the
childbirth with mother and the child, and seeing the face in the
nine months through your pregnancy and feeling the hand of
love from the person who knows you during the pregnancy, is a
big huge help to all women and I wish everybody could have it.
I'm not saying like, you know O B s are excellent too, doctors
checking you and going to office very dry, I don't think it should
be like that. I think it should be more sensitivity, because each individual is different and their needs especially, and you're talking
about women that don't have their families.

Similarly, N8 (Canadian-born), conveys her confidence in both
midwifery and medical care: "I'm a strong believer in women and I
like the idea that midwives and women stick together, because I think
that women really do have some good instincts about each other so
that was sort of the comforting about why I wanted a midwife. But
the doctor that I had chosen was wonderful, and, basically had similar experiences for both pregnancies and childbirth." This final quote
signifies solidarity with other women (rather than the family, as expressed by N7 above). The focus on support from and solidarity
with other women emphasizes autonomy and independence, which
might indicate a greater sense of agency and control. This difference
(the pattern emerges from the data) also demonstrates the relevance
of identity in explaining birth preferences. Relatively privileged
women indicate that they prefer midwives because they engender a
sense of solidarity (as women), and provide support and autonomy
from spouses, while immigrant women who express preferences
for midwives claim that midwives can serve as substitutes or supplements for family. For Canadian-born women, more meaning is attached to the birth event through the choice of a care provider,
whereas for immigrant women the meaning of the birth event seems
to be established through culture and family tradition.

ANALYZING INTERSECTIONALITY, INEQUALITY ... AND IDENTITY?

I have argued that improving global maternal health requires a wide,
inclusive, view of the experiences of women and their preferences for

care and support. In part, as I have suggested, this exploration can be done within theoretical and methodological commitments to transversalism, which insists on international, integrative approaches, and action. The data from the Canadian research site provide some of this dialogue, as interview participants were from diverse backgrounds, many from the global South. Inclusion of women from immigrant communities seems to be a good way to start to develop an understanding of the multiplicity of ideas and experiences that, ultimately, affect maternal health and well-being. The other countries in the larger study will provide additional perspectives and insights on this matter, as well as on the relationships between women, health systems, and the state. Such an approach also responds to Paul Farmer's call for transnational approaches to the study of health and inequality (2005, 18).

The health disparities literature, or the social determinants of health (SDH), can contribute to the theoretical framework by emphasizing the importance of investigation and understanding of "contextual factors above the level of the individual." In this volume, Wiebe's analysis of the struggle for reproductive justice in the First Nations community of Aamjiwnang and Walks's investigation of the reproductive experiences of butch lesbians, transmen, and genderqueer individuals contribute to this literature. They, and other works in this vein, ask what social, political, and economic dynamics affect preferences for (maternal) health care. How are power relations expressed in these preferences? In this chapter, I have only begun to examine possible answers to these questions. In a previous section, I noted that there was no documented maternal health disparity in Canada; maternal mortality ratios are not disaggregated in Canada the way they are in the United States. However, it is well-known and well-documented that there is a "healthy immigrant effect," despite the obvious benefits of universal health care. The "healthy immigrant effect" identifies the pattern whereby immigrants arrive in relatively good health, but their health status deteriorates over time. That this pattern applies to maternal and reproductive health as well is a plausible extrapolation (see Ray et al. 2007; Hyman and Dussault 2000; see also Beiser 2005; McDonald and Kennedy 2004; and Oxman-Martinez, Abdool, and Loiselle Léonard 2000).

Although Iris Young and Laurel Weldon recommend that "political theory would do well to disengage social group difference from the logic of identity" (Young 2000, 82), and point out that "it is the intersection of social *structures*, not identities, to which the concept refers" (Weldon 2008, 202), there are several important questions that can only be answered with the conceptual integration of identity. For example: how does unequal social position (determined by race, ethnicity, country of origin, s e s , sexual orientation, and so on), and/or culture[8] affect health? What can cultural heterogeneity or other differences in maternal health preferences reveal about the distribution of power and resources? Whereas international agencies and imperatives, such as the Millennium Development Goals, establish a worthy global agenda that focuses on the reduction of death and suffering, improvement of health indicators might not be the only goal worth pursuing. There are many symbolic, identity-generating and -sustaining elements of care during pregnancy and childbirth that should be balanced through public policy. When they are not appropriately balanced, women try to create these experiences as they navigate medical and cultural terrain. This is often much easier for privileged women, in this case Canadian-born primarily white women. There are also more identity-related considerations among Canadian-born women (for natural, woman-centred care, time to communicate with practitioners, more autonomy and control). Many immigrant women seemed to concur with participant E3, who stated, "The major goal is to make you alive and the baby alive. How you get to that does not really matter to me because when you carry the baby in your pregnancy, there's only one prayer that you have, that is you want to stay alive, you want the baby be alive and well. How you get to that destination does not really matter so far it is achieved." Many immigrant women emphasized the importance of care, time, and support, but wanted and expected this from family rather than health practitioners, and requested instead better (medical) health system access and information. However, for these women access to obstetrical care was also a marker of elevated social status, and therefore an expression of identity. Aboriginal women, by way of contrast, do seem to emphasize the importance of identity and custom (in addition to, or as a separate consideration from, safe motherhood), and consider the reclaiming of the birth experience to be a way to decolonization (Simpson 2006, 28–9). Identity also helps to explain *why* the intersecting vectors of gender and immigrant status produce unique effects.

Also important to recognize, and to emphasize, is that the dynamics of public-private distinctions are often experienced very differently by Canadian-born and immigrant women, and these experiences reflect tangible, structural elements of inequality and identity. The quotes in the preceding section reveal that immigrant women tend to think about their experiences of pregnancy and childbirth as well as preferences for care providers in the context of the family, whereas Canadian-born women tend to resist this frame, and emphasize instead the importance of solidarity with other women. Therefore, it is reasonable to conclude that differences in the ways in which preferences and experiences are framed are related to the structural elements of inequality, which are experienced differently by Canadian-born and immigrant women. But it is also important to recognize that differences in preferences for care during pregnancy and childbirth are constitutive of culture and express identity.

CONCLUSION

This research empirically tests the conceptual claims and methodological potential of intersectionality to capture and elucidate some of the components that contribute to complex inequality. It seeks to understand the relationship between, or intersections among, various measures of inequality and identity. The interpretation of data suggests that there is much to learn about privileged women and vulnerable women, their relationship to the health system, society, and the state, in addition to the myriad ways in which public and private realms are experienced. The intersecting vectors of gender and immigrant status in particular reveal unique effects, such as divergent preferences for care during pregnancy and childbirth and the justifications for these preferences. It was noted above that the "healthy immigrant effect" likely presents in the domain of maternal health, although there are no data collected on differences in maternal mortality ratios in different populations within Canada. Immigrant women in the study, the overwhelming majority of whom preferred medical care for pregnancy and childbirth among available options, also spoke of barriers in navigating that care. Many spoke about language barriers, and being overwhelmed by the difficulties of understanding their doctors throughout the process. Even women who were fluent in English found communication challenging during stressful and emotional times. Therefore, the tangible elements of inequality, in this case language, indicated barriers to access and care and, perhaps, affected outcomes, but seemed to be distinct from the identity-based preferences.

However, the identity-based elements were present and compelling. Preferences for medical care among immigrant women expressed markers of privilege and status, while exceptional preferences for midwives expressed the need for the support of family and its surrogates. Canadian-born women explained preferences for midwifery care in terms of solidarity, women-centredness, empowerment, and autonomy from spouses.[9] Medical interventions were often resisted, and such resistance was critical to the construction of identity. These preferences and expressions of resistance were also important in generating meaning with regard to the events of pregnancy and childbirth, particularly among Canadian-born women. The cultural inscription of pregnancy and childbirth as private events, to be experienced and celebrated only within the narrow realm of the family, tends to strip pregnancy and childbirth of broader social meanings. Therefore, choice of care provider, and justification for that choice, in the language of solidarity, autonomy, and the reclaiming of nature becomes critically important in creating broader social meaning from the birth event. For immigrant women, many countries and cultures of origin seem to accord more sociocultural meaning to the birth event. In addition, public and private domains are often constructed very differently, with more social blurring of the lines that create sharp distinctions in North America (although this blurring of private and public realms is not necessarily liberating for women). There is little, if any, evidence of the need among immigrant women to ascribe additional or new meaning to pregnancy and childbirth through choice of care providers. The intersection of gender and immigrant status therefore reveals distinct patterns of reproductive preferences that might be invisible in maternal health analyses that focus on pregnancy and childbirth as universal experiences. Disaggregation of women as a single social category is critical for reproductive and maternal health research in all parts of the globe precisely because pregnancy, childbirth, and care options are politicized in complex ways and reveal elements of both inequality and identity.

NOTES

1 This divergence in social and political goals is also evident in feminist debates on abortion, which was, and in some cases is, the sine qua non of

gender equality. However, abortion rights were primarily the goal of affluent white women, while African-American women, as noted above, struggled to gain the right, and some basic support for the right, to determine, free of state coercion, when and under what circumstances to bear children (see Schoen 2005; Roberts 1998).

2 One recent contribution applies the concept of intersectionality to several health-related case studies, but does not apply or test intersectionality as a research paradigm or methodological approach. In other words, the case studies assert various intersections but do not thoroughly examine or test them (Hankivsky 2011).

3 In this study, "preferences" refer to the choices that individual women make about care during pregnancy and childbirth. In some cases these choices were made in accordance with a prior, imagined ideal, and in others they reflect a constrained reality, wherein the range of available choices is quite limited, for various reasons. What is most relevant in this study, in regard to preferences, are the ways in which women articulated their options and went about, or planned to go about, navigating them. In many cases, immigrant women's preferences are shaped by their experiences in their countries of origin, although this is not true for all immigrant women. Further, many immigrant women who participated in the study had given birth in Canada as well, and so their preferences reflected different sets of context-specific factors. It is not the purpose of this research to hypothesize and then draw conclusions about the causes of various preferences, but rather to document diverse patterns of preferences as a means of testing theory concerning intersectionality and identity. In order to do this, it is important to identify and explain the prevalence of inequality and identity-health connections; their specific causes are a separate concern, one that is well beyond the scope of this research.

4 The Cuban site of the research was developed differently. I had the assistance of two researchers, who conducted the research in two separate parts of the country. In total, twenty-seven women provided written narratives in response to questions very similar to those used in the Canadian interviews. These narratives (written, due to the risks associated with the use of recording devices in that country), included women from urban and rural environments. The transcripts of these narratives have been analyzed through latent discourse analysis. Research in Honduras was developed and conducted in partnership with the Canadian Red Cross, which has established intervention sites and strategies for improving maternal, neonatal, and child health. Data were collected in March 2011 in four different communities, and included sixty-five interviews with women who had given birth within the past two years. Four research assistants from the

area (Department of Copán) conducted the semi-structured interviews, which were subsequently transcribed. Analysis of this data is in progress.

5 These universally shared experiences are social rights. Marshall argued that social rights developed in Great Britain following the development of civil and political rights.

6 One notable exception is Boesten (2010).

7 Other key indicators do demonstrate disparities. For example, a 2009 study reports that the infant mortality rate for the non-Aboriginal population was 6.0 per 1,000 live births, whereas the infant mortality rate for the Aboriginal population in Canada was 12.0 per 1,000 live births (Lalonde, Butt, and Bucio 2009, 958). The infant mortality rate in Inuit communities is reported to be approximately four times as high as the overall Canadian rate (Stout and Harp 2009, 8).

8 See Farmer (1999, 6–7) for a discussion of the (problematic) difference between inequality and culture.

9 The articulation of these preferences reflects the justification for midwifery's resurgence. As Adrienne Rich (1995, chapter 6) explains, historically midwives had much more scientific and evidence-based approaches to childbirth than medical doctors and surgeons did. Midwives also had much better rates of uncomplicated birth and lower rates of maternal and infant mortality. Over time, midwives lost professional status and space for practice to medical doctors for a variety of reasons. The emergence of the licensed, professional midwife in the 1990s and 2000s in Canada was facilitated by arguments related to practical expertise in addition to feminist approaches, such as woman-centred care, autonomy (of the birthing mother), continuity of care, and the development of a long-term relationship between midwives and the birthing mother and her family. It also developed as a rejection of the medical approach to pregnancy and birth as illness, rather than a normal, healthy, "natural" life event (see Rich 1995, 141; Macdonald 2007, 58–9). Moreover, the new midwifery challenges "technocratic birth" (Robbie Davis-Floyd in Macdonald 2004, 53), and cultivates images of both tradition and nature (Macdonald 2004, 53), which appeal to Canadian-born women who have learned to be properly suspicious of medical expertise and technological advancements. If the challenge has been for "new" Ontario midwives to strike a balance between tradition and modernity (Macdonald 2004, 56–7), this challenge has been taken up by consumers of midwives' services, who want solidarity, connection, and meaning in the context of highly accessible and fully funded medical and hospital services.

BIBLIOGRAPHY

Aronowitz, Robert. 2008. "Framing Disease: An Underappreciated Mechanism for the Social Patterning of Health." *Social Science & Medicine* 67(1): 1–9.

Bedolla, Lisa García. 2007. "Intersections of Inequality: Understanding Marginalization and Privilege in the Post-Civil Rights Era." *Politics and Gender* 3(2): 232–47.

Beiser, Morton. 2005. "The Health of Immigrants and Refugees in Canada." *Canadian Journal of Public Health* 96(2), S30–44.

Boesten, Jelke. 2010. *Intersecting Inequalities: Women and Social Policy in Peru, 1990–2000*. University Park: Penn State Press.

Brodie, Janine. 2009. "Putting Gender Back In: Women and Social Policy Reform in Canada." In *Gendering the Nation-State: Canadian and Comparative Perspectives*, Yasmeen Abu-Laban, ed., 165–84. Vancouver: U B C Press.

C I H I (Canadian Institutes for Health Information). 2004. *Giving Birth in Canada: Providers of Maternity and Infant Care*. Ottawa: C I H I.

Collins, Patricia Hill. 2000. "It's All in the Family: Intersections of Gender, Race, and Nation." In *Decentering the Center: Philosophy for a Multicultural, Postcolonial, and Feminist World*, Uma Narayan and Sandra Harding, eds., 156–76. Indianapolis: Indiana University Press.

– 1998. *Fighting Words: Black Women and the Search for Justice*. Minneapolis: University of Minnesota Press.

– 1997. "Defining Black Feminist Thought." In *The Second Wave: A Reader in Feminist Theory*, Linda Nicholson, ed., 241–59. New York: Routledge.

Crenshaw, Kimberlé. 1998. "A Black Feminist Critique of Antidiscrimination Law and Politics." In *The Politics of Law*, David Kairys, ed., 356–80. 3rd ed. New York: Basic Books.

– 1991. "Mapping the Margins: Intersectionality, Identity Politics, and Violence Against Women of Colour." *Stanford Law Review* 43(6): 1241–99.

Farmer, Paul. 2005. *Pathologies of Power: Health, Human Rights, and the New War on the Poor*. Berkeley: University of California Press.

– 1999. *Infections and Inequalities: The Modern Plagues*. Berkeley: University of California Press.

Grossman, Joanna L. 2009. "Pregnancy and Social Citizenship." In *Gender Equality: Dimensions of Women's Equal Citizenship*, Linda C. McClain and Joanna L. Grossman, eds., 233–50. New York: Cambridge University Press.

Hancock, Ange-Marie. 2007a. "Intersectionality as a Normative and Empirical Paradigm." *Politics and Gender* 3 (2): 248–53.

– 2007b. "When Multiplication Doesn't Equal Quick Addition: Examining Intersectionality as a Research Paradigm." *Perspectives on Politics* 5 (1): 63–79.

Hankivsky, Olena, 2011. *Health Inequities in Canada: Intersectional Frameworks and Practices*. Vancouver: U B C Press.

Heymann, Jody, Clyde Hertzman, Morris L. Barer, and Robert G. Evans, eds. 2006. *Healthier Societies: From Analysis to Action*. New York: Oxford University Press.

Hoyert, Donna L. 2007. "Maternal Mortality and Related Concepts." *Vital and Health Statistics* 3(33). Analytical and Epidemiological Studies, US Department of Health and Human Services and the C D C.

Hoyert, Donna L., Isabella Danel, and Patricia Tully. 2000. "Maternal Mortality, United States and Canada, 1982–1997." *Birth* 27(1): 4–11.

Hyman, Ilene, and Gilles Dussault. 2000. "Negative Consequences of Acculturation on Health Behaviour, Social Support and Stress among Pregnant Southeast Asian Immigrant women in Montreal: An Exploratory Study." *Canadian Journal of Public Health* 91(5): 357–60.

Jackson, Vicki C. 2009. "Citizenships, Federalisms, and Gender." In Seyla Benhabib and Judith Resnick, eds., *Migrations and Mobilities: Citizenship, Borders, and Gender*, Seyla Benhabib and Judith Resnick, eds., 439–85. New York: N Y U Press.

Jenson, Jane. 2009. "Citizenship in the Era of 'New Social Risks': What Happened to Gender Inequalities?" In *Gendering the Nation-State: Canadian and Comparative Perspectives*, Yasmeen Abu-Laban, ed., 185–202.Vancouver: U B C Press.

Joachim, Jutta. 2003. "Framing Issues and Seizing Opportunities: The U N, N G O s, and Women's Rights." *International Studies Quarterly* 47(2): 247–74.

Johnson, Candace. 2008. "The Political 'Nature' of Pregnancy and Childbirth." *Canadian Journal of Political Science* 41(4): 889–913.

Kershaw, Paul. 2009. "Care*fair*: Gendering Citizenship 'Neoliberal' Style." In *Gendering the Nation-State: Canadian and Comparative Perspectives*, Yasmeen Abu-Laban, ed., 203–19. Vancouver: U B C Press.

Lalonde, André B., Christine Butt, and Astrid Bucio. 2009. "Maternal Health in Canadian Aboriginal Communities: Challenges and Opportunities." *J O G C* 2009(31): 956–62.

Levy, Barry S., and Victor W. Sidel, eds. 2006. *Social Injustice and Public Health*. New York: Oxford University Press.

Lombardo, Emanuela, Petra Meier, and Mieke Verloo, eds. 2009. *The Discursive Politics of Gender Equality: Stretching, Bending, and Policy-Making*. New York: Routledge.

Macdonald, Margaret. 2007. *At Work in the Field of Birth: Midwifery Narratives of Nature, Tradition and Home*. Nashville: Vanderbilt University Press.

– 2004. "Tradition as a Political Symbol in the New Midwifery in Canada." In *Reconceiving Midwifery*, Ivy Lynn Bourgeault, Cecilia Benoit, and Robbie-Davis Floyd, eds., 46–66. Montreal & Kingston: McGill-Queen's University Press.

Marmot, Michael, and Richard G. Wilkinson. 2006. *Social Determinants of Health*. 2nd ed. New York: Oxford University Press.

Marshall, T.H. 1964. *Class, Citizenship and Social Development*. New York: Doubleday.

McCall, Leslie. 2005. "The Complexity of Intersectionality." *Signs* 30(3): 1771–800.

McClain, Linda C., and Joanna L. Grossman, eds. 2009. *Gender Equality: Dimensions of Women's Equal Citizenship*. New York: Cambridge University Press.

McDonald, James Ted. 2004. "Insights into the 'Healthy Immigrant Effect': Health Status and Health Service Use of Immigrants to Canada." *Social Science and Medicine* 59: 1613–27.

Nash, Jennifer, C. 2008. "Re-thinking Intersectionality." *Feminist Review* 89: 1–15.

Nazroo, James Y. and David R. Williams. 2006. "The Social Determination of Ethnic/Racial Inequalities in Health." In *Social Determinants of Health*, eds. Michael Marmot and Richard G. Wilkinson, 238–66. 2nd ed. New York: Oxford University Press.

Nestel, Sheryl. 2006. *Obstructed Labour: Race and Gender in the Re-emergence of Midwifery*. Vancouver: U B C Press.

Oxman-Martinez, Jacqueline, Shelly N. Abdool, and Margot Loiselle-Léonard. 2000. "Immigration, Women and Health in Canada." *Canadian Journal of Public Health* 91(5): 394–5.

Rapp, Rayna. 2000. *Testing Women, Testing the Fetus: The Social Impact of Amniocentesis in America*. New York: Routledge.

Ray, Joel G., Marian J. Vermeulen, Michael J. Schull, Gita Singh, Rajiv Shah, and Donald A. Redelmeier. 2007. "Results of the Recent Immigrant Pregnancy and Perinatal Long-Term Evaluation Study (R I P P L E S)." *Canadian Medical Association Journal* 176(10): 1419–26.

Rich, Adrienne. 1995. *Of Woman Born*. New York: Norton.

Roberts, Dorothy E. 2009. "Race, Gender, and Genetic Technologies: A New Reproductive Dystopia?" *Signs* 34(4): 783–804.

– 1998. *Killing the Black Body: Race, Reproduction, and the Meaning of Liberty*. New York: Vintage.

Schoen, Johanna. 2005. *Choice and Coercion: Birth Control, Sterilization, and Abortion in Public Health and Welfare*. Chapel Hill: University of North Carolina Press.

Shklar, Judith. 1991. *American Citizenship: The Quest for Inclusion*. Cambridge, M A : Harvard University Press.

Simpson, Leanne. 2006. "Birthing as an Indigenous Resurgence: Decolonizing our Pregnancy and Birthing Ceremonies." In *Until Our Hearts are on the Ground: Aboriginal Mothering, Oppression, Resistance and Rebirth*, D. Memee Lavell-Harvard and Jeannette Corbiere Lavell, eds., 25–33. Toronto: Demeter Press.

Stout, R., and R. Harp. 2009. *Aboriginal Maternal and Infant Health in Canada: Review of On-Reserve Programming*. British Columbia Centre of Excellence for Women's Health and Prairie Women's Health Centre of Excellence. April.

Tripp, Aili Mari. 2006. "The Evolution of Transnational Feminisms: Consensus, Conflict, and New Dynamics." In *Global Feminism: Transnational Women's Activism, Organizing, and Human Rights*, Myra Marx Ferree and Aili Mari Tripp, eds., 51–78. New York: N Y U Press.

Weldon, S. Laurel. 2008. "Intersectionality." In *Politics, Gender, and Concepts*, Gary Goertz and Amy Mazur, eds., 193–218. New York: Cambridge University Press.

World Health Organization (W H O). 2005. *World Health Report. Make Every Mother and Child Count*. Geneva: W H O Press.

Young, Iris Marion. 2000. *Inclusion and Democracy*. New York: Oxford University Press.

Yuval-Davis, Nira. 2006. "Human/Women's Rights and Feminist Transversal Politics." In *Global Feminism: Transnational Women's Activism, Organizing, and Human Rights*, Myra Marx Ferree and Aili Mari Tripp, eds., 275–95. New York: N Y U Press.

PART TWO

The State of Reproduction

5

Quebec's Constitutional Challenge to the Assisted Human Reproduction Act: Overlooking Women's Reproductive Autonomy?

VANESSA GRUBEN AND ANGELA CAMERON

On 24 April 2009, the Supreme Court of Canada heard the appeal in *Attorney General of Quebec v. Attorney General of Canada* (QCCA 2008, 1167). In this case, the Quebec government challenged the validity of the Assisted Human Reproduction Act (AHRA)[1] on the grounds that certain sections of the Act[2] are *ultra vires* the Parliament of Canada under the Constitution Act, 1867 (c.3, U.K.); that is, they fall outside the legislative authority of Parliament.[3] The Quebec Court of Appeal concluded that the impugned provisions are *ultra vires* Parliament. The attorney general of Canada appealed the decision to the Supreme Court. Nearly twenty months later, the Supreme Court declared many of these provisions unconstitutional. In doing so, it gutted the AHRA, which, with the exception of Quebec, was Canada's only comprehensive legislation governing reproductive technologies.

The response to the Court's decision was decidedly mixed, both in terms of its jurisprudential impact and its effect on the practice of assisted reproductive technologies in Canada. In our view, the Supreme Court's decision fell short in several respects, most notably in failing to recognize the potentially negative effects of reproductive technologies on women and the importance of national protection against such effects. While the AHRA was neither a complete nor an ideal legislative regime governing vital aspects of women's reproductive autonomy,[4] it provided much-needed, *nation-wide* protection for women's equality rights (for feminist critiques of AHRA, see

Harvison Young 2005; Ariss 1996; Cameron 2008; and Hnatiuk 2007). The Court's failure to acknowledge the gendered effect of this legislation is perhaps not surprising, given that women's reproductive autonomy was largely absent from the parties' submissions and the lower court decision.

We argue that the possibility of negative gendered effects of reproductive technologies supports the conclusion that the Act properly fell within the legislative authority of the federal government by virtue of its criminal law power.[5] In our view, the protection and promotion of women's reproductive autonomy constitutes a valid criminal law purpose, and the AHRA, which established prohibitions and penalties to achieve this purpose, was validly enacted as criminal law. With respect, the Court erred in failing to reach this conclusion. By striking down the legislation, the Court has left women vulnerable to potential abuses of reproductive technologies. Its decision has crippled these imperfect protective mechanisms and has left a legal vacuum to be filled only when and how each province and territory see fit, resulting in a piecemeal approach to the regulation of reproductive technologies.

In this chapter we first delineate what we mean by reproductive autonomy. Second, we offer a brief history. Third, we explain how the AHRA affected women's reproductive autonomy. Fourth, we briefly summarize the Supreme Court of Canada's decision. Fifth, we argue that the provisions of the AHRA, which had as their purpose and effect the protection of women's reproductive autonomy, properly fell within Parliament's legislative authority over criminal law and that the majority of the Court erred in concluding otherwise. Finally, we examine the potential consequences of the Court's gutting of the AHRA and the legislative gap that has arisen as a result of their decision.

REPRODUCTIVE AUTONOMY

At a very basic level, "autonomy" means having the personal freedom or "liberty to follow one's will" (Oxford English Dictionary, 2nd ed.) Most definitions presume that autonomy requires that individuals have the ability "to choose and act in ways that are consistent with their goals and values" (McLeod 2002, 1). Traditional liberal definitions further add that autonomy requires that "individuals have the right to make their own informed choices" (Jackson and Sclater 2009, 1). Together, these definitions are suggestive of a normative understanding of autonomy that is very individualistic and emphasizes both one's *right* and *ability* to make independent choices and act on them as one sees fit. Translating this standard definition of autonomy into our context, reproductive autonomy, then, reads as the right and the ability to "choose and act in ways that are consistent with one's own *reproductive* goals and values." Broadly understood, it involves the ability to make choices about when to have children; the use of birth control; who to have children with; abortion; where, when, and how to give birth; the use of reproductive technologies; or even the use of sex- or gene-selective abortion.

However, this liberal understanding of autonomy is incomplete in that it fails to capture significant factors that influence women's ability to make our own choices and act on them. First, critical theorists point to the reality that "we are not isolated and essentially self-interested individuals," as the traditional definition of autonomy might assume, but rather are "necessarily socially embedded" (Jackson and Sclater 2009, 11; McLeod 2002, 105). As a result, our ability to act on our own will is often dependent on – or restricted by – other people. For example, in this volume, Gustafson and Porter illustrate how women's reproductive lives are enacted within the context of the family. Second, as Emily Jackson and Shelly Day Sclater argue, when applying the concept of autonomy to our reproductive decisions in this typically individualistic way, the tendency is to assume that it requires giving individuals a great degree of privacy. In other words, exercising reproductive autonomy requires "being able to shield ... our most private thoughts and choices from the critical gaze of others," including that of the state (Jackson and Sclater 2009, 1). Underlying this belief is a common assumption, as described by Theresa Glennon (2009, 149), that "regulation stands in opposition to autonomy while the unfettered market" and laissez-faire governance "enhances" it. The notion of "privileging privacy" ignores the reality that "being free from interference in our choices" does not do much to help disadvantaged groups, who often "lack the means and opportunities" – the ability – to exercise their freedom to choose (Glennon 2009, 149). Feminist scholars have emphasized how the historical oppression of women continues to both shape their decision-making and restrict their free exercise of autonomy (Sherwin 2007, 171).

To counteract this political and practical turn, we apply the term "relational autonomy" in place of normative liberal understandings of autonomy.[6] Relational autonomy takes account of the reality that "our development and, indeed, our entire lives *as* individuals *require* our interdependence with others" (Jackson and Sclater 2009, 11) Specifically, as Sherwin explains, it demands "consideration of the types of choices facing agents and the [social] forces that may be structuring those choices" (2007, 17). A crucial feature of most relational accounts is the belief that because individuals are socially embedded, protecting autonomy may require the positive provision of resources by the state in some circumstances and not simply noninterference, as traditionally held (Jackson and Sclater 2009, 11). Glennon argues that this is especially true in the area of assisted reproduction because "for those unable to reproduce without assistance, the inability to access such assistance" quite severely limits their reproductive autonomy" (2009, 15).

Taking all of this into consideration, the promotion of reproductive autonomy is not just about having negative freedom. Rather, it places an obligation on the state to "foster the conditions" necessary to enable people to make these choices (Baylis, Rodgers, and Young 2008, 97). This may involve anything from the provision of childcare to ensuring safe access to abortion services (Sherwin 1992, 116).

HISTORY OF THE AHRA

The legislative and social history of the AHRA is long and complex. It represents the culmination of a number of contentious processes, and contains within it a number of compromises on ethically and morally controversial issues. Because it deals with so many divisive aspects of reproductive technologies (e.g., commodification of reproduction) and genetic science (e.g., cloning), gutting the AHRA does more than simply change the contours of constitutional law and the balance of power between Quebec and the federal government. Canadians from across the country have dedicated significant resources to the creation of the AHRA and, most important, have reached some kind of consensus on enormously controversial issues.[7]

Since 1989, Canadians have been actively debating the use and regulation of all aspects of reproductive technologies. In that year, the Royal Commission on New Reproductive Technologies (the Commission) was struck by the federal government to study the unregulated and emerging area of reproductive technologies. In 1993, it produced a lengthy report, including 293 recommendations (Royal Commission on New Reproductive Technologies 1993). The Commission, headed by Dr Patricia Baird, took the issue of women's reproductive autonomy as a starting point, and many of its recommendations reflect this (52–9).[8] Following the release of the Commission report, legislation governing reproductive technologies was introduced and heatedly debated by members of Parliament, the Canadian public, and media, not once but twice.[9] In response to reactions to the Bill, in 2001, the House of Commons Standing Committee on Health reviewed the draft legislation, including extensive testimony from various stakeholders.

The AHRA has been met with continued opposition by members of the Bloc Québecois (a nationalist party at the federal level) on the grounds that it violates the division of powers between the federal and provincial governments. The following is an excerpt from the debates in the House of Commons on the second iteration of the Bill. Pauline Picard is a member of Parliament elected on the BQ slate, and said, in 1996: "I do not know how many times I have read the Constitution Act. According to sections 92(7) and (8) of the act of 1867, and based on the interpretation made by the courts, health and social services should come under the exclusive jurisdiction of Quebec. But this did not prevent the federal government from getting constantly involved, since as early as 1919" (House of Commons Debates 1996). In fact, Quebec passed its own legislation dealing with various aspects of reproductive technologies during the debates leading up to the AHRA.[10]

Despite continued opposition from the BQ, rooted in its concerns about the division of powers, in March 2004 the federal government introduced the AHRA. Less than two years later, the attorney general of Quebec (AG Quebec) filed a reference with the Quebec Court of Appeal that was heard in early September 2007 (Pursuant to the Court of Appeal Reference Act, R.S.Q. c. 23).

The AG Quebec challenged the constitutionality of thirty-two provisions of the AHRA (s. 8–19, 40–53, 60, 61–8). Twenty of the impugned provisions had not yet come into force at the time of the hearing.[11] The Court of Appeal found all thirty-two provisions *ultra vires*, that is, constitutionally invalid. These provisions regulate donor consent (s. 8), prohibit collection of gametes from minors (s. 9),[12] prohibit the unlicensed creation of embryos (s. 10), and prohibit the unlicensed practice of transgenics (s. 11). They regulate compensation for altruistic surrogate mothers (s. 12), prescribe the premises where reproductive technologies may be practised (s. 13), and regulate information collection and disclosure (ss. 14–19) and the destruction of reproductive materials (s. 16). The impugned provisions also create a licensing regime for activities such as research with human embryos and clinical trials (ss. 40–4). Finally, they include the enforcement provisions (ss. 45–53), the penalties for breaching the Act (ss. 60–4); the promulgation of regulations (ss. 64–7); and the equivalency provision (s. 68). The Court of Appeal concluded that these provisions were *ultra vires* Parliament because assisted human reproduction did not fall within Parliament's power to enact criminal law but, rather, fell within the province's power to regulate health (Court of Appeal, 2008 Q C C A 1167, paras. 10, 128–37).

The attorney general of Canada (A G Canada) appealed the decision to the Supreme Court of Canada. Although no other provincial government had challenged the A H R A, the attorneys general of New Brunswick, Saskatchewan, and Alberta intervened before the Supreme Court in support of the A G Quebec. The appeal was heard on 17 April 2009. After many months, the Court rendered its decision on 22 December 2010 (Reference re Assisted Human Reproduction Act, 2010 SCC 61). As is discussed below, the majority of the Supreme Court upheld much of the Quebec Court of Appeal's decision. It declared most of the impugned provisions to be *ultra vires* on the basis that they regulated the medical aspects of assisted human reproduction procedures. However, sections 8, 9, 12, and 60 (as well as certain administrative and enforcement provisions) were upheld on the basis that only they were validly enacted by Parliament under the criminal law power and were therefore constitutional.

THE AHRA AND WOMEN'S REPRODUCTIVE AUTONOMY

The Constitution Act, 1867 lists the powers reserved to each level of government. However, areas such as health care and reproductive technologies were not contemplated by the framers of the 1867 Act, and so are negotiated (and litigated) as between the levels of government. According to Canadian constitutional law principles, to fall within the jurisdiction of the federal or provincial government the main purpose (or pith and substance) of a law must be squarely within the jurisdiction of that particular level of government.

Technical arguments regarding the scope of the federal/provincial division of powers and related jurisprudence dominated the arguments made by the parties and the judgments (see Respondent's Factum; Appellant's Factum, Court of Appeal, QCCA 2008, 1167). The ongoing struggle for constitutional power between the province of Quebec and Parliament provided the backdrop for the litigation, and drove the arguments, analysis, and conclusions. We argue that in the context of reproductive technologies, constitutional jurisdiction as between levels of government is not clear-cut,[13] and in the absence of bright dividing lines those ambiguities must be resolved with women's reproductive autonomy in mind. Canadians and lawmakers have spent decades debating how best to protect women, and their children, from the possibilities of gendered exploitation and subordination offered by these technologies (Cameron, Gruben, and Kelly 2010). These central concerns, we argue, were overlooked in this litigation and the resulting decisions.

In the following discussion, we illustrate how the regulation of women's reproductive autonomy was a central, although not the sole, concern of the AHRA. We include the many ways in which the AHRA regulated women's reproductive autonomy, but do not take a position on the substance of that regulation. The subject matter of the AHRA is "disparate"; regulating reproductive science on the one hand and reproductive autonomy on the other (Jackman 1994; Campbell 2002). This is not surprising, given the unique history of the AHRA, which the Commission envisioned would be two separate statutes. Thus, the task of determining the "pith and substance" of this legislation was particularly challenging. The AG Canada attempted to unify them by arguing that the subject of the AHRA is the "artificial creation of human life" (Appellant's Factum). The AG Quebec instead narrowly focused on the medical aspects of the impugned provisions, characterizing them as related to "infertility treatments" (Respondent's Factum). In our view, the "artificial creation of human life" is technically correct, as it captures the breadth of the AHRA. However, in characterizing the pith and substance so broadly, there was a significant risk that the impact of the AHRA on women's reproductive autonomy would be overlooked and the fundamental role that women play in reproduction would be ignored. Unfortunately, this risk was realized, as illustrated by the reasons of Justices LeBel, Deschamps, and Cromwell.

Reproductive technologies[14] take place primarily on the bodies of women, and, as such, represent a critical site for the contestation of women's reproductive autonomy and equality. As Sanda Rodgers (2007, 189) argues: "Women's reproductive autonomy is key to women's equality and essential to full and constitutionally protected membership in the Canadian state." Reproductive technologies deeply affect women's reproductive autonomy and a woman's ability to control her own fertility (Deech and Smajdor 2007, 77). On the one hand, these technologies may promote women's reproductive autonomy. For example, they may enable a woman to bear children later in life either by using her own previously frozen eggs, donor eggs, or a surrogate mother, giving her greater control over her fertility and maximizing her ability to navigate a career and motherhood and to choose her preferred family form. However, these technologies may seriously undermine women's reproductive autonomy, and "have the potential to become factors in the suppression of women's autonomy and integrity if they are mismanaged, injudiciously regulated, or if their very availability services to further prejudicial attitudes and assumptions" (Deech and Smajdor 2007, 95).

The effect on women's reproductive autonomy extends to those provisions that have been struck down. At the outset, the AHRA explicitly recognizes the protection of women's reproduction as one of its principal purposes in its declaration of principles: "2.(c) while all persons are affected by these technologies, women more than men are directly and significantly affected by their application and the health and well-being of women must be protected in the application of these technologies" (Carter 2006, 32).[15]

A number of other declaratory principles affirm that reproductive technologies affect women's reproductive autonomy. Section 2(b) declares that reproductive technologies must be employed in a way that protects and promotes individual health, dignity, and rights. Section 2(d) requires "free and informed consent" as a "fundamental condition" of the use of reproductive technologies. Section 2(f) declares that trade and commodification of one's reproductive function and materials is prohibited because of the risk of exploitation. Each of these principles – health, dignity, consent, and freedom from exploitation – is fundamental to the free and equal exercise of women's reproductive autonomy.

Given the pervasiveness of the principle of reproductive autonomy in the declaratory section, it is not surprising that many of the substantive provisions of the AHRA directly regulate women's reproductive autonomy, in some areas limiting reproductive autonomy and in others promoting reproductive autonomy. These provisions can broadly be categorized as reproductive services, consent and reproductive autonomy, and reproductive health and well-being.

Reproductive Services

Perhaps most obviously, the AHRA limits reproductive services. First, the AHRA sets out strict limits on surrogacy. The AHRA bans commercial surrogacy by prohibiting the payment of consideration to a woman who acts as a surrogate (s. 6). This prohibition limits the reproductive autonomy of infertile women, because it removes commercial surrogacy as one way to create her family. It has been argued that this ban severely restricts a woman's access to reproductive technologies because of the inordinately long wait times for donated ova and the difficulties in finding a woman to act as an altruistic surrogate (Hnatiuk 2007). Further, the AHRA restricts reimbursements to altruistic surrogates by limiting payment to certain receipted expenses incurred while pregnant (s. 12).[16] These provisions, rightly or wrongly, limit women's reproductive autonomy.[17]

The AHRA also limits reproductive services by prohibiting the purchase of reproductive materials. Again, these provisions, rightly or wrongly, profoundly affect women's reproductive autonomy. Most obviously, the AHRA removes a woman's choice to sell her ova. Further, the prohibition affects a woman's access to reproductive technologies; it has been argued that payment for gametes significantly decreases the supply of gametes available for use in assisted reproduction (Turkmendag, Dingwall, and Murphy 2008, 283). This gamete shortage directly impairs a woman's ability to conceive a child using either donor ova or sperm. Notably, these are choices that are available to women in many other countries (see, for example, Spar 2006).

Consent and Reproductive Autonomy

Consent is essential to the protection and promotion of women's reproductive autonomy. Reproductive technologies only promote reproductive autonomy where women freely consent to their use. The AHRA entrenches the principle of informed consent in three contexts: consent to the use of reproductive material or embryos (s. 8); consent to the use of the technologies (s. 14); and consent to the collection, use, and disclosure of health reporting information, which is important for protecting the health and well-being of women using these technologies.

The AHRA promotes consent in four ways. First, the AHRA requires consent to be obtained in writing. For example, s. 8 prohibits the use of one's reproductive material for the purpose of creating an embryo without the donor's written consent (s. 8[1]). Similarly, section 14 requires the donor's written consent to the collection, use, and disclosure of personal information. Second, the AHRA allows a donor to withdraw her consent to the use of her reproductive material or a donated embryo. The regulations promulgated under section 8 permit the withdrawal of consent as long as it is in writing (s. 8 regs, s. 5[2]) and before the reproductive material (s. 5[2][a]) or embryo has been used (s. 14[2][a]). Third, the AHRA requires an individual to undergo counselling before donating reproductive material or undergoing an assisted reproduction procedure (s. 14[2][b]). Mandatory counselling arguably assists people in making free and informed decisions in this context (Royal Commission on New Reproductive Technologies 1993, 460–2). Finally, the AHRA establishes the age of capacity for participating in these technologies to be twenty-one.[18]

Consent and reproductive autonomy are intricately connected. Indeed, "the ethical justification of informed consent stems from its promotion of autonomy" (Berg et al. 2001, 11). Free and informed consent is especially important given the potential for coercion or undue pressure to participate in these technologies. For example, a woman may be pressured to donate ova or surrogacy services to family members or to another woman in exchange for reproductive services (often known as "egg sharing") (Royal Commission on New Reproductive Technologies 1993, 593; Ruperelia 2007). Further, a woman may be pressured by her partner to undergo risky procedures on the basis that she "must exhaust every possibility" for conceiving a genetically related child (Deech and Smajdor 2007, 89). The consent and counselling mechanisms described above seek to address these risks of exploitation.

Notably, the AHRA only regulates consent to the situations described above (Rivard and Hunter 2005, 29). The AHRA does not regulate consent to the medical treatment per se, which is appropriately left to the provinces.

Women's Health and Well-being

Finally, the AHRA seeks to protect and promote the health and safety of women using reproductive technologies. Although women may undertake any number of risky medical procedures, few have the potential to profoundly affect their reproductive autonomy like reproductive technologies.[19] Even though both men and women may suffer from infertility or wish to create their families using reproductive technologies, "it is women who bear the risks and burdens of treatments, and who will usually bear the blame and carry the stigma when treatment is deemed unnatural or unethical" (Deech and Smajdor 2007, 87). Thus, safeguards are necessary to ensure the safe and ethical use of reproductive technologies on the bodies of women.

Numerous health risks are associated with the use of reproductive technologies. Women who use donated reproductive materials, whether sperm, ova, or embryos, are at risk of acquiring various pathogens from these materials (Rivard and Hunter 2005, 77–8). There is room in the AHRA to regulate the safety requirements of donated sperm, ova, and embryos. Although the safety of donor sperm is currently regulated by the federal semen regulations promulgated under the Food and Drugs Act (FDA), it is possible that these regulations will be incorporated into any regulations promulgated under the AHRA regarding the safety of donated ova and embryos (Semen Regulations, SOR/96-254; Rivard and Hunter 2005, 78).[20] In addition, a woman who undergoes infertility treatments often takes a number of drugs, many of which have mild to severe side effects and in rare cases may be fatal.[21]

The procedures themselves also raise a number of health concerns. For example, the number of embryos implanted when a woman is undergoing in vitro fertilization may negatively affect her health. Where numerous embryos are implanted, there is a greater risk of multiples, which, in turn, carries increased risks to the woman's health including pre-eclampsia, pregnancy-induced hypertension, and increased chance of a caesarian section, which itself carries a number of health risks. Finally, the development of new reproductive technologies, such as egg freezing, certainly affects a woman's health and reproductive autonomy and must be pursued with this in mind.

Finally, reproductive technologies threaten women's well-being and reproductive autonomy when they are used in a discriminatory manner. Unfortunately, there has been a long history of discrimination against lesbian women, both single and couples, as well as single mothers by choice, in the use of reproductive technologies. For instance, in British Columbia, lesbians were denied access to reproductive technologies by fertility clinics on the basis of their sexual orientation (*Korn v. Potter*, [1996] B.C.J. No. 692 (B.C.S.C.)).

The AHRA contains three mechanisms to protect the health and safety of women. First, it creates a licensing regime to ensure that the use of reproductive technologies is closely monitored (AHRA, s. 10). Section 10 lays the groundwork for the licensing regime by prohibiting the use of any gametes or embryos except in accordance with the regulations (not yet drafted).[22] In other words, section 10 serves as the basis for the regulatory regime governing the use of reproductive materials for the controlled activities set out in the AHRA.

Second, the AHRA created the now defunct Assisted Human Reproduction Agency of Canada, which is charged with administering and enforcing the AHRA's regulatory regime (ss. 21–39). The agency plays several roles. As mentioned above, it supervises the practice of reproductive technologies and in doing so ensures that they are being used safely, ethically, and in a non-discriminatory manner. Further, the agency plays a fundamental role in providing much needed uniformity across Canada. For example, to effectively monitor the safety of these technologies, there must be a single authority collecting all relevant information. Similarly, a single body is necessary for the tracing functions set out in the act. For a donor-conceived offspring to be able to ascertain whether he or she is genetically related to another individual, there can only be one repository for the identifying information (s. 18[4]).

Third, the AHRA authorizes the collection, use, and disclosure of health reporting information from donors, persons undergoing human reproductive procedures, and donor-conceived children, which is considered essential to protecting health and welfare in this context. These provisions govern the collection of information from individuals using reproductive technologies and authorize the use and disclosure of this information for numerous purposes. Most notable is the creation of a personal information registry that will be used, in part, to identify "health and safety risks, potential and actual abuses of human rights, or ethical issues associated" with the use of reproductive technologies (s. 18[1]). This information will also be used for research and statistics, ultimately promoting the safe and ethical use of reproductive technologies in women (s. 15[5]). Interestingly, the AHRA requires consent to the collection, use, and disclosure of personal information as a condition of using reproductive technologies (s. 14).

The safe and ethical use of reproductive technologies promotes reproductive autonomy because it ensures that these technologies are used in the best interests of women. However, these health and safety provisions also have the potential to constrain a woman's ability to determine for herself under what circumstances she may use these technologies. Perhaps most glaring is the prohibition on donating reproductive materials or undergoing reproductive technologies where a woman does not consent to the collection, use, and disclosure of her personal information in accordance with the AHRA (Gruben 2009). Further, the AHRA may restrict a woman who wants to undergo home insemination (Cameron 2008). It may be that these are justifiable incursions on a woman's reproductive autonomy but we must not ignore the fact that this legislation has a real and profound effect on women's ability to choose when, how, and under what circumstances a woman wishes to employ reproductive technologies, even under the auspices of protecting women's health and well-being.

THE DECISION OF THE SUPREME COURT OF CANADA

Twenty months after the hearing, the Supreme Court of Canada released its long-awaited decision on the constitutionality of the AHRA. The Court's decision was split. Four judges (McLachlin C.J. writing) concluded that the AHRA fell within the scope of Parliament's criminal law power. Four judges (LeBel and Deschamps J.J. writing) concluded that the AHRA was *ultra vires* Parliament, because it regulated matters of provincial jurisdiction, namely hospitals, property and civil rights, and matters of a merely local nature. Justice Cromwell cast the deciding vote. In brief reasons, he concluded that most of the impugned provisions fell within provincial jurisdiction. However, he found that certain provisions were validly enacted pursuant to the criminal law power. These were section 12, which regulates the commodification of reproductive material and services, including the commercial surrogacy and the commodification of gametes, and section 8, which requires consent before the use of one's gametes or embryos; both were deemed to be *intra vires* Parliament. Finally, those provisions relating to the administration and enforcement of the prohibited activities (ss. 5–7), to which all parties had agreed, were determined to be validly enacted pursuant to Parliament's criminal law power. The sections of the AHRA requiring mandatory counselling, the disclosure of health information before engaging in assisted reproductive procedures, and the protection of women's health and well-being – including the regulatory framework to oversee the use of reproductive technologies – fell outside the legislative authority of Parliament.

The reasons of McLachlin C.J., and LeBel J. differ in several respects, including the overall approach to the division of powers analysis, the proper scope of Parliament's criminal law power, and the permissible overlap of federal legislation into areas of provincial jurisdiction; they also diverge in the pith and substance of the impugned provisions. Although their reasons are extensive, we offer only a brief overview of the decisions as they pertain to our concerns with women's reproduction here.

McLachlin C.J. examined the legislation as a whole and concluded that it fell within Parliament's criminal law power. In her opinion, the pith and substance of the impugned provisions was to establish a regulatory regime that would "prevent or punish practices that may offend moral values, give rise to serious public health problems and threaten the security of donors, donees and those not yet born" (para. 32). In reaching this conclusion, McLachlin C.J. adopted an expansive view of the criminal law power. In her opinion, Parliament may enact legislation pursuant to its criminal law power to address questions of morality, health, and security, among others. These categories are not fixed and will continue to evolve over time, as "the criminal law must be able to respond to new and emerging matters that go to the health and security of Canadians and the fundamental values that underpin Canadian society" (para. 43). With respect to public health harms in particular, she explained that federal legislation that addresses human conduct that has an injurious or undesirable effect on the public rightly falls within the criminal law power (para. 54).

In the course of her analysis, McLachlin C.J. recognized the potential threat to women's health and well-being posed by reproductive technologies and the role of the AHRA in protecting those interests and reducing the risks to women and their resulting children. In particular, she noted a number of the risks to women's health: "Sperm and ova from infected donors pose grave risks to the health of both the women who receive them and the resulting offspring. Retrieval of ova may cause serious health problems for women, as the process uses drugs that can induce ovarian hyper-stimulation syndrome, a potentially dangerous condition. Multiple pregnancies, a common outcome of assisted reproductive, may post health risks to women (high blood pressure, kidney trouble, and difficult delivery) and to resulting offspring (cerebral palsy, poor eyesight, and breathing problems" (para 97). McLachlin C.J. also recognized the potential for abuse of these technologies and the "prospect of novel harms to society, as the Baird Report amply documents. The 'commodification of women and children' (p. 718); sex-selective abortions ... octogenesis with the potential to 'dehumanize motherhood'; 'baby farms' ... discrimination based on ethnicity or genetic status ... and exploitation of the vulnerable" (para. 100). However, her decision fell short of analyzing how these threats relate to women's reproductive autonomy more specifically.

LeBel and Deschamps JJ. took a starkly different approach. In their opinion, the impugned provisions of the AHRA were in pith and substance related to the regulation of a medical practice that is, in and of itself, beneficial. Their reasons fail to identify the unique gendered risks inherent in the use of reproductive technologies. As a result, they are largely silent on the impact of reproductive technologies on women's reproductive autonomy. LeBel and Deschamps JJ. adopted a much narrower view of Parliament's criminal law power, which they concluded requires a "real evil and a reasonable apprehension of harm" (para. 240). LeBel and Deschamps JJ. concluded "assisted human reproduction was not then, nor is it now, an evil to be suppressed" (para. 251). Instead, they took the view that "assisted human reproduction amounts to a step forward for the constantly growing number of people dealing with infertility" (para. 254). It is like "other fields of medical practice ... such as ... organ transplants or grafts" (para. 254). Their failure to recognize the unique, gendered risks inherent in the use of reproductive technologies and

the important role of the A H R A in minimizing those risks led LeBel
and Deschamps JJ. to conclude that the requisite harm or evil did
not exist, and accordingly that the impugned provisions of the A H R A
are *ultra vires* Parliament.

Cromwell J.'s reasons were very brief and did not explicitly address
the nature of reproductive technologies or their potential for harm or
abuse. However, his conclusion that the bulk of the impugned provisions are *ultra vires* lead us to conclude that, like LeBel and Deschamps
JJ., he did not recognize the unique risks arising from the use of reproductive technologies.

THE CRIMINAL LAW POWER AND WOMEN'S REPRODUCTIVE AUTONOMY

In our view, the impugned provisions of the A H R A that promote
and protect women's reproductive autonomy should have been upheld as *intra vires* pursuant to Parliament's criminal law power.
Although it is arguably narrower following the Supreme Court's decision, Parliament's authority to legislate in the area of criminal law
is generally understood to be quite broad (Reference re: Firearms
Act (Can.), [2000] 1 S.C.R. 783 at para. 28). Parliament has the
"discretion" to determine the interests it wishes to safeguard and the
activities it wishes to suppress by penal prohibition (*R. v. Hydro-
Quebec*, [1997] 3 S.C.R. 213 at para. 119). As Estey J. stated in
Scowby v. Glendinnning ([1996] 2 S.C.R. 226 at 237): "A crime is an
act which the law, with appropriate penal sanctions, forbids; but as
prohibitions are not enacted in a vacuum, we can properly look for
some evil or injurious or undesirable effect upon the public against
which the law is directed. That effect may be in relation to social,
economic or political interests; and the legislature has had in mind
to suppress the evil or to safeguard the interest threatened."[23] As a
result, "criminal law finds its expression in a broad range of legislation" (Firearms, para. 29), not just in the Criminal Code.[24] In our
view, this includes the impugned provisions of the A H R A, in part
because of the impact on women's reproductive autonomy.

Legislation is generally considered to be criminal law where it is
"a valid criminal law purpose backed by a prohibition and a penalty" (Firearms, para. 27). In the following section we discuss each of
these criteria, and conclude that the A H R A satisfied all three.

1. A Note on Women's Reproductive Autonomy and the Criminal Law

Framing women's reproductive autonomy, and reproductive technologies generally, within the criminal law has been seen by some commentators as problematic at a number of levels.[25] The most pressing of these concerns has been an ethically rooted reluctance to regulate women's reproductive autonomy through the criminal law. Criminalizing activities such as surrogacy or egg donation attaches a social stigma to these activities that undermines women's choices and agency. This is particularly true, as is the case with the AHRA, when the associated penalties are harsh.[26]

There are several reasons, however, why we argue that the impugned provisions of this legislation should have been upheld under the criminal law power. Before this decision, the federal criminal law power had been interpreted to be plenary,[27] which gives Parliament the choice of whether to merely regulate potentially harmful activities without penalty or to criminalize them. The AHRA itself contains protections from criminalization for women using reproductive technologies. The Act only criminalizes third parties (such as fertility doctors or surrogacy agents) who may exploit women accessing their services (s. 4–7). In our view, this was an appropriate use of Parliament's plenary power to criminalize that avoids harsh punishment for women exercising reproductive autonomy, while maintaining a regulatory framework.[28] Second, the AHRA can be amended to be entirely regulatory instead of criminal, while remaining under the federal criminal law power that allows for national standards. We argue that a better approach would have been to amend the AHRA in consultation with the provinces to address any concerns related to existing criminal penalties, rather than to seek to have it declared unconstitutional. Possible amendments might have included the reduction or elimination of harsh punishments for third parties.

2. Criminal Law Purpose

Protecting and promoting women's reproductive autonomy is a valid criminal law purpose. Many of the impugned provisions fall squarely within the well-recognized criminal law purposes of morality,

security, and public health (Reference re Validity of Section 5(a)
Dairy Industry Act, [1949] S.C.R. 1 (Margarine Reference). See also
Firearms, para. 31). These provisions sought to entrench Canadians'
fundamental values vis-à-vis women's reproductive autonomy and
to prevent the misuse of these technologies that could be injurious
to women.

It is clear that the "criminal law serves an essential moral function
by identifying and vindicating fundamental social values" (Healy
1994–95, 905) The AHRA represents years of consultation with
Canadians regarding these complex social issues, beginning with the
Commission and continuing through numerous sessions of debate in
Parliament. In its report, the Commission acknowledged that the
regulation of reproduction "will affect the way people think about
their rights and responsibilities to each other and to future generations" (Commission, 49). Thus, in exploring these difficult issues,
the Commission was guided by a number of principles, including
individual autonomy, equality, respect for human life and dignity,
protection of the vulnerable, and the non-commercialization of reproduction; all engage fundamental social values.

Even a brief look at a few of the difficult questions underlying the
impugned provisions reveal that they are of fundamental social significance and have a profound effect on human dignity. For example,
to what extent should women be remunerated for participating in
surrogacy arrangements? Is the sale of gametes inherently wrong or
should some form of remuneration be permitted to ensure that there
are sufficient gametes available to those who require them? What is
the appropriate limit on the number of offspring conceived from one
gamete donor? Under what circumstances, if any, should we allow
the use of an individual's gametes after he or she has died? Is it necessary for both donors to consent to the disposition of their frozen
embryos or should they be bound to their earlier agreements? Should
we allow women to freeze their eggs for use at a later time in the
absence of a compelling medical reason to do so? As with many
questions of profound social significance, there are opposing views
on the answers. This divergence of opinion does not remove the
AHRA from the criminal law sphere. There is no question that there
is considerable disagreement about how best to regulate reproductive technologies in Canada. A great deal of ink has been spilled
on a wide variety of issues relating to reproductive technologies,
much of it on the proper limits on women's reproductive autonomy.

The difficulty in reaching a consensus on these issues is evinced by the fact that the Commission took several years in preparing its recommendations and that it took close to a decade thereafter for Parliament to enact the A H R A. This does not, in and of itself, preclude the A H R A from qualifying as criminal law. As Angela Campbell (2008, 81) notes, there are often diverging opinions on questions of profound social significance in society, including bigamy, prostitution, and assisted suicide, that are nevertheless considered to be valid criminal prohibitions.

In addition, the purpose underlying many of the impugned provisions was to protect the health and safety of women using reproductive technologies. The protection of public health and safety is a well-recognized criminal law purpose and "the scope of the federal power to create criminal legislation with respect to health matters is broad" (R J R -MacDonald Inc. v. Canada (Attorney General), [1995] 3 S.C.R. 199 (R J R MacDonald), para. 32). As discussed, women who undergo these procedures are exposed to many risks to their physical and psychological health. The A H R A seeks to minimize the potential harm these women face in several ways. First, the A H R A not only prohibits certain activities but also tightly controls others, including many A H R procedures. It does so by creating a series of exemptions for individuals who, and facilities that are, licensed by the agency to carry out authorized procedures. This licensing regime authorizes the agency to monitor licensees to ensure that authorized procedures are carried out in a safe and ethical manner (A H R A, ss. 40–53). Second, the information provisions require physicians to collect significant health and personal information from all those involved in reproductive technologies and authorize extensive use and disclosure of this information for a number of purposes including "the identification of health and safety risks" as well as monitoring for the abuse and misuse of these technologies (s. 18). Third, the rigorous consent requirements described above seek to prevent the exploitation of women and their reproductive capacity (s. 14).

Respectfully, we argue that LeBel and Deschamps JJ.'s analyses are flawed because they characterize reproductive technologies only as "beneficial" and fail to recognize the unique and gendered risks associated with the use of these technologies. Indeed, the justices erroneously equate these technologies with other medical procedures, such as organ transplant (Respondent's Factum, para. 110; see also

Tremblay 2003, 519). In our view, their approach discounts the importance of women's reproduction and the potential for harm in this context at both an individual and societal level.

While we have pointed to the potential for harm to individual women, Maureen McTeer also notes that the misuse of reproductive technologies results in "societal harm." She explains: "The notion of harm ... would reflect a more accurate view of human life as more than a mere exercise of physical survival. It would also allow for the protection of those most vulnerable to any abuses that might result from the use and development of technology in the field of human reproduction and genetics, such as women ... the disempowered and the poor" (1995, 893).

To conclude that the potentially injurious effects of reproductive technologies are not as serious as Sunday shopping (*Lord's Day Alliance of Canada v. Attorney General of British Columbia*, [1959] S.C.R. 497), tobacco (*RJR-MacDonald*), hockey helmets (as AG Canada argued), or the environment (*Hydro-Quebec*, [1997] 3 S.C.R. 213 at para. 119) undermines the fundamental importance of women's reproduction.

Further, earlier Supreme Court of Canada jurisprudence did not require the subject matter of criminal legislation to be intrinsically "harmful or evil." This novel and narrow characterization is a notable departure from the Court's usual language, and fails to accurately capture the nature of reproductive technologies. Although there is a potential risk of serious harm to women and their children arising from the use of reproductive technologies, when properly used these technologies may result in a much wanted child. On the other hand, the mere fact that reproductive technologies may have beneficial effects does not cancel Parliament's legislative authority over them. The Supreme Court has, on many occasions, concluded that legislation falls within the criminal law power where the subject matter has had potentially injurious effects but is not intrinsically harmful. For example, the Supreme Court has held that the Food and Drug Act is validly enacted federal legislation under the criminal law power (*Schneider v. The Queen*, [1982] 2 S.C.R. 112 [*Schneider*]). The subject matter of the FDA, food and drugs, is inherently beneficial but if misused poses a risk to public health and safety. For example, prescription drugs have beneficial therapeutic effects; but are potentially life-threatening if they are used inappropriately. Similarly, the Supreme Court has found that the regulation of lotteries and firearms fall within the criminal law power, yet they are not intrinsically "evil," but rather have potentially injurious effects if misused (*R. v. Furtney*, [1991] 3 S.C.R. 89; Firearms Act).

Finally, some have argued that criminal law is not the most effective or preferred way to regulate reproductive technologies (Healy 1994–95, 905). As mentioned, some have argued that the criminal law should not be used to regulate reproductive technologies for a variety of reasons including that these technologies develop rapidly and outpace the inherently rigid criminal law (Caulfield 2002, 20) and that criminalizing activities related to human reproduction might actually result in further harm to women because these activities are driven underground (Harvison Young and Wasunna 1990, 239; Harvison Young 2005, 123). While these concerns may be well-founded, "the efficacy of a law, or lack thereof, is not relevant to Parliament's ability to enact it under the division of power analysis" (Firearms Act, para. 57). In other words, the AHRA does not have to answer every possible critique to withstand constitutional scrutiny.

3. Prohibitions and Penalties

The AHRA establishes a series of prohibitions backed by penalties. The AHRA prohibits outright certain activities, such as commercial surrogacy arrangements, and creates a series of exemptions for others. For example, the AHRA prohibited anyone from undertaking an AHR procedure except where she has a license to do so. All were subject to criminal penalties, either fine or imprisonment (AHRA, ss. 60–1).[29] The latter, together with the ancillary provisions implementing the AHRA, were the subject of the constitutional challenge (ss. 40–59). The fact that these provisions are not outright prohibitions does not disqualify them as criminal law. It is well-settled that "exemptions from a law do not preclude it from being prohibitive and therefore criminal in nature" (Firearms Act, para. 39). Indeed, complex licensing schemes such as those found in the AHRA, like the Firearms Act and the Canadian Environmental Protection Act, have been upheld as constitutional in a number of cases (Firearms Act; *Hydro-Québec*, [1997] 3 S.C.R. 213).

CONCLUSION: THE POTENTIAL EFFECTS
ON WOMEN'S REPRODUCTIVE AUTONOMY

We believe that the Court's decision will almost certainly have a negative impact on women's reproductive autonomy and has increased the potential for serious harm to and abuse of women using these technologies and the children born of them.

The Court's decision has left an enormous gap in the regulation of reproductive technologies. Before the decision, the A H R A was the only comprehensive legislation regulating reproductive technologies in Canada. Quebec is the only province that has chosen to regulate in this area. To date, no other province has indicated that it will fill the gap left behind and enact legislation that addresses the unique challenges arising from the use of reproductive technologies. This is not surprising. For a number of economic and political reasons, provinces and territories have a spotty record in protecting women's biological and social reproductive autonomy. The best examples are in family law where the provinces and territories hold clear jurisdiction. For example, while the A H R A protects the anonymity of gamete donors, the legal status of the donor remains undetermined in most provinces, despite the fact that legal parentage falls squarely within their domain. This means, for example, that the rights and responsibilities of the donor vis-à-vis donor offspring are left undefined. These concerns are particularly relevant to women-led[30] families that have chosen to exclude donors as legal parents, yet despite their wishes, a number of Canadian courts have granted donors parental rights (Cameron, Gruben, and Kelly 2010). At a more general level, women's social and biological reproduction rights have been unevenly treated across provinces and territories.[31] Notably, as Thompson-Philbrook addresses more extensively in chapter 9 of this volume, access to abortion services is alarmingly uneven across Canada (see also Rodgers 2007).

Even if legislation is enacted at the provincial level, it will almost certainly be a patchwork approach. Women and children in different provinces will be subject to varying levels of protection. Take, for example, limitations on the number of embryos that can be implanted into a woman's uterus. The health risks to women and children arising from the implantation of multiple embryos are well-recognized. Indeed, a panel of experts commissioned by the Ontario government recently confirmed the severity of these risks to the pregnant woman by adding pre-eclampsia, gestational diabetes, anemia, and premature labour to the numerous risks to the resulting offspring. Women and any resulting children who live in a province, such as Quebec, that has adopted a single embryo transfer policy will certainly be better protected than those who live in provinces that have not.

In the final analysis, a partial, imperfect national legislative regime such as the AHRA is preferable to the legal vacuum that now exists following the finding of *ultra vires*. This vacuum will now only be filled by provinces and territories when and how they see fit. This type of piecemeal approach is, we submit, highly unsatisfactory in a field as important as women's reproductive autonomy.

NOTES

1 S.C. 2004, c. 2.

2 Sections 8 to 19, 40 to 53, 60, and 61 to 68.

3 In the legal context, law-making authority is divided between the federal and provincial legislatures pursuant to the Constitution Act, 1867 (c. 3, UK), which is commonly referred to as "the division of powers." Where a court concludes that either the provincial or federal legislatures does not have power to enact a certain law and has overstepped its constitutional law-making authority, the legislation is said to be *ultra vires* and is considered unconstitutional.

4 We use the term *reproductive autonomy* to refer to individual women's choices regarding whether and how to biologically reproduce including access to abortion, contraception, and to safe, effective reproductive technologies. As we discuss above, we also use this term to refer to systemic barriers to both social and biological reproductive equality and autonomy that face women as a group, and which are disproportionately experienced by marginalized women (see Rodgers 2007).

5 While it is true that Canadian constitutional law doctrines of "double aspect" and "necessarily incidental" apply in this case, a discussion of the implication of these is beyond the scope of this paper.

6 McLeod (2002, 110) posits that autonomy has more to do with "self-trust."

7 That is not to say that the status quo should have remained, but rather that diverse issues such as stem cell research and sperm donation should

have been revisited separately and deliberately, rather than throwing out the entire Act and regulatory regime.

8 For feminist critiques, see Ariss (1996) and Majury (1994).

9 These two earlier versions of the AHRA "died" before a vote was taken because the session of Parliament in which they were initially introduced ended.

10 See, for instance, the filiation of children born of assisted procreation (1991) RSQ c. C-I-1, s. 451. In 2007, An Act Respecting Clinical and Research Activities as regards Assisted Human Reproduction and Amending Other Legislative Provisions was tabled before the Quebec National Assembly, but never passed. An examination of the merits of Quebec's legislation is beyond the scope of this chapter, which is principally concerned with the piecemeal approach that will exist across the country where reproductive technologies are regulated on a province by province basis.

11 AHRA, ss. 12, 14–19, 24(1)(a)(e)(g), and 40–59.

12 Under most circumstances.

13 Most commentators argue that it is shared between the federal and provincial governments (see Jackman 1994, 2, 18; Martin 1989, 2; Rivard and Hunter 2005, 29).

14 With the non-invasive exception of sperm donation.

15 Unlike a preamble, a declaration of principle is an integral part of legislation and has some legal force.

16 These expenses have yet to be set out in the regulations.

17 The Commission found that Canadian opinions on commercial surrogacy varied widely (Commission, 669). Those against commercial surrogacy argue that it dehumanizes and degrades women's reproductive capacity (674). In contrast, those who support commercial surrogacy argue that it is acceptable on the basis that a woman has a right to control her own body free from state interference (Commission, 679; Busby and Vun 2010).

18 Further, the AHRA establishes age restrictions on the use of reproductive technologies, a condition for the capacity to consent (s. 6[4]).

19 Abortion is another example.

20 There is increased risk with respect to ova donation, because ova are generally fresh. Sperm are cryopreserved, quarantined, and after a six-month waiting period are tested for HIV. There is little to no possibility of egg quarantine and, therefore, there are greater health risks associated with the use of fresh ova.

21 For example, in the United Kingdom, Temilola Akinbolagbe developed ovarian hyperstimulation syndrome following a cycle of I V F, suffered a heart attack as a result, and died shortly thereafter (Deech and Smajdor 2007, 88). For a complete list of the possible side effects see "The H F E A Guide to Infertility (2007/8)," available online at http://www.hfea.gov.uk/docs/Guide2.pdf.

22 Except possibly home insemination (Cameron 2007).

23 As cited in Hydro-Quebec, para. 121.

24 For examples, see the Food and Drugs Act, R.S. 1985, c. F-27; the Tobacco Act, S.C. 1997, c. 13; the Firearms Act, S.C. 1995, c. 39; and the Canadian Environmental Protection Act, R.S.C. 1985, c. 16 (14th supp.).

25 Campbell (2008, 79) highlights three principle concerns: (1) a lack of consensus as to which activities should be criminalized; (2) the criminal law is too blunt; and (3) criminalization will limit scientific breakthroughs. For other instances see Caulfield (2001, 335) and Young and Wasunna (1990, 239).

26 Penalties include fines of up to $500,000 and prison terms of up to ten years (A H R A ss. 60, 61).

27 Plenary means a power with formal, regulatory steps and gradations that may fall short of actually criminalizing an activity. For instance the federal criminal law power has been used to regulate tobacco advertising, even where tobacco itself is not illegal (see *R J R MacDonald Inc. v. Canada (Attorney General)*, [1995] 3 S.C.R. 199).

28 This position may be seen by some as paradoxical given the use of the criminal law to restrict women's reproductive autonomy in the context of abortion, as discussed by Wilson J. in *Morgentaler*. A detailed discussion of this issue is beyond the scope of this chapter. However, we do note the important distinction between the use of Parliament's use of the criminal law plenary power to legislate in a wide variety of areas, such as assisted human reproduction, and the use of the Criminal Code to criminalize certain behaviour, which may be found to violate the Charter.

29 Prohibited activities are punishable by a fine of up to $500,000 or imprisonment of up to ten years. Controlled activities are punishable by a fine of up to $250,000 or imprisonment of up to five years.

30 Families led by lesbians or single mothers by choice who have used anonymous sperm donors to conceive their children (see Cameron, Gruben, and Kelly 2010).

31 For instance, for many years Quebec fertility doctors were permitted to deny artificial insemination to lesbians and single women (see Scala in this volume; Barratt, Greenbaum, Masella, and Paquette 2001).

BIBLIOGRAPHY

Ariss, Rachel. 1996. "The Ethic of Care in the Final Report of the Royal Commission on New Reproductive Technologies." *Queen's Law Journal* 22: 1–50.

Barratt, Amy, Mona Greenbaum, Brigitte Masella, and Nicole Paquette. 2001. *Access to Fertility Services for Lesbians: A Question of Health*. Montreal: Lesbian Mothers Association of Quebec, 2001.

Baylis, Francoise, Sandra Rogers, and David Young. 2008. "Ethical Dilemmas in the Care of Pregnant Women: Rethinking 'Maternal-Fetal Conflicts.'" In *The Cambridge Textbook of Bioethics*, Peter A. Singer and A.M. Viens, eds., 97–103. Cambridge: Cambridge University Press.

Berg, Jessica W., et al. 2001. *Informed Consent: Legal Theory and Clinical Practice*. 2nd ed. Oxford: Oxford University Press.

Busby, Karen, and Delaney Vun. 2010. "Revisiting the Handmaid's Tale: Feminist Theory Meets Empirical Research on Surrogate Mothers." *Canadian Journal of Family Law* 26 13.

Cameron, Angela. 2008. "Regulating the Queer Family: The Assisted Human Reproduction Act." *Canadian Journal of Family Law* 24: 13–94.

Cameron, Angela, Vanessa Gruben, and Fiona Kelly. 2010. "De-Anonymising Sperm Donors in Canada: Some Doubts and Directions." *Canadian Journal of Family Law* 26. 95–148.

Carter, Ian. 2006. "Playing the Youth Card: The Impact of the Declaration of Principles in the Youth Criminal Justice Act." *C.R.* 32: 232–41.

Caulfield, Timothy. 2001. "Clones, Controversy, and Criminal Law: A Comment on the Proposal for Legislation Governing Assisted Human Reproduction." *Alberta Law Review* 39: 335.

– 2002. "Bill C-13 The Assisted Human Reproduction Act: Examining the Arguments Against a Regulatory Approach." *Health Law Review* 11: 20.

Deech, Ruth, and Anna Smajdor. 2007. *From IVF to Immortality: Controversy in the Era of Reproductive Technology*. Oxford: Oxford University Press.

Glennon, Theresa. 2009. "Regulation of Reproductive Decision-Making." In *Regulating Autonomy: Sex, Reproduction and Family*, Shelley Day Sclater, Fatemeh Ebtehaj, Emily Jackson, and Martin Richards, eds., 149–68. Portland, OR: Hart Publishing.

Gruben, Vanessa. 2009. "Assisted Reproduction Without Assisting Over-Collection: Fair Information Practices and the Assisted Human Reproduction Agency of Canada." *Health Law Journal* 17: 229.

Harvison Young, Allison. 2005. "Let's Try Again ... This Time With Feeling: Bill C-6 and New Reproductive Technologies." *UBC Law Review* 38: 123.

Harvison Young, Alison, and A. Wasunna. 1990. "Wrestling with the Limits of Law: Regulating Reproductive Technologies." *Health Law Journal* 6: 239.

Healy, Patrick. 1994/1995. "Statutory Prohibitions and the Regulation of New Reproductive Technologies under Federal Law in Canada." *McGill Law Journal* 40: 905.

Hnatiuk, Dana. 2007. "Proceeding with Insufficient Care: A Comment on the Susceptibility of the Assisted Human Reproduction Act to Challenge Under Section 7 of the Charter." *University of Toronto Faculty of Law Review* 65: 39

Jackman, Martha. 1994. "The Constitution and the Regulation of New Reproductive Technologies." In *Royal Commission on New Reproductive Technologies, Legal and Ethical Issues in New Reproductive Technologies*. Ottawa: Supply and Services Canada.

Jackson, Emily, and Shelley Day Sclater. 2009. "Introduction: Autonomy and Private Life." In *Regulating Autonomy: Sex, Reproduction and Family*, eds. Shelley Day Sclater, Fatemeh Ebtehaj, Emily Jackson, and Martin Richards, 1–16. Portland, OR: Hart Publishing.

Majury, Diana. 1994. "Is Care Enough? Proceed with Care: Final Report of the Royal Commission on New Reproductive Technologies." *Dalhousie Law Journal* 17: 279.

Martin, Sheila. 1989. *Women's Reproductive Health, The Canadian Charter of Rights and Freedoms, and the Canada Health Act*. Ottawa: Canadian Advisory Council on the Status of Women.

McLeod, Carolyn. 2002. *Self-Trust and Reproductive Autonomy*. Cambridge: MIT Press.

McTeer, Maureen. 1995. "A Role for Law in Matters of Morality." *McGill Law Journal* 40(4): 893.

Overall, Christine. 1987. *Ethics and Human Reproduction: A Feminist Analysis*. Winchester: Allen & Unwin.

Rivard, Glenn, and Judy Hunter. 2005. *The Law of Assisted Human Reproduction*. Markham: LexisNexis Canada.

6

On Reproductive Citizenship: Thinking about Social Rights and Assisted Reproduction in Canada

ALANA CATTAPAN

On 10 May 2009, hundreds of demonstrators marched on Queen's Park with strollers in tow to demand that the Government of Ontario expand its funding of in vitro fertilization. Fondly called the "pram push," the demonstration took place on Mother's Day and was intended to bring the infertility community together and "convince the Ontario government that infertility was a medical condition like diabetes and high blood pressure, and therefore should be funded under the Ontario Health Insurance Plan" (Horibe 2010, 35).

As the "pram push" was being planned in Ontario, a bill was being debated in Quebec's Assemblée nationale that would fund three cycles of IVF for citizens of the province. Building on Premier Jean Charest's related election promise, the bill was seen by many as a sign of the Government of Quebec's continued dedication to pronatal policies, including baby bonuses, affordable childcare, progressive parental leaves, and an already existing tax credit for assisted reproductive services. As Charest said, "A couple that wants children must get all the help possible," implying that it is the government's responsibility to provide such help (Peritz 2008).

These examples are by no means the only instances of recent actions attempting to broaden access to assisted reproductive technologies (ARTs). Court cases, petitions, expert panels, and legislation are only some of the methods that have been used in Canada and elsewhere to foster increased access to ARTs. Taken together, they reveal how some Canadians have started to understand access to

ARTs in terms of rights. The arguments used by the organizers of the "pram push" point to how IVF might be seen as a right under universal health care, while the Government of Quebec's funding announcement was presented in terms of the state's obligation to help Québécois build families.

These rights claims, to a family and access to medical services, are nothing new. Indeed, from the right to have a family to the right to health care services established by Canada's public health care system, the language of rights used to promote public funding of ARTs builds on pre-existing notions of what we are entitled to as citizens. Further, it builds on longstanding state interventions into motherhood and parenthood more generally, adding to a long history of social programs responding to parents', and most often, mothers' needs, particularly for parents who are white, middle- to upper-class, heterosexual, and able-bodied, and who also have legal status as citizens. Framing access to ARTs in Ontario, Quebec, and across the country in terms of a right to reproductive technologies enables us to see ARTs as part of this ongoing history of reproductive citizenship; as something that the state owes us; an entitlement deserved by citizens of the state.

Though they are nothing new, these rights are being used in a new way. The right to "found a family" has been included in the United Nations' *Universal Declaration of Human Rights* since 1948, but has generally been interpreted and applied as a negative rather than a positive right (Washenfelder 2004). People may have the right to found a family free from the influence of external forces, but whether or not they have a right to public funding so that they can create a family is a very different question. And though the right to equitable health care services in Canada is clear, it still remains unclear whether infertility should be treated as an illness or disorder to be "cured" via IVF.

Furthermore, these rights claims are different because they mark a shift in the relationship between citizenship and procreation that has been historically rooted in notions of a civic responsibility to bear children within the context of a "traditional family." Though parents have long been accorded access to social services and social capital because they have children, the demand for the state to enable reproduction at the time of conception has only emerged since the advent of ARTs, and only substantively in the very recent past (Turner 2001, 192).

Finally, these rights represent a new sort of response to the retrenchment of social policy reforms since the 1990s that have changed how reproduction in Canada is governed. The "rolling back" of social services has, according to the feminist political economy and social policy literatures, left families reeling, as they are forced to take responsibility for the reproductive labour that the state has stopped subsidizing. Janine Brodie (2008, 179) refers to the outcomes of these social policy reforms as "individualizing," insofar as the consequent social policy regime "places steeply rising demands on people to find personal causes and responses to what are, in effect, collective social problems." The demand for public funding for IVF treatments works to individualize infertility in the way that Brodie suggests by relying on a medical understanding of infertility. As an illness to be cured, infertility is to be treated on an individual basis, a perspective that obscures the widely experienced factors that often lead to infertility, including but not limited to sexually transmitted infections, advanced maternal age, and the continued presence of high levels of environmental toxins. The emphasis of public debate on individual access to infertility treatment renders the very important and collectively felt issue of infertility prevention relatively insignificant.

What emerges then is that "reproductive citizenship" – the balance of rights and duties that citizens and the state share to enable reproduction – is changing with the regulation of ARTs. Extending from feminist and queer studies scholarship that have theorized citizenship as a matter of belonging, recognition, and participation, reproductive citizenship identifies how longstanding state interest in a growing citizenry and the governing of who can "reproduce with whom and under what social and legal conditions" is expanding to accommodate the way that people have come to think about aspects of reproduction itself as a right of citizenship (Richardson and Turner 2001, 330). Examined in the context of social policy retrenchment and the increasing reliance on individual subjects as the deserving recipients of public services, reproductive citizenship also points to the individualizing and exclusionary tendencies of the contemporary governance of reproduction.

In this chapter, I argue that attempts to regulate ARTs in Canada have continued the individualizing and exclusionary trends occurring in reproductive citizenship over the past thirty years. These trends, previously evident in the retrenchment of childcare benefits, family allowances, primary health care, and other reforms made to Canada's social policy regime, are replicated in attempts to govern ARTs in Canada. This is most clear in the ways that the policy process has privileged a medical model of infertility that frames fertility as an issue of individual concern, resulting in the exclusion of certain social groups.

In the first section of this chapter, I explore the concept of "reproductive citizenship" employed in the work of Bryan S. Turner to explicate the relationship between citizenship, social rights, and childrearing. In the next section, I apply this concept to the history of parental duties and entitlements administered through social policy in Canada since the 1900s, demonstrating how reproductive citizenship has changed over time, with recent social policy reforms decreasing parental entitlements by focusing on the individual as their primary subject. Then, I provide a short history of public policy governing assisted reproduction in Canada, with the subsequent section assessing how this process has replicated the individualizing tendencies of social policy reform, notably by privileging a medical model of infertility and instituting barriers to access for certain marginalized groups. To conclude, I address new developments in the governance of ARTs, suggesting that though existing federal policy has replicated the problematic tendencies of recent social policy reforms, new initiatives may change things once again.

THEORIZING REPRODUCTIVE CITIZENSHIP

In "The Erosion of Citizenship," sociologist Bryan S. Turner (2001) describes how traditional routes to citizenship in the United Kingdom, namely people's roles as workers, soldiers, and parents, have changed with the decline of the post-war welfare state. He writes that with the rise of precarious labour and technological advances in the military, people are less and less able to make rights claims and receive entitlements as soldiers and workers, though reproduction remains a key element of contemporary citizenship. Parenthood, he writes, continues to give citizens access to certain social rights and works to re-inscribe certain social norms.

Perhaps the greatest contribution of Turner's work is his use of the term "reproductive citizenship" to describe how citizens' contributions as parents are closely tied to their access to certain social rights. He uses this term to describe how social capital, "family security systems, various forms of support for mothers, and health and educational provision for children," have been accorded to parents, resulting in a complementary relationship of rights and obligations that began, in the case of Canada, with the establishment of programs like Mothers' Allowance (Turner 2001, 193). This harkens back to longstanding notions of reproduction as duty, serving the "demographic interests" of the state, wherein childbearing and childrearing are, indeed, services, rewarded with corresponding entitlements (Remmenick 2010, 319).

Turner's reproductive citizenship builds on a long history of literature on citizenship in the post-war welfare state, extending from T.H. Marshall's understanding of citizenship as tied to social rights. Citizenship for Marshall, as for Turner, reaches beyond one's formal status as a citizen to address a sense of belonging to a political community and an assurance of a basic standard of living through access to certain social services. However, Turner does not merely theorize reproductive citizenship as increased access to the rights of citizenship given to parents, but also as a lack of the same. Extending from Brenda Cossman's work on sexual citizenship, reproductive citizenship is about "practices of inclusion and exclusion, of belonging and otherness, and the many shades in between" (2007, 5). Put simply, reproductive citizenship is a means of describing the myriad ways that people have come to think about their reproduction in terms of "belonging, recognition and participation" – as part of the rights that they deserve as citizens, whether or not they receive them (Cossman 2007, 3).

Reproductive citizenship is a useful concept for a number of reasons. First, it gives a name to the relationship between procreation and the rights and responsibilities of citizenship, offering a lens through which to observe change over time. In doing so, it provides a way to view the evolving interactions between citizens and the state from their historic associations with civic duty to contemporary articulations of entitlement. Second, reproductive citizenship allows us to differentiate between rights claims associated with reproduction and those tied to sexuality. Though sexual and reproductive citizenship are closely related and overlap in numerous ways, Turner writes that scholarship on sexual citizenship does not adequately describe the relationship between citizenship and reproduction. Sexual citizenship is a theoretical framework used to explore how certain sexual minorities are often granted legal rights as long as they are "privatized, deradicalized" and "deeroticized" – economically productive and nondescript (Bell and Binnie 2000, 3). Reproductive citizenship is a more useful concept for exploring the relationship between citizenship and reproduction, because, although the sexual citizenship literature may reveal the ways that sexual minorities have been denied access to the rights associated with parenting, it largely fails to identify those rights as tied to the "demographic objective[s] of securing and sustaining the connection between reproduction and citizenship" (Turner 2001, 197).

Reproductive citizenship also builds on feminist citizenship theory by making an analytical distinction between the gendered and reproductive elements of citizenship. Feminist citizenship theory has identified how male-centric notions of citizenship have assumed women to be dependent on a male breadwinner within the context of a nuclear, heterosexual family, leaving women out of the rights and duties of citizenship beyond their roles as mothers, wives, and, occasionally, as incidental labourers (Lister 1997). Examining the reproductive rather than the gendered aspects of citizenship shifts the focus of study slightly, from the ways that reproductive labour has been used to limit women's experience of citizenship to examining how reproductive labour has (for women and for men) been used as currency in making rights claims.

Finally, reproductive citizenship points to the ways that particular groups have been excluded from the rights associated with parenting. From the difficulty that many queer Canadians have experienced accessing assisted reproductive services (Cameron 2008) to the forced sterilization of the "mentally deficient," the study of reproductive citizenship explores who is and is not seen to be a desirable reproductive subject. Turner himself identifies how social services linked to parenthood have been provided only to "traditional" families that can replicate a nuclear, heterosexual ideal. In doing so, he states that fertility and reproductive capacity are analogous to the "social, cultural, and biological goals of parenthood," thereby excluding parents engaged in non-reproductive or homosexual relationships (Turner 2001, 196).

Despite the many contributions of Turner's work, reproductive citizenship forms only a part of his larger argument about the evolution of citizenship rights, and consequently his work does not fully explain the nature of reproductive citizenship or what it has historically entailed. For example, his explanation of reproductive citizenship in the post-war period is limited to the statement that entitlements were granted in relation to citizens' roles as workers, soldiers, and parents. As such, the long and diverse history of reproductive citizenship, before and since the decline of the welfare state, is reduced to an exchange of entitlements for citizens' reproductive labour.

In the rest of this chapter, I will expand upon Turner's theory by providing a selective history of reproductive citizenship in Canada from the late nineteenth century to the contemporary period, focusing primarily on social policy. Then I will provide a short history of the development of public policy on assisted reproduction in Canada, describing how it extends the trajectory of recent social policy reforms, replicating their non-universal, individual-focused approach.

SOCIAL POLICY AND REPRODUCTIVE CITIZENSHIP

The relationship between parents, the state, and the rights and obligations of citizenship has an exceptionally long history. The idea of "mothers of the nation" (re)producing workers, soldiers, and parents draws on even older ideas about the nation itself as mother or father. The role of women-as-mothers was considered, in many cases, in the eighteenth and nineteenth centuries to be at least as important as men-as-soldiers, and their contributions were seen as a public good and as a duty of citizenship, though entitlements corresponding to this duty were slow to come (Blom 2000, 16–17).

Such entitlements did emerge, however, in the early twentieth century, when states in the West intervened with policies intended to address their declining populations. France, for example, viewed its lack of population growth as a major crisis, as a threat to the nation, and as a failure of the virility of the *patrie*. Providing paid maternity leave to women who could not otherwise afford to take time off was one way that the Government of France sought to address infant mortality, allowing women to take care of their children, and providing a social service to working mothers (Jenson 1986).

In Canada, similar citizen entitlements were also instituted in the early twentieth century. Though there were a few existing state-funded programs to support mothers, including a pre-school opened at British Columbia's Infant's Hospital (Finkel 2006, 70, 75) and some social assistance provided to deserted wives (Prentice, Bourne, et al. 1988, 208), churches or charitable organizations were the primary social service providers before the First World War. This would change when Mothers' Allowance was first introduced in Manitoba in 1916, followed soon after by Saskatchewan, Alberta, British Columbia, and Ontario. These programs, available only to poor but "virtuous" widowed or deserted mothers, were based on the logic of a family supported by a male breadwinner: namely that families without a male wage earner necessarily needed support. These early iterations of Mothers' Allowance also built on the momentum of the moral and social reform movements trying to keep families together and the children of the destitute out of more expensive publicly funded orphanages (Finkel 2006, 100).

At the beginning of the Second World War, entitlements expanded. Maternity leave in Canada was introduced in 1941, and though this leave was unpaid, some benefits were available through the newly introduced Unemployment Insurance Program. Daycare programs were established for mothers "working in industries essential to the war effort" through federal-provincial cost-sharing programs during the Second World War (Mahon 1997, 397). Further, in the early 1940s, the Mackenzie King government funded family allowances, providing parents with funds to subsidize child-rearing. Paid directly to women, family allowances were a means through which the Government of Canada could mitigate demands for higher wages, reducing the need for employers to pay salaries that could independently support entire families, while giving many women the financial capacity to leave their jobs outside the home, and to return to their duties as mothers and wives (Brodie 1996, 129–30; Finkel 2006, 130–3). More and more, the citizen duty to reproduce was met in Canada, as elsewhere in the West, with entitlements that recognized women as contributing members of society first and foremost through their reproductive labour.

In this way, parental entitlements were an important element of the welfare state, though the post-war period stressed the importance of the male-headed family as the avenue for entitlement. Federal funding for childcare was eliminated in 1946, and the benefits that had been granted to pregnant women through the Unemployment Insurance program were terminated soon thereafter. The cancellation of these benefits took place just as the King government's Family Allowance Program was renewed and expanded, "encouraging women to return home to bear and to care for children" by providing funds to women that would offset their lost income in leaving the workforce (Mahon 1997, 397).

The reliance of social policy on a male-breadwinner model thus shaped reproductive citizenship in the post-war period. Men and women had access to very different social welfare entitlements, with women's access to services largely dependent on their non-engagement with the paid labour force and tied to their role as mothers. Even when women did participate in waged labour, unemployment insurance included particular provisions for married women and women who lost their jobs during pregnancy or shortly thereafter that made it particularly difficult for these women to access their benefits (Pulkingham 1998).

In the 1970s, crisis led to uncertainty about the viability of the Keynesian economic model. Social spending was seen to be problematic by some governments because it would limit market expansion, "dampening economic growth, protecting inflexible labour markets, hindering labour force participation, [and] fostering welfare dependency" (Jenson and Saint-Martin 2003, 81–2). The expansive welfare state that relied on notions of universal entitlement was slowly replaced by a model in which social assistance came to be seen as a "'hand up' as opposed to a 'hand out'" – to be used briefly to facilitate the entry or re-entry of citizens into the labour force, rather than as a means to establish a minimum standard of living (McKeen 2009, 78).

Scholars have often cited the 1995 federal budget as a critical juncture in this shift. While the cutting of social spending occurred before 1995 (through, for example, the changes to eligibility requirements for employment insurance), the "downloading" of services that occurred through the elimination of the Canada Assistance Plan and the establishment of the Canada Health and Social Transfer in the 1995 budget has been widely identified as a key moment in the erosion of the Canadian social safety net. Coupled with the changes to employment insurance, cutbacks to social movement organizations, and changes to childcare benefits, the federal government's provision of services to Canadians *qua* Canadians gave way to a new model of governance in which the responsibility for social reproduction and income support became the responsibility of citizens themselves, through the market, their families, or their communities (Jenson and Saint-Martin 2003, 80).

This ascendency of a neo-liberal politics, as outlined above, changed the way that parental entitlements are granted. With the remaining social programs aimed not at ensuring a basic standard of living, but instead at putting the unemployed back into the labour force as quickly as possible, reproductive citizenship is increasingly tied to employment. Living on social assistance, particularly for families, is exceedingly difficult, and recipients have to continually justify their need for support.

These social policy reforms have, as Brodie has observed, altered how mothers, and particularly single mothers, are able to access social services. Though single mothers were once entitled to social assistance to ensure that they would be capable of focusing on their childrearing duties until their children were of school age, public policy is now "reshaping the social identities of single mothers" from the time that they give birth, limiting "their capacity to make claims on the state by redefining them as [a] welfare problem – as undeserving, employable, and dependent" by limiting access to employment insurance and other forms of social assistance (Brodie 1995, 58). Similarly, the replacement of the universal Family Allowance (providing funds to all families with children) with the income-dependent Child-Tax Benefit in 1992 changed the way that parents-as-parents access social assistance, substituting a program in which all parents were entitled to income support with one in which only the poorest parents are provided with minimal income supplements, thereby "reinforcing work incentives for parents" by making it more appealing to be underemployed, overworked, and underpaid than to remain on social assistance (McKeen 2009, 74).

Though these examples are but a few of the ways that social services provisions have changed with the decline of the welfare state, they represent the way that the parental (and largely maternal) obligation to engage in childrearing is being replaced by a model in which parental entitlements are tied up with employment. Whereas services were once provided to parents and families in the welfare state, more and more it is largely as individual workers that people are seen as legitimate (reproductive) citizens, and it is in their capacity as citizen-workers that they able to acquire income supports to raise their families.

Turner argues that reproductive citizenship (particularly in the age of ARTS) is as active as ever, and although it repeats the historical exclusions of some marginalized groups, state supports for parenting continue to promote the "demographic objective of securing and sustaining the connection between reproduction and citizenship" (2001, 197). At the same time, he suggests, given economic liberalization and the ever-more prevalent nature of casual and precarious labour, entitlements for workers are less and less forthcoming. However, the Canadian case demonstrates a more complex relationship between parental and employment entitlements than Turner's work would suggest. The history of reproductive citizenship in Canada shows that reproductive citizenship and entitlements tied to employment are increasingly intertwined. Mothers, as mothers, are no longer entitled to supports. Rather it is as workers in need of training, or as the poorest-of-the-poor who need a "hand up" to get back into the labour market, that parental entitlements are now distributed.

The shift away from welfarism in the last few decades has marked a new chapter of reproductive citizenship, wherein income support distributed through the male-breadwinner model has been replaced by individualizing social policies that assume temporary need on the part of the citizen-worker. The governed subject is increasingly the individual, self-sufficient, employable citizen, rather than the citizen-parent who provides their reproductive labour for the public good.

GOVERNING ASSISTED HUMAN REPRODUCTION

This self-sufficient citizen is, in part, the basis of Canadian public policy governing ARTs. Though public policy governing assisted reproduction has the potential to expand the cradle-to-grave social safety net to include conception, the development of relevant public policy has focused on infertility as a matter of individual rather than collective concern. Reproduction itself has been recognized, in this policy process, as a social good, however the focus on individual solutions, particularly through the privileging of a medical model of reproduction that disregards preventive care and excludes certain populations, has resulted in a policy framework wherein individual citizens are largely responsible for infertility care, either by acquiring a particular medical diagnosis, or by financing treatment themselves.

The beginning of this process is most often traced to the birth of the first child conceived via in vitro fertilization in Britain in 1978. Though it took several years for the technology to be made available to Canadians, the idea of reproduction without sexual intercourse captured the imagination of the public, and debate was taken up quickly, particularly among feminist and religious groups. This eventually led, in 1989, to the calling of the Royal Commission on New Reproductive Technologies to determine how to regulate these technologies, and to find some sort of moral middle ground between those lauding reproductive technologies for their libratory potential and those condemning their capacity to be used in ways oppressive to women and disrespectful of human dignity.

The Royal Commission spanned four years, cost tens of millions of dollars, consulted more than 40,000 Canadians, and produced thousands of pages of research. In November 1993, it released its two-volume final report, *Proceed with Care*, which laid the groundwork for federal regulation of ARTs. The report justifies federal action and then outlines the scope of potential policy by making recommendations for infertility prevention programs, the prohibition of certain technologies, and the licensing and regulation of others, including the development of a federal agency to oversee the implementation of these latter provisions. It also includes recommendations for provincial governments, health care professionals and their administrative bodies, patients themselves, industry stakeholders, employers, and school boards.

On the whole, the Royal Commission's recommendations present ARTs as both an issue of national concern and of private interest. *Proceed with Care* focuses on identifying the importance of national regulation of ARTs to uphold the shared values of Canadians, the most important of which is seemingly the maintenance of human dignity through the non-commercialization of human life. *Proceed with Care* emphasizes again and again the idea that attributing monetary value to genetic material is completely unacceptable and any practices that might lead to the commodification of reproductive tissue or, in the case of surrogates, gestation, must be banned. At the same time, it emphasizes the importance of giving Canadians a broad menu of choices in their reproductive lives, and promotes reproductive autonomy by providing a regulatory agency to ensure that Canadians can continue to access ARTs, but to do so within certain limits.

In the months following the release of *Proceed with Care*, the federal government consulted with provincial and territorial governments, aware of the national importance of regulating ARTs, as well as the jurisdictional difficulties presented by federal intervention into a matter of health care services. In July 1995, then-Health Minister Diane Marleau, with the support of the provincial governments, called for a voluntary moratorium on the technologies seen to be the most ethically reprehensible, including many that the Royal Commission had recommended for criminalization.

Soon after, in June 1996, then-Health Minister David Dingwall introduced legislation – Bill C-47, the Human Reproductive and Genetic Technologies Act – as part of a two-part legislative process that would definitively ban "unacceptable practices" under the newly introduced Act, and would then proceed to regulate other ARTs in conjunction with provincial/territorial governments (Health Canada 1996, 14). However, C-47 died on the order paper when a federal election was called in 1997. Discussion about how to develop a comprehensive pan-Canadian strategy on ARTs continued through Health Canada's *Reproductive and Genetic Technologies Overview Paper* (1999), its consultations on sexual and reproductive health (1999), and the release of a workbook designed to promote dialogue between the federal government and stakeholder groups (2000), though no substantive progress was made. A private member's bill attempting to ban human cloning was introduced in the interim, and though it was debated extensively in Parliament and in the Standing Committee on Health, it too died on the order paper.

In 2001, then-Minister of Health Allan Rock presented draft legislation for the Standing Committee on Health to review. The resulting report, *Assisted Human Reproduction: Building Families*, was tabled in December 2001, and urged the Government of Canada, once again, to introduce legislation as soon as possible. Bill C-13, the Assisted Human Reproduction Act (AHRA), received first reading in the House of Commons in October 2001; however, this proposed legislation also failed to pass before an election was called. The bill was reintroduced in February 2004, and it received royal assent in April of that year.

In short, the Assisted Human Reproduction Act codifies the boundaries for reproductive choice first set out by the Royal Commission, repeated in the voluntary moratorium and in early attempts at legislation. Criminalizing some activities, regulating others, and leaving others completely outside of the regulatory scheme, the AHRA effectively sets parameters for the use of ARTs and related research. It also established an agency, Assisted Human Reproduction Canada,

to regulate yet-to-be-developed technologies and to settle new ethical questions as they arise. Furthermore, as the AHRA builds on
many of the principles set out by the Royal Commission, it attempts
to strike the same balance that the Commissioners sought to achieve
between reproductive autonomy and a need for the federal government to protect Canadians from the unforeseen implications of
ARTS.

Since the passage of the AHRA, a number of challenges to its legitimacy have been raised. For example, there have been charges
that the Act has resulted in threats of prosecution that have intimi-
dated many would-be parents, donors, and surrogates, keeping them
from participating openly and safely in assisted reproductive procedures. As a result, the criminalization of sperm and egg purchase
has led to a dearth of available gametes and surrogates, driving
patients abroad and "underground" (Expert Panel on Infertility and
Adoption 2009, 128). Furthermore, as is outlined in more detail by
Gruben and Cameron's contribution to this volume, the Act was
challenged by the Government of Quebec, which asked the Quebec
Court of Appeal whether assisted reproduction falls within the federal government's legislative jurisdiction. The Court of Appeal ruled
in favour of the Government of Quebec, stating that the federal government did not have the authority to regulate broadly on matters of
health. The decision was appealed, and heard by the Supreme Court
of Canada, which, in its 2010 judgment, agreed with the Government of Quebec, overturning a number of the Act's provisions. The
provisions no longer in effect include those establishing Assisted
Human Reproduction Canada, and the agency was closed in March
2013. Other court cases addressing parental rights and the desire of
donor offspring to know the identity of their donors have been revealing areas of ethical, political, and moral concern that are not
addressed by the AHRA or by subsequent regulations.

Because few of AHRA's provisions have ever been implemented,
provincial governments, pressured by interested citizens, have started to take action. Frustration with the lack of legislation, in addition
to the cost-prohibitive nature of services like IVF, led the Government
of Quebec to establish its own accreditation bodies to regulate ARTs,
and further, to institute a refundable tax credit to offset the costs of
infertility care. This was replaced in 2010 with public funding for
assisted reproductive services, including three cycles of IVF. This
new funding is intended to give eligible citizens of Quebec equitable

access to A R T s. Similarly, the Government of Manitoba has also offered a tax credit to reimburse 40 per cent of the cost of certain assisted reproductive services since October 2010, and in 2009, the Government of Ontario's Expert Panel on Infertility and Adoption released a report supporting public funding for certain A R T s.

REPRODUCTIVE CITIZENSHIP AND ASSISTED REPRODUCTION IN CANADA

Though policy marking the boundaries of permissible assisted reproduction in Canadian society differs vastly from programs like Family Allowances and childcare benefits that gave parents financial support to raise their children, policy governing A R T s has continued the trajectory of reproductive citizenship in Canada by extending state interventions into parenthood. Whereas the governing of reproduction has conventionally been associated with childrearing, through public health campaigns, daycare, social assistance, and education policy, the federal regulation of A R T s allows some measure of governing conception as well. By delimiting the boundaries in which people can use A R T s, the A H R A and the debate that preceded it identified assisted reproductive services as within the purview of the state. In doing so, the A H R A establishes A R T s as a means through which to address infertility, with subsequent provincial policies to fund I V F extending the "cradle-to-grave" social safety net backwards to the womb.

More than simply regulating reproduction, federal public policy governing A R T s is part of a larger shift in reproductive citizenship that occurred in the 1980s onwards, away from the universalist tendencies of the welfare state. Extending the retrenchment of childcare benefits, federal health care transfers, and employment insurance, the A H R A and its predecessors have replicated the individualizing and exclusionary tendencies of recent changes to Canada's social policy regime. This has occurred in several ways, namely through the privileging of individual choice tied to a medical model of infertility, and the related exclusion of marginalized populations.

The idea that legislation would set the boundaries for reproductive choices was, as mentioned above, a fundamental element of the Royal Commission's recommendations, and was taken up by proposed legislation and codified in the A H R A. This meant balancing individual and collective interests, and the extent to which the legislative framework established by the Royal Commission and taken up in the ensuing efforts to codify some of its recommendations achieved this balance has been the subject of much scrutiny. Alison Harvison Young, for example, has examined the Canadian approach to governing A R T s in comparison with that of the United States, and asserts that the Canadian legislation assumes that it is both "possible and desirable to control these technologies in order to protect the public interest, and that government can and should do so" (Harvison Young 1998, 44).

Others have examined the legislative framework laid out by the Royal Commission on its own terms, finding that it takes a liberal approach deeply committed to individual autonomy. In "Experts, Non-experts, and Policy Discourse: A Case Study of the Royal Commission on New Reproductive Technologies," Francesca Scala describes how the "themes and concepts of the pro-choice movement" emerged in the consultations held by the Royal Commission, particularly in briefs and testimony from women's groups. For many of these groups, A R T s were an extension of the debates over abortion that took place just before and during the first stages of the Royal Commission, and these groups, concerned about a slippery slope of "choice," saw A R T s as a matter of reproductive autonomy above all else. The focus on reproductive autonomy advanced by women's groups worked to support and legitimate the Royal Commission's recommendations, which constructed "reproductive technologies as neutral, necessary, and client-centered" (Scala 2002, 9). Though consideration of reproductive autonomy is critical to any public debate over A R T s, the emphasis in the public hearings on "the language of abortion politics, that is, the emphasis on equality of access, individual autonomy, and reproductive choice" supported the Commission's framing of A R T s as an individual concern; one of many options available to individuals entitled to reproductive freedom (9).

Scala's work is particularly useful because she demonstrates how the liberal individual rights discourse, taken from the rhetorical trappings of the abortion debate and advanced by the Royal Commission, is intimately tied up with a medical model of infertility. Scala contrasts the Royal Commission's recommendation that infertility treatments should be provided within the context of a single-payer health insurance system with the related recommendation that I V F should only be funded for women with bilateral fallopian tube blockage, since evidence-based medicine has deemed the treatment "experimental" for other indications. In doing so, she demonstrates how these two recommendations together allowed the Royal Commission to place infertility care within a publicly funded health care system, while effectively leaving most of those seeking care to their own devices, forcing individuals to become the managers of their own care, responsible for treating their infertility. Further, she shows how, by embedding this care within the context of provincial health care programs, which for the most part only fund medically necessary treatments and services, these recommendations imply that not only is infertility broadly conceived as a medical condition, but as one that necessitates medical intervention. As such, Scala suggests, these recommendations have worked to simultaneously individualize and medicalize the regulation of A R T S.

These recommendations take for granted that infertility is understood as a medical condition treated via medical intervention, to the extent that bearing a child through assisted conception is a treatment for a physiological condition. This view is clearly articulated in testimony to the Royal Commission, when one witness described infertility "not [as] a disease insofar as it can be caught from someone else who has it. But if a broken leg can be considered a disease, than infertility is a disease too ... because it's something that's not functioning" (Royal Commission on New Reproductive Technologies 1993, 172). This medical approach to infertility stands in opposition to social approaches that understand infertility simply as involuntary childlessness, including those who have a partner who is physiologically incapable of reproduction, being in a relationship where one is incapable of biological reproduction with one's partner, or being single. Despite the commissioning of research addressing self-insemination among lesbians, and its discussion of the social stigma of infertility, it was medical, not social, infertility that was taken up by the Royal Commission: its explicit definition of "infertility" deemed a couple infertile when they had been married or cohabitating for at least two years, had not used contraception during that period, and had not had a pregnancy.

This medical model of infertility used by the Commission was critiqued by the feminists who had originally called for the Commission because of its continuation of the medicalization of childbirth, moving agency in reproduction away from women. Viewing infertility as an illness or condition and A R T S as its cure was a perspective that was seen to embed childbirth even deeper within the western medical paradigm. For those interested in opposing the medicalization of reproduction and promoting home birth, for example, ARTs were seen as yet another way that the medical establishment was taking control over women's bodies and their reproductive capacity (Sawicki 1991), not to mention excluding queer Canadians.

This identification of ARTs as a threat to women's autonomy was understood in relation to another feminist concern, that ARTs were a means to "deflect attention from other potential causes of infertility such as environmental pollution, work hazards, [and] smoking," though both critiques long predated the Commission (Sawicki 1991, 72). To address this issue, the Commission dedicated a significant portion of its report to examining and making recommendations to address the causes of infertility, including environmental and workplace hazards, sexually transmitted diseases, smoking, and the tendency of Canadian women to bear children at an ever-older age. However, it was the Commission's ART-specific recommendations to make legislation banning certain practices and to regulate others that were most readily taken up by the Government of Canada. Since the Commission, the federal government has engaged in some initiatives to decrease infertility (including the development of its *Framework for Sexual and Reproductive Health* and *The Canadian Guidelines for Sexual Health Education*); nevertheless, investment and initiatives to reduce infertility have been negligible in relation to the resources and priority given to the regulation of ARTs. By focusing on the prohibition and regulation of ARTs without considering infertility as a broader social issue, the public policy governing assisted reproduction in Canada has largely ignored the factors causing infertility, with policy-makers choosing the concrete deliverable of legislation over the complex challenge of developing public health initiatives for preventive care. Taken together with supports like increased state-funded childcare programs that would help women reproduce at an age where they are more likely to do so effectively, or campaigns to reduce environmental and workplace hazards that harm reproductive health, the AHRA could perhaps be taken as advancing the interests of Canadians, but, alone, it fails to acknowledge the collective nature of the problem.

Important to note is that the medical model of infertility promoted by the Commission is not exclusively a means of individualizing the governing of reproduction. Indeed, the provision of public funding to a non-essential medical service could easily be seen as an expansion of universal health care, and the expansion of state-funded parental entitlements. Furthermore, it is often argued that the funding of I V F actually reduces health care spending by enabling people using I V F to engage in more cycles if necessary, leading to safer choices about how many embryos to implant and reducing multiple births. However, by establishing infertility as an individual medical issue to be cured, and funded, for only the very few, the public policy on assisted reproduction in Canada also privileges the interests of the individual over those of the collective and effectively promotes a two-tiered approach to providing assisted reproductive services. Those with certain medical indications are entitled to care; those without the required medical indicators, but with sufficient funds, can receive the treatment they desire; and those without either diagnosis or financial resources are restricted by circumstance in their reproductive choices. The autonomy enabled by the privileging of the medical model is thus only substantive autonomy for some, and a restricted autonomy for others.

The focus on the individual and the exclusions of public policy on A R T s are not limited to those advanced by the rhetoric of individual choice and a medical model of infertility. Returning to Turner's work, A R T s offer the potential to end the exclusion of queer Canadians from the citizenship entitlements tied to parenthood by providing new means for individuals to become parents without engaging in heterosexual intercourse. Much like liberal feminist arguments supporting A R T s that the idea of women's reproductive autonomy and "supremacy of the rational agent" (Scala 2002, 108) promotes reproductive choice, Turner views A R T s as potential agents of change that theoretically enable a broadening of reproductive citizenship.

In reality, Turner continues, this is simply not the case. In the United Kingdom, relevant public policy has derailed the potential of A R T s by continuing to limit access, re-inscribing the historic norms of reproductive citizenship. These arguments extend to the Canadian case and particularly the A H R A, despite its explicit prohibition of discrimination on the basis of sexual orientation and marital status. In practice, certain citizens have been unable to access A R T s as a result of the Act, which has entrenched, rather than reduced, related social disparities.

In her "Regulating the Queer Family: The Assisted Human Reproduction Act," legal scholar Angela Cameron describes some of these exclusions by demonstrating how a number of the Act's provisions disadvantage queer Canadians seeking to use ARTS. For example, the prohibition of artificial insemination outside of licensed facilities infringes on the longstanding practice in the queer community to self-inseminate using a known donor. Women are no longer legally able to self-inseminate using the sperm donor of their choice but rather, under the AHRA, have to pay for treatment in a licensed clinic. Walks's contribution to this volume further discusses the social and legal barriers to reproduction and parenting that continue to be faced by butch lesbians, transmen, and genderqueer individuals. Writing specifically about situations in which gay men and lesbian couples wish to use ARTS to reproduce together, Cameron demonstrates how the prohibition on self-insemination, coupled with prohibitively strict sperm donation requirements for donations provided by queer men limit the options of queer men and women who want to reproduce together, biologically, without having sexual intercourse. These donation requirements, which stipulate that "queer men may only donate sperm to a willing donor with a special application by their doctor, a medical screen, and a dispensation from the Minister of Health," put gay men in the position of either complying with these stringent requirements, having sex with women, or acting outside of the law by going ahead with self-insemination (Cameron 2008, 110). Cameron further describes how the Act's prohibition of commercial surrogacy not only disadvantages gay men, who disproportionately require a surrogate, but also how the criminalization of commercial surrogacy may prevent compensated surrogates from seeking medical attention, putting them in a more vulnerable position than might otherwise be the case (Cameron 2008, 110).

Rhetorical inclusion but practical exclusion has long occurred for single men and women. For single women trying to get pregnant using artificial insemination, until amendments were made in 2012, the AHRA required ARTS to take place in licensed facilities obligating single women and queer couples to engage in a clinical experience at their own expense or break the law. Single men not only face the difficulties in obtaining both egg and surrogate faced by gay men, but also face strong social stigmas against single-male parenting. In both cases, ARTS are presented as a solution to medically indicated infertility, not as a means for single people to engage in biological reproduction, and discourses about access are, and have long been, focused on the needs of (most often heterosexual) couples.

Whether or not people have a diagnosis of infertility, for those who need them, finding surrogates and egg donors is a significant challenge, one made even more difficult for those who might otherwise be able to pay, given the AHRA's restrictions on providing financial incentives to surrogates and donors. While this latter restriction was intended to enable equal access to ARTs and to prevent the commercialization of reproduction, in reality it has largely resulted in a market-based two-tier system in which those with sufficient financial resources are able to access ARTs abroad, or to contravene the law by paying surrogates and donors. Those without the funds to do so are left with limited options for assisted biological reproduction.

The medical model of infertility, taken together with the exclusions that it enables, perpetuates the neo-liberal turn in reproductive citizenship. The privileging of the individual as the subject of public policy, wherein individually diagnosed subjects are responsible for their own infertility, has dominated discourses that frame reproduction as a solely personal issue. This is particularly evident in the Commission's recommendations to provide funded care for only a few infertile patients, leaving the rest to fund their own treatments or to go without. Further, the exclusions of marginalized populations (including single women, single men, lesbian and gay Canadians, and people with low socio-economic status) from accessing ARTs replicates longstanding exclusions of marginalized populations from parental entitlements.

The history of state intervention, and indeed, regulation, as to who is entitled to reproductive supports and who is not, continues through public policy on ARTs. This is true not only in the ways that public policy on ARTs has extended the governance of reproduction to conception itself, but further, in the ways that it replicates the individualizing and exclusionary trends present in recent social policy reforms. Like many social welfare programs, the governing of ARTs, and particularly the pre-eminence of the medical model of infertility in relevant public policy, has been a marker of a shift toward an individualizing logic.

CONCLUSION: EXPANDING
REPRODUCTIVE CITIZENSHIP

This long history of public policy regulating assisted reproductive technologies in Canada is, therefore, an extension of the history of policy governing parenthood: a continuation of reproductive citizenship. Though the emphasis of policy regulating ARTs is on parental entitlements and responsibilities before conception rather than on prenatal services or provisions after children are born, the attempted regulation of ARTs simply marks a different component of a longstanding relationship between parents and the state. Though it is clear that public policy debate emerged with the development of assisted reproductive technologies and public concern about their implications, the ascendency of a neo-liberal politics that emphasizes personal choice and individualism in reproduction has been mirrored in the development of public policy on ARTs, beginning with the Commission. The utility of Turner's "reproductive citizenship" thus becomes apparent insofar as it gives us the capacity to view ARTs as both an extension and continuation of longstanding government interventions into reproduction. In applying Turner's concept to the long history of policy governing reproduction in Canada, the nuances of reproductive citizenship become clear.

Since the passage of the AHRA, it seems that reproductive citizenship, as it relates to ARTs, is changing again. As mentioned above, citizens in Ontario, as elsewhere, have been coming together to demand expanded funding for ARTs, and particularly IVF, as a right of citizenship. The Government of Ontario initially recognized this demand, endorsing the recommendations of the Expert Panel on Infertility and Adoption to fund greater access to ARTs through the Ontario Health Insurance Plan. The report of the expert panel suggests that funded services, to be provided by medical practitioners, in licensed clinics, would extend to single people and same-sex couples, though these recommendations are yet to be implemented.

In Quebec, such claims to services have already been recognized, first with a tax credit for the use of ARTs, and more recently with the establishment of state funding for the same, administered through the Ministry of Health and Social Services. In addition to those experiencing medical infertility, same-sex couples and single women have been receiving publicly funded care in Quebec since 2010. However, because the cost of providing ARTs in the province has been higher than anticipated, the Ministry of Health and Social Services has been considering new eligibility guidelines that, according to some reports, may rely solely on medical understandings of infertility, effectively terminating funded access to same-sex couples and single women (Fidelman 2013). Despite potential new limitations on access to services, reports of long waiting lists, and the ongoing ability of wealthier residents to jump the queue by looking for care outside of the province, the new funding is, at the very least, reducing the financial costs of accessing A R T s for some residents of Quebec. For those ineligible for the program due to age, number of I V F cycles, or otherwise, the Quebec government offers a 50 per cent tax credit for infertility-related expenses. In Manitoba too, the eligibility requirements for the 40 per cent tax credit are minimal, requiring only that the services claimed are administered by a "licensed practitioner or fertility treatment clinic" or are related prescriptions (Manitoba Finance 2011).

Although the prohibitive provisions of the A H R A still prevent certain groups from engaging with A R T s as they would like, and though infertility is still widely viewed as a medical rather than a social issue, reproductive citizenship in Canada continues to evolve through public policy governing A R T s. These new provincial initiatives suggest that the medical model of infertility is expanding to include more social understandings, and that state investment in conception is on the rise. Embracing an individual model, but one in which the state is responsible for rights provisions, citizens are "uploading" responsibility for A R T s, claiming that the state's interest in having a growing population of healthy citizens may be best achieved through public funding of I V F. Though the implications of these new claims to positive rights to A R T s are beyond the scope of this chapter, it is clear that the perceived right to A R T s, taken together with nascent programs institutionalizing this right, may lead to a model of reproductive citizenship wherein it is the state's obligation to ensure that potential parents are able to reproduce.

It follows that reproductive citizenship is a useful analytical model to study the changing relationship of rights and responsibilities between parents and the state. Through the exploration of Turner's work and its application to the Canadian case, this chapter has traced the evolution of reproductive citizenship from earlier notions of reproduction as a civic duty to contemporary policy governing assisted reproduction. In doing so, it has pointed to the ways in which policy governing A R T s has extended some of the underlying assumptions of the neo-liberal turn in social policy, particularly by employing a medical model of infertility that privileges certain actors, and by supporting choice in reproductive services without making provisions for universal access, while simultaneously addressing an assumed understanding of the public good. What remains is how to continue to move forward on public policy governing assisted reproduction that addresses both individual and collective interests, finding a balance between public and private, access and control.

BIBLIOGRAPHY

Bell, David, and Jon Binnie. 2000. *The Sexual Citizen: Queer Politics and Beyond*. Cambridge: Polity.

Blom, Ida. 2000. "Gender and Nation in International Comparison." In *Gendered Nations: Nationalisms and Gender Order in the Long Nineteenth Century*, Ida Blom, Karen Hagermann, and Catherine Hall, eds., 3–26. New York: Berg.

Brodie, Janine. 1995. *Politics on the Margins: Restructuring and the Canadian Women's Movement*. Halifax: Fernwood.

– 1996. "Restructuring and the New Citizenship." In *Rethinking Restructuring: Gender and Social Change in Canada*, Isabella Bakker, ed., 126–40. Toronto: University of Toronto Press.

– 2008. "Putting Gender Back In: Women and Social Policy Reform in Canada." In *Gendering the Nation-State: Canadian and Comparative Perspectives*, Yasmeen Abu-Laban, ed., 165–84. Vancouver: U B C Press.

Cameron, Angela. 2008. "Regulating the Queer Family: The Assisted Human Reproduction Act." *Canadian Journal of Family Law* 24: 101–21.

Cossman, Brenda. 2007. *Sexual Citizens: The Legal and Cultural Regulation of Sex and Belonging*. Stanford: Stanford University Press.

Fidelman, Charlie. 2013. "Fertility Programs Too Lax, Group Says: Stricter Criteria and Guidelines, Including Age Limits Needed." *The Montreal Gazette*, 23 May 2013, A3.

Finkel, Alvin. 2006. *Social Policy and Practice in Canada: A History*. Waterloo, O N: Wilfrid Laurier University Press.

Harvison Young, Alison. 1998. "New Reproductive Technologies in Canada and the United States: Same Problems, Different Discourses." *Temple International and Comparative Law Journal* 12: 43–86.

Health Canada. 1996. *New Reproductive and Genetic Technologies: Setting Boundaries, Enhancing Health*. Minister of Supplies and Services.

Horibe, Joanne. 2010. "From Patient to Advocate." *Creating Families* 5(2): 34–8.

Jenson, Jane. 1986. "Gender and Reproduction: Or, Babies and the State." *Studies in Political Economy* 20: 9–46.

Jenson, Jane, and Denis Saint-Martin. 2003. "New Routes to Social Cohesion." *Canadian Journal of Sociology* 28(1): 77–99.

Lister, Ruth. 1997. "Dialectics of Citizenship." *Hypatia* 12(4): 6–21.

Little, Margaret Hillyard. 1994. "'Manhunts and Bingo Blabs': The Moral Regulation of Ontario Single Mothers." *The Canadian Journal of Sociology* 19(2): 233–47.

Mahon, Rianne. 1997. "Child Care in Canada and Sweden: Policy and Politics." *Social Politics*: 382–418.

Manitoba Finance. 2011. *Personal Tax Credits. Department of Finance, Province of Manitoba.* http://www.gov.mb.ca/finance/pcredits.html.

McKeen, Wendy. 2009. "The Politics of the National Children's Agenda: A Critical Analysis of Contemporary Neoliberal Social Policy Change." In *Public Policy for Women: The State, Income Security, and Labour Market Issues*, Marjorie Griffin Cohen and Jane Pulkingham, eds., 71–93. Toronto: University of Toronto Press.

Ministry of Children and Youth Services, Expert Panel on Infertility and Adoption, 2009. "Raising Expectations: Recommendations of the Expert Panel on Infertility and Adoption." http://www.children.gov. on.ca/htdocs/English/infertility/report/index.aspx.

Peritz, Ingrid. 2008. "Kissing Babies isn't Enough." *The Globe and Mail*, 22 November, F3.

Prentice, Alison, P. Bourne, G. Brandt, B. Light, W. Mitchinson, and N. Black. 1988. *Canadian Women: A History.* Toronto: Harcourt Brace Jovanovich.

Pulkingham, Jane. 1998. "Remaking the Social Divisions of Welfare: Gender, 'Dependency,' and UI Reform." *Studies in Political Economy* 56: 7–48.

Remmenick, Larissa. 2010. "Between Reproductive Citizenship and Consumerism: Attitudes Towards Assisted Reproductive Technologies among Jewish and Arab Israeli Women." In *Kin, Gene, Community: Reproductive Technologies Among Jewish Israelis*, Daphna Birenbaum-Carmeli and Yoram S. Carmeli, eds., 318–39. New York: Berghahn Books.

Richardson, Eileen H., and Bryan S. Turner. 2001. "Sexual, Intimate or Reproductive Citizenship." *Citizenship Studies* 5(3): 329–38.

Royal Commission on New Reproductive Technologies. 1993. *Proceed with Care: Final Report of the Royal Commission on New Reproductive Technologies.* Ottawa: Minister of Government Services Canada.

Sawicki, Jana. 1991. *Disciplining Foucault: Feminism, Power, and the Body*. New York: Routledge.

Scala, Francesca. 2002. *Experts, Non-experts, and Policy Discourse: A Case Study of the Royal Commission on New Reproductive Technologies*. Ottawa: Carleton University.

Turner, Bryan S. 2001. "The Erosion of Citizenship." *British Journal of Sociology* 52(2, June): 189–209.

Valverde, Mariana, and Lorna Weir. 1997. "Regulating New Reproductive and Genetic Technologies: A Feminist View of Recent Canadian Government Initiatives." *Feminist Studies* 23(2): 419–23.

Washenfelder, Chantelle. 2004. "Regulating A Revolution: The Extent of Reproductive Rights in Canada." *Health Law Review* 12(2): 44–52.

7

Deinstitutionalizing Pregnancy and Birth: Alternative Childbirth and the New Scalar Politics of Reproduction[1]

STEPHANIE PATERSON

On 22 February 1982, Jean Ritz died of anoxia in a Kitchener-Waterloo hospital just hours after being "caught" at home by two community midwives.[2] The coroner determined that the anoxia had been caused by "infection which was introduced into the uterine cavity as a result of rupture of the amniotic membrane" (Office of the Chief Coroner, 20 May 1982). After this finding, the coroner, Dr Jack Burger, made two recommendations: first, that the College of Physicians and Surgeons of Ontario (CPSO) and the College of Nurses of Ontario (CNO) work together to develop standards of practice and curriculum leading to a licensing system for midwifery in the province; and second, to make available to interested parties literature on home and hospital births (Office of the Chief Coroner, 20 May 1982).[3] Despite the traumatic outcome for the Ritz family, Clayton Ruby, lawyer for the Ritzes and their midwife during the inquest, maintained support for home birth, noting, "The acceptance of the idea of home birth as an equal alternative to hospital birth is, in my opinion, very sensible."

The Ritz Inquest is significant in the history of midwifery for several reasons. Most important, it brought widespread professional and public attention to the recently revived practice of midwifery, leading to public discussion about legalization and integration into the provincial health care system (see Bourgeault et al. 2001; Paterson 2010). Moreover, the inquest revealed widespread public concern over the safety of home births, leading to vociferous debate on the subject. As early as 1981, home birth advocate and midwifery supporter Eleanor Barrington speculated that home birth would become the "motherhood issue of the eighties" (Barrington 1981). While the College of Physicians and Surgeons of Ontario discouraged the few willing physicians who attended home births with threats of punishment, midwifery advocates attempted to raise public awareness with pamphlets, posters, and lectures and seminars outlining the benefits of home birth. Debate continued during the 1980s as home birth became one of the most contentious issues surrounding regulated midwifery, along with issues such as entry to practice, governance systems, and curriculum.

Underlying the debate over home birth sparked by the Ritz inquest is a debate about space and place (MacDonald 2007; see also Rothman 1982, Van Wagner 1991). As MacDonald (2007, 128–9) aptly notes, "In Canada, home birth – unlike in many European nations where home birth has always been allowed – was a radical use of domestic space, the supreme example of women's control over reproduction … a potent symbol of an autonomous midwifery profession in Canada … and a clear example of the trend toward the 'demedicalization' of everyday life." I wish to expand on this idea. Specifically, I suggest that the home birth debate was not only a debate about space and place, but also implicated a broader debate over contemporary governance arrangements within the arena of reproductive politics, a debate that was reawakened during the late 1960s and early 1970s with the emergence of the alternative birth movement (A B M) throughout the United States and Canada. In other words, the home birth debate was not just a debate about space and place, but also a debate about scale.

Originating in political geography, scale refers to "the level of geographic resolution at which a given phenomenon is thought of, acted upon or studied" (Agnew 1997, 100; 2002, 16). As a theoretical construct, scale enables us to explore the ways in which the home birth debate was intimately wrapped up in a debate about contemporary governance arrangements in the area of reproductive politics. Moreover, scale provides a lens through which to consider the degree of (dis)continuity between alternative childbirth advocates across time and space, providing an opportunity in which to consider the dynamic re-emergence of midwifery and the ways in which midwifery became a site of identity formation for both those giving and receiving midwifery care.

In what follows, I elaborate on the theoretical construct of scale, and, after providing brief overviews of the Ontario health care governance regime and the A B M, explore the ways in which A B M advocates deployed spatial discourses to disrupt, fragment, or transform the biomedical multiscalar arrangements that shaped reproductive politics at the time. I then turn to the resulting multiscalar arrangements ushered in by the 1991 Midwifery Act in Ontario. In particular, I argue that A B M problematized two scales that figured prominently in the biomedical governance arrangement: the body and the household. Applying these ideas to biomedical governance in Ontario, I demonstrate that the New Midwifery Movement[4] was able to disrupt, but not transform, the multiscalar arrangements that had governed childbirth and reproduction in the province for decades. Overall, I aim to show that body and home were constructed and used as scales of social and political identity formation that both continued and fractured biomedical discourses in the arena of reproductive politics.

THE POLITICS OF REPRODUCTION:
A QUESTION OF SCALE?

Literature on the politics of scale has proliferated during the past decade, producing excellent analyses explaining the topography of states, especially "glocalization" (Swyngedouw 1997), welfare state reform (Peck 2002; Masson 2006; Mahon 2009), the role of political parties in the production of scale (Agnew 1997, 2002), the role of networks in the production of scale (Cox 1998; Masson 2006), and the relationship between the production of scale and social reproduction (Marston 2000, 2004; Marston and Smith 2001; McDowell 2001; Mahon 2005). Rooted in political geography, and inspired by Marxian and post-structural analyses of space and time (see Lefebvre 1991[1974]; Soja 1989), scalar theory has been adopted by political scientists and policy scholars interested in unpacking the state and its implications for political, economic, and social (re)organization and mobilization (for overviews see Keil and Mahon 2009; Marston 2004; see also the special volume of *Social Politics*, 2005).

Rather than viewing the state as an ontological given, scalar theory enables researchers to explore the state as a series of socially constructed arenas and associated processes, decentring the "methodological nationalism" featured in many studies (Mahon et al. 2007). Viewing the state as a series of scales requires researchers to focus on the interconnections and relational dimensions between scales as a subject for empirical inquiry rather than an assumed fact. Studies within this approach have revealed important insights about both state initiatives and group mobilization. From this perspective, shifts in state structure, during the neo-liberal period for example, have proven much more complex than a simple "hollowing out" (see Jessop 2002). Furthermore, groups need not engage the national scale to initiate policy change (see, for example, Masson 2006; Mahon 2005, 2006, 2009).

The implications of this approach for policy studies are considerable. As Mahon (2009, 207) observes, "It is not a question of a simple, singular hierarchy structuring interscalar arrangements and the social relations embedded therein. Rather, there is a multiplicity of diversely structured, overlapping interscalar rule regimes operative in and across diverse policy fields. While these arrangements clearly influence what happens at the local scale, sufficient room often exists for local actors to modify the effects." Such an approach, then, enables researchers to expose the complex ways in which state and society interact to initiate change.

Although the concept of scale has been refined and nuanced within theoretical treatments (for a discussion, see Marston 2000, 2004; Brenner 2001), perhaps the most widely used definition comes from Agnew (1997, 100): "the focal setting at which spatial boundaries are defined for a specific social claim, activity or behaviour." This definition is useful in that it embodies two important elements of scales, the material and the discursive (see Delany and Leitner 1997; Marston 2000, 2004; Masson 2006). Scale is not an ontological certainty; rather, social agents constructed scale through discursive processes and material practices. Moreover, as noted by Massey (1994), scale is constructed through (and constructs) social relations, which is reiterated by Marston and Smith (2001, 617) in their claim that "scale-making should be understood as an embodied process undertaken by social agents themselves shaped by gender, race, class and geography operating within particular historical contexts."

Although Agnew's oft-cited definition provides the conceptual grounding for scale, on its own it obscures the relational dimension of scales; that is, scales can only be understood in relation to other scales (Brenner 2001; Keil and Mahon 2009; Mahon et al. 2007).

This conceptual feature distinguishes scales from other concepts central to spatial theory, including, but not limited to, space and place. According to Agnew (2002, 15–16, also cited in Guenther 2006, 553), "space represents a field of practice or an area in which an organization or set of organizations (such as states) operate, held together in popular consciousness by a map image or narrative story that makes space whole and meaningful," whereas place "represents the encounter of people with space. It refers to how everyday life is inscribed in space and takes on meaning for specified groups of people and organizations." Building on this work, Guenther (2006, 553) defines scale as the "layering of spaces and places, a nested hierarchy of spaces of different size, such as local, regional, national and global."

Unlike space or place, scales reflect a particular, though neither static nor uncontested, hierarchical relational ordering of spatially bounded political locales.[5] This analytic feature also serves to distinguish scalar theory from approaches such as institutionalism and multi-level governance. Similar to scalar theory, these approaches emphasize sites of contest and political action; however, unlike scalar theory, they do not question the ways in which those sites are discursively constituted and constructed with reference to other arenas of political action. In contrast, from the perspective of scalar theory, these temporally and spatially contingent orderings are referred to as "scalar fixes," which are constituted by scalar discourses in which specific scales – national, sub-national, local, institutional, and so on – and the actors associated with them are assigned various roles within interscalar rule regimes. Canadian federalism, then, is a particular scalar fix that is neither static nor uncontested.

Scalar fixes are both the object and subject of political contest. As an *object* of political contest, scale jumping gives social agents opportunities to strategically engage state actors operating at particular scales in an attempt to have their claims addressed (Smith 1992). For example, Kitchin and Wilton (2003) demonstrate the ways in which disability activists in Canada and Ireland strategically identify and act on particular fields of action existing across different scales. As a *subject* of political contest, re-scaling processes reflect the dynamic nature of scale production. According to Swyngedouw (1997, 142), rescaling refers to "a series of socio-spatial processes that changes the importance and role of certain geographical scales, reasserts the importance of others, and sometimes creates entirely new significant scales" (see also Mahon et al. 2007). For example, Masson's (2006) work on feminist activism in Quebec demonstrates the ways in which women used and constructed the "regional" scale as an important focal point for feminist politics.

While emphasis within this literature is most often placed on "state" scales – such as global, national, regional, and local – bodies and households, although often under theorized, also play an important role in the politics of scale (see Marston 2000, 2004; see also the debate between Brenner 2001 and Marston and Smith 2001, as well as Peck 2002; Tyner 2000; Cidell 2006). Feminist theorists, although not speaking in the language of scale, have convincingly demonstrated that both the body and home are spatially bounded sites for specific claims, activities, or behaviours. Butler's (1990; 1993) work, for example, reveals the body to be an important site of resistance within the politics of identity. Similarly, the works of black feminists have challenged the notion of second-wave white feminists that "homes" were inherent sites of oppression (see hooks 2000; Hill Collins 1990). Instead, the home, like the body, is an important, if not complex, site of resistance and identity formation.

Moreover, as demonstrated by feminist and critical-policy scholars, both bodies and homes are implicated in the complex spatial ordering of political regimes – they are implicated in the rationalities of government and play a key role in constructing each other, as well as other scales. On the one hand, policies impel and position subjects, constituting the everyday (e.g., Bacchi 1999; 2010). On the other hand, however, bodies and households are also sites of resistance to particular representations of both policy problems and subjects. Bodies and households, then, are not only sites of claims-making, activities, and behaviours, but are also important sites of identity construction. The politics of reproduction is thus an important site of inquiry into the production of scale.

THE SCALAR POLITICS OF REPRODUCTION: ONTARIO HEALTH CARE GOVERNANCE AND THE ALTERNATIVE BIRTH MOVEMENT

In articulating a new vision of childbirth, one in which women were central, the A B M sought to disrupt the biomedical scalar fix that had emerged during the post-war era. By the late nineteenth century, biomedicine was emerging as a hegemonic discourse in both Canada and the United States. Premised on advances in science and backed by the state, biomedicine claimed birth as a "medical" event, thereby radically altering the birthing experiences of women throughout much of the West (Mitchinson 1993, 2002; for an overview, see Rushing 1993). Until this time, midwives had been the primary birth attendants to Canadian and American women and babies were caught in homes. The ascendance of biomedicine was assisted by urbanization and modernization, and by the mid-twentieth century the majority of babies were born in hospitals.

By this time, a new scalar fix in the field of Canadian health care was emerging premised on both biomedicine and universalism, giving way to a complex multiscalar governance arrangement that served to displace the prominence of women in the birthing process. At the federal scale, the Medical Care Act of 1966 established a universal pre-paid insurance system for medical services based on a fifty/fifty cost-sharing program with the provinces. Also established in 1966, the Canada Assistance Plan covered expenses for services falling outside provincial health insurance plans.[6] The cost-sharing arrangements were altered significantly in 1977 with the implementation of Established Programs Financing, which replaced the cost-sharing structure with a block-funding system based on a combination of tax-points and direct transfers, effectively reducing the federal contribution to health care services.

In 1984, the universal nature of Canadian health care was reasserted with the Canada Health Act. The Act integrated medical and hospital acts and explicitly articulated five key values of the health care system, including universality, accessibility, comprehensiveness, portability, and public administration. These arrangements have both fostered and constrained the federal role in health care. Though health care discourse is anchored in talk of "national standards," provinces faced, until recently, very little federal intervention in health care service provision. As a result, there are considerable differences among health care systems across the country.

At the provincial scale, governments are responsible for the design and implementation of health care service provision and insurance systems. In Ontario, this is achieved mostly through the Ontario Health Insurance Program (O H I P), as well as public and private hospital acts. Coverage through insurance is one way provinces can exert their power in health care. For example, midwifery is legal in Alberta, but is not publicly funded. Similarly, access to abortion is limited in some provinces through lack of insurance coverage. Moreover, while provincial governments must commit to the five principles of health care, reductions in federal funding have increased provincial governments' discretion in health care spending. Thus, despite some leverage by the federal government, the dominant scale within the interscalar rule regime in health care is the provincial government.

The dominance of provincial and federal governments has meant that the municipal scale has played a limited role in health care governance. At the municipal scale, the government is largely responsible for public health initiatives, education, and awareness, which fall outside the CHA.

Perhaps more important than the municipal scale are the institutional scales – hospitals, clinics, and so on – the sites at which health care is provided. At these sites, provincial and local scales interact in important ways. For example, whereas provincial governments are responsible for hospital administration through a board of directors, with no requirement for local representatives on the board, the boards are "community focused," suggesting an important role for local discourses to operate at this scale.

As noted above, the ascendance of modern medicine and its corresponding multiscalar governance arrangement displaced birthing women and midwives as key birth attendants; physicians and their team of "experts" were now responsible for childbirth. Women were taught to fear childbirth and accepted interventions such as anesthetic, episiotomies, and c-sections. Birthing took place on the doctor's schedule, not the woman's. Women were often isolated from their partners and families, and left to labour alone until the physician was ready to deliver the baby. Once born, the infant was taken away from the mother, bathed, and brought back only for scheduled feedings. For many women, the processes of pregnancy and birth were disembodied experiences to which they contributed little and during which they received little emotional support. The resulting biomedical "scalar fix" constituted birth as something that "happens to" women and constructed the "institutional" scale (i.e., hospitals) as *the* appropriate birthplace.[7] As described above, within biomedical multiscalar arrangements, the institutional scale both governs (through procedures and routines) and is governed (by various state and sub-state scales, as well as by local scales). The scale of the "body," in contrast, is constructed as passively governed, constituted solely by its relation to other scales.

By the 1960s, many women were becoming disillusioned with medicalized births and sought a "better way." The natural childbirth movement, originating in the 1930s, opened a discursive space in which to challenge this approach to birth. The literature devoted to natural childbirth encouraged women to resist medical pain relief measures and instead to take control over pain management, using, for example, Bradley or Lamaze methods. Initially these approaches had little impact on biomedical births; however, a new legion of childbirth educators trained in "natural" techniques for pain management began teaching women and their partners how to manage pain without medical intervention. Childbirth classes became important sites of resistance to medicalization, creating networks of women to share ideas, books, and techniques.

In addition to childbirth classes, an emerging literature that merged natural childbirth with feminist principles provided an important launching point for discussing new ideas about birth. Some of the important publications of the time included Hazell's (1969) *Commonsense Childbirth*, Lang's (1972) *Birth Book*, Kitzinger's (1984, originally published in 1962) *The Experience of Childbirth* and *Education and Counselling for Childbirth* (1977), Gaskin's (1975) *Spiritual Midwifery*, and Arms' (1975) *Immaculate Deception*, which lined women's bookshelves throughout the United States and English Canada. In 1985, Canada's contribution to this literature came from Barrington's (1985) *Midwifery is Catching*. Like her American counterparts, Barrington's book contains graphic photos of women during birth and provides a detailed overview of the decline and re-emergence of midwifery.[8]

Although not all of these publications are "radical,"[9] they share a number of common features. First, they emphasize the importance of women reclaiming control of their bodies, particularly during pregnancies and birth. Second, by emphasizing women's subjective, intuitive knowledge of their own bodies, the books demonstrate the politics of reproduction and illuminate the struggles for knowledge and control. From this perspective, all of these works challenge the commonly held belief that birth is a medical act. Third, within this context, all of the publications seek to foster women's voice in reproductive politics. This was to be done through reorienting women to the processes of pregnancy and birth so they could reclaim reproduction from medical dominance. Finally, all of these publications, as well as the movement they reflected and, in turn, strengthened, outlined alternative visions of birth that challenged the biomedical model.

In sum, all of these works visualize a new scalar politics of childbirth, effectively problematizing two scales central to biomedical multiscalar arrangements in Canada and the United States: the passive body and the institutional scale. In so doing, A B M advocates were able to decentre the institution/hospital as the main site in which to give birth, opening the door for legitimizing home birth as an alternative to medicalized hospital births. As women mobilized about these ideas in Ontario, policy change became a certainty. However, the resulting multiscalar arrangement and interscalar rule regime served to disrupt, rather than transform, the biomedical scalar fix. As I will show, such rescaling processes constructed identities that both continued and disrupted biomedical discourses in reproductive politics.

OF HOMES AND HOSPITALS: THE ALTERNATIVE BIRTH MOVEMENT AND THE RESCALING OF REPRODUCTION

Noted above, the contemporary biomedical scalar fix constructs the scale of the body as a passive entity, which is divided by form and function and "acted on" by skilled physicians in hospital settings. In this context, birth is something that "happens to" women, rather than something they "do" (Hazell 1969). In addition, at the institutional scale, the hospital is constructed as the only safe place in which to give birth, due to the presence of physicians (i.e., "skilled experts") and equipment that can identify and address complications *when* they arise. In problematizing these scales, A B M advocates sought to reclaim the body as an active entity, directing and controlling birth, which is something that women do, and remove birth from the gaze of medical science by returning it to the home.

Scalar discourses (re)constituting the body were central to the A B M, among both moderates and radicals. This reconstitution addressed two elements of biomedicine: allopathism and the presumed passivity of bodies. Regarding allopathism, Arms (1975, 119) writes, "Woman gives birth, and she is one with the process." Kitzinger (1977, xi) reminds potential childcare educators that, "Many women value the presence of another woman who understands what they are feeling, and no machine can ever take the place of a good midwife, both in terms of seeing what is happening – not just to the uterus but to the whole woman – and in giving encouragement and help of the right kind at the right time." These ideas are articulated more clearly in the 1984 edition of *The Experience of Childbirth*, where Kitzinger writes, "Pregnant women are not merely 'maternity patients,' childbearing bodies being checked for pathology, nor 'antenatal pupils' learning techniques to cope with labour" (13). Kitzinger also challenges the tendency of biomedicine to divide pregnancy into "stages" and challenges the instrumentalism of the medical model of birth. Similarly, Canadian writer Eleanor Barrington (1985, 19) argues: "The holism in midwifery refers to the whole woman, for her whole reproductive cycle, in her whole environment. A pregnant woman is a physical, emotional, and social being, and none of these factors can be safely ignored. Similarly, no one event in her reproductive cycle can be adequately analyzed without reference to what has come before."

In addition to allopathism, the A B M challenged the presumed passivity of birthing patients among physicians. Some advocates argued that biomedical science both assumes and renders women passive. For example, Lang (1972, 2) claims that the dehumanization of childbirth occurred because "women are thought of as brainless children." Later, in documenting the history of the role of medical science in pregnancy and birth, she argues, "In [Dr James Y.] Simpson's first anesthetized delivery, the inhalation lasted twenty minutes. Consciousness was obliterated as was the pain and the voluntary efforts of the woman. The labour of childbirth had been shifted from the woman to her attending physician" (14). Arms (1975) attributes this outcome to the "immaculate deception," the fear of childbirth that has prompted women to hand over authority to "experts." She claims, "So woman lost her intuitive knowledge of childbirth and replaced it with fearful expectations of tortu[r]ous agony" (1975, 13).

In addition to explaining the causes and consequences of passivity, A B M advocates documented women's struggles for change. For example, Lang's work also documents the active subject in birth, challenging the assumptions held and reinforced by medical science. In addition to providing first-person birth stories and advice to those contemplating home births, she writes, "In light of this type of treatment, we women are now taking the responsibility of childbirth out of the hospital, into our own hands ... Women are learning how to listen once more to their long buried instinctive selves."

Arms (1975) makes similar claims, recounting women's struggles against biomedical obstetric care.

More moderate advocates emphasized women's "responsibility" for their pregnancies and births, aligning alternative birth discourse with emergent neo-liberal discourse. For example, Hazell (1969, 21) claims, "I began to discover to my amazement that there were some women who enjoyed having babies, and surprisingly these were the women who took responsibility for their labors, did not use drugs during the process, and refused to relinquish their integrity to the hospital." Later she advises, "It [the American way of birth] can be changed only by us. And we can change it only if we face squarely each aspect of it and ask ourselves, 'How can I do this the best possible way for *me?*' [...] Birth is a joy in direct proportion to our personal investment in it; it will be a nightmare in direct proportion to our abdications of the responsibilities entailed" (37–8). The notion of responsibility and change is echoed in Kitzinger (1984).

At the same time, however, in reconstituting the body as an active, embodied subject, A B M advocates deployed discourses that were classist, heteronormative, and racialized. Much of the A B M literature reflects the experiences of white, educated women. Reflective of the liberal feminism of this time, Hazell (1969), Barrington (1981; 1985), and Kitzinger (1977; 1984) explicitly assume a middle-class audience. For example, in chapter 4 of *Midwifery is Catching*, Barrington (1985, 55) explains, "Analysis of the current midwifery clientele denies both the designation 'lunatic' and relegation to a fringe. Whereas parents who sought midwifery in the early 1970s belonged to the counterculture, the current clientele is mostly mainstream. Within one decade the 'hippie' ideas and birth practices spread back into the middle-class suburbs from whence the counterculturalists originally came."

Where Barrington's work is defensive, demonstrating the normality of alternative birth options, Kitzinger outlines the potential of middle-class women to "educate" those of lower classes. In a chapter entitled, "Underprivileged Women in Childbirth," Kitzinger (1977, 115) writes: "The challenge is not simply to instruct women in the anatomy and physiology of the reproductive organs and in techniques of adjustment to labour but to help them towards something which is even more valuable: discovering possibilities of choice, of voluntary decision and action, of self-direction, and of what those in the middle class think of as basic human dignity and responsibility."

This middle-class perspective is also apparent in *The Experience of Childbirth*, when Kitzinger (1984, 50) suggests, "Having a baby at home need not be costly. The main expense involved at home is secondary to the birth itself and is connected with getting adequate domestic help for the period which used to be called 'lying in.'" She suggests that one might find domestic services through one's local government or social service agencies.

Heteronormativity and racialized images are also invoked in many of the works. The family unit of which Kitzinger (1977; 1984) and Hazell (1969) speak clearly resembles the patriarchal nuclear family. For example, in Kitzinger's (1984, 50) discussion of hiring domestic help, she notes that such help is not necessary if one's partner can take a week off, since, "it's an opportunity for the man to improve his domestic skills." Similarly, in decrying the over-medicalization of birth, Hazell (1969, 34) asserts, "The husband is systematically excluded from the position of authority in his family, as soon as his wife becomes pregnant, to be replaced by the doctor." And although Gaskin (1975) endorses communal living arrangements, she does so from a heteronormative perspective, emphasizing reciprocal relationships between men and women.

Although race was very rarely discussed explicitly, important racialized images appear throughout the works. Kitzinger (1977) effectively bundles race and class into the category of "underprivileged women," discussed above. Racialized images also appear in Barrington's history of midwifery in Canada, which barely acknowledges the birth experiences of First Nations women or the role of midwifery therein, the persistence of home births in specific ethnic communities, and the ways in which the new midwifery was reconstituted by white women acting on racialized women in the South (see also Nestel 2000, 2006; Johnson 2009). And although Arms (1975) and Lang (1972) advocate for social justice, with Lang calling for global social justice and an end to sexism and racism, the birth experiences and images presented are those of white heterosexual and able-bodied women (see also Gaskin 1975). Such perspectives serve to obscure the agency of lesbian or transwomen, women of colour, women with disabilities, and poor women in reproductive politics. Importantly, the idea of the "educated white woman" educating poor, minority women about their bodies and raising children would become a key strategy in securing policy change in Ontario (Nestel 2000, 2006; Mason 1990).

In rejecting the allopathic orientation and presumed passivity of bodies characterizing biomedicine, the A B M discursively reconstituted the (white, hetero, middle-class) body as an active, embodied subject, reclaiming and reasserting authoritative knowledge of birth and using such knowledge to direct one's own pregnancy and birth. Not only is birth something that women do, it is also a "natural" and "normal" function. As a natural and normal function, there is often little need for medical intervention. Birth is reconceptualized as a social, relational event, not one subject to medical scrutiny. Within this reconceptualization, women, not physicians, are the experts in their pregnancies and births and therefore should determine how and where birth will take place and who shall assist and attend. This rescaling of the body implicated a simultaneous rescaling of institutions.

Scalar discourses problematizing the institutional scale simultaneously demonized hospitals, associating them with places of death and disease and, in some cases, oppression, and reinforced notions of homes as safe and nurturing spaces. Hazell (1969, 223) argues, "Women come into the hospital healthy and often leave having acquired some sort of infection. Babies are particularly susceptible because neither they nor their mothers have resistance to the variant strains of bacteria found in hospitals. To remedy this, we need to get obstetrics completely out of the general hospital and make home delivery more feasible for those who wish it." Moreover, in describing the "ideal" birth system, Hazell's (1969, 224–32) "Maternity Motel Complex" emulates the middle-class household right down to the "mother's helpers" to assist with childcare and support for first-time mothers, as well as the "hairdresser, a masseuse, and a manicurist" (231). She writes, "You feel as if you had been on a vacation" (231). Moreover, Hazell goes so far as to suggest that home birth babies are healthier both physically and mentally.

These ideas are echoed in later works. Before describing what women typically experience in hospitals, Lang (1972, 16) observes, "But where has all this innovation of modern medicine brought us today? We, as women, are still forced to endure some of the most outrageous insults possible. We are still expected to labor and bear our children in hospitals, which are centers of disease and infection." Arms (1975, 51) notes, "When a pregnant woman checks into the American hospital to give birth to her child, she may not be fully aware that she is automatically stepping into an institution that is solely designed for the treatment of disease and disorder." Kitzinger (1985, 45) similarly argues, "Having a baby is a normal life crisis. It is not an illness ... Unless there are reasons why it is best for the baby to be born in hospital (either medical or 'social' reasons, which include not having sufficient room), home is therefore often the best place to have a baby." Home, then, was constructed as a site of nurturing and bonding, free from the gaze of biomedicine, and took on a more prominent role in the scalar politics of reproduction. In reifying home and hospital, ABM scalar discourses sought to displace the hospital as a key scale within the biomedical scalar fix.

The scalar discourses deployed by ABM advocate problematized two scales central to biomedical multiscalar arrangements: the body and the institution. In challenging the allopathic orientation and the presumed passivity of bodies, the ABM constituted the body as a key site of resistance to medical intervention and, in some cases, sexist domination. At the same time, however, such constructions served to reinforce class, race, and homosexual oppression. That is, only some bodies were active agents. In reconstituting birth as a social and relational event, rather than a medical condition, ABM advocates were able to argue for the home as the best place to give birth. In Ontario, both of these scales, the body and the home, would take on a new role in the resulting multiscalar arrangement of the 1990s.

ALTERNATIVE BIRTH IN ONTARIO: DISRUPTING THE BIOMEDICAL SCALAR FIX

Above, I argued that the ABM problematized two scales central to the biomedical scalar fix, reconstituting the pregnant and parturient body as active and the home as a viable, and in many cases the best, place to give birth. The influence of this material in Canada has been documented by Daviss (1999; 2001) and reiterated by my personal interviews conducted with key players in the Ontario ABM. In particular, the New Midwifery Movement (NMM), which emerged from the ABM, sought to transform the biomedical multiscalar arrangement and its corresponding interscalar rule regime, as encoded in the complex governance regime in the province outlined above. I suggest that the NMM was effective in disrupting, but not transforming, this particular scalar fix. Specifically, while the NMM reconstituted the role of individuals and homes within the new scalar politics of reproduction, the dominance of biomedical scalar discourses remains and is embedded within midwifery legislation.[10]

By the mid-1980s, a perceived impending health care crisis, spurred in part by the growing influence of neo-liberal discourse, was shaping public discussions on health care. A number of factors contributed to this perception. In the face of economic crises and new discourses of state and economy, health care costs were spiralling. Moreover, shrinking federal contributions led provincial health ministers to seek out new ways to provide health care services. Somewhat ironically, the influence of neo-liberalism provided a discursive space in which to discuss alternative health care services, which in the context of reproductive health was compounded by shortages in obstetric care providers throughout the province.[11] One alternative that was gaining visibility throughout the province was midwifery services.

During the late 1970s, the N M M emerged from the A B M.[12] The A B M established a group of women who reclaimed community midwifery, as well as consumer groups dedicated to advocating the care of midwives. Although legalization and regulation were not immediate goals, the opportunity was provided in 1983, when the Conservative government announced the Health Professions Legislative Review (H P L R) and invited midwives to submit a proposal for self-regulation. In 1985, the H P L R Committee recommended that midwifery be established as a self-regulated profession, but suggested that the task of developing and implementing such a system was well beyond the purview of the committee. In response, the government appointed the Task Force for the Implementation of Midwifery in Ontario (T F I M O), to be led by feminist lawyer Mary Eberts, with members Rachel Edney (a family physician), Karen Kauffman (an obstetric nurse who taught at Ryerson), and Alan Schwartz, a policy advisor for the Ministry of Health who had also been responsible for the H P L R.

Both the H P L R and the T F I M O invited submissions from various groups. H P L R participants were also invited to review and comment on other submissions, and to respond to particular comments from other groups. The T F I M O invited written submissions and invited groups to make oral presentations outlining their positions on various issues regarding midwifery, such as governance systems, curriculum, mode of entry, and scope of practice. In both venues, scalar discourses were deployed in important ways. For example, during the H P L R, the College of Physicians and Surgeons of Ontario argued: "Birthing rooms are being developed in order to provide a more home-like atmosphere for labour and delivery ... The safest place for delivery is in the hospital-based delivery area. ... Birthing centres may be an alternative to hospital deliveries. A birthing centre is a non-hospital, non-home setting for a delivery that offers a more "home-like" atmosphere but must be adjacent to, or part of, a hospital facility so that emergencies can be readily treated." This position reflects considerable ambivalence toward home. On the one hand, the C P S O acknowledges the comforts home provides and thus the importance to "provide a more home-like atmosphere" in an attempt to humanize childbirth. On the other hand, however, hospitals are "safe" places, in which medical experts can attend to impending emergencies quickly and efficiently. Lacking such experts and technological equipment, homes are thus not appropriate for births.

In response, midwifery advocates appropriated scalar discourses stemming from the A B M. In emphasizing the need for choices in childbirth and birthplace, advocates decentred the institutional scale in reproduction and reconstituted the body and the home within multiscalar arrangements.[13] For example, the second submission of the Midwives' Coalition[14] to the H P L R explains, "Using midwives in community settings and to provide home care either for delivery itself or to facilitate early postpartum discharge would lower costs involved in hospital centred care" (70). Here we see the convergence of scalar discourses constituting the home as an appropriate site of birth and neo-liberal discourse, as well as the ways in which midwifery services would redefine hospital births.

Scalar discourses similar to those of the A B M were also deployed in submissions to the T F I M O. For example, the submission from the A O M reconstitutes the body as an active, embodied agent: "The growing use of the midwife as a birth attendant is an indication that women are assuming a greater degree of responsibility for their pregnancy and birth." And, "[The medical] model is disease oriented with the emphasis on pathology and curative treatment. The medical model tends to focus on specific organs and systems. Viewed from the perspective of the medical model pregnancy becomes a mechanical event, separate from the woman's body, with the needs of the mother and fetus often in conflict ... In this model the pregnant woman becomes a passive object upon which procedures are performed." Similarly, the submission by the Ottawa chapter of the Midwifery Task Force included anecdotes and personal stories of home birth, which served to heighten the importance of the home as a site at which to birth and to destabilize the importance of the hospital: "I felt I could relax better at home in an environment where I would have no distractions from the natural process that my body, mind, and spirit were moving through ... The people that receive you in hospital are strangers to you."

The result of this public dialogue on midwifery was the Midwifery Act, 1991, which enables licensed midwives to catch babies in hospitals, homes, and birthing clinics. College of Midwives regulations enable women to engage in "informed choice" about procedures and interventions, within the boundaries of safe care, and advocates choice of birthplace (see also Sharpe 2004a, 2004b; Mason 1990; Paterson 2010, 2011). Both of these enabling regulations institutionalized the scalar discourses problematizing the scales of the body and the institution. Put another way, the Midwifery Act recognizes and fosters the agency of women (i.e., active bodies) by allowing them to choose how and where they give birth (including, and perhaps most important among midwives, home birth). In effect, the act has disrupted the biomedical scalar fix by altering the previous multiscalar arrangement and interscalar rule regime that precluded homes as birth sites and bodies as active agents. Subsequently, bodies and homes have emerged as more prominent scales within the scalar politics of reproduction.

Specifically, the Midwifery Act disrupts the biomedical scalar fix in three key ways. First, it reconfigures the home within the multiscalar arrangement. That is, in contrast to the biomedical multiscalar arrangement, midwifery legislation situates the home as a site within the hierarchical ordering of political locales. Through regulations describing the "appropriate" conditions under which women can birth at home, the home is implicated in the governance structure of midwifery. Recent studies have demonstrated the ways in which women resist these regulations to ensure they can birth at home (see Sharpe 2004a; Murray 2008). Second, in practice, the act has redefined hospital births. On the one hand, physician-attended births have changed in response to demands from ABM advocates. As noted above, physicians had been making concerted efforts to make hospital or clinic births more "home-like." On the other hand, midwife-attended hospital births are in many ways "deinstitution-alized." As documented by MacDonald (2007), midwives and the women they serve disturb the medicalized tendencies of hospital births by resisting particular procedures and routines and by encouraging home-like settings. MacDonald (2007, 165) writes of her interview participants who had hospital births, "Though they were all concerned with past and potential interference they associated with the hospital – such as epidurals and teaching rounds – midwifery care mediates the space for them in important ways, mitigating against the institutional feel and its potential embodied effects." Thus, the institutional scale is being redefined and renegotiated under the provisions of the legislation. Finally, the resulting interscalar rule regime has fractured the authority of physicians, integrating not only other licensed health care professionals such as midwives, but also lay people (i.e., pregnant women) in determining their course of care.

These changes reflect an important fracturing of the biomedical scalar fix, with newly constructed scales and reconstructed old ones. However, the construction and use of scales of social and political identity formation also reproduced biomedical discourses in the arena of reproductive politics, which has limited the complete transformation of the biomedical scalar fix. At present, the more than 400 licensed midwives in the province catch 7 per cent of Ontario's babies (Ontario Maternity Care Expert Panel 2006), 20 per cent of whom are caught in homes (College of Midwives of Ontario 2008). While the low numbers of women in midwifery care is due largely to the limited supply of midwives, with long waiting lists common in many areas throughout the province, more important is the relatively low number of home births, which has caused concern among many practising midwives (see, for example, Sharpe et al. 2009). Consider, for example, that in the Netherlands, midwives attend about 85 per cent of all births, 30 per cent of which are home births.

Moreover, biomedical discourse remains hegemonic and potentially limits the authority of both women and their midwives (see Paterson 2010, 2011). In many cases, midwives must defer to the authority of physicians and all care is assessed within the boundaries of "safety," which is defined and practised with reference to biomedical discourse. Thus, it is midwives with reference to biomedicine, not pregnant women, who determine which pregnancies are suited for homebirths. Finally, although the current scalar politics of reproduction includes the home and a potentially redefined institutional scale, the hierarchical ordering of scales remains intact. In sum, the provincial scale remains the key – although by no means the sole – player in the new scalar politics of reproduction. Continued support for midwifery, including material resources, while popular at local levels, will largely be decided at the provincial scale.

CONCLUSION

The preceding analysis revealed the ways in which advocates of alternative birth used and constructed scale to initiate a new scalar politics of reproduction. Alternative Birth Movement literature problematized two scales featured prominently in the biomedical multiscalar arrangements of Canada and the United States, the body and the institution. ABM advocates challenged the allopathism of biomedicine, arguing that pregnancy was not something to be treated. In addition, ABM advocates illuminated the agency of women during pregnancy and birth. In problematizing the passivity of bodies within the biomedical scalar fix, the ABM exposed the potential harms of hospital births and the merits of home births, positing strong arguments for home births. In practice, these principles enabled advocates of the subsequent New Midwifery Movement in Ontario to challenge the biomedical scalar fix. In so doing, NMM advocates constructed and used scales of social and political identity formation that both continued and fractured biomedical discourses in the arena of reproductive politics. Particularly, the biomedical scalar fix has been disrupted, but not transformed.

This analysis contributes to the literature on the politics of childbirth in a number of ways. First, despite a flourishing literature regarding Ontario midwifery, very little explores the (dis)continuity between the ABM and the NMM (c.f. Daviss 2001). Thus, there is little understanding of the dynamic re-emergence of midwifery and how midwifery became an embodied practice and a site of identity formation for both those giving and receiving midwifery care. Second, very little literature to date explores the role of the state (for exceptions, see Bourgeault 2004; Paterson 2010). Yet this is crucial to our understanding of midwifery politics. Although neither the ABM nor the NMM were explicitly advocating a new politics of scale within the area of reproduction, their claims had important implications for contemporary multiscalar arrangements. How birth

was thought about, advocated, and practised was intricately connected to governance arrangements. Third, but related to the previous point, while much of the literature on Ontario midwifery
explores advocacy and professionalization, the discursive politics of
midwifery, including their implications for governance, has been
overlooked (for exceptions, see MacDonald 2004, 2007; Spoel and
James 2006; Paterson 2010, 2011). Not only were A B M and N M M
advocates constructing and performing their identities, they were
also rescaling reproduction in important ways. The preceding analysis then, premised on the theoretical construct of scale, demonstrates
the important interconnections between states and groups in their
attempts to generate change.

NOTES

1   I would like to thank Francesca Scala, Marlene K. Sokolon, Jenna
    Germaine, and Matthew Brett for comments on earlier versions of this
    paper.
2   Midwifery discourse places emphasis on the role of the mother in birthing.
    Rather than "delivering" babies, midwives "catch" them. Community mid-
    wives refer to midwives who are not nurse-midwives. Some were foreign
    trained, while others gained their skills through some form of apprentice-
    ship with other midwives and/or sympathetic physicians.
3   At this time, midwifery was alegal; while there was no explicit legal prohi-
    bition against midwifery, obstetric care fell within the accepted boundaries
    of biomedicine. Thus, midwives were in danger of being charged for prac-
    tising medicine without a license.
4   The New Midwifery was a movement spawning from the A B M that was
    dedicated to reviving, reforming, and regulating midwifery throughout
    Canada. See Shroff (1997) for a detailed overview.
5   Although it should be noted that the "hierarchical" nature of such order-
    ings has been contested (see Mahon 2009 for a discussion). Furthermore,
    some have argued that the concept of scale must move beyond areal scales
    to include those that transcend defined spatial boundaries, such as net-
    works (see Cox 1998). Finally, it should not be assumed that interscalar
    relations within any given polity are neatly bounded and organized into
    such domains as national, local, etc. Rather, interscalar relations are com-
    plex mappings that overlap particularly constructed policy fields within
    and across states (see Mahon 2009).

6 CAP was replaced in 1996 by the Canada Health and Social Transfer, a block funding system directed at spending for health and education. In 2005, the CHST was replaced by two separate funding systems, the Canada Health Transfer and the Canada Social Transfer.

7 This is not to suggest that American and Canadian health care systems have followed similar trajectories. Indeed, the United States' market system is markedly different from Canada's public system. While these are important differences that deserve closer scrutiny in the scalar politics of reproduction, they are not the focus of the present analysis. As explained above, the purpose of the analysis is to untangle the ways in which politics was embedded in debates about childbirth. How these ideas were operationalized within particular contexts and informed specific scalar strategies is taken up in the second part of this paper.

8 Barrington's work has been criticized as bourgeois and racialized (see Nestel 2000; 2006). Similar issues arise with the other books mentioned here, although to my knowledge a detailed analysis of the ABM literature along these lines has yet to be conducted.

9 For example, Hazell, Kitzinger, and Gaskin take as given (and natural) the heterosexual unit; at the same time, however, Gaskin challenges the nuclear family and instead advocates communal living. Both Lang and Arms locate medicalized birth in gender oppression, but tend to reflect different strains of feminism: Lang's language is more radical whereas Arms' is more liberal. Kitzinger is also more liberal. For example, when she explains why she refers to the baby as "it," she writes, "But I knew I would suggest militant feminism if I used 'she' every time" (1977, xii).

10 For example, regulations regarding consultation and transfer of care, as well as choice of birthplace, are premised on biomedical assessments and "diagnosis" of particular conditions. See Murray 2008; Paterson 2010 and 2011 for more detailed discussions.

11 This is not meant to suggest that neo-liberalism was the only or the most important factor (see Paterson forthcoming).

12 For a more detailed overview, see Bourgeault (2000; 2006), Bourgeault et al. (2004), Daviss 1999; 2001), Biggs (2004), and Shroff (1997).

13 It is important to note however, that there were some important discursive shifts. For example, ABM advocates emphasized "natural" birth, i.e., birth free from interventions, whereas NMM advocates emphasized "normal" birth, i.e., a "low-risk" birth, which is the "expertise" of the midwife. ABM advocates also discuss normal birth, but the meaning is social rather than medical. Similarly, while some ABM advocates focused on choice, others

emphasized control over the birth process (see Paterson 2010 for a detailed discussion).

14 The Midwives' Coalition included the Ontario Nurse Midwives Association, the Ontario Association of Midwives (as it was called at the time), and the Midwifery Task Force of Ontario, a consumer group.

BIBLIOGRAPHY

Agnew, J. 1997. "The Dramaturgy of Horizons: Geographic Scale in the 'Reconstruction of Italy' by the New Italian Political Parties." *Political Geography* 16: 99–122.

– 2002. *Place and Politics in Modern Italy.* Chicago: University of Chicago Press.

Arms, S. 1975. *Immaculate Deception: A New Look at Women and Childbirth in America.* Boston: San Francisco Book Company / Houghton Mifflin Book.

Bacchi, C. 1999/2005. *Women, Policy and Politics: The Construction of Policy Problems.* Thousand Oaks: Sage Publications.

– 2010. *Analysing Policy: What's the Problem Represented to Be?* Don Mills: Pearson Education.

Barrington, E. 1985. *Midwifery is Catching.* Toronto: Vintage Books.

– 1981. "The Rebirth of an Old Custom." *The Globe and Mail,* 4 July.

Biggs, L. 2004. "Rethinking the History of Midwifery in Canada." In *Reconceiving Midwifery*, I. Bourgeault, C. Benoit, and R. Davis-Floyd, eds., 17–45. Montreal & Kingston: McGill-Queen's University Press.

Bourgeault, I.L. 2006. *Push! The Struggle for Midwifery in Ontario.* Montreal & Kingston: McGill-Queen's University Press.

– 2000. "Delivering the 'New' Canadian Midwifery: The Impact on Midwifery of Integration into the Ontario Health Care System." *Sociology of Health and Illness* 22(2): 172–96.

Bourgeault, I.L., C. Benoit, and R. Davis-Floyd. 2004. "Introduction." In *Reconceiving Midwifery*, I. Bourgeault, C. Benoit, and R. Davis-Floyd, eds., 3–14. Montreal Kingston: McGill-Queens University Press.

Bourgeault, I.L., E. Declercq, and J. Sandall. 2001. "Changing Birth: Interest Groups and Maternity Care Policy." In *Birth by Design: Pregnancy, Maternity Care, and Midwifery in North America and Europe*, R. Devries, C. Benoit, E. Van Teijlingen, and S. Wrede, eds., 51–69. New York: Routledge.

Brenner, N. 2001. "The Limits to Scale? Methodological Reflections on Scalar Structuration." *Progress in Human Geography* 25(4): 591–614.

Butler, J. 1990. *Gender Trouble: Feminism and the Subversion of Identity.* London: Routledge Press.

– 1993. *Bodies that Matter. On the Discursive Limits of "Sex."* New York: Routledge Press.

Cidell, J. 2006. "The Place of Individuals in the Politics of Scale." *Area* 38(2): 196–203.

College of Midwives of Ontario. 2008. *Annual Report.* Toronto: College of Midwives of Ontario.

Cox, K. 1998. "Spaces of Dependence, Spaces of Engagement and the Politics of Scale, or: Looking for Politics." *Political Geography* 17(1): 1–23.

Daviss, B.A. 2001. "Reforming Birth and (Re)Making Midwifery in North America." In *Birth by Design: Pregnancy,Maternity Care, and Midwifery in North America and Europe,* R. DeVries, C. Benoit, E. van Teijlingen, and S. Wrede, eds.,70–86. New York: Routledge.

– 1999. *From Social Movement to Professional Midwifery Project: Are We Throwing the Baby out with the Bath Water?* M A thesis in Canadian Studies. Ottawa: Carleton University.

Delany, D., and Leitner, H. 1997. "The Political Construction of Scale." *Political Geography* 16: 93–7.

Gaskin, I. 1977. *Spiritual Midwifery.* Summertown, PA: The Book Publishing Company.

Guenther, K. 2006. "'A Bastion of Sanity in a Crazy World': A Local Feminist Movement and the Reconstitution of Scale, Space, and Place in an Eastern European City." *Social Politics: International Studies in Gender, State, and Society* 13(4): 551–75.

Hazell, L. 1969. *Commonsense Childbirth.* New York: Putnam.

Hill Collins, P. 1990. *Black Feminist Thought: Knowledge, Consciousness and the Politics of Empowerment.* London: Routledge.

hooks, b. 2000. *Feminist Theory: From Margin to Centre.* Cambridge: South End Press.

Jessop, B. 2002. *The Future of the Capitalist State.* Cambridge, UK: Polity Press.

Keil, R., and R. Mahon, eds. 2009. *Leviathan Undone: Towards a Political Economy of Scale.* Vancouver: U B C Press.

Kitchin, R., and R. Wilton. 2003. "Disability Activism and the Politics of Scale." *Canadian Geographer* 47(2): 97–115.

Kitzinger, S. 1977. *Education and Counselling for Childbirth.* New York: Macmillan Publishing Co.

– 1984[1962]. *The Experience of Childbirth.* London: Penguin Books.

Lang, R. 1972. *Birth Book*. California: Genesis Press.

Lefebvre, H. 1991[1974]. *The Production of Space*, trans. D. Nicholson-Smith. Oxford: Blackwell Publishing.

MacDonald, M. 2007. *At Work in the Field of Birth: Midwifery Narratives of Nature, Tradition, and Home*. Nashville: Vanderbilt University Press.

Mahon, R. 2005. "Rescaling Social Reproduction: Childcare in Toronto/Canada and Stockholm/Sweden." *International Journal of Urban and Regional Research* 29(2): 341–357.

– 2006. "Of Scalar Hierarchies and Welfare Redesign: Childcare in Three Canadian Cities." *Transactions of the Institute of British Geographers* 31(4): 452–66.

– 2009. "Of Scalar Hierarchies and Welfare Redesign: Child Care in Four Canadian Cities." In *Leviathan Undone*, Roger Keil and Rianne Mahon, eds., 209–30. Vancouver: UBC Press.

Mahon, R., C. Andrew, and R. Johnson. 2007. "Policy Analysis in an Era of 'Globalization': Capturing Spatial Dimensions and Scalar Strategies." In *Critical Policy Studies*, M. Orsini and M. Smith, eds. Vancouver: UBC Press.

Mahon, R., and R. Keil. 2009. "Introduction." In *Leviathan Undone*, Roger Keil and Rianne Mahon, eds., 3–26. Vancouver: UBC Press.

Marston, S. 2000. "The Social Construction of Scale." *Progress in Human Geography* 24(2): 219–42.

– 2004. "A Long Way from Home: Domesticating the Social Production of Scale." In *Scale and Geographic Inquiry*, E. Sheppard and R. McMaster, eds., 170–91. Oxford: Blackwell Publishing.

Marston, S., and N. Smith. 2001. "States, Scales, and Households: Limits to Scale Thinking?" *Progress in Human Geography* 25(4): 615–19.

Mason, J. 1990. *The Trouble with Licensing Midwives*. Ottawa: CRIAW/ICREF.

Massey, D. 1994. *Space, Place and Gender*. Minneapolis: University of Minnesota Press.

Masson, D. 2006. "Constructing Scale/Contesting Scale: Women's Movement and Rescaling Politics in Quebec." *Social Politics* 13(4): 462–86.

McDowell, L. 2001. "Linking Scales: Or How Scales about Gender and Organizations Raise New Issues for Economic Geography." *Economic Geography* 1(4): 227–50.

Mitchinson, W. 1993. "The Medical Treatment of Women." In *Changing Patterns: Women in Canada*, S. Burt, L. Code, and L. Dorney, eds., 391–421. Toronto: McClelland and Stewart.

– 2002. *Giving Birth in Canada, 1900–1950.* 2nd ed. Toronto: University of Toronto Press.

Murray, B. 2008. "How Authoritative Texts Reinforce the Medical Model of Birth." *British Journal of Midwifery* 16(4): 212–17.

Nestel, S. 2006. *Obstructed Labour: Race and Gender in the Re-emergence of Midwifery.* Vancouver: U B C Press.

– 2000. "Delivering Subjects: Race, Space, and the Emergence of Legalized Midwifery." *Canadian Journal of Law and Society* 15(2): 187–215.

Ontario Maternity Care Expert Panel. 2006. *Maternity Care in Ontario 2006: Emerging Crisis, Emerging Solutions.* Toronto: Ontario Women's Health Council.

Paterson, S. 2010. "Feminizing Obstetrics or Medicalizing Midwifery? The Discursive Constitution of Midwifery in Ontario." *Critical Policy Studies* 4(2): 127–45.

– 2004. "Ontario Midwives: Reflections on a Decade of Regulated Midwifery Practise." *Canadian Woman Studies* 24(1): 153–8.

– 2011. "Midwives, Women, and the State: (De)Constructing Midwives and Pregnant Women in Ontario, Canada." *Canadian Journal of Political Science* 44(3): 483–505.

Peck, J. 2002. "Political Economies of Scale: Fast Policy, Interscalar Relations, and Neoliberal Workfare." *Economic Geography* 78(3): 331–60.

Rothman, B. Katz. 1982. *In Labor: Women and Power in the Birthplace.* New York: W.W. Norton.

Rushing, B. 1993. "Ideology in the Reemergence of North American Midwifery." *Work and Occupations* 20(1): 20–46.

Sharpe, M. 2004a. "Exploring Legislated Midwifery: Texts and Rulings." In *Reconceiving Midwifery,* I.L. Bourgeault, C. Benoit, and R. Davis-Floyd, eds., 150–66. Montreal & Kingston: McGill-Queen's University Press.

– 2004b. *Intimate Business: Woman-Midwife Relationships in Ontario, Canada.* P h D dissertation: University of Toronto.

– 1997. "Ontario Midwifery in Transition: An Exploration of Midwives' Perceptions of the Impact of Midwifery Legislation in its First Year." In *The New Midwifery: Reflections on Renaissance and Regulation,* F.M. Shroff, ed., 201–44. Toronto: Women's Press.

Shroff, F.M. 1997. "Introduction: Midwifery – From Rebellion to Regulation: The Rebirth of an Ancient Calling." In *The New Midwifery: Reflections on Renaissance and Regulation,* F.M. Shroff, ed., 15–40.

Smith, N. 1992. "Geography, Difference and the Politics of Scale." In *Postmodernism and the Social Sciences*, J. Doherty, E. Graham, and M. Malek, eds., 57–79. London: Macmillan Press.

Swyngedouw, E. 1997. "Neither Global nor Local: "Glocalization" and the Politics of Scale." In *Spaces of Globalization: Reasserting the Power of the Local*, K. Cox, ed., 137–66. New York: Guilford Press.

Soja, E. 1989. *Postmodern Geographies: The Reassertion of Space in Critical Social Theory*. London: Verso.

Tyner, J. 2000. "Migrant Labour and the Politics of Scale: Gendering the Philippine State." *Asia Pacific Viewpoint* 41(2): 131–54.

Van Wagner, V. 1991. *With Women: Community Midwifery in Ontario.* Master's thesis, York University, Toronto.

8

With Breast Intentions: Breastfeeding Policy in Canada

MARLENE K. SOKOLON

"We reclaim the inherent right to govern our own bodies."
Ann Simonton, quoted in Yalom 1997, 244

Breastfeeding policy is a touchstone issue for feminism because it highlights the inextricable tensions between the bio-physicality of the female body and larger cultural, political, and economic structural arrangements that affect gender roles.[1] The practice of breastfeeding directly confronts tensions between women's reproductive and productive lives, as it confers on women a greater reproductive burden than men. It is also at the centre of debates about whether women should seek gender equality by minimizing gender differences or whether, by recognizing the inextricable reproductive differences, women should exert pressure to adjust the current patriarchal, social, and economic structures to accommodate female bodies (Carter 1995; Blum 1999; Kedrowski and Lipscomb 2008). In addition, breastfeeding also represents the tension between human biology and cultural constructs, because it is a biological practice with historical, cultural, and social variations that are infused with religious, political, and moral meanings (Stuart-Macadam 1995). Hence, breastfeeding proves a crucial issue not only for feminist theory but for understanding how public policy reflects, modulates, and exasperates the inherent tensions embedded in this complex and variable practice.

In this chapter, I examine the current Canadian approaches to breastfeeding by examining the publications and discourses surrounding contemporary policy. I focus principally on the Health Canada 2004 *Exclusive Breastfeeding Duration* recommendation but also examine several other official government documents and court rulings that contribute to the Canadian policy discourse. In the second part of the chapter, I analyze this discourse in light of three main critiques associated with breastfeeding policy: over-medicalization, an idealized view of nature, and a romanticized view of motherhood and the family. The Canadian discourse is found to reflect the critiques of all three approaches. Canadian breastfeeding policy, for example, defines success as measured in infant nutrition and morbidity indicators without paying equal and necessary attention to public and workplace accommodations. I conclude with two recommendations that would re-orient the discourse on breastfeeding in Canada. First, rather than promoting a one-size-fits-all recommendation, policy should promote a woman-friendly practice that accommodates a wide variation in infant feeding decisions; and second, breastfeeding policy discourse should not be isolated or fractured from the broader experience of women's reproductive health, such as abortion, menstruation, and menopause. With the emphasis on a broader discourse, policy changes affecting public and economic spaces are not conceptualized to solely benefit infant-feeding or health indicators; instead, breastfeeding should be conceptualized within the larger holistic of women's reproductive lives as a practice that involves the nexus of biology and culture and of production and reproduction.

CANADIAN POLICY ON BREASTFEEDING

After very low breastfeeding rates following the Second World War, the practice of breastfeeding in Canada began steadily increasing in the 1960s. Currently, according to the 2003 Canadian Community Survey, approximately 85 per cent of Canadian women initiate breastfeeding, although rates vary across regions, levels of education, ethnicity, and socio-economic status (Millar and Maclean 2005; Chalmers, Levitt et al. 2009; Nathoo and Ostry 2009). A more recent survey in 2006 estimated that, in several regions, the average is now closer to 90 per cent initiation rates (Public Health Agency 2009). Canadian women initiate breastfeeding, and at a much higher rate than, for example, American women, who have approximately 68.4 per cent initiation rates (Hausman 2003). Canadian rates vary significantly across regions (Newfoundland and Labrador have rates of 63 per cent compared with British Columbia, which has 93 per cent), education (only 71 per cent of women with less than secondary graduation breastfeed, compared with 89 per cent with post-secondary education), and socio-economic status (74 per cent of those in the lowest income category breastfeed, as compared with 89 per cent of women in the highest income category). Rates of breastfeeding also vary according to ethnicity; the 2001 Aboriginal Peoples Survey, for example, found approximately 73 per cent initiation rates across First Nations, Inuit, and Métis mothers, although this rate also varies according to region. There is a significant drop across all groups in the duration of breastfeeding (22 per cent stop breastfeeding after one month and only 47 per cent breastfeed for longer than four to six months) and much lower rates of exclusive breastfeeding at six months (the average is between 14.4 per cent and 17 per cent). Based on the current situation, where the vast majority of women initiate breastfeeding but then discontinue the practice, recent breastfeeding policy in Canada has focused on two goals: first, increasing duration rates of exclusive breastfeeding and second, increasing the breastfeeding rates of targeted groups, such as those living in certain regions, those of a lower socio-economic class, or those ethnic groups with lower initiation rates than "successful" white, older, middle- to high-income, well-educated breastfeeding mothers (Dubois and Girard 2003; Black, Godwin et al. 2008).

Since the early 1980s, which saw scandals involving the exploitation of women in developing countries by formula companies, the Canadian government has officially supported initiatives by the World Health Organization (w H O) about the marketing of breast milk substitutes and the promotion of breastfeeding guidelines. However, due partially to the fact that the Canadian Constitution gives authority over health care primarily to the provinces, this support for international guidelines has never been enacted into law (Nathoo and Ostry 2009). Instead of legal guidelines, the federal government has focused on educational campaigns targeting hospitals, health care professionals, and new mothers. In 2004, Health Canada adopted the changes made in 2001 by the w H O; the new recommendation for breastfeeding duration in Canada is outlined in its publication, *Exclusive Breastfeeding Duration* (Health Canada 2004). Although this publication clearly stresses "it is not intended to be an all-inclusive document on breastfeeding" and does refer to other research and information, it includes both a justification for this new recommendation and a list of implications for this initiative. In this publication, Health Canada uses the WHO definition of exclusive breastfeeding: "the practice of feeding only breast milk (including expressed breast milk) ... allows the baby to receive vitamins, minerals or medicine. Water, breast milk substitutes, other liquids and solid foods are excluded." Accordingly, the main breastfeeding recommendation for Canadians states "exclusive breastfeeding is recommended for the first six months of life for healthy term infants, as breast milk is the best food for optimal growth. Infants should be introduced to nutrient-rich, solid food with particular attention to iron at six months with continued breastfeeding for up to two years and beyond."

As outlined in the document, the principal rationale for this change in policy from four to six months of exclusive breastfeeding is scientific evidence, which indicates that exclusive breastfeeding "confers additional protection against gastrointestinal infections." This evidence, based on a study in Belarus, found that babies breastfed exclusively for six months had a lower risk of gastrointestinal infection (one or more occurrences) than babies exclusively breastfed for only three months. The publication goes on to stress that there is no justification or evidence that shows how six-month exclusive breastfeeding affects infant growth rates or iron status. It also adds that other studies on the effect of exclusive breastfeeding on respiratory tract infections, allergies, obesity, and cognitive development have been "inconclusive, insufficient, or have not shown substantial differences." The document further justifies the change from four to six months of exclusive breastfeeding by citing the maternal health benefits conferred by delayed menses, which can improve maternal iron deficiency but which cannot "be relied upon as a foolproof method of contraception." In addition, based on two studies of Honduran women, the document also indicates "a small but statistically significant" potential weight loss of, on average, 0.42 kilograms (approximately 1 pound) in comparison with women not exclusively breastfeeding for six months. Thus, the main justifications for this policy change are twofold: first, six-month exclusively breastfed babies statistically have fewer occurrences (one or more) of gastrointestinal infections; and, second, breastfeeding women may have less risk of iron deficiency and experience a weight loss of 0.42 kg.

Health Canada's *Exclusive Breastfeeding Duration* also outlines ten implications that result from its new recommendation to increase exclusive breastfeeding from four to six months. The first implication mentioned encourages health professionals to implement the recommendation at national, provincial, and community levels, with "special consideration" for applying it at the individual level. The fourth through sixth implications outline the role of vitamin supplements, introduction of solid food at six months, monitoring of infant growth rates, and special attention for infants born of iron-deficient mothers. In point seven, the publication acknowledges that "some mothers may not exclusively breastfeed to six months for personal and/or social reasons and they should also be supported to optimize their infant's nutritional well-being." The penultimate implication notes that "the implementation of this recommendation can be maximized through the provision of adequate social support to breastfeeding women by increasing community, public health, hospital and workplace efforts." Finally, the document emphasizes Health Canada's support for the implementation of the UNICEF/WHO Baby-Friendly Initiative. This initiative focuses on the implementation of WHO Codes at the hospital level to evaluate hospital practices that are deemed obstacles to the promotion of breastfeeding (Levitt, Kaczorowski et al. 1996; Palda, Guise et al. 2004).

In comparison with other educational literature on breastfeeding, this government document proposes comparatively moderate benefits for both mother and child as justifications for the policy change. Although the document stresses that it is not intended to be an "all-inclusive" publication, there is no mention here of, for example, Sudden Infant Death Syndrome. In other Canadian government publications, such as *Sudden Infant Death Syndrome (SIDS)*, Health Canada (2005) indicates that breastfeeding "may giv[e] some protection against SIDS." This claim is highly controversial, since unlike exposure to tobacco products or not placing the child to sleep in the prone position, there is no conclusive evidence linking breastfeeding with a reduced risk of SIDS (see, for example, Henderson-Smith, Ponsonby et al. 1998; Moon and Fu 1997; Vennemann, Bajanowski et al. 2007). In contrast, scientific evidence suggests that the use of pacifiers actually reduces the risk of SIDS more than breastfeeding; however, due to concerns (also not scientifically supported) that pacifiers may cause "nipple confusion" in the infant, the promotion of pacifiers is rarely mentioned (and is not mentioned on the Canada Health webpage) as a recommendation to reduce the risk of SIDS (Tonz 2000; Callaghan, Kendall et al. 2005). The new policy also mentions only moderate benefits to maternal health as a justification for changing to six-month exclusive breastfeeding. The document does not mention, for example, as other Health Canada information websites do (Health Canada 2008), the purported connection between breastfeeding and a reduced risk of breast cancer. The scientific evidence for this reduced risk for the population at large remains inconclusive; there is stronger evidence, however, that breastfeeding does reduce the risk of breast cancer in women who possess certain gene mutations, such as the B R C A 1 . Unfortunately, this same mutation may also be connected to the extreme physical discomfort that some women have while breastfeeding, which often results in them discontinuing the practice (Jernström, Lubinski et al. 2004).

Exclusive Breastfeeding Duration also does not overtly promote breastfeeding as a means of achieving an idealized or pre-pregnancy weight but rather indicates that six months of exclusive breastfeeding may result in the relatively small weight loss of approximately 0.42 kgs in comparison with women not exclusively breastfeeding. This moderate claim stands in sharp contrast to the American Women, Infant, and Children program (W I C) breastfeeding promotion in New York State, launched in October 2010.[2] In a series of television advertisements, breastfeeding was promoted by W I C as a diet program (New York State 2010). The television spots employed the typical advertising strategies of diet plans by broadcasting an image of a thin woman showing off her "fat pants" and claiming to have lost 18 kg (40 lbs), not on a "fad diet," but by breastfeeding her baby. Breastfeeding, the voiceover tells its audience, burns up to 500 calories, which is further claimed to be "equivalent to two hours of aerobic exercise."

Health Canada's literature on exclusive six-month breastfeeding presents a modest justification for policy change, although the larger policy discourse referred to in this publication makes broader claims for the benefits for breastfeeding. Important to note is that there is scientific evidence indicating health benefits of breastfeeding for both the mother and child, especially for the first few months after birth. Nevertheless, the scientific evidence cited supporting breastfeeding is often based on very few, non-replicated studies. In addition, the conclusiveness of the scientific studies and the relative degree of benefit conferred by breastfeeding is often exaggerated, as is the case in the

WIC advertisements above. For example, in her examination of the politics of breastfeeding, Palmer (1993) notes that breastfed babies have psychological and emotional benefits and are less likely to develop diabetes, childhood cancer, SIDS, long-term bowel disease, future coronary heart disease, and eczema, while having higher IQs; she also indicates benefits to the mother, including reduced risk of endometrial cancer, bone disease, and breast cancer (see also, for example, Jelliffe and Jelliffe 1978; Boswell-Penc 2006). Although there are studies that do indicate such benefits, as Law notes, the advocacy literature tends to promote the benefits of breastfeeding and the risks of bottle-feeding in strict categorical terms without discussing the controversies and debates concerning the data within the epidemiological community or the fact that "reliable and meaningful statistics on the effects of infant feeding methods are notoriously difficult to come by" (Law 2000, 414; see also Knaak 2006; Valaitis, Hesch et al. 2000; Clifford 2003; Blier 2006; Kramer, Matush et al. 2007; Twells and Newhook 2010). More important, as Law (2000, 422) further argues, the relative health and psychological advantages to breastfeeding can be marginal and do not take into account the complexity of intertwined risks and benefits to "family, work practices, child care decisions, social goods and labor relations."

This focus on health indicators with the marginalization of other relevant factors in infant feeding decisions is reflected in the Canadian *Exclusive Breastfeeding* publication. As noted above, this document primarily changes the Canadian policy recommendation from four to six months of exclusive breastfeeding due to additional protection against gastrointestinal infections. Within the section outlining the implications of this policy change, for the discussion of vitamins, the initiation of complementary food and growth patterns are of primary importance. Not until points seven and nine does the text focus on supporting woman who chose to not breastfeed for personal and/or social reasons and on the ramifications that this recommendation has for Canadian work and public space accommodations. Thus, while the document acknowledges that infant feeding choices are connected to social and individual variation and socioeconomic issues, these issues are not central to the implications of the recommendation and are visibly given less prominence than a potential reduction of instances of gastrointestinal infections for infants or weight loss of 0.42 kg for the nursing mother.

THEORETICAL ASSUMPTIONS OF
BREASTFEEDING POLICY IN CANADA

The Canadian policy on breastfeeding reflects several underlying, embedded assumptions that hinder a comprehensive understanding of the tensions and complexity of the breastfeeding experience for both women and children in Canada. The main focus of official policy has been on general or universalized guidelines, based on biological indicators, regarding the appropriate or proper breastfeeding practice. Although the *Exclusive Breastfeeding* document does emphasize that "special consideration is needed when applying this recommendation at the individual level," it is also an adoption of the W H O definition of and guidelines for breastfeeding and, as such, it promotes a world-wide medically based standard for a human cultural practice that has longstanding historical, social, and socioeconomic variations. Included in these guidelines is an emphasis on a child-centred discourse of "baby-friendly" hospital initiatives intended to promote practices that increase breastfeeding rates, especially targeting "unsuccessful" groups, such as women in certain ethnic groups or of lower socio-economic status. The Canadian policy emphasizes a medical perspective that assumes a highly essentialized view of a women's body as a reproductive body with a corresponding idealized perspective of nature, motherhood, and the family. Such discourse also assumes strong moralizing judgments long associated with breastfeeding practices. What is missing from the Canadian policy discourse is a "woman-friendly" perspective that recognizes the diversity of acceptable infant-feeding goals and understands the practice within the larger scope of a woman's reproductive life.

REINFORCEMENT OF THE MEDICALIZATION
OF BREASTFEEDING

Although this point has already been made, it is important to re-emphasize that the justification for Canadian policy on breastfeeding is based primarily on scientific medical evidence that relies on biomedical indicators, such as infant growth and morbidity. Also noted above, since health care is primarily a provincial power, the policy at the federal level is principally an educational campaign targeting both medical professionals and new mothers to promote the health benefits of breastfeeding. Although the infant formula industry was invited to the first meeting to discuss breastfeeding policy in Canada, by the early 1990s the actors involved in policy development were restricted to pro-breastfeeding advocacy groups, government officials, and health care associations and professionals (Nathoo and Ostry 2009). As Nathoo and Ostry (2009) also note, this partnership among government, medical professionals, and advocacy groups such as La Leche League Canada is remarkable, since many of these advocacy groups had been previously associated with the natural childbirth movement, which promoted mother-to-mother knowledge in opposition to the medicalization of childbirth and infant nutrition (represented, in this partnership, by both government and medical professionals). The current strong coalition can still break down when medical or scientific evidence conflicts with advocacy goals; for example, both W H O and Health Canada do not necessarily recommend breastfeeding, for instance, in situations where there is a risk of mother-to-child transmission (M T C T) of viral infection, as can be the case with H I V (see Savage and Lhotska 2000). Conflict can also arise when medical evidence supports supplementing premature babies' diet with formula or discontinuing breastfeeding when mothers abuse alcohol or other controlled substances (see O'Connor, Merko, et al. 2004; Riordan and Wambach 2010). Breastfeeding advocates also challenge studies on the transmission of environmental toxins in breast milk (see Berlin and LaKind et al. 2002; Boswell-Penc 2006; Boersma and Lanting 2008). In many of these cases, advocacy groups readily cite and support scientific research that confirms the benefits of breast milk but argue against any scientific studies that do not support breastfeeding practices (Law 2000).

Despite some conflict, by the end of the twentieth century in Canada a fairly secure coalition between breastfeeding advocacy groups and the medical profession had developed. The change in policy from exclusive breastfeeding for four to six months was made, for example, by the Expert Advisory Panel on Exclusive Breastfeeding. This panel consisted of medical professionals such as nurses and pediatricians as well as academics specializing in nursing, nutritional sciences, and medical education (Health Canada 2004). Other advisors to Canadian breastfeeding policy include the Infant Feeding Expert Advisory Group. This group includes experts in allergy sensitivity, infant nutrition, breastfeeding research, infant development, and lactation consultants (Health Canada 2010). Thus, in Canada, the only actors involved in policy formation include medical professionals, scientific experts such as those in nutrition and development, and lactation consultants in association with breastfeeding advocacy groups.

The current breastfeeding policy, with the support of these advocacy groups, justifies its recommendations with reference to indicators of infant nutrition and maternal health benefits. Although Health Canada tends to be cautious in its citation of health claims of breastfeeding, as Knaak (2006) notes, its documents do not always include the full range of evidence available; for example, Health Canada cites evidence that breastfeeding improves bonding between mothers and children but not data revealing that, for some mothers, breastfeeding was not relationship-enhancing but painful and burdensome (e.g., Nigro 1998; Law 2000; Giles 2003; Kouba 2007). Furthermore, as Knaak (2006) also points out, considering the close connection between medical expertise and breastfeeding advocacy, if researchers and educators are not vigilant about the ideological investments in their research, there is the potential for the foundational ethics of medical-based expertise to be undermined. Taking this potentiality into account, it is possible to question the reason that Canadian policy literature on s I D s promotes breastfeeding but not the use of pacifiers, despite research that indicates a role for pacifiers. Furthermore, it is possible to question why the only women's groups involved as actors in policy development are breastfeeding advocates, to the exclusion of a broader participation of women's advocacy groups.

The current policy is also problematic because it focuses on an educational campaign privileging a medical model policy that defines successful breastfeeding by initiation and duration rates and infant-centred indicators of growth and morbidity. Importantly, the promotional campaign based on these medical indicators has not been shown to be responsible for increasing rates of breastfeeding (Nathoo and Ostry 2006). Ironically, rates and duration of breastfeeding are more likely to increase when success can be measured not by medical indicators but by a woman's personal experience and individual goals (Nathoo and Ostry 2006; Harrison, Morse et al. 1985). Furthermore, despite Health Canada's relatively moderate justifications for exclusive breastfeeding benefits, it downplays the importance of other crucial implications in its recommendations, such as work and public accommodations. A supportive workplace environment, such as access to maternity leave or in-house accessible daycare, can be as crucial as indicators of gastrointestinal infections in a woman's decision to breastfeed or to continue breastfeeding her child. As Paterson's analysis of the medicalization of midwifery in this volume also indicates, scrutiny of this policy underscores the shift of authority over reproduction to medical experts, here exemplified by the medical model of breastfeeding. This one-size-fits-all model recommends six-month exclusive breastfeeding as the proper choice for all women without equal attention paid to the difficulties of this bio-cultural practice, as well as its larger connection to women's reproductive lives.

REINFORCEMENT OF BREASTFEEDING AS "NATURAL"

Canadian policy privileges not only the discourse of the medical model but also discourse that emphasizes breastfeeding as a natural activity. In a Public Health Agency of Canada publication called *10 Great Reasons to Breastfeed* (2009), the conclusion stresses that "breastfeeding is natural" and breastfeeding activists, too, have long argued that it is a natural practice. The word "natural," as Bartlett (2005, 18, 12–41) emphasizes, is an overloaded term with "many layers of meaning" and is particularly problematic in the discourse on breastfeeding. The term is often used in a physiological or biological sense to describe the fact that, as mammals, human beings evolved lactation to feed infants (Carter 1995; Stuart-Macadam 1995; Latteier 1998). In this sense, "natural" refers to the biological or physiological functioning of the female reproductive body. Breastfeeding, however, is not understood as natural, in the sense of an innate, effortless, or involuntary biological act; rather, most new mothers require a great deal of guidance and support for successful breastfeeding. As one new mother put it: "Natural, my butt. We are not born with any innate ability to nurse. Don't ask me how the first people figured it out" (Gore 1998, 78). "Natural," in this sense, is understood in the language of the La Leche League as "a womanly art" (Wiessinger 2010) or as Palmer's (1993) "born talent" (see also Giles 2003).

The naturalness of breastfeeding, therefore, is conceived as a sociobiological activity that requires social support and is maintained by cultural norms. The Canadian policy on exclusive breastfeeding, for example, recognizes the importance of developing sociocultural support for breastfeeding by recommending "adequate social support ... [through] community, public health, hospital, and workplace efforts" (Canada Health 2004). Inadequate social support for breastfeeding mothers, especially in the early weeks, is an oft-cited reason for the discontinuation of exclusive breastfeeding or breastfeeding altogether (see Kehler, Chaput et al. 2009). The 2004 recommendation also supports hospital initiatives, such as the baby-friendly practice, because inadequate support at hospitals also affects breastfeeding rates (Daneault, Beaudry et al. 2004; Spiby, McCormick et al. 2009). In addition, Canadian policy discourse stresses the importance of constructing cultural norms to support this biological activity. The webpage for the Breastfeeding Committee of Canada (BCC), a Health Canada Initiative, clearly states: "The vision of the BCC is to establish breastfeeding as the cultural norm for infant feeding within Canada" (Breastfeeding Committee of Canada 2010). Other government publications support this position and stress the multicultural approach to supporting breastfeeding practices (Agnew, Gilmore et al. 1997). Therefore, the use of the term "natural" in policy discourse to describe breastfeeding does not imply a biological activity in contrast to a cultural construct; rather, "natural" is understood as referring to a biological activity intertwined with cultural norm construction and social support (Stuart-Macadam 1995).

Despite this stress on the naturalness of breastfeeding as biocultural practice, breastfeeding is labelled as natural in the discourse that opposes it to the "artificiality" of infant formula (Wolf 2001; for examples see Palmer 1993; Baumslag and Michels 1995). Early promotion of breastfeeding in the 1960s stressed its naturalness in contrast to the medicalization of birth and the commercialization of infant formula, both of which undermined a woman's *natural* identity as a mother (Carter 1995). Because this discourse reintroduced a dichotomy between natural breastfeeding and artificial bottle-feeding, it simultaneously reinforced essentialist connotations associated with the purpose of the breast into the discourse (Arneil 2000). At the protest rally, for example, where Ann Simonton "reclaim[ed] our inherent right to govern our bodies," Yalom goes on to note that many participants held placards reading "our breasts are *for the newborn*, not for men's porn" (Yalom 1997, 244). In other words, in our newly claimed right to govern our bodies, the discourse still supported the female body as an essentialist body –

a woman's breast is *for* babies. This essentialized view of the breast continues to echo in more recent discourse on breastfeeding; as one supporter stated, "women have breasts for a reason, and it is ridiculous to suggest an artificial substitute when the real thing is clearly better" (*USA Today* 2005). Or, as the poet Deborah Abbott reflected: "my breasts are those of a woman who has lived long and well ... they have done their work and lie on my chest like fruit upon the ground" (Yalom 1997, 255). This language emphasizes that breasts have a function and work to do. In the struggle to reclaim breasts from the over-sexualization found in North American culture, such discourse has re-introduced and re-emphasized that a woman's true identity is found in her reproductive role. As Lee emphasizes in this volume, this discourse undermines an understanding that a woman's body is neither *for* men's sexual pleasure nor *for* baby's nutritional needs (Latteier 1998; Yalom 1997; Hausman 2003).

Furthermore, since western culture ascribes a moral authority to nature in which the natural is viewed as superior and "good," the language of breastfeeding as natural also reintroduces into the discourse an additional moralized judgment (Daston and Vidal 2003). In contemporary studies, infant feeding decisions are described as a "moral minefield" in which women can be judged and judge themselves as saints or sinners depending on whether they breastfeed or not (Murphy 1999; MacLean 1990; Knaak 2006). Such moralizing judgments of breastfeeding in the West have a long history in the sacred image of the nursing Madonna in the Middle Ages as well as in religious documents that emphasized the breastfeeding mother as the "true mother" and condemned the employment of wet-nurses as "an abomination in the eyes of the lord" (Yalom 1997). This imagery of the Virgin Mary as the archetype of a breastfeeding mother is not completely lost in the contemporary imagination; for example, Robin Fountain describes her struggle with breastfeeding in contrast to the images of the loving and peaceful Virgin and Child iconography (Fountain 1998). In most contemporary discourse, however, this overtly religious language has been replaced with the "naturalness" of breastfeeding; yet, the moral overtones remain. Knaak (2005) emphasizes that, in Canada, breastfeeding is "the moral gold standard for mothering." Women who breastfeed, and do so exclusively for six months, are labelled "successful," whereas women who are members of groups that have less "successful" rates of breastfeeding are targeted for governmental educational campaigns (for an example of research targeting such groups see Coulibaly, Seguin et al. 2006). The degree to which breastfeeding advocacy dismisses or ignores its tendency to use moralizing language is reflected, for example, in Palmer's view that "whin[ing] about not making mothers feel guilty is such a cop-out" (Palmer 1993, 83). Considering the long history of moral judgments connected to breastfeeding practices, the use of the word "natural" in the Canadian government's *10 Great Reasons to Breastfeed* educational document and its support for breastfeeding as the "cultural norm" imposes another bureaucratic judgment on women who do not breastfeed.

REINFORCEMENT OF ROMANTICIZED VIEW
OF MOTHERHOOD AND THE FAMILY

The Canadian policy on breastfeeding also reflects a romanticized or idealized view of motherhood and the family. As noted above, Canadian discourse defines successful breastfeeding by initiation and duration rates. This means that, in Canada, the successful breastfeeding mother tends to be white, older, well-educated, and from a middle- to upper-class income bracket. She also tends to have workplace employment that offers generous maternity leave benefits. Such women also tend to be part of a traditional heterosexual family, which includes a male either as the primary breadwinner or as an engaged and supportive partner. The same statistics also point out racial and class disparities in breastfeeding practices and are used to target such groups for educational campaigns. Women who are deemed unsuccessful at breastfeeding tend to be younger mothers, not of European descent, or single mothers who often are not part of an idealized and conservative traditional family. As Hausman (2003) points out, such statistics simply reflect larger racialized and class-related health disparities. Although Canadian policy stresses health care, community, and workplace support to achieve exclusive breastfeeding, it does not pay equal or enough attention to the implications of exclusive breastfeeding for the woman's and her family's (traditional or not) resources, both as an investment in the activity of breastfeeding and as a drain on other enterprises, such as her wage labour. The reality is that not all mothers have partners who are either willing or able to perform other responsibilities, such as housework, child care, or wage labour while the mother devotes time and resources to exclusive breastfeeding for six months (Blum 1999).

Nor is it the case that all mothers wish to devote their time and resources to extended exclusive breastfeeding.

The Canadian policy also assumes that, in terms of financial resources, the mother is not the sole or primary breadwinner in the
family. In the government's economic assessment of breastfeeding,
the cost of her lost wages tends not to be considered a determinant.
The typical argument for the economic savings of breastfeeding cites
the lower cost of breastfeeding in comparison with infant formula,
as well as potential economic savings in medical care payments or in
workplace sick days due to infant illness (see Baumslag and Michels
1995; Riordan and Wambach 2010). In *10 Great Reasons to
Breastfeed* (2009), the eighth reason is that "Breastfeeding saves you
money! Without question, breastfeeding saves hundreds – even
thousands – of dollars." What is often not calculated in these "savings" is the financial cost to the woman and her family of her lost or
reduced wages during her maternity leave or move to part-time
work; in addition, there are potential long-term financial consequences for the mother's career advancement and promotion, savings, and long-term pension contributions. Most important, the
recommendation that a woman exclusively breastfeed for six months
assumes that the mother and not her partner is always the most appropriate parent to take extended leave to care for their child.
Embedded in this assumption is the supposition that the partner's
and not the mother's wages contribute more to the family's financial
stability. Without this assumption of female domesticity and idealized family arrangements, workplace accommodations could not be
mentioned ninth in the implications of a policy promoting exclusive
six-month breastfeeding. Importantly, the coalition between conservative breastfeeding advocates and other feminist groups breaks
down on this assumption that policy should reflect traditional family arrangements with male breadwinners (Arneil 2000).

Breastfeeding policy and much of the medical model underlying it
also conceptualizes an idealized view of the mother and child as a
unit with unconditionally identical interests. Jennifer Peddlesden,
former co-chairman of the Breastfeeding Committee for Canada, for
example, supported the theory that "mother and babies are intended
to function as one unit for months after birth" (*Weaned Prematurely*
1999). Lactating specialists, some of whom are advisors on Canada's
Infant Feeding Expert Advisory Group, also emphasize that "the
breastfeeding mother-baby dyad is a single psychological organism"

(Riordan and Wambach 2010; Hausman 2003). This idealized view is also reflected on the covers of breastfeeding books, which often bear a striking resemblance to images of the nursing Madonna in the Middle Ages: in both the medieval paintings and contemporary book covers, serene images of perfectly calm and content breastfeeding babies look up at smiling and relaxed mothers. Such images fail to represent the wide range of emotions many women feel about their experience of motherhood, including feelings of ambivalence regarding one's child, sense of emotional detachment at failures to breastfeed or other aspects of mothering, or the frustration felt by the constant demands of their children (for examples of first-person narratives, see Lawrence 2007; Berry 2009; Restaino 2009). Even the language of the Baby-Friendly Initiative assumes a unit or dyad in which one can promote breastfeeding as a "baby-friendly" policy, because presumably the baby's needs are never in conflict with her mother's needs. This idealized view of motherhood does not recognize that both the mother and child are agents that do not always have identical needs or demands (see Hausman 2003; Hrdy 1999). This is not to suggest that women's interests are necessarily or always antithetical to their newborn children's needs or that, as agents, women do not choose to breastfeed their children or exclusively breastfeed their baby for six months. Instead, the dyad or unit perspective of mother and child is highly problematic because it undermines the complexity of the decision-making process and collapses conflicting needs and goals concerning infant feeding decisions. Of equal importance, the Canadian policy that emphasizes this idealized view of motherhood as a "unit" or "dyad" detaches the practice of breastfeeding from the larger domain of women's reproductive lives, which includes mothering long after weaning and other aspects of women's reproductive health.

RECOMMENDATIONS FOR A RE-ORIENTATION OF BREASTFEEDING POLICY

Breastfeeding in Canada represents a touchstone issue or a "central dilemma of feminism" (Carter 1995). On the one hand, breastfeeding offers relative nutritional and epidemiological advantages for infants and mothers and, for many women, promotes bonding with their new child. On the other hand, as a bio-cultural practice, breastfeeding epitomizes a woman's heavier reproductive burden, which can place the practice in conflict with other needs and goals of the mother and her family. The current Canadian policy to recommend an increase of exclusive breastfeeding emphasizes health benefits, such as fewer instances of gastrointestinal inflections and delayed menses, while giving less prominence to the corresponding social and workplace support needed to achieve this goal.

Thus, one main weakness of the current breastfeeding policy in Canada is that it places demands on women and their bodies with no real corresponding service provisions, other than recommending public and workplace support, necessary for women to meet Health Canada's recommendation. In Canada since 1997, it has been the courts that have provided some protection for public and workplace accommodation, in the legal decision of *Poirier v. British Columbia* and the controversy over Swiss Chalet Restaurant's decision to participate in a national breastfeeding promotion (see Arneil 2000; Law 2000; Nathoo and Ostry 2009. See also Woodard 1997). The *Poirier* ruling, argued from the basis of non-discrimination based on sex, found that accommodation must be made for breastfeeding women in the workplace. On the one hand, this accommodation was seen as a victory for a woman's right to breastfeed; on the other hand, the ruling can be seen as limited, since workplace accommodation can be met by making minimal provisions for pumping breast milk. Therefore, like the WTO definition that includes "expressed breast milk" as part of exclusive breastfeeding, this ruling focused on breastfeeding as defined by the goal of infant nutrition. As Arneil argues, such accommodation is simultaneously a retrenchment of understanding and a reduction of the complexity of a woman's reproductive body to that of the ideal disembodied "male" worker. Moreover, as this is a provincial ruling, considerable variation in a woman's right to breastfeed in public or in the workplace exists across the provinces. As many scholars have noted, this limited support is inadequate; for breastfeeding to be a realistic choice for many women, adequate maternity leave and adaptations to the workplace for breastfeeding women cannot be penultimate in a list of implications but must be weighted as a central contributor to infant feeding decisions (Spisak and Gross 1991; Heymann and Kramer 2009).

The advocacy to increase workplace and public accommodation, however, still does not address the complexity surrounding breastfeeding policy. Increasing work and public space accommodations may help to remedy constraints currently imposed on women who choose to breastfeed but such improvements do not benefit women who choose not to breastfeed. Current policy does suggest that, for both personal and social reasons, some women choose not to breast-feed exclusively and that such "parents need to be supported and given appropriate information to enable informed decisions to en-sure optimal infant nutrition." However, since Health Canada in the same document defines breastfeeding as *the optimal infant nutrition*, women who choose not to breastfeed are considered targets for education campaigns (author's emphasis; for targeting certain groups see Berry 2009). Respect for diversity in infant feeding deci-sions requires the real possibility that there can be more than one proper, rational, or correct choice: if six months of exclusive breast-feeding is the only proper choice, than realistically there is no choice (Knaak 2005; see also Kedrowski and Lipscomb 2008). As an alter-native to the medicalized model, which focuses on success defined as duration and initiation rates, many scholars, including Lee and Nathoo and Ostry in this volume, have suggested that successful breastfeeding be defined by a woman's perspective of her own breastfeeding experience or her own infant-feeding goals (see also Harrison, Morse et al. 1985; Nathoo and Ostry 2009).

In contrast to the medical model and its focus on a baby-friendly policy, it is imperative to develop a woman-friendly perspective that understands breastfeeding decisions as complex and holistic, since any given infant-feeding decision is based on a cost-benefit analysis connected to other desires and constraints of individual and family needs (Law 2000). A woman-friendly perspective includes support-ing a diversity of breastfeeding experiences, from the woman who does not breastfeed to the woman who breastfeeds longer than the typical western cultural expectations. A woman-friendly perspective supports a range of possibilities for discontinuing the practice, from economic choices to the rarely examined lower sexual desire many women experience during breastfeeding, which is often a factor in the mother's choice to wean (LaMarre and Paterson et al. 2003). Such a woman-friendly perspective stands outside and beyond universal medical indicators and does more to reflect the individu-al, bio-cultural, and socio-economic diversity of the practice of breastfeeding.

Finally, the current Canadian policy tends to detach or isolate infant-feeding decisions from the broader context of a woman's re-productive life. This disconnect is even highlighted in the recent judicial rulings and Health Canada recommendations to re-orient the workplace to accommodate the lactating mother; as noted above, both the *Poirier* decision and the Health Canada definition of exclusive breastfeeding focus on providing for infant nutrition. Correspondingly, workplace accommodations in Canada do not focus on protecting the broader needs of a lactating female worker, such as protecting potential psychological benefits for the mother while breastfeeding or the cultural variations of breastfeeding practices. Focusing breastfeeding on infant nutrition essentially detaches and fractures the experience of breastfeeding from the wider context of a woman's reproductive life. In contrast, breastfeeding can be understood as a bio-cultural activity that is part of a broader and meaningful reproductive life; as Gustafson and Porter describe in this volume, reproductive life includes a wide understanding of relational and situational influences on a woman as she "moves" through the stages in her life.

CONCLUSION

Understanding breastfeeding within this broader context of women's "reproductive lives" requires a theoretical and policy approach that seeks wider accommodation for breastfeeding not primarily based on infant nutrition but as part of the life of an embodied female experience. This woman-friendly approach would provide a new emphasis for work and public space accommodations beyond the longstanding focus on the needs of newborn infants. Although a baby-friendly perspective may be an easier sell than a woman-friendly approach, arguments based on infant nutrition isolate breastfeeding from the stages of a female reproductive life. "Who would not support," as one of my students remarked, "something good for cute little babies?" In contrast, the embodied woman has a reproductive system that is not always so cute. The embodied woman not only provides nutrition for cute babies, but also possesses a body that may contract nipple soreness, breast infections (mastitis), or thrush. This body may have an unwanted pregnancy or have difficulty reproducing and require emotionally draining and physiologically dangerous hormones to attempt IVF. It is an embodied life that menstruates, with all its potential complications of ovarian cysts, endometriosis, and monthly "weepy days," and it is a life that experiences menopause, potentially accompanied by years of hot flashes, fatigue, and osteoporosis. Women have a reproductive life that cares for children long after they are weaned and, often simultaneously, supports sick and aging parents. Understanding breastfeeding as part of a stage in this reproductive life means that accommodations for breastfeeding are not reducible to infant nutrition; rather, it is all stages of a reproductive female body that need accommodation within these wider social and economic spaces.

In contrast, by viewing breastfeeding primarily through the lens of infant health indicators, the Canadian policy adopts a discourse that promotes an idealized view of breastfeeding as "natural," with the "successful" mother properly providing her breast for her baby's nutritional needs. The current policy both downplays the relevance of larger social and economic considerations by relegating work and public accommodations to secondary on the list of implications of its main breastfeeding recommendations. Furthermore, when made, the recommendation for public accommodation is based on securing infant nutrition rather than on accommodating a women's reproductive body. This focus on infant nutrition perpetuates a discourse that isolates and fractures the experience of breastfeeding from the larger context of the complexity of women's reproductive lives. Breastfeeding policy, therefore, does continue to present a touchstone issue for feminism as it highlights the persistently fragmented approach in Canada to accommodating a fully embodied female reproductive life.

NOTE

1 I would like to thank the participants of the Fertile Ground Workshop at Concordia University (September 2010), Jenna Germaine, and the anonymous reviewers for their comments on a previous version of this paper.

BIBLIOGRAPHY

Agnew, Teresa, Joan Gilmore, et al. 1997. "A Multicultural Perspective of Breastfeeding." Ottawa: Minister of Public Works and Government Services Canada.

Arneil, Barbara. 2000. "The Politics of the Breast." *Canadian Journal of Women and the Law / Revue Femmes et Droit* 12: 346–70.

Apple, Rima. 2006. *Perfect Motherhood*. New Brunswick: Rutgers University Press.

Bartlett, Allison. 2005. *Breastwork*. Sydney: University of New South Wales Press.

Baumslag, Niomi, and Dia Michels. 1995. *Milk, Money, and Madness: The Culture and Politics of Breastfeeding*. Westport: Bergin & Garvey.

Berlin, Cheston M., Judy S. LaKind et al. 2002. "Conclusions, Research Needs, and Recommendations of the Expert Panel." *Journal of Toxicology and Environmental Health* 65: 1929–35.

Berry, Patricia. 2009. "Because I Don't Want To." In *Unbuttoned*, Dana Sullivan and Maureen Connelly, eds., 124–32. Boston: Harvard Common Press.

Black, Ray, Marshall Godwin, et al. 2008. "Breastfeeding Among the Ontario James Bay Cree." *Canadian Journal of Public Health* 99(2): 98–101.

Blier, Pierre. 2006. "Pregnancy, Depression, Antidepressants, and Breast-Feeding." *Review of Psychiatric Neuroscience* 31(4): 226–8.

Blum, Linda. 1999. *At the Breast*. Boston: Beacon Press.

Boersma, E.R., and C. Lanting. 2008. "Environmental Exposure to Polychlorinated Biphenyls (PCBs) and Dioxins." In *Short and Long Term Effects of Breast Feeding on Child Health*, Berthold Koletzko, Kim Fletcher Michaelsen et al., eds., 271–87. New York: Kluwer Academic/Plenum Publishers.

Boswell-Penc, Maia. 2006. *Tainted Milk*. Albany: State University of New York Press.

Breastfeeding Committee for Canada. 2010. "Breastfeeding Canada." Accessed 19 August. http://breastfeedingcanada.ca/.

Callaghan, Ann, Garth Kendall et al. 2005. "Association Between Pacifier Use and Breastfeeding, Sudden Infant Death Syndrome, Infection and Dental Malocclusion." *International Journal of Evidence-Based Healthcare* 3(6): 147–67.

Carter, Pam. 1995. *Feminism, Breasts, and Breast-Feeding*. New York: St. Martin's Press.

Chalmers, Beverley, Cheryl Levitt, et al. 2009. "Breastfeeding Rates and Hospital Breastfeeding Practices in Canada: A National Survey of Women." *Birth* 36(2): 22–32.

Clifford, Tammy J. 2003. "Breast Feeding and Obesity: The Evidence Regarding Its Effects on Obesity is Inconclusive." *British Medical Journal* 327(7420): 879–80.

Coulibaly, Ramata, Louise Seguin, et al. 2006. "Links between Maternal Breast-Feeding Duration and Quebec Infants' Health." *Maternal Child Health Journal* 10: 537–43.

Daneault, Suzzane, Micheline Beaudry, et al. 2004. "Psychosocial Determinants of the Intention of Nurses and Dietitians to Recommend Breast-feeding." *Canadian Journal of Public Health* 95(2): 151–4.

Daston, Lorraine, and Fernando Vidal, eds. 2003. *The Moral Authority of Nature*. Chicago: University of Chicago Press.

Dubois, Lise, and Manon Girard. 2003. "Social Inequalities in Infant Feeding during the First Year of Life." *Public Health Nutrition* 6(8): 773–83.

Fountain, Robin. 1998. "If It Was Good Enough for Mary." In *The Reality of Breastfeeding*, Ann Benson Brown and Kathryn Reed McPherson, eds., 97–100. Westport: Bergin & Garvey.

Giles, Fiona. 2003. *Fresh Milk*. New York: Simon and Schuster.

Gore, Ariel. 1998. *The Hip Mama Survival Guide*. New York: Hyperion.

Harrison, Margaret J., J.M. Morse, et al. 1985. "Successful Breast Feeding: The Mother's Dilemma." *Journal of Advanced Nursing* 10: 261–9.

Hausman, Bernice. L. 2003. *Mother's Milk: Breastfeeding Controversies in American Culture*. New York: Routledge.

Health Canada. 2004. "Exclusive Breastfeeding Duration." http://www.brandonrha.mb.ca/export/sites/brandonrha/galleries/pdf/Having_a_Baby/Canada_Health_Breastfeeding.pdf.

Health Canada. 2005. "Sudden Infant Death Syndrome (s i d s)." Accessed 19 August 2010. http://www.hc-sc.gc.ca/hl-vs/babies-bebes/sids-smsn/index-eng.php.

Health Canada. 2008. "Breast Cancer." Accessed 10 September 2013. http://www.phac-aspc.gc.ca/cd-mc/cancer/breast_cancer-cancer_du_sein-eng.php.

Health Canada. 2010. "Membership of the Infant Feeding Expert Advisory Group." Accessed 19 August 2010. http://www.hc-sc.gc.ca/fn-an/nutrition/infant-nourisson/eag-gce-inf-nour-membership-membres-eng.php#sum.

Henderson-Smart, D.J., A.L. Ponsonby, et al. 1998. "Reducing the Risk of Sudden Infant Death Syndrome: A Review of the Scientific Evidence." *Journal of Paediatric Child Health* 34: 213–19.

Heymann, Jody, and Michael S. Kramer. 2009. "Public Policy and Breast-Feeding: A Straightforward and Significant Solution." *Canadian Journal of Public Health* 100(5): 381–3.

Hrdy, Sarah Blaffer. 1999. *Mother Nature: A History of Mothers, Infants, and Natural Selection.* New York: Random House.

Jelliffe, Derek B., and E.F. Patrice Jelliffe. 1978. *Human Milk in the Modern World.* Oxford: Oxford University Press.

Jernström, H., J. Lubinski, et al. 2004. "Breast-Feeding and the Risk of Breast Cancer in BRCA1 and BRCA2 Mutation Carriers." *Journal of the National Cancer Institute* 96(14): 1094–8.

Kedrowski, Karen M., and Michael E. Lipscomb. 2008. *Breastfeeding Rights in the United States.* Westport: Praeger.

Kehler, Heather L., Katie H. Chaput, et al. 2009. "Risk Factors for Cessation of Breastfeeding Prior to Six Months Postpartum among a Community Sample of Women in Calgary, Alberta." *Canadian Journal of Public Health* 100(5): 376–80.

Knaak, Stephanie. 2005. "Breast-Feeding, Bottle-Feeding and Dr. Spock: The Shifting Context of Choice." *Canadian Review of Sociology and Anthropology* 42(2): 197–216.

Knaak, Stephanie. 2006. "The Problem with Breastfeeding Discourse." *Canadian Journal of Public Health* 97(5): 412–14.

Kouba, Jean. 2007. "Some Women Found Breast Feeding Physically and Emotionally Demanding." *Evidence-Based Nursing* 10(2): 62.

Kramer, Michael S., Lidia Matush, et al. 2007. "Effect of Prolonged and Exclusive Breast Feeding on Risk of Allergy and Asthma." *British Medical Journal* 335(7624): 815–18.

LaMarre, Amanda K., Laurel Q. Paterson, et al. 2003. "Breastfeeding and Postpartum Maternal Sexual Functioning." *The Canadian Journal of Human Sexuality* 12(3–4): 151–68.

Latteier, Carolyn. 1998. *Breasts: The Women's Perspective on an American Obsession.* New York: The Haworth Press.

Law, Jules. 2000. "The Politics of Breastfeeding: Assessing Risk, Dividing Labor." *Signs* 25(2): 407–51.

Lawrence, Jen. 2007. "Unhinged." In *Between Interruptions*, Cori Haward, ed., 143–53. Toronto: Key Porter Books.

Levitt, Cheryl A., Janusz Kaczorowski, et al. 1996. "Breast-Feeding Policies and Practices in Canadian Hospitals Providing Maternity Care." *Canadian Medical Association Journal* 155(2): 181–8.

Luke, Barbara. "Weaned Prematurely." 2009. *Alberta Report*, 24 May: 26.

MacLean, Heather. 1990. *Women's Experience of Breast Feeding.* Toronto: University of Toronto Press.

Millar, Wayne J., and Heather Maclean. 2005. *Health Reports.* Ottawa: Statistics Canada. Health Statistics Division 16: 23–34.

Moon, Rachel Y., and Linda Y. Fu. 2007. "Sudden Infant Death Syndrome." *Pediatrics in Review* 28(6): 209–14.

Murphy, Elizabeth. 1999. "Breast is Best: Infant Feeding Decisions and Maternal Deviance." *Sociology of Health and Illness* 21(2): 187–208.

Nathoo, Tasmin, and Aleck Ostry. 2009. *The One Best Way: Breastfeeding, Politics, and Policy in Canada.* Waterloo: Wilfred Laurier University Press.

New-York-State. 2010. "NYSDOH WIC Breastfeeding Campaign 2." Accessed 21 October. http://www.youtube.com/watch?v=qjo WWUYDKQM.

Nigro, Mary Blanchet. 1998. "How I Stopped Worrying and Learned to Love the Bottle." In *The Reality of Breastfeeding*, Amy Benson Brown and Kathryn Read McPherson, eds. Westport: Bergin and Garvey.

O'Connor, Deborah L., Susan Merko, et al. 2004. "Human Milk Feeding of Very Low Birth Weight Infants During Initial Hospitalization and after Discharge." *Nutrition Today* 38(3): 102–11.

Painter, Kim. "SIDS Guidelines Stir Up a Storm." 2005. *USA Today*, 25 October: 6d.

Palda, Valerie. A., Jeannie-Marie Guise, et al. 2004. "Interventions to Promote Breast-Feeding: Applying the Evidence in Clinical Practice." *Canadian Medical Association Journal* 170(6): 976–8.

Palmer, Gabrielle. 1993. *The Politics of Breastfeeding.* New York: Harper Collins.

Public Health Agency of Canada. 2009. "10 Great Reasons to Breastfeed Your Baby." Accessed 19 October 2010. http://www.phac-aspc.gc.ca/hp-ps/dca-dea/stages-etapes/childhood-enfance_0-2/nutrition/reasons-raisons-eng.php.

Public Health Agency of Canada. *What Mothers Say: The Canadian Maternity Experiences Survey.* Ottawa, 2009. http://www.phac-aspc.gc.ca/rhs-ssg/survey-enquete/ref-eng.php.

Restaino, Jessica. 2009. "Drained." In *UnButtoned*, Dana Sullivan and Maureen Connolly, eds., 142–50. Boston: Harvard Common Press.

Riordan, Jan, and Karen Wambach. 2010. *Breastfeeding and Human Lactation.* Boston: Jones and Bartlett Publishers.

Savage, Filicity, and Lida Lhotska. 2000. "Recommendations on Feeding Infants of HIV Positive Mothers." In *Short and Long Term Effects of Breast Feeding on Child Health*, Berthold Koletzko, Kim Fletcher

Michaelsen, et al., eds., 401–2. New York: Kluwer Academic/Plenum Publishers.

Spiby, Helen, Felicia McCormick, et al. 2009. "A Systematic Review of Education and Evidence-Based Practice Interventions with Health Professionals and Breast Feeding Councillors on Duration of Breast Feeding." *Midwifery* 25: 50–61.

Spisak, Shelly, and Susan Shapiro Gross. 1991. *Breastfeeding and Human Lactation*. Washington: National Center for Education in Maternal and Child Health.

Stuart-Macadam, Patricia. 1995. "Biocultural Perspectives on Breast-feeding." In *Breastfeeding: Biocultural Perspectives*, Patricia Stuart-Macadam and Katherine A. Dettwyler, eds., 1–38. New York: Walter de Gruyter.

Tonz, Otmar. 2000. "Breastfeeding in Modern and Ancient Times." In *Short and Long Term Effects of Breast Feeding on Child Health*, Berthold Koletzko, Kim Fletcher Michaelsen et al., eds., 1–21. New York: Kluwer Academic/Plenum Publishers.

Twells, Laurie, and Leigh Ann Newhook. 2010. "Can Exclusive Breastfeeding Reduce the Likelihood of Childhood Obesity in Some Regions of Canada?" *Canadian Journal of Public Health* 101(1): 36–9.

Valaitis, Ruta, Richard Hesch, et al. 2000. "A Systematic Review of the Relationship between Breastfeeding and Early Childhood Caries." *Canadian Journal of Public Health* 91(6): 411–17.

Vennemann, M., T. Bajanowski, et al. 2007. "Do Risk Factors Differ between Explained Sudden Unexpected Death in Infancy and Sudden Infant Death Syndrome." *Archive of Disease in Childhood* 92: 133–6.

Wiessinger, Diane. 2010. *The Womanly Art of Breastfeeding*. New York: Ballantine.

Wolf, Jacqueline H. 2001. *Don't Kill Your Baby*. Columbus: Ohio State University Press.

Woodard, Joe. 1997. "Let it All Hang Out, Modestly." *Alberta Report* 24(46).

Yalom, Marilyn. 1997. *A History of the Breast*. New York: Ballantine Books.

9

Doctor Knows Best: The Illusion of Reproductive Freedom in Canada

JULIA THOMSON-PHILBROOK

Ask a Canadian what differences exist between Canadian and American cultures, and single-payer health insurance is usually the first answer. Depending on individual interests, a plethora of other social values are potential seconds. Higher education funding. Gun control. Capital punishment. Gay marriage. First Nations. Language. Multiculturalism. Abortion.

Wait, abortion? Certainly, unlike Canada's neighbour to the south, where abortion debate appears increasingly vitriolic and the two-year election cycle of state and national representatives keeps abortion near the top of the public agenda, public opinion polls over the last decade consistently show that a majority of Canadians support legal abortion and current abortion policy.[1] Dr Henry Morgentaler, whose name is synonymous with the Canadian pro-choice movement, was named to the Order of Canada, Canada's highest civilian honour, in 2008.[2] No government has seriously tried to re-criminalize abortion since the Senate defeated Bill C-43 in 1992, and in the 2011 election, Prime Minister Stephen Harper promised to keep abortion off the table in a Conservative government (Church 2011). It appears that a consensus in favour of legal abortion is considerably more entrenched in Canada than it is in the United States.

Is this consensus reflected in Canadian law? Certainly many prominent Canadians believe that abortion is a constitutional "right" in Canada, and speak of abortion as though this were the case. For example, the Abortion Rights Coalition of Canada's spring 2009 newsletter argues, "Anti-abortionists seem offended by the claim that the debate is closed, with the issue settled by the Supreme Court in 1988. Equitable access to legal abortion has been deemed fundamental to women's constitutional rights" (Arthur 2009, 1). In a 2006 speech in Toronto, then-m p candidate for the Liberal Party Michael Ignatieff explained his return to Canada after many years in the United States in part because, "I didn't want to live in a country where a woman's right to choose is still a battleground as opposed to an acquired Constitutional right" (Bryden 2006). "Ordinary" Canadians also struggle to correctly identify Canadian abortion policy: while 21 per cent know that Canada does not restrict abortion at all, a staggering 41 per cent of Canadians are under the impression that abortions are legal only in the first trimester (Angus Reid 2010). The latter, of course, is the framework established by the American Supreme Court in *Roe v. Wade*, and has nothing whatsoever to do with Canadian abortion policy.

It would surprise many, then, to learn that the US Supreme Court found abortion to fall under the protection of the US Bill of Rights, while the Canadian Supreme Court refused to explicitly tie the practice to the constitutional rights of women in Canada. The US Supreme Court found in *Roe v. Wade* (1973) that the implicit constitutional right to privacy extended to abortion. Significantly, seven out of the nine American justices joined the majority opinion, creating a precedent that established the right of women to choose (Garrow 1998). The threat of reversal looms,[3] but as Fallon (2006) points out, the notion that reversing the *Roe* precedent would somehow "wipe the legal slate clean" (611) and allow the courts to "escape the abortion wars" (612) are fallacies, not least because of the nationalization of abortion politics encouraged by the decision.

In Canada, however, the Canadian Supreme Court struck down the existing abortion law in *R. v. Morgentaler* (1988) because it was too complicated, not because a woman had the right to abortion itself. And while five out of the seven justices voted to strike down the existing criminal law that regulated abortion, only three of those argued that a woman had a constitutional right to abortion in Canada. Further, these five justices created three opinions, each of which no more than two justices signed. As such, no clear precedent emerged out of the *Morgentaler* decision, much less a clear constitutional right to choose for Canadian women.

In this chapter, I compare and contrast Canadian and American abortion politics to show that the respective judicial sagas that culminated in the *Roe* and *Morgentaler* decisions reflect the fundamental institutional differences between the two countries. The traditions found in the Westminster parliamentary system reduced the scope of judicial challenges in Canada compared with those in the United States. Canadian women's groups initially struggled for attention precisely because the notion of parliamentary supremacy and the lack of constitutionally established rights prevented them from making legitimate claims for abortion rights. Once the constitutionally entrenched Charter of Rights and Freedoms took effect in 1982, women and women's groups were already backbenchers in the abortion debate, leading to a court challenge fundamentally different from *Roe*. In the United States, however, women's groups were able to bring their grievances directly to the Supreme Court, because the United States enjoys a long history of both judicial review, the doctrine that subjects legislative and executive actions to judicial oversight, as established in *Marbury v. Madison* in 1803; and a Bill of Rights, adopted in 1791. These key differences shaped movement strategies and help to explain the drastically different opinions found in *Roe* and *Morgentaler* and their subsequent aftermaths. Specifically, the *Morgentaler* decision led to two distinct trends in Canadian abortion politics.

First, and as discussed in more detail below, *Morgentaler* legitimized the traditional medical discourse instead of adopting a rights-based one, leaving women seeking abortions dependent on doctors. The *Roe* opinion, on the other hand, rejected the medical discourse in favour of a rights-based one. While Americans legitimately argue over a woman's right to choose, and the concept of "fetal rights" or the "right to life" has taken hold amid a rights-based discourse, Canadians would be more apt to point to a doctor's right to perform an abortion than a woman's right to obtain one.

Second, because the Canadian Supreme Court reiterated Parliament's authority to legislate abortion in the *Morgentaler* decision, the House of Commons remains the key to establishing abortion rights in Canada. Policy-makers have largely been able to avoid the subject since the Mulroney government's failed attempt to re-criminalize abortion in 1992, insisting instead that doctors decide. In other words, Parliament hides behind the traditional medical discourse used in *Morgentaler* to leave a political hot potato untouched.

Pro-choice groups need legislation – or even potential legislation – to bring the issue back to the forefront of Canadian politics, and the absence of such legislation leaves these groups in a compromising and vulnerable position as they remain on the fringes of Canadian politics. Comparatively, in the United States after *Roe*, pro-choice groups became the legitimate representatives of pro-choice Americans. Ironically, while *Roe* may have sparked one of the most contentious and enduring policy debates in American history, women's reproductive rights remain at the forefront of the American psyche. In Canada, the medical establishment guards reproductive freedom, and abortion policy itself remains a mystery to many Canadians. As a result, women have little recourse in the Canadian political system or sympathy or understanding among the public when provinces restrict abortion access.

I do not argue that American women enjoy a level of access to abortion that Canadian women do not. In fact, both countries have states and provinces where women have difficulty obtaining safe abortions.[4] Significant hurdles often make it difficult to access safe and legal abortions in many states, and I do not intend to dismiss these barriers to abortion access. However, American women enjoy a constitutional right to choose abortion, although various limits, notably funding restrictions, work to limit access. In Canada, women remain in the shadows of abortion policy, and abortion rights are inherently more precarious.

DOCTOR KNOWS BEST: THE ESTABLISHMENT OF MEDICAL DISCOURSE IN NORTH AMERICA

Before the late nineteenth century, abortion was readily available in both the United States and the British Empire, including Canada. If they could not afford doctor's fees, or if they could not find a doctor willing to perform one, women could visit midwives or apothecaries and obtain abortions relatively easily.

Only after doctors objected to the circumstances under which women were receiving the procedure did the United States begin to criminalize it. In fact, the criminalization of abortion in the nineteenth century resulted from a group of organized doctors seeking to maximize their economic status and to further professionalize medicine (Mohr 1978; Luker 1984; Tatalovich 1997). Certainly, the case of Madame Restell, a famous abortionist practising in New York

City in the nineteenth century, infuriated doctors, not least because she called herself a physician despite having no training (Carlson 2009). Policy-makers in all fifty states complied with the newly established doctors' associations and passed legislation regulating abortion, first to establish acceptable abortion providers and set gestational limits according to quickening, then to make abortion illegal altogether, occasionally with some exceptions for the life of the mother as determined by her doctor.[5] This legislative progression saw doctors wrest control from midwives and apothecaries, the Madame Restells, and women themselves, and become the gatekeepers of the procedure.

In Canada, before Confederation, rules and regulations followed the laws of the United Kingdom,[6] where the Ellenborough Act of 1803 decried "certain other heinous offences, committed with ... intent to procure the miscarriage of women ... have been of late also frequently committed" and banned abortion after quickening. In 1837, legislation dropped the quickening distinction to make all abortion illegal. The Dominion of Canada followed suit in 1869.

In Canada, as in the United States, Tatalovich (1997) argues that a fear of unlicensed individuals performing dangerous abortions on women drove doctors and others to encourage the ban on abortions. The trial of Dr Emily Stowe, a homeopathic doctor trained in the United States and refused a licence by Ontario's medical establishment, centred on her sex and her suitability to practise medicine (Backhouse 1991). Backhouse argues that the desire to regulate abortion came out of physicians' fear of declining birthrates among "the better class of inhabitants" (1991, 166), partially due to the ready access to abortion, but also notes that doctors resented the loss of patients and fees to unlicensed "abortionists."

Regardless, doctors in both the United States and Canada sought to legislate abortion to wrest control of the procedure. In this, they were overwhelmingly successful. While at the beginning of the nineteenth century women largely enjoyed access to contraceptive and abortion services, by its end Canadian and American doctors had successfully lobbied governments to make the procedure illegal, often with heavy penalties for both abortionists and the women who sought them. Thus, the nineteenth century saw the creation of a "medical discourse" surrounding abortion, just as Nathoo and Ostry in this volume (chapter 11) point out the medicalization of breastfeeding, while Paterson (chapter 7) and Johnson (chapter 4) speak to the privileging of medical expertise in birthing practices.

The establishment of this discourse is significant for many reasons, but particularly because it helped cement the American and Canadian medical establishments' control over the abortion issue and established similarly narrow policy legacies in both countries. Jenson points out that discourse functions "by setting boundaries to political action and by limiting the range of actors that are accorded the status of legitimate participants, the range of issues considered to be included in the realm of meaningful political debate, the policy alternatives feasible for implementation, and the alliance strategies available for achieving change" (1987, 65). In other words, once the medical discourse gained acceptance, doctors and policy-makers became the sole legitimate participants of the debate, and as such, controlled the scope of the debate and the means for policy change.

Accordingly, most of the prominent actors in the initial abortion reform movements in the twentieth century were doctors. For example, British doctor Aleck Bourne, a member of the Abortion Law Reform Association, challenged the British law against abortion in 1939. Bourne was found to be acting in "good faith" when procuring a miscarriage for a young woman, and the success of the defence essentially offered doctors a means to provide legal abortions in certain circumstances. Because English common law continued to guide Canadian policy, the Bourne defence likely also applied to Canadian doctors, although Tatalovich (1997) is careful to point out that it was never tested. In Canada, doctors led the abortion reform movement in the 1960s (Tatalovich 1997; Brodie, Gavigan, and Jensen 1991). Similarly, in the United States, doctors were the driving force behind the abortion liberalization movement of the 1950s. Doctors were clearly at the forefront of the abortion reform movements in both Canada and the United States.

This is not to suggest that women's groups were not actively protesting abortion restrictions and demanding legislative change. The abortion reform movement truly exploded in the late 1960s and early 1970s with the second wave of feminism, and several pro-choice groups emerged to lobby their respective government elites for abortion policy reform. In 1966, the National Organization for Women (NOW) was founded in the United States, followed by the National Action League for the Repeal of Abortion Laws (NARAL) in 1969.[7] In Canada, the Canadian Association for the Repeal of the Abortion Law (CARAL) organized in 1974.[8] These groups joined the national discussions surrounding abortion, and in many cases became representatives of certain groups of pro-choice women.[9] Yet women's groups were relatively insignificant actors in these abortion debates, precisely because the medical discourse allowed doctors and policy-makers to control the scope of the debate. Further, pro-choice groups used a rights discourse and not a medical one, so they had difficulty establishing themselves as legitimate actors in the abortion reform debate.

Further constraining women's pro-choice groups from legitimate participation were the Canadian and American institutional configurations. First, the federal systems potentially allowed both federal and regional governments to legislate abortion, creating confusion among the reform movement and policy-makers. Second, the parliamentary system in Canada allowed policy-makers to ignore pro-choice groups altogether, while the presidential system in the United States created a plethora of hoops through which potential legislation had to jump.

Both countries have federal systems that make jurisdiction over abortion far from clear. In Canada, the federal government regulates the Criminal Code, but the provinces are responsible for health care delivery. Because abortion has historically been subject to criminal statutes, it has historically been regulated at the federal level. However, as the providers of care, the provinces also have an important stake in the debate.

In the United States, the states regulate criminality and therefore abortion. Pro-choice groups faced fifty state laws requiring reform. However, abortion is arguably also under federal jurisdiction through the interstate commerce clause of the US Constitution. The Supreme Court determined in *Gibbons v. Ogden* (1824) that the interstate commerce clause allows the federal government to regulate commercial transactions between states. In the case of abortion, as some states began to offer abortion on demand, and as women travelled between states to undergo the procedure, the federal government arguably had a legitimate constitutional stake in abortion policy. While today both countries have moved toward a greater nationalization of abortion politics, the dual jurisdiction over abortion still exists. For example, both federal and state governments have passed rules and regulations concerning abortion funding that have been upheld by the Supreme Court.[10]

In Canada, the parliamentary system allowed policy-makers to maintain party discipline and effectively dismiss pro-choice groups altogether. Further, the Westminster parliamentary system that Canada uses tends to produce majority governments, allowing the executive branch to control the scope of debate and policy change. Thus, successive majority governments were able to focus abortion policy discussion on the needs of doctors. After all, abortion remained in the Criminal Code, so it was clearly up to the federal government to decriminalize the procedure. Policy-makers preferred this route because it allowed them to avoid blame for abortion policy, pointing instead to the responsible doctors who supported legislative change (or the status quo).

In the United States, numerous veto points, or "areas of institutional vulnerability where a mobilization of opposition can thwart a policy reform" (Richardt 2003, 90), allowed for confusion and diluted initiatives. This is because a separation of powers characterizes the presidential system, and legislation requires consent from a bicameral legislature as well as the executive branch. While the system undeniably allowed women more access to policy-makers than their Canadian counterparts, doctors, pro-life groups, and religious leaders also had access.

Thus, the medical discourse and the dominant institutional configurations meant that Canadian and American policy-makers could effectively ignore women altogether. The medical discourse also allowed policy-makers to crown doctors and their legal representatives as the sole legitimate actors in the debates, and the institutional configurations helped to limit the participation of women altogether and drown out women's claims. In the United States, various state medical and law associations, along with their national counterparts, the American Medical Association (AMA) and the American Law Institute (ALI), enjoyed considerable access to the state legislatures and therefore the ability to influence the public agenda. As a result, "women's interests were not as well represented as those of lawyers, doctors, and public health personnel" (Rubin 1982, 25). Further, the two dominant party associations refused to incorporate abortion into their platforms (Crotty 1984). In Canada, the Canadian Medical Association (CMA) and the Canadian Bar Association

(C B A) testified before House committees on abortion policy reform while women's groups protested outside (Jenson 1992; Gavigan 1992). Canadian "debates about state regulation ... occurred as if the pregnant women had little interest and few rights in the matter" (Jenson 1992, 16), and the C M A used rhetoric that featured responsible doctors seeking to best treat their patients under the threat of prosecution (Haussmann 2001). At the federal level only the New Democratic Party (N D P) would actively promote a woman's right to choose.

It should come as no surprise, then, that the legislation that came out of the American states and Canada that were ultimately tested in *Roe* and *Morgentaler* made doctors the gatekeepers of abortions. With the notable exceptions of New York, Hawaii, Washington, and Alaska, which essentially passed laws allowing abortion on demand according to gestational limits, the remaining forty-six states were slow to reform abortion laws, or else passed laws that allowed abortion in certain cases, including rape, incest, and when a woman's "health" was in danger. Doctors, of course, determined the severity of these threats and therefore the appropriateness of the procedure when assessing their pregnant patients. In Canada, abortion reform in 1969 created the therapeutic abortion committee (T A C) system, which defined legal abortions as those performed in "accredited" or "approved" hospitals after a team of three doctors, none of which would perform the procedure in question, determined that continuation of the pregnancy would endanger the life or health of the mother. Thus, doctors in Canada decided who was eligible for an abortion, public health personnel determined where one could take place, and women were left at their mercy.

Clearly, legislative reform had proven a completely inadequate medium for the pro-choice groups to reform abortion policy and shift away from the medical discourse. In their analysis of social movements and political opportunity structures, Meyer and Staggenborg (1996, 1648) suggest that "the availability of additional institutional venues for action encourages movements suffering defeats to shift targets and arenas to sustain themselves." According to this proposition, pro-choice groups in both Canada and the United States, ignored during abortion reform debates, should alter their strategies. As Rubin confirms, if the "legislatures were unsatisfactory, another route was open to the reformers – litigation" (Rubin 1982, 29). Indeed, in both countries, the reform movements eventually bypassed the legislatures and took their demands straight to the courts. Yet the means by which they did so were profoundly different. Each case therefore requires separate attention.

THE CONSTITUTIONALIZATION
OF AMERICAN POLITICS

By the 1960s, constitutional challenges to laws by social movements through litigation had become extremely popular in the United States. In *Marbury v. Madison* (1803), the Supreme Court awarded itself the power of judicial review, including the role of arbiter between the federal government and citizens through its interpretation of the US Bill of Rights. In subsequent decisions, the Court found that this review extended to state laws as well. By appealing to its power of judicial review, citizens could stymie the legislative process by questioning the constitutionality of state and federal laws before the Court. Following the successful example set by the National Association for the Advancement of Colored People (N A A C P), which culminated in the landmark 1954 *Brown v. Board of Education* decision, the pro-choice movement abandoned legislative tactics, and victory in the courts became the ultimate strategy (Rubin 1982; Tatalovich 1997; Scheppele 1996).

The judicial challenge allowed the movement to detract from the medical discourse and advance a rights-based one. Indeed, Jane Roe was a Texan woman seeking an abortion, and she claimed the right to choose abortion based on the recent finding by the Court in *Griswold v. Connecticut* (1965) that the implicit-privacy clause of the Bill of Rights covered contraception for unmarried persons. Roe hoped the Court would extend this implicit-privacy clause to include a right to choose abortion as well, arguing that women had the right to choose abortion away from the prying eyes of the state. Roe's defence team consisted of two young female lawyers supported by various pro-choice groups. Roe and her legal team therefore catapulted women to the forefront of the abortion debate, successfully inserting women into a debate that had previously focused on the medical establishment.

Also remarkable was the participation of women in the judicial challenge, independent of their doctors. The court heard thirty-six *amicus curiae* briefs, which allowed the pro-choice movement to challenge the medical discourse that constrained abortion policy debate. "Through presenting *amicus curiae* briefs, women as individuals and in groups ... were accepted into the judicial policy process" (Stetson 2001, 253–4). Examples of groups that filed briefs in support of abortion rights included the American Women's Medical Association, New Women Lawyers, National Abortion Action Coalition, and the National Organization of Women and Women's Health and Abortion Project. Most of these groups had been shut out of the legislative debates in the 1960s and early 1970s.[11]

In January 1973, the *Roe* decision ruled that the implicit-privacy clause covered a woman's right to choose abortion. The justices therefore shifted the abortion discourse from a medical to a rights-based one because they created a *constitutional right* to choose abortion in the first trimester and a limited right to abortion in the second and third trimesters. Abortion was no longer a procedure that required the approval of a male doctor; rather, it was a woman's right to receive an abortion if she deemed it necessary. Significantly, the decision also made the justices of the Supreme Court the guardians of American abortion policy.

The *Roe* decision was therefore a critical juncture (Collier and Collier 1991), a policy choice that re-oriented the political landscape and is difficult to reverse. *Roe* abruptly veered abortion policy away from its century-old, rigid medical discourse and legitimized the rights-based discourse the pro-choice groups had been using. As Jenson (1987) suggests, everything about abortion politics shifted along with the discourse: the legitimate participants, the political alliances, the alternative policy options, and the range of issues considered relevant to the debate. Pro-choice groups won a seat at the table because policy-makers could no longer defer solely to the medical profession. In fact, during the first trimester, placing abortion decisions in the hands of doctors was arguably unconstitutional.

Thus, the *Roe* decision forever changed the landscape of American abortion politics. Perhaps most significantly, a counter-movement that also uses a rights-based discourse emerged. In 1973, in response to *Roe*, the National Right to Life Committee formed. Pro-life groups before *Roe* were "not very strong and well organized" (Stetson 2001, 254), but *Roe* "unleashed a political backlash as the pro-life counter-offensive was mobilized" (Tatalovich 1997, 59). Arguably, because the judicial arena closed immediately following *Roe* – no court would turn around and reverse a decision so quickly – activity in the legislature became a crucial aspect of the pro-life strategy. As the counter-movement moved into one arena, the movement itself had to follow (Meyer and Staggenborg 1996).

In the post-*Roe* abortion politics landscape, movement strategies centre on either maintaining the status quo or reversing the decision. Either way, the only way to remove the constitutional right to choose is through constitutional amendment, or by convincing the Court to reverse precedent. Presidents nominate justices, and so the pro-life counter-movement believes that by electing pro-life presidents, the Court will eventually be composed of enough members to gut *Roe* (Tatalovich 1997; Rubin 1982). They have enjoyed some success, particularly with the restriction of public funds for abortion services. Notably, *Casey v. Pennsylvania* (1992) dispensed with the trimester framework, creating instead a right to choose abortion until "viability."[12]

Further, party associations at both the state and federal levels began to take sides. The Democrats, "at the insistent urging of [the pro-choice movement], included a plank in their [1976] platform that stated, "We feel that it is undesirable to attempt to amend the U.S. constitution to overturn the Supreme Court decision permitting abortion," while Republicans countered in their platform that the party favoured "a continuance of the public dialogue on abortion and supports the efforts of those who seek enactment of a constitutional amendment to restore protection of the right to life for unborn children" (Rubin 1982, 98). With these battle lines drawn, policy-makers began offering movement and counter-movement access to their ranks. As a result, abortion has become increasingly contentious in American legislatures, particularly as the two-year terms for many state and federal representatives create a continuous election cycle.

In summary, *Roe* established a woman's constitutional right to choose abortion away from the prying eyes of the state, made the Supreme Court the guardian of abortion policy, and dispensed with the medical discourse surrounding abortion, allowing pro-choice (and some pro-life) groups to become legitimate representatives of women in abortion debates. However, precisely because it abandoned the prevailing medical discourse in favour of a rights-based one, *Roe* also encouraged the mobilization of the anti-abortion, pro-life counter-movement that has successfully curbed access in many states in the decades since the *Roe* decision and gave rise to an increasingly contentious abortion policy debate that thrives in the short American election cycle. However, while it may seem that a woman's right to choose is under constant threat in the United States, the fact remains that the Supreme Court has to reverse *Roe* in order to take it away – and reversing *Roe* would cause a litany of new judicial challenges that ought to make the Court reluctant to do so (Fallon 2006).

The Canadian experience has been remarkably different.

DOCTOR STILL KNOWS BEST: REPRODUCTIVE "FREEDOM" IN CANADA

As stated in the introduction, two main factors explain why the Canadian abortion policy legacy, steeped in its medical discourse, outlived its American counterpart. First, Canadian political institutions offered little room for pro-choice groups to establish themselves as legitimate representatives of women in the abortion debate. The double whammy of parliamentary supremacy, which holds that Parliament reigns supreme over all other branches of government, and executive federalism, where intergovernmental negotiation – crucial for health policy in Canada – is dominated by executives from the provincial and federal levels (Watts 1989), limits the number of potential avenues for influence. The parliamentary system also allows policy-makers to deny abortion interest groups leverage in the legislative system, particularly through both party discipline and closed caucus meetings.

Second, the medical discourse of abortion politics continues to dominate in Canada because the *Morgentaler* decision was about a doctor's right to determine patient care, not a woman's inherent right to choose abortion. A shift to a rights-based discourse could only occur if the Court found that a woman had a right to abortion in the first place. Thus, while *Morgentaler* did encourage a pro-life counter-movement to mobilize, neither side has since enjoyed victories to sustain support or interest among the Canadian public, because neither is a legitimate actor according to the medical discourse currently in place. As Meyer and Staggenborg (1996, 1647) point out: "In the long run, neither side can maintain itself without victories." The state of Canadian abortion policy therefore does not readily sustain movement and counter-movement activities, and both sides exist in relative obscurity.

As in the United States, Canada's abortion reform movement of the 1960s focused on the image of conscientious, ethical, and responsible doctors hoping to protect themselves from unwarranted prosecution. Thus, "women, organized as women demanding specific and particular gender rights, had as yet no status as political actors" (Jenson 1992, 25). Instead, the Canadian Medical Association, the Canadian Bar Association and members of Parliament shaped the 1969 abortion reform legislation. While several pro-choice groups submitted resolutions to the government, "none [gained] recognition as major actors in the debate" (Jenson 1992, 31). The result was a law that ensured that abortion policy would remain outside the realm of women and therefore the pro-choice movement (Haussmann 2001; Jenson 1992). Abortions would be legal within "accredited" hospitals, and only when that hospital's TAC, made up of three doctors, not including the one performing the abortion, determined that the continuation of pregnancy would endanger the "life or health of the mother."

Section 251 left almost every political actor, legitimate or not, wholly unsatisfied. As Jenson points out, while many more women had access to abortion than ever before, the law "nevertheless, in general, [subjected] women to the vagaries of doctors' and hospitals' judgment of the morality and politics of abortion" (1992, 37). In addition, "as the law came into effect, it became evident that the interpretation of the words [life or health of the mother] varied widely across the country" (Dunsmuir 1993). National party associations were eager to maintain the medical discourse and therefore avoid blame for abortion policy altogether. The two most important party associations, the Liberals and the Conservatives, steadfastly refused to present abortion as a fundamental right of women in their platforms (Young 2000). Further, discord among doctors in Canada – particularly over the right to offer abortions outside of "accredited" hospitals – meant infighting among even the legitimate participants of the abortion debate. Not surprisingly, eager to establish a constitutional right to abortion similar to the one in *Roe*, the pro-choice movement took the cause to the Canadian Supreme Court.

However, judicial challenges in Canada were more difficult than in the US, mainly because the courts did not have the same level of power to review legislation as their American counterparts. Historically, the Canadian court system arbitrated disputes between levels of government, not between the government and citizens. Although the Canadian Bill of Rights became law in 1960, the Court was loathe to use it to strike down legislation. The Bill of Rights was a mere statute, subject to revision by Parliament. Morgentaler's first attempts to use the courts to reform Canadian abortion laws illustrate this reality.

Morgentaler challenged the 1969 reforms by setting up his own freestanding abortion clinic in Montreal. He was clearly in violation of the Criminal Code, because he did not receive "consent" from a T A C, or perform the procedure in an accredited institution. So, too, were the pregnant women who sought abortions in his clinic, although section 251 punished those providing illegal abortions much more severely than the women obtaining the procedure. In 1970, the Quebec government arrested and tried Morgentaler. In his defence, he argued that despite ignoring Criminal Code abortion regulations, he was innocent of all charges. He invoked both the "Bourne defence" of 1939, and Section 45 of the Criminal Code, which absolved doctors of criminal negligence if they could prove "a surgical procedure was performed for the benefit of the patient with reasonable care and skill and with regard to the health of the patient" (Tatalovich 1997, 74). His case largely focused on his right as a doctor to practise as he saw fit and the rights of provinces to regulate the provision of care.

Although a Quebec jury acquitted him, the Court of Appeal reversed the decision. Morgentaler appealed to the Supreme Court, but it refused to hear his case. Canada's highest court seemed determined to show judicial restraint, refusing to shape policy outside the legislatures (Scheppele 1996; Tatalovich 1997; Jenson 1992). "If people did not like the abortion statute, the Court argued, they would have to go to Parliament to get it changed. The courts would stay out of it" (Scheppele 1996, 34).

Though it was a defeat for the abortion reform movement, the case allowed doctors to become the advocates for abortion rights in Canada. Throughout the 1970s, Morgentaler established himself as the face of the pro-choice movement, generally with the full support of the pro-choice groups that were forced to battle within the confines of the medical discourse and without the luxury of judicial review. Yet this avenue for change – using a doctor to challenge abortion laws who used a defence that focused on a doctor's autonomy and not a woman's right to reproductive freedom – led to the relative obscurity of pro-choice groups and women in general as they struggled to establish themselves as legitimate participants in the debate.

Although he spent time in jail after his acquittal was overturned in 1974, Morgentaler continued to perform illegal abortions in his clinic upon his release, and refused to conceal his actions. Morgentaler was constantly in the Quebec court system battling prosecution for performing illegal abortions. One of his appeals made it to the Supreme Court, which found in *Morgentaler v. the Queen* (1976) that section 251 of the Criminal Code was within the scope of Canadian criminal law and did not violate the Canadian Bill of Rights. Soon after, the newly elected Parti Québécois announced that the province would no longer enforce the abortion laws.

Victorious in Quebec, Morgentaler set up a clinic in Toronto, Ontario, where officials arrested him in 1983, along with two of his partners, Drs Smoling and Scott. Again, a jury acquitted them, but the Ontario Court of Appeal overturned the decision, and the Morgentaler team appealed to the Supreme Court. This time, Morgentaler mounted a constitutional defence because the Charter of Rights and Freedoms had recently been entrenched into the Canadian constitution. The Charter granted to the Canadian courts a power of judicial review similar to that in the United States and a list of rights that federal and provincial legislation had to respect. It also provided pro-choice groups with a chance to alter the discourse away from its medical constraints. Women could now challenge section 251 of the Criminal Code because it violated their constitutional rights as citizens. However, perhaps because Morgentaler was now the recognized and respected leader of the reform movement, pro-choice groups chose to throw their weight behind him and his legal team.

Morgentaler's legal team preferred to use an almost exclusively medical discourse. "Dr Morgentaler's lawyer wished to emphasize the narrow question of physicians' rights and their fears of prosecution" (Haussmann 2001, 72). However, the two questions before the Court were whether section 251 violated a woman's right to "security of the person" in section 7 of the Charter, and whether or not abortion was outside the scope of the federal government's legislative powers. Morgentaler's lawyers did, however, discourage pro-choice groups from filing supporting briefs, and the Court forbade them to act as interveners. Unlike the American pro-choice groups, then, which were allowed to submit *amici curiae* briefs in *Roe*, Canadian pro-choice groups still remained on the periphery of the abortion constitutional case.

In January 1988, the Supreme Court ruled in favour of Drs Morgentaler, Smoling, and Scott in three separate opinions. It ruled that section 251 of the Criminal Code was unconstitutional because it infringed on a woman's "security of the person," but the majority justices could not agree as to why, leading to three majority opinions. Two held that the law created two separate violations to security of the person: first, under threat of criminal sanction, a woman should not be forced to carry a fetus unless she meets criteria "unrelated to her own priorities and aspirations" because it violates her bodily integrity, and second, that the TAC system delays necessary medical treatment. In a concurring opinion, two other justices ignored the bodily integrity aspect altogether in favour of the "right of access to medical treatment." Only one justice held that a woman had a constitutional right to end her pregnancy, free from state interference, at the beginning of her pregnancy. Most significantly, all five justices in the majority, albeit in separate opinions, held that Parliament could regulate abortion – just not using the TAC or "accredited" hospital frameworks. The decision therefore ties a woman's security of the person to ease of access to medical treatment.

Though the Court found that the 1969 abortion legislation created unnecessary burdens on pregnant women, it fell far short of finding a constitutional right to abortion in the Charter, instead ruling that abortion was within the scope of the federal government's powers to regulate criminal activity. As such, there was no critical juncture, no shift in discourse, no shift in Canadian abortion politics. The Court handed abortion decisions right back to doctors and the abortion question right back to Parliament. Thus, while many believe the *Morgentaler* decision established a constitutional right to choose abortion, that belief is simply not true. Rather, *Morgentaler* rejected the status quo because it made it difficult for patients to get proper medical treatment from their doctors, and with some constitutional guidelines, sent the question right back to Parliament. The Court treated abortion as a medical procedure, not a right, and that, as Brodie et al. (1992) argue, makes Parliament, not the Court, the gatekeeper of Canadian abortion policy. Indeed, two subsequent court cases, *Borowski v. Canada* (1989) and *Tremblay v. Daigle* (1989), refused to find a right to personhood for the fetus in the

Charter, effectively closing the judicial avenue for pro-choice and pro-life groups altogether.

Because the Westminster parliamentary system, coupled with Canadian federalism, allows the parties and the executive to effectively avoid sticky political issues, neither the pro-choice movement nor the pro-life counter-movement have been able to keep up appearances on the national stage. Quite simply, the Canadian pro-choice movement and pro-life counter-movement are not big players on the Canadian political scene.[13] Even the Senate's defeat of Bill C-43, the only attempt by a government since *Morgentaler* to recriminalize abortion, was arguably defeated because the C M A threatened to stop providing abortions altogether out of concern for prosecution against doctors (Thomson 2005).

The Liberal and Conservative parties refuse to include abortion in their platforms, although several individual members of Parliament or party members have pledged their support to one side or the other. However, strong party discipline ensures that even these members toe the party line: abortion is "settled," according to previous Liberal Prime Minister Chrétien (Hebert 2000); Liberal Prime Minister Martin promised to discourage private member abortion bills under his government (Aubry 2004); and Conservative Prime Minister Stephen Harper has repeatedly promised to keep abortion off the legislative agenda (O'Neil and Curry 2004; Puzic 2006; Church 2011). The rise of the N D P to official opposition status in 2011 means that for the first time, a party committed to abortion rights is a major player on the national scale. However, it is unclear whether the party will push for abortion protections in the upcoming parliamentary session.

In summary, there is no prolonged battle over abortion in Canada. Rather, the Canadian pro-choice and pro-life movements operate largely on the periphery of abortion politics. Even the president of C A R A L complained in 2005 that funding is difficult to find for both sides because of the impermeability of the political parties (Thomson 2005).

Yet the invisibility of the abortion debate, and the absence of a binding precedent establishing a woman's right to end her pregnancy, means that abortion services are inherently precarious in Canada. While successive Canadian governments have maintained that abortion falls under the Canada Health Act of 1984, which stipulates that all provinces must offer medically necessary services to receive federal funding for health care,[14] there is no constitutional protection for a woman's right to choose, precisely because of parliamentary supremacy and the enduring nineteenth-century medical framework that surrounds abortion policy.

WOE IS THE CANADIAN WOMAN: THE ILLUSION OF REPRODUCTIVE FREEDOM IN CANADA

I am certainly not the first to sound the alarm regarding reproductive freedom in Canada. Pro-choice groups, including CARAL and its successor, the Abortion Rights Coalition of Canada, have long been warning that abortion services are on the decline. Ten years ago, the Canadian Medical Association included a brief in one of their journals that noted that abortion services were "a patchwork quilt with many holes," arguing that "the availability of abortions in Canada now depends on a woman's location and the size of her pocketbook" (2001, 847). A researcher at Canadians for Choice, posing as a pregnant woman seeking an abortion, published a widely cited critique of the availability of abortion services across the provinces and at Canadian hospitals and clinics (Shaw 2006).

Nor am I trying to argue that American women enjoy greater access to abortion services than their Canadian counterparts. Certainly, in many American states, the lack of clinics and funding for abortion services makes abortion an unrealistic option for many pregnant women. For example, Mississippi only has one abortion clinic, and that clinic operates under the constant threat of closure by state authorities (Brown 2012). Rather, I argue that in the United States, policy-makers and the public pay attention to the subject and recognize a woman's legitimate stake in the debate. This legitimate participation by American women in the debate stems from the establishment of a right to abortion in *Roe*, even though many vehemently disagree with the Court's decision. American pro-choice and pro-life groups are highly visible interest groups at both the state and federal levels. Even the recent debate over health care legislation in 2008 came down to the availability of public funds for abortion. In the United States, women have a place at the table when it comes to abortion policy.

Conversely, I argue that the *Morgentaler* decision has had two important effects on Canadian abortion policy. First, it continued to legitimize the medical discourse surrounding abortion and to deny women a prominent place in abortion policy discussions. Second, the decision reiterated Parliament's role as the gatekeeper of abortion policy, and policy-makers are quite happy to point fingers at the medical establishment to avoid the difficult issue altogether. Further, the joint effects of party discipline and the propensity for majority governments in the Canadian system has allowed successive governments to deny pro-choice groups prominent roles on the national stage.

As a result, the provinces have slowly chipped away at abortion services, either blatantly, as in New Brunswick, which refuses to pay for abortions provided outside the province or in private clinics within it, or more clandestinely, as in Manitoba, where only two hospitals and one clinic perform the procedure, all within 100 km of the American border (Canadians for Choice 2006). If you are a pregnant woman in Manitoba living on Hudson Bay, you must travel over 1,000 km to get to the nearest hospital or clinic that provides abortions.

Reproductive freedom in Canada is therefore inherently fragile, precisely because of the enduring medical discourse that surrounds abortion and the institutional configurations that allow governments and policy-makers to shut out women's voices. As Joyce Arthur, a prominent pro-choice advocate, succinctly summarizes, "Legislatures don't like to touch the abortion issue; it's a messy issue and can hurt political careers because of its divisiveness. This can work in [the pro-choice groups'] favour, because it means no abortion restrictions will be passed, but it also work against [them], because no enhancement of abortion services will happen either" (quoted in Thomson 2005).

In other words, while Harper may have promised to keep abortion off the table, inaction may be the best possible policy choice for pro-life Canadians, and the greatest threat to reproductive freedom in Canada, particularly as the shortage of doctors who provide abortions grows, and fewer medical schools offer comprehensive abortion training. It may seem counter-intuitive to hope that a Conservative government would pass a bill re-criminalizing abortion, but at least then pro-choice groups will have another chance to wrest control of the abortion question and establish a rights-based discourse for Canadian abortion politics.

NOTES

1 For example, a 2001 Léger Marketing poll found that nearly half of Canadians support legal abortion, compared with 37.6 per cent against; a 2005 Gallup poll found that a majority of Canadians were satisfied with the country's abortion laws; a 2008 Angus-Reid poll found that half of Canadians support legal abortion; an EKOS Politics poll in 2010 found that 52 per cent of Canadians identify as pro-choice, while only 27 per cent identify as pro-life.

2 While Morgentaler's appointment was not without controversy, a 2008 Angus Reid poll showed that 60 per cent of Canadians supported the decision and another 66 per cent believed he was a hero to Canadian women (Brennan 2008).

3 While the US Supreme Court has modified its original decision in subsequent cases, notably in *Webster v. Reproductive Services* (1989) and *Planned Parenthood of Southeastern Pennsylvania v. Casey* (1992), it has thus far continued to reaffirm *Roe v. Wade*'s core finding, that abortion falls under the purview of the implicit privacy clause of the Fourteenth Amendment (Tatalovich 1997; Garrow 1998). For a detailed discussion of the implicit right to privacy and the Court's subsequent decisions, please see David Garrow's book, *Liberty and Sexuality: The Right to Privacy and the Making of Roe v. Wade* (1998).

4 To learn more about the varied access to abortion for American and Canadian women, see NARAL's State Report Cards (www.naral.org) and the 2006 Canadians for Choice study by Jessica Shaw, "Reality Check: A Close Look at Accessing Abortion Services in Canadian Hospitals" (www.canadiansforchoice.ca).

5 In 1821, Connecticut passed the first law limiting pharmaceutical abortions through apothecaries; over the next ten years, all the states passed legislation that made abortion a crime unless the life of the mother was in danger.

6 The legislative history of abortion in Canada is necessarily tied to that of the United Kingdom prior to the Statute of Westminster in 1931.

7 After the *Roe* decision in 1973, NARAL changed its name but maintained the same acronym, to become the National Abortion and Reproductive Rights League.

8 Similarly, CARAL became the Canadian Abortion Rights Action League after 1988.

9 I say "certain groups of pro-choice women" because many third- and fourth-wave feminists have criticized the second-wave movement, of

which these pro-choice groups were a part, for representing middle-class white women instead of women as a whole. For an example, see Rebecca Walker's *To Be Real: Telling the Truth and Changing the Face of Feminism* (1995).

10 *Harris v. McRae* (1980) upheld Medicaid restrictions on abortion provision, and *Webster v. Reproductive Health Services* (1989) allowed states to prohibit the use of public funding for abortions.

11 The American Medical Association and the American Bar Association also submitted amici curiae briefs to the Court in favour of abortion law reform independently from the pro-choice and feminist groups.

12 Although the shift to "viability" arguably marks a return to the medical discourse framework, giving doctors the right to establish when viability occurs, *Casey* has done little to refute the rights-based discourse upon which modern American abortion politics are based.

13 Sylvia Bashevkin (1996) points that that pro-choice movement leaders felt the pro-life counter-movement, particularly REAL women, had access to elites in the Mulroney government. How much influence they had is another matter. Mulroney tried once to re-criminalize abortion after the 1988 *Morgentaler* decision, but the proposed legislation was relatively favourable to women seeking abortions in the first trimester. The Liberal Chrétien government, in power from 1993 to 2006, refused to grant access to either side.

14 Arguably, not all governments have curtailed or cut funding according to the Act when provinces fail to provide abortions. While the Liberal governments of the 1990s and early 2000s were vocal about their commitment to abortion services under the Act, it remains to be seen whether or not a majority Conservative government will be quite as vigilant.

BIBLIOGRAPHY

Angus Reid Public Opinion. 2008. "Half of Canadians Want Abortion to Remain Legal." Accessed 2 August 2011. http://www.angusreidglobal. com/polls/32518/half_of_canadians_want_abortion_to_remain_legal/.

Angus Reid Public Opinion. 2008. "Most Canadians Unaware of Lack of Restrictions on Abortion." Accessed 2 August 2011. http://www. angusreidglobal.com/polls/43161/most-canadians-unaware-of-lack-of-restrictions-on-abortions/

Arthur, Joyce. 2009. "Women's Rights Are Not up for Debate." *Activist: The Voice of Abortion Rights in Canada* (Spring)1: 6. Accessed 2 August 2011. http://www.arcc-cdac.ca/newsletters/spring-2009.pdf.

Aubry, Jack. 2004. "Truth or Spin: Abortion and Private Members' Bills." *Edmonton Journal*, 14 June.

Backhouse, Constance B. 1991. "The Celebrated Abortion Trial of Dr. Emily Stowe, Toronto, 1879." *Canadian Bulletin of Medical History* 8: 159–87.

Bashevkin, Sylvia. 1996. "Losing Common Ground: Feminists, Conservatives and Public Policy during the Mulroney Years." *Canadian Journal of Political Science* 29(2): 211–42.

Brennan, Richard. "Three in Five Support Morgentaler Honour." *Toronto Star*, 9 July. http://www.thestar.com/news/canada/2008/07/09/three_in_five_support_morgentaler_honour.html.

Brodie, Janine, Shelley Gavigan, and Jane Jenson, eds. 1992. *The Politics of Abortion*. Toronto: Oxford University Press.

Brown, Robbie. 2012. "Mississippi's Lone Abortion Clinic, Given Temporary Reprieve, Fields Rush of Calls." *New York Times*, 2 July. http://www.nytimes.com/2012/07/03/us/mississippis-lone-abortion-clinic-given-temporary-reprieve-fields-rush-of-calls.html?_r=0.

Bryden, Joan. 2006. "Ignatieff Comes out Swinging with Anti-American Remarks." *Kamloops Daily News*, 31 March.

Carlson, A. Cheree. 2009. *The Crimes of Womanhood: Defining Femininity in a Court of Law*. Chicago: University of Illinois Press.

Church, Elizabeth. 2011. "Anti-Abortion Rally Takes to the Hill." *The Globe and Mail*, 12 May.

Collier, Ruth Berins, and David Collier. 1991. *Shaping the Political Arena: Critical Junctures, the Labor Movement, and Regime Dynamics in Latin America*. Princeton: Princeton University Press.

Crotty, William J. 1984. *American Parties in Decline*. Boston: Little Brown.

Dunsmuir, Mollie. 1993. "Abortion: Constitutional and Legal Developments." *Current Issue Review* 89-10E.

Eggertson, Laura. 2001. "Abortion Services in Canada: A Patchwork Quilt with Many Holes." *Canadian Medical Association Journal* 164(6): 847–50.

EKOS Marketing. 2010. "Canadians Decisively Pro-Choice on Abortion." Accessed 2 August 2011. http://www.ekospolitics.com/wp-content/uploads/full_report_april_11.pdf.

Fallon Jr, Richard H. 2006. "If *Roe* Were Overruled: Abortion and the Constitution in a post-*Roe* World." *Saint Louis University Law Journal* 51: 610–53.

Gallup. 2005. "Most Canadians, Britons Satisfied with Abortion Laws." Accessed 2 August 2011. http://www.gallup.com/poll/16663/most-canadians-britons-satisfied-abortion-laws.aspx.

Garrow, David J. 1998. *Liberty and Sexuality: The Right to Privacy and the Making of Roe v. Wade.* Berkeley: University of California Press.

Gavigan, Shelley. 1992. "Morgentaler and Beyond: Abortion, Reproduction and the Courts." In *The Politics of Abortion*, ed. Janine Brodie, Shelley Gavigan, and Jane Jenson, 117–51. Toronto: Oxford University Press.

Jenson, Jane. 1992. "Changing Discourse, Changing Agendas: Political Rights and Reproductive Policies in France." In *The Women's Movements of the US and Western Europe: Consciousness, Political Opportunity and Public Policy*, Mary Katzenstein and Carole Mueller, eds., 64–88. Philadelphia: Temple University Press.

Jenson, Jane. 1992. "*Getting to Morgentaler: From One Representation to Another.*" In *The Politics of Abortion*, Janine Brodie, Shelley Gavigan, and Jane Jenson, eds., 15–55. Toronto: Oxford University Press.

Haussmann, Melissa. 2001. "Of Rights and Power: Canada's Federal Abortion Policy 1969–1991." In *Abortion Politics, The Women's Movement, and The Democratic State*, Dorothy McBride Stetson, ed., 63–86. New York: Oxford University Press.

Hébert, Chantal. 2000. "A Referendum to Regret." *Guardian* (Charlottetown, Prince Edward Island), 9 November.

Léger Marketing/Canadian Press. 2001. "The Opinions of Canadians on Abortion." Accessed 18 September 2013. http://www.leger360.com/admin/upload/publi_pdf/011112eng.pdf.

Luker, Kristin. 1984. *Abortion and the Politics of Motherhood.* Berkeley: University of California Press.

Meyer, David S., and Suzanne Staggenborg. 1996. "Movements, Countermovements, and the Structure of Political Opportunity." *The American Journal of Sociology* 101(6): 1628–60.

Mohr, James C. 1978. *Abortion in America: The Origins and Evolution of National Policy.* New York: Oxford University Press.

O'Neil, Peter, and Bill Curry. 2004. "Harper Rejects Changing Abortion Law: Polls Put Tories in First Place." *Calgary Herald*, 10 June.

Puzic, Sonja. 2006. "Tories Would Curb Access to Abortion, Activists Warn." *The Globe and Mail*, 21 January.

R. v. Morgentaler, [1988] 1 S.C.R. 30.

Richardt, Nicole. 2003. "A Comparative Analysis of the Embryological Research Debate in Great Britain and Germany." *Social Politics: International Studies in Gender, State and Society* 10 (vol. 1): 86–128.

Roe v. Wade, [1973] 410 U.S. 113.

Rubin, Eva R. 1982. *Abortion, Politics and the Courts:* Roe v. Wade *and Its Aftermath.* Westport: Greenwood Press.

Scheppele, Kim. 1996. "Constitutionalizing Abortion." In *Abortion Politics: Public Policy in Cross-Cultural Perspective*, Marianne Githens and Dorothy McBride Stetson, eds., 29–54. New York: Routledge.

Shaw, Jessica. 2006. *Reality Check: A Close Look at Accessing Abortion Services in Canadian Hospitals.* Ottawa: Canadians for Choice.

Stetson, Dorothy McBride. 2001. "US Abortion Debates 1959–1998: The Women's Movement Holds On." In *Abortion Politics, Women's Movements, and the Democratic State*, Dorothy McBride Stetson, ed., 247–67. New York: Oxford University Press.

Tatalovich, Raymond. 1997. *The Politics of Abortion in the United States and Canada.* Armonk: M.E. Sharpe.

Thomson, Julia. 2005. *Roe v. Morgentaler: Comparative Abortion Policy Development in the United States and Canada.* Master's thesis, Concordia University, Montreal, QC.

Walker, Rebecca, ed. 1995. *To Be Real: Telling the Truth and Changing the Face of Feminism.* New York: Anchor Books.

Watts, Ronald L. 1989. *Executive Federalism: A Comparative Analysis.* Kingston, ON: Institute of Intergovernmental Relations, Queen's University.

Young, Lisa. 2000. *Feminists and Party Politics.* Ann Arbor: University of Michigan Press.

PART THREE

The Discursive Politics of Reproduction: Subjectivity, Discourse, and Power

Girl Power and the Pill: Unpacking Web-based Marketing for Alesse and Yasmin

LISA SMITH

"By taking the Pill you're taking control" (Alesse, 2009).
"After all, it's your body!" (Yasmin, 2009).

Even though direct-to-consumer advertising is not permitted in Canada, pharmaceutical companies *are* able to market directly to prospective and current customers on the Internet. This has resulted in the rise of web-based marketing campaigns created by pharmaceutical companies seeking to build customer loyalty to a particular brand. In contemporary North American society, the emergence of web-based marketing of prescription drugs highlights the increased presence of pharmaceutical companies in the daily lives and homes of individuals (Fox and Ward 2008). Individuals are able to easily access information about pharmaceutical products. Web-based marketing is a new and important site where the social meaning of a pharmaceutical product is constructed, and social scientists ought to examine and deconstruct the content of these campaigns. In the case of the oral contraceptive pill – or the pill, as it is commonly called – the two most prominent campaigns are those for Alesse, manufactured by Wyeth, and Yasmin, manufactured by Bayer. On both websites, using the pill is presented as a way for a young woman to assert her independence and individuality because it allows her to manage her fertility, health, appearance, and emotions. According to the Alesse and Yasmin websites, a girl on the pill is a girl who is empowered, a girl who embodies "girl power." The object of this paper is to deconstruct the content of these websites, and in particular the mobilization of discourses of "girl power," to illuminate current social trends in pill use, as well as representations of young femininity in online media.

To situate the use of discourses of "girl power" by the pharmaceutical companies in the websites, I begin by considering how feminist demands for agency have informed the cultural representation of the pill since its inception; however, there have been significant changes in the pill's use in Canada that need to be considered. First, as Lupton (1995) argues, late-modern societies are characterized by a shift toward the neo-liberal subject – a subject that is self-regulating, meaning that there is an increased emphasis placed on individual responses to social and health problems. Because of this, pharmaceutical companies are more likely than ever to market directly to consumers, as opposed to just physicians. Second, the pill has always been considered a lifestyle drug (Tone 2001; Watkins 1998), meaning it can be used to treat conditions that are at the margins of health and illness. However, as I will examine in this paper, the secondary benefits of pill use, such as prevention of acne and more regular periods, have risen to equal the pill's status as a contraceptive. Finally, when the pill was first approved the majority of users were married women in their twenties (McLaren 1990). In Canada today, the majority of pill users are young single women between the ages of fifteen and twenty-five, and their reasons for using it are varied: from contraception to controlling acne to regulating periods (Black et al. 2004, Wilkins et al. 2000). Use of the pill has come to be a key symbol of the capacity of a young woman to control her body, as opposed to an object associated with women more generally. The Alesse and Yasmin websites reflect these changes, and contribute to contemporary understandings of individual choice and empowerment within the context of young women's use of the pill.

The emphasis the websites place on power and control portray the pill user as a powerful and independent subject; and yet, the websites equally construct her, and young women more generally, as fundamentally problematic and thus in need of the control offered by the pill. Making sense of this tension highlights that while women always make choices in relation to reproductive technologies, they are equally governed by the manner in which those choices are constructed within wider systems of social meaning. As Ruhl (2002, 643) keenly observes, "contemporary debates about birth control and fertility are unique in their emphasis on *self*-control." The content of the Alesse and Yasmin sites demonstrates that contemporary discourses about the pill are unique in their emphasis on the need for young women to engage in self-control of their bodies while simultaneously presenting the pill as the only option for a girl fully in control of her body and life. As Gonick (2006) and Harris (2004) note, it is the tension between "girl power" and "girls at risk" that shapes the discursive field that constitutes young women as subjects in contemporary North American societies. Similarly, even though the Alesse and Yasmin websites situate pill use as an individual choice, a young woman who fails to use the pill is a threat to herself as well as to society more generally.

FEMINISM AND THE PILL

In western democratic societies, a woman's liberation is still thought to be contingent on her capacity to make choices in matters relating to reproduction. This belief creates a strong imperative for pill use because it is perceived to be the only woman-centred and "reliable" birth control device. Reflecting this belief, the recent fiftieth anniversary of the pill was marked by articles in prominent newspapers and magazines across Canada, all of which heralded the device as the single most important invention in the twentieth century for women (Allemang 2010, Gibbs 2010). According to these articles, the pill gave women reproductive freedom and thus equally gave them political freedom. As McLaren observes, the desire to control reproduction in some way is common to most human societies. What varies "is a particular society's procreative ideology" (1990, 23) "or the way that a society thinks about and organizes reproduction" (Ruhl 2002, 642). Over the past hundred years, choice – and in particular reproductive choice – has figured prominently in feminist philosophy and politics (Albury 1999). Choice continues to shape how we think about and understand use of the pill. In part, we can make sense of this due to historical feminist struggles for personhood, and by extension, agency.

Speaking broadly, liberal feminists have tended to argue that women and men are fundamentally equal and deserve the same access to rights and status (see Mill 1869 [1977], Wollstonecraft 1792 [1975]).

Within liberal philosophy, "One of the core principles ... is the universal human capacity to reason; rationality in the liberal sense rests in the individual's capacity to remove himself from the particularities of his circumstances" (Ruhl 2002, 644). Autonomy of the mind is based on the individual's capacity to subvert the body. Women were often characterized as unable to attain the idealized state of liberal personhood because their reproductive system tied them to uncontrollable natural processes, such as menstruation and menopause. But no state was more a threat to a woman's autonomy than pregnancy, which can occur "spontaneously" and in the absence of one's will (Ruhl 2002, 651).

As Tone (2001) and Watkins (1998) have observed, the pill was an innovation of science; but its invention was contingent upon a system of social values and beliefs, which emphasized the importance of a woman-centred contraceptive as *the* solution to the modern woman's problem. The call for women-centred control of reproduction was heard across feminist philosophy in the latter half of the twentieth century. The radical-feminist philosopher Shulamith Firestone argued that a feminist revolution required "the full restoration to women of ownership of their own bodies" and the "seizure of control of human fertility" by women (1970, 11). Marxist-feminist philosopher Mary O'Brien insisted that freedom for women from domination required the freedom to choose parenthood (1981, 21). The influential existential feminist, Simone de Beauvoir (1952), argued that a woman's reproductive system limited her capacity to act as an autonomous individual. According to de Beauvoir, a woman's embedded status as a "natural," rather than a "rational," subject was particularly evident in pregnancy: "Ensnared by nature, the pregnant woman is plant and animal, a stock-pile of colloids, an incubator, an egg; she scares children proud of their young, straight bodies and makes young people titter contemptuously because she is a human being, a conscious and free individual, who has become life's passive instrument" (de Beauvoir 1952, 495). According to de Beauvoir, for a woman to attain the desired status of an autonomous subject she had to regulate and control her body, and in particular her reproductive body. For this reason, de Beauvoir argued that access to reliable contraception and abortion were essential preconditions to freedom for women (1952, 513).

The link between a woman's freedom and her control of her fertility found a practical political expression in the tireless campaigning of birth control activist Margaret Sanger. In *Women and the New Race*, she stated, "Millions of women are asserting their right to voluntary motherhood. They are determined to decide for themselves whether they shall become mothers, under what conditions and when. This is the fundamental revolt referred to. It is for women the key to the temple of liberty" (1920, 5). Sanger emphatically believed that women's freedom was equal to freedom from unplanned pregnancy. Because the pill allowed a woman to decide when she would become pregnant, it allowed her to enter the public sphere as a rational individual, capable of making choices because she was no longer constrained by the material conditions of her body.

Despite her emphasis on the importance of women's reproductive choice, Sanger was also a fierce advocate of population control. Unfettered fertility, particularly of the "unfit under class" meant the degeneration of women, and the population as a whole: "Even as birth control is the means by which woman attains basic freedom, so it is the means by which she must and will uproot the evil she has wrought through her submission. As she has unconsciously and ignorantly brought about social disaster, so must and will she consciously and intelligently *undo* that disaster and create a new and a better order" (Sanger 1920, 5–6). According to Sanger, a woman is implicated in the engineering of a better future as she regulates her fertility. The notion that fertility is a woman's choice, but also that the right exercise of that choice is a social responsibility that will shape wider social conditions, is still present in contemporary discourses that inform the politics surrounding the use of the pill; however, as I will examine, it appears in new ways and with new subjects as the target.

In spite of the fact that reproductive politics are still coloured by the issue of choice, there is an increasing tendency to recognize the complex nature of this concept. As Ruhl observes, the degree to which fertility is controllable, or indeed the body more generally, always "lie[s] midway between rational control and 'simple' biology." She points out that pregnancy is sometimes planned, sometimes unplanned, but is rarely a fully engineered process (2002, 655). The appeal to choice has very real practical and theoretical limitations, as the assertion that individual choice exists often fails to provide a deeper examination of the power relations within which choices are made. The belief in late-modern societies that choice exists for everyone invites the notion that one ought to act responsibly by making the "right" choice. Against this backdrop, choice is not an absolute reality, but is instead a social construct through which we come to understand our actions within the wider context of social relationships.

Currently, there exists a growing body of historical scholarship on the pill. May (2010), McLaren (1990), and Tone (2001) provide compelling analyses of the place of the pill in recent history, highlighting the controversies that were sparked by its development. While these accounts are useful and important, the tendency to historicize the pill creates the impression that women no longer struggle with its use and that there is nothing new to examine. The pill has been cast off as an *old* reproductive technology, in favour of analyses of *new* reproductive technologies, such as IVF, and preventive sexual technologies such as the HPV vaccine. In both Canada (see Connell and Hunt 2010) and the United States (see Wailoo et al. 2010), the campaigns that promote the HPV vaccine call on young women to actively regulate their sexuality through preventive pharmaceutical strategies. In a similar fashion, the pill is part of the rise of "Big Pharma" in contemporary society. And yet, its connection to the history of women more generally requires a nuanced analysis to consider how the past ties into the present when women use the pill.

RECONCEIVING THE PILL

As Granzow (2007, 47) argues, "the same discourse that reveals an assumed direct correlation between control (over the body) and increased choice [and autonomy] (in women's lives), is in operation today." Yet there is an ongoing tendency to see the pill as reflecting a woman's expression of choice. In doing so, we ignore how the pill is constitutive of specific feminine subjects at different times, places, and spaces (Cream 1995). When the pill was first released, the majority of users were white middle-class married women (Watkins 1998). Advertisements emphasized that the pill was the ideal accessory for a married woman interested in spacing and limiting pregnancies (Tone 2001). Different constructions of choice are at play when we consider use of the pill by Puerto Rican women as research subjects before the pill was released for general consumption in the United States (see Cream 1995) or among unmarried college women in the 1960s on American college campuses (see Bailey 1997). It is important to consider the subtle changes in how control and choice come into play based on the context and the subject in question.

Following Butler (1990), I see femininity as an ever-changing identity that is brought into existence through meaningful acts, like using the pill. Cream (1995) argues that using the pill has become an accepted and expected act by a heterosexual woman in western democratic societies. According to Cream, it is one of the most significant ways she asserts her identity as a woman. Yet, in Canada, the story of the pill is no longer as strongly attached to women in general, nor is its use always primarily attached to fertility control. The majority of Canadian pill users are young women between the ages of fifteen and twenty-five (Black et al. 2004). Some young women will start using the pill as young as thirteen or fourteen, even before they are sexually active, as a precautionary measure, and most will stay on it for upwards of ten years, seeking the benefits of shorter periods and clearer skin (Wilkins et al. 2000).

Unlike condoms or diaphragms, which arguably have limited uses, individuals can and will use pharmaceuticals, like the pill, to achieve other ends beyond their primary intended function (Flower 2004, Fox and Ward 2008). In fact, the pill has long been identified as one of the first "lifestyle drugs" – meaning it is used to treat conditions that lie at the margins of health and illness. Pharmaceutical companies have long touted the benefits of using the pill to dissuade concerns over continual use in the absence of an identified illness (Tone 2001 2007; Watkins 1998). The concept "lifestyle drug" refers to a pharmaceutical that is used to enhance quality of life as opposed to treating a particular medical condition (Fox and Ward 2008, 857). The changing characteristics of users and usage of the pill have resulted in companionate shifts in how it is being sold as a cultural commodity by pharmaceutical companies. The pill is now marketed as being the ideal accessory for a young woman fully in control of her body and life.

Use of the pill by young women has been supported by relaxed sexual mores (Baker 2008), as well as rising concerns over the sexual health of young people. Fifty years ago this concern might have prompted state programs compelling parents to regulate their children's behaviour. Significant advancements in knowledge in the health sciences and the development of pharmaceuticals, like the pill, have meant that the response to sexual health problems is increasingly found in the use of pharmaceutical technologies on behalf of the individual adolescent (Alderman 2003). In light of these changes, it is not surprising that pharmaceutical companies marketing the pill have shifted their focus to a much younger demographic and emphasize the pill's status as a multi-use lifestyle drug. Though there are remnants of the discourse of "choice" that were present when the pill was first released, there are significant differences, which reflect the unique status of young women within modern liberal states.

GETTING GIRLS ON THE PILL

Late-modern societies are characterized by an intensification of individualization, meaning there is an increased emphasis on individual, as opposed to state-based responsibility for health and welfare (Beck 1992). The new emphasis placed on the individual has led to significant changes in the ways in which young women are regulated. As Harris observes:

> In the modern period of the late nineteenth century, youth were disciplined directly by the state and its agents so that they would develop slowly, under close supervision, to serve a unified and progressive nation. Later modern times, however, are characterized by dislocation, flux, and globalization, and demand citizens who are flexible and self-realizing ... Direct intervention and guidance by institutions have replaced by self-governance; power has devolved onto individuals to regulate themselves through the right choices. The social and economic logic of late modernity compels people to become self-inventing and responsible citizens who can manage their own development and adapt to change without relying on the state. (2004, 3)

The ideal young female subject is characterized by her heightened sense of individual autonomy. She pursues her freedom and autonomy by consulting various experts to maximize her health, wealth, and happiness. As Rose observes, we are governed by these "therapies of freedom" and governance in this case "is something we do to ourselves, not something done to us by those in power" (1990, 213).

The heightened expectation for individual responsibility for all manner of social problems is exemplified in calls for empowerment. As Cruikshank observes, despite seeming to be an intensely personal process, being empowered "is no longer a personal or private goal ... taking up the goal of self-esteem is something we owe society, something that will defray the costs of social problems" (1993, 328). Both women and girls are encouraged to make choices that will express their individuality and lead to a sense of empowerment, which is increasingly related to the consumer decisions they make (Gill 2008). While in the past beauty routines were paramount, a woman's relative empowerment is, increasingly, measured by her capacity to seek out the appropriate expert advice and technologies to manage her short- and long-term health (Lupton 1995).

The rise of "healthism" and the growing prominence of pharmaceutical solutions to everyday "problems" have led to what Fox and Ward (2008) call the "pharmaceuticalisation of everyday life." Pharmaceutical advertising increasingly situates the consumption of pharmaceuticals as the act of a responsible individual, who is interested in personally identifying and caring for her body (Fox and Ward 2008; Fishman 2004). Against this backdrop, pharmaceutical marketing has become a "de facto arm of large-scale public health projects, working together with the government and the medical industry to manage and organize targeted populations" (Connell and Hunt 2010, 73). In this context, empowerment is linked to the individual's capacity to identify and seek out the appropriate pharmaceutical given her particular set of "problems."

Contemporary understandings of girls, girlhood, and use of the pill are situated within the wider context of individualism, empowerment, and healthism. But these social trends are equally shaped by the unique status of young women in late-modern societies. As Driscoll observes, the term "girl" does not refer to a particular age, but rather refers to a type of female subjectivity, the form of which is constructed and demarcated by a given society (2002, 4). In most twenty-first-century western cultures, "girl" refers to a stage in a woman's life when she is "immature and malleable" and in the process of becoming a woman (Driscoll 2002, 4). In this paper, I draw on a more specific cultural usage of the term "girl" to refer to feminine adolescence and early adulthood, which Driscoll refers to as a sub-category of "girl culture" more generally. "Girl culture" in this context does not necessarily refer to pre-teen or tween phenomena, although it shares similar characteristics.

Over the past fifty years, youth have emerged as an integral population in constructing the future; however, according to Harris, "it is

young women, rather than youth in general, who are now the subjects of this scrutiny and regulation" (2004, 2). Over this same period, the representation of girls in media and popular culture has
increased exponentially (Driscoll 2002, Gonick 2006, Mazzarella
and Pecora 2007, McRobbie 2000). The manner in which a young
woman becomes a woman has become an issue of public interest.
New discourses have emerged from diverse fields, from psychology
and health sciences to popular culture, all of which attempt to guide
a young woman's conduct in relation to herself during this period of
transition. These discourses represent "girls" or young women as
"one of the stakes upon which the future depends" (McRobbie
2000, 4). Harris argues that young women have emerged as the
"vanguard of new subjectivity ... Power, opportunities, and success
are all modeled by the 'future girl'" – a kind of young woman celebrated for her "desire, determination and confidence to take charge
of her life, seize chances, and achieve her goals" (2004, 1). As young
women become responsible for the future, they are celebrated, but
they are equally governed and regulated by expectations placed on
their behaviour. The tension inherent in the discursive field, which
presently defines girls and girlhood in late-modern societies, is best
exemplified in the discourse of "girl power."

   "Girl power" has emerged as one of the most important phrases
in making sense of young female identity in late modern society.
"Girl power" represents a "new girl": assertive, dynamic, and un-
bound from the constraints of passive femininity. The phrase "girl
power" was first popularized in the 1990s by Riot Grrrl bands,
such as Bikini Kill: "These bands challenged the sexism and racism
of punk rock, expressing a general desire to make things better for
girls" (Currie et al. 2009, 7). For these bands, "girl power" was for
women who were either teens or in their early twenties. Gonick
(2006, 6) observes, "Girl Power celebrates the fierce and aggressive
potential of girls as well as the reconstitution of girl culture as a
positive force embracing self-expression through fashion, attitude,
and a Do-It-Yourself (DIY) approach to cultural production."

   In spite of its counterculture roots and even though the initial girl
power movement was intensely anti-consumerist, the message of girl
power was quickly picked up within mainstream culture to market
products to young women. The message behind girl power was
picked up by more mainstream music groups, most notably the Spice
Girls, and has echoed throughout numerous television programs,

such as *Buffy the Vampire Slayer* and *Sabrina the Teenage Witch*. Today, a variety of consumer campaigns promote diverse products from T-shirts to lipstick as empowering young women (Gill 2008).

While it might seem that "girl power" is one-dimensional, Currie et al. (2009, 15) point out that "'girl power' is a discursive field within which competing meanings associated with 'being a girl' are made available within popular culture." The emergence of "girl power" cannot be separated from a series of opposing discourses that construct young women as weak, vulnerable, and in need of special care and guidance (Gonick 2006, Harris 2004). Gonick (2006) characterizes this counter-trend as "Reviving Ophelia," which refers to a popular psychology book published in the 1990s. This more fragile incarnation of the modern girl "is a sign of disordered development and [is] a threat to the new social order" (2006, 15). Similarly, Harris (2004) identifies the "at-risk" girl. With both cases, young women are portrayed as harbouring chaotic emotions, engaging in out-of-control behaviours, and making inappropriate consumption choices. Thus, while girl power portrays young women as potentially strong and powerful feminine subjects, girls who embody "Reviving Ophelia" or "at-risk" girls are compromised by their in-between status and are characterized by disordered development. Because young women are constantly represented as teetering on the edge of becoming unstable, they are often identified as an "at risk" or "high risk" population in need of guidance, intervention, and regulation to prevent them from becoming disordered (Mazzarella and Pecora 2007).

In this way, the discourses that construct young women as power-*ful* and autonomous, such as girl power, and the discourses that construct young women as power*less*, problematic, and dependent, reflect the complex positioning of young women as subjects in late modern society. As Harris (2004, 32) observes, under neo-liberalism, "success and failure are constructed as though they were dependent on strategic effort and good personal choices." Yet the belief in individual choice and responsibility obscures the economic, social, and cultural factors that structure the options before a young woman.

The tendency within girl studies has been to examine the emergence of girl power within psychology, the consumption of clothing and beauty products, and within the television, film, and music industries. Far less attention has been paid to the deployment of discourses of girl power within the domain of sexual health and the use of pharmaceutical technologies. As a product that regulates multiple aspects of the body and emotions, and that is used by a large number of young women, I argue the pill is an incredibly important device to consider when seeking to understand the modern characterization of girls and girl culture.

METHODOLOGY

In what follows, I present findings from a discourse analysis of web-based marketing campaigns for Alesse and Yasmin, and in particular the deployment of discourses of girl power. Feminists have long pointed out the importance of examining power, knowledge, and discipline when it is not tied to a single institution and cuts across "a variety of social spheres and spaces such as family, workplace, media, etc." (Gill 2007, 63). Similarly, Currie (1997) and Smith (1990) point to the importance of paying attention to the scripts that discipline women's bodies as part of their everyday life. Advertisements are key sites for understanding how contemporary formations of femininity are communicated to women (Bartky 1998; Bordo 1993; Driscoll 2002, Gill 2007). They "form part of the 'public habitat of images' that work to discipline and regulate women's relationship to their own bodies" (Gill 2007, 63). These scripts are found in fashion magazines and on television; however, a growing number are found online.

In conducting my analysis of Alesse and Yasmin's websites I have examined the text as discourse that constitutes young women, meaning the information and images on the website are engaged and linked into a complex set of social relationships that produce and structure identity. In the *Archeology of Knowledge*, Foucault defines discourse as "an entity of sequences of signs," (1969, 141) which attribute particular meanings to specific objects and subjects. As discourse becomes organized into a system or network that brings together disparate institutions and structures, a discursive formation or field emerges, making it possible for certain statements to be "true" or "sayable." While uniform discourses are rare, it is still possible to distill from them common principles, while at the same time pulling out the tensions between opposing statements. Following Hall, my aim in conducting an analysis of the websites was to consider the knowledge that was being produced (1997, 45). I therefore examined what kinds of meaningful statements were being made by the websites about girls and how they used the pill. I considered the visual and auditory content of the websites, as well as the text. After viewing and reading the materials I noted repeated words, ideas, and concepts and drew out common themes. To be clear, I am not examining the actual impact of the websites on users' identities. Nor do I mean to imply that advertisements simply impose meanings on their viewers, who accept them uncritically and without examination. The aim of my analysis is to consider how the websites propose a particular way of regulating and organizing the conduct of young women (Hall 1997, 46).

Alesse and Yasmin are both brands of the oral contraceptive pill, produced by Wyeth and Bayer respectively. Pharmaceutical companies invest millions of dollars in ensuring that patients will go to their doctor and ask not just for the pill, but specifically for Alesse or Yasmin. The introduction of campaigns on the Web reflects Wyeth and Bayer's recognition that young women, the primary users of the pill, are comfortable accessing information on the Internet. The Yasmin and Alesse websites are not the same. They reflect varying degrees of a discursive field. As I mentioned in the previous section, the discourse of girl power incites a young woman to seek out self-knowledge and to assert this knowledge by choosing to use the pill. Empowerment in this context is based on a young woman's capacity to make "good" choices arising from an individual desire to control her fertility, body, and emotions. On the flip side, a young woman is equally portrayed as not always being able to make the right choices on her own. She is compromised by her in-between status; her body and emotions are often out of control and she requires guidance, intervention, and regulation.

UNPACKING ONLINE MARKETING
FOR ALESSE AND YASMIN

Upon entering the Alesse and Yasmin websites, one is transported into a stereotypical depiction of what makes up a young woman's world. The visual space of the Alesse website, a pink and white room, reflects the physical accessories of a young woman's life: a single bed, a make-up bag, a diary, and a cell phone. Various items, such as pieces of paper with notes scribbled on them, photos of friends, and pillows are artfully scattered to suggest a personalized space. The Yasmin website mimics the layout of a young woman's magazine like *Teen Beat* or *Cosmopolitan*. Throughout the site there are candid Polaroids of smiling young women in artless embraces with friends. There is a calendar with marked dates, such as "Lunch with Kathy," "Start pill today," and "Paper due." A blinking pink cell phone, an iPod and a purple day planner hover on the site, inviting the user to access different informational pamphlets.

The sites are not sexually suggestive at all and in fact hardly mention sexual activity. The central message of the sites is that a young woman is a unique individual. The choices she makes express her individuality. In both websites, as soon as the user enters, she is greeted with upbeat generic "teen" music. The Yasmin website has only one music option; however, on the Alesse website, the user can change the music to meet her tastes. Does she prefer "Rock," "Hard Rock," "Urban," "Electronica," or "New Country"? There are links to the band websites, and free downloads are merged with a section that compares different forms of contraception. The ability to choose what type of music will be played as a backdrop is a reflection of the general message behind Alesse's advertising campaign: that a young woman is in the process of defining who she is as a unique individual through the choices she makes. This message is also found in "Alesseisms." These phrases are prompted by the question, "Tell us what Alesse means for you?" They are meant to indicate the range of meanings that Alesse can have for a young woman. Users can send electronic T-shirts to their friends with their favourite Alesseism, such as "I'm Reallestic" or "I'm Flalesse." Both Yasmin and Alesse's websites fully embrace the notion that for a young woman, "consumption and lifestyle are key to identity," and that "success and young femininity are connected through notions of choice, versatility, beauty and cleverness" (Harris 2004, 22).

Fully embracing the girl power mantra, the Yasmin website emphasizes that taking the pill is an individual project, referring to "*my* health," "*my* Pill," and "*my* Yasmin diary" (emphasis added, Yasmin 2009). The Alesse website is more explicit, and states: "*You* have taken the responsibility for your sexuality and decided to take control" (emphasis added, Alesse 2009). Both the Alesse and Yasmin websites emphasize that being empowered and being a powerful young woman is based on the capacity to make "good" choices relating to fertility *and* general health. Further, the Alesse (2009) website places even more emphasis on the need for a young woman to act in a generally responsible manner toward her body: "If you put aside time to care for yourself, you'll benefit from your efforts. And it doesn't take much. A few regular check-ups and some common sense skin care tips can go a long way." Here, we see that the site ties the habit of pill use into a wider set of beneficial daily habits.

As Granzow observes, "The same discourses used in the campaign for the invention and introduction of The Pill, and the same discourse that reveals an assumed direct correlation between control (over the body) and increased choice (in women's lives), is in operation today" (2007, 47). Previous discourses emphasized the absolute need for women to control fertility. In the Alesse and Yasmin websites, we see that fertility control is downplayed and taking the pill is characterized as an essential accessory in and of itself for young women.

While it might seem that these campaigns situate young women as powerful and independent subjects, the websites also exclude young women and establish them as a problematic population in need of care, control, and regulation. These discourses, what Gonick (2006) calls "Reviving Ophelia" and Harris (2004) calls "girls at-risk," portray young women as chaotic and out of control.

Both the Alesse and Yasmin websites emphasize the internal processes of change and chaos as a young woman goes through puberty and approaches adulthood. In both websites, the questions that pop up as the user scrolls over different objects and spaces, such as relationship problems, the need for breast self-exams and fears surrounding doctor visits, indicate the internal processes of transition and change that a young woman is going through. According to both websites, these transitions create responsibilities in relation to the body, one of which is to be on the pill, both for controlling fertility and "other" benefits. While a young woman may have come to one of the websites interested in learning about fertility control, she quickly learns that she has many other "problems" to worry about, which the pill can help her with.

Both sites place a particular emphasis on acne. On the Alesse website, a discussion of acne is found in the site preamble, "Other Benefits," and in the section "Your Skin." According to the Alesse website, acne can appear without warning and gets "in the way" of a young woman living her life. The Yasmin website also discusses the benefit of the pill for alleviating premenstrual symptoms and lightening blood flow. "Users of birth control pills have less menstrual blood loss and more regular cycles. There may be a decrease in painful menstruation and premenstrual syndrome symptoms" (Yasmin 2009). The Alesse website also affirms that taking the pill will result in lighter and more regular periods and "less severe cramps" (Alesse 2009). An irregular period and the symptoms associated with premenstrual syndrome (P M S) are constituted as problems that constrict a young woman's free movement. Planned periods and the absence of P M S allow her to ensure that her body does not interfere with her life. Again, the Alesse website goes even further. The user is also informed that her long-term health can benefit from using the pill: "While the Pill is an effective method of birth control, it has many other benefits that you may not be aware of ... The Pill can also reduce the likelihood of developing ovarian cysts, endometrial cancer, ovarian cancer and benign breast disease" (Alesse 2009). While the Yasmin website focuses on localized problems like acne and menstruation, the Alesse website presents the pill as a useful drug for keeping potential maladies at bay both in the short and long term.

The Alesse website also highlights that a young woman's emotions are out of control and in need of careful handling. Her sexuality and desire are presented as potentially dangerous and disruptive to her relationship with her parents, her partner, and herself. Discussions about contraception are portrayed as embarrassing and difficult. "Talking about contraception may seem odd, but once you do, you and your partner will both feel better" (Alesse 2009). In both websites, the tone is very patronizing, emphasizing that despite being empowered, the user is still in many ways innocent, sexually demure, and often uncomfortable with her body. As the Alesse website points out, a young woman's out-of-control emotions and desires can get in the way of her better judgment. "Find time to talk before you both get carried away with the moment" (Alesse 2009). Both the Alesse and Yasmin websites instruct a young woman to approach her body in a rational and calculated manner. She is told that the future can be planned and controlled if she is willing to be responsible and take the appropriate steps.

The content of the Yasmin and Alesse websites are not unified instances of the discourse of "girl power" and "Reviving Ophelia"/"girls at-risk," but rather variations on a theme, designed by marketing experts in the hopes of enticing young women to purchase a product, the oral contraceptive pill. In spite of the differences in degree, both sites reveal a common tension. While a young woman is expected to make a personal choice that represents her unique qualities as an individual, in the face of what would seem to be unlimited options, in fact she is directed toward one choice. She is expected to choose to use the pill. Other choices, which are not as effective or far-reaching, would reflect a lapse in her judgement as a responsible individual.

As Driscoll notes, advertising directed at young women often represents them as being "in need of instruction" and "guidance" (2002, 95). In the Alesse website, the narrative voice alternates between that of a helpful and knowing girlfriend and that of a kind and cool aunt, both of whom urge a young woman to recognize what she already knows is best for her. In the same way that magazines are instructional, the Alesse website educates the user about the physical changes she is going through and also directs the way she should conduct herself in relation to her developing body. Her problematic state requires attention to detail and routine, but it also requires the consultation of knowledgeable adults, such as her parents, and experts, such as doctors and pharmacists. According to the websites for Yasmin and Alesse, whether she is ultimately successful in being empowered or not lies in whether she is able to gain access to and continually consume the pill. In this context, "[s]uccess and failure are constructed as though they were dependent on strategic effort and good personal choices ... However, these designations have much more to do with economic and cultural resources than personal competencies" (Harris 2004, 32).

Despite attempting to portray diversity, using multi-ethnic models and diverse age groups, the Alesse and Yasmin websites clearly target young middle- and upper-class women who are more likely to have access to health care and the support of their families in making birth control choices (Harris 2004, 23). By portraying the choice to use the pill as individual, despite the fact that it is textured by social factors, young women who are not able to or who choose not to use the pill are constructed as failing to live up to the neo-liberal ideal of responsibility. A young woman's failure to use the pill may be socially characterized as a more general personal failure; however, her perceived lack of individual responsibility in these cases is often judged in isolation from any social and economic disadvantages that might limit her access to the pill.

Finally, both sites suggest that young women are empowered by the control offered by the pill, and yet when we think back to Ruhl

(2002) we are reminded that the control of biological processes is always complicated and contingent. Despite the fact that the Alesse website promises the user protection from getting "carried away" with her emotions, there are still many issues that the pill cannot resolve, particularly the issue of the transmission of sexually transmitted infections (STIs). Though young women are protected from pregnancy, they need to remain in control and use a condom regardless. The Alesse website situates this responsibility as a question of rational and calculated behaviour and individual control. "Safety is your responsibility. Each one of us is responsible for practicing safe sex" (Alesse 2009). "While there are no medical means to prevent STIs, a combination of good personal hygiene, safe sex practices and healthy living can help to avoid them" (Alesse 2009). The pill's effectiveness as a contraceptive can be affected by many factors, such as time of use and use of antibiotics. Further, genital warts and herpes can both still be contracted even with the use of a condom. Alesse's disclaimer is complicated by the reality that even responsible behaviour is incapable of resolving the unpredictable nature of disease in the context of sexual relations. Further, Holland et al. found that the negotiation of sexual encounters is shaped by "social constraints which legitimate sexual pressure from men, including violence, and provide a model of sexual behaviour for young women which can be described as passive femininity" (1994, 23). Under this model, young women are expected to make their bodies available for uninterrupted heterosexual lovemaking, and in many ways the pill legitimates this.

De Beauvoir and Sanger sought freedom for women through technology. But technologies are social objects that come to have meaningful histories of their own, as is made clear in this volume by Scala's, Cattapan's, and Cameron and Gruben's examinations of reproductive technologies. The pill is now intimately connected with young femininity in most modern liberal states. While it has created new types of bodily control, which many women may value, it has equally opened up new avenues of regulation. I do not intend to reinstate the notion that young women are in need of care and attention, or to reify the belief that they are in fact a population "at risk." Rather, I wish to point out how the discourse used in the Alesse and Yasmin websites constructs a conflicting representation that is at the heart of contemporary feminine subjectivity: the claim that a young woman is meant to be the author of her own destiny ignores the social forces that define the parameters of this project and obscures the reality that choices always involve varying degrees of constraint and control on the part of the individual. This tension is amplified in the context of the pill, because the subjects addressed are young women, and at issue is their sexual health.

CONCLUSION

"My aim has been to emphasize, by the use of concrete examples and neglected facts, the need of a new approach to individual and social problems. Its central challenge is that civilization, in any true sense of the word, is based upon the control and guidance of the great natural instinct of sex. Mastery of this force is possible only through the instrument of birth control" (Sanger 1922, 1).

For Margaret Sanger, the dream of the pill represented women's freedom, but also a social utopia made possible by the technological control of women's bodies. Her political views were strongly supported by many feminist philosophers of the time, who emphasized the importance of women being able to control their reproductive processes to act as free-minded autonomous subjects capable of rational decision-making. While the issue of choice continues to colour contemporary use of the pill, I have argued that there is an intensification of individuality in decision-making and an increased emphasis placed on young women as key decision-makers in reproductive politics. As exemplified in the Alesse and Yasmin websites, young, heterosexual women are expected to make personal decisions about pill use. Yet the choices made available to them are limited by their problematic status, as well as by social and economic factors that limit their access to the pill. I do not contend that women should not use the pill. What I wish to throw into relief is how the construction of the pill is as complicated now as it was when it was first released for consumption.

As Tone and Watkins (2007, 5) point out, "a drug's value is measured not only by its pharmacological effect but also by the cultural contexts in which it is made, circulated and used." In Canada, marketing for the pill targets young women and draws heavily on the popular discourse of "girl power," as well as the conflicting notion that young women are an "at risk" population in need of special care and concern. In both sites, a young woman is characterized as active, independent, and sexually powerful while at the same time represented as an individual at risk for being overwhelmed by her unruly body, emotions, and sexual urges. Ultimately, these seemingly opposing positions work together to reinforce the modern young woman as both the subject of her own responsible conduct as well as an object reflecting the wider anxieties of late liberalism, such as individual control, and social and economic inequalities. In marketing to young women over the Internet, the Alesse and Yasmin websites present controlling fertility through the pill as the ultimate choice facing a young woman. By communicating this information, the sites seem to be benevolently responding to a social need that will ultimately lead to the empowerment of all young women. Yet, the websites, constructed by pharmaceutical companies, seek to meet a financial end, selling a product to a consumer, with the assistance of doctors and other medical professionals. As such, it is perhaps to be expected that the sites uncritically present young women who do not take the pill as failing to live up to the responsibilities of the ideal young feminine subject. What is troubling is that the websites are in many ways merely synthesizing general social views that continue to characterize teenage motherhood, acne, P M S, and in some cases even cancer as the sole result of an individual girl's power, and pill use as the only rational response to these problems.

BIBLIOGRAPHY

Alesse. (2009). Retrieved 13 July 2009. http://www.alesse.ca.
Albury, R. 1999. *The Politics of Reproduction: Beyond the Slogans.* Sydney: Allen and Unwin.
Alderman, E., J. Rieder, and M. Cohen. 2003. "The History of Adolescent Medicine." *Pediatric Research* 54(1): 137–47.
Bailey, Beth. 1997. "Prescribing the Pill: Politics, Culture and the Sexual Revolution in America's Heartland. *Journal of Social History* 30(4): 827–56.
Baker, Maureen. 2008. "Restructuring Reproduction: International and National Pressures." *Journal of Sociology* 44(1): 65–81.
Black, Amanda, Diane Francoeur, and Timothy Rowe. 2004. "Consensus Canadien sur la Contraception." *Directives Cliniques de la S O G C* 143: 158–74.
Butler, Judith. 1990. *Gender Trouble.* New York: Routledge.

Casper, Monica, and Laura Carpenter. 2008. "Sex, Drugs, and Politics: The HPV Vaccine for Cervical Cancer." *Sociology of Health & Illness* 30(6): 886–99.

Connell, E., and A. Hunt. 2010. "The HPV Vaccination Campaign: A Project of Moral Regulation in an Era of Biopolitics." *Canadian Journal of Sociology* 35(1): 63–82.

Cream, J. 1995. "Women on Trial: A Private Pillory." In *Mapping the Subject: Geographies of Cultural Transformation*, S. Pile and N. Thrift, eds. London: Routledge.

Cruikshank, Barbara. 1993. "Revolutions Within: Self-government and Self-esteem." *Economy and Society* 22(3): 327–44.

Currie, Dawn. 1997. "Decoding Femininity: Advertisements and Their Teenage Readers." *Gender & Society* 11(4): 453–77.

Currie, D., D. Kelly, and S. Pomerantz. 2009. *"Girl Power": Girls Reinventing Girlhood*. New York: Peter Lang.

de Beauvoir, Simone. 1952. *The Second Sex*. New York: Vintage Books.

Driscoll, C. 2002. *Girls: Feminine Adolescence in Popular Culture and Cultural Theory*. New York: Columbia University Press.

Firestone, S. 1970. *The Dialectic of Sex: The Case for Feminist Revolution*. New York: William Morrow and Company.

Flower, R. 2004. "Lifestyle Drugs: Pharmacology and the Social Agenda." *Trends in Pharmacological Sciences* 25(4): 182–5.

Foucault, Michel. 1984. "The Politics of Health in the Eighteenth Century." In *The Foucault Reader*, P. Rabinow, ed., 273–90. New York: Pantheon.

Foucault, Michel. 1991a. "Governmentality." In *The Foucault Effect: Studies in Governmentality*, G. Burchell, C. Gordon, and P. Miller, eds., 87–104. Chicago: University of Chicago Press.

Fox, Nick, and Katie Ward. 2008. "Pharma in the Bedroom… and the Kitchen… The Pharmaceuticalisation of Daily Life." *Sociology of Health & Illness* 30(6): 856–68.

Gill, Rosalind. 2007. *Gender and the Media*. Cambridge: Polity Press.

Gill, Rosalind. 2008. "Empowerment/Sexism: Figuring Sexual Agency in Contemporary Advertising." *Feminism & Psychology* 18(1): 35–60.

Gonick, Marnina. 2006. "Between 'Girl Power' and 'Reviving Ophelia': Constituting the Neoliberal Girl Subject." *NWSA* 18(2): 1–23.

Granzow, Kara. 2007. "De-constructing 'Choice': The Social Imperative and Women's Use of the Birth Control Pill." *Culture, Health & Sexuality* 9(1): 43–54.

Hall, Stuart. 1997. *Representation: Cultural Representations and Signifying Practices*. Buckingham: Open University Press.

Harris, Anita. 2004. *Future Girl: Young Women in the Twenty-First Century*. New York Routledge.

Harris, Anita. 2005. "Discourses of Desire as Governmentality: Young Women, Sexuality and the Significance of Safe Spaces." *Feminism & Psychology* 15(1): 39–43.

Holland, J., C. Ramzanoglu, S. Sharpe, and R. Thomson. 1994. "Power and Desire: The Embodiment of Female Sexuality." *Feminist Review* 46: 21–38.

Johnson, Lesley. 1993. *The Modern Girl: Girlhood and Growing Up*. Buckingham: Open University Press.

Lupton, Deborah. 1995. *The Imperative of Health: Public Health and the Regulated Body*. London: Sage.

Martin, Kelly, and Zheng Wu. 2000. "Contraceptive Use in Canada: 1984–1995." *Family Planning Perspectives* 32(2): 65–73.

May, Elaine Tyler. 2010. *America and the Pill: A History of Promise, Peril, and Liberation*. Basic Books.

Mazzarella, S., and N. Pecora. 1999. *Growing Up Girls: Popular Culture and the Construction of Identity*. New York: Peter Lang.

Mazzarella, S., and N. Pecora. 2007. "Girls in Crisis: Newspaper Coverage of Adolescent Girls." *Journal of Communication Inquiry* 31(1): 6–27.

McLaren, Angus. 1990. *A History of Contraception*. Oxford: Basil Blackwell.

McRobbie, A. 2000. *Feminism and Youth Culture*. New York: Routledge.

Mill, John Stuart. 1869[1977]. *The Subjection of Women*. New York: Dover.

O'Brien, M. 1981. *The Politics of Reproduction*. Boston: Routledge & Kegan Paul.

Rose, Nicolas. 1990. *Governing the Soul: The Shaping of the Private Self*. London: Routledge.

Ruhl, Leslie. 2002. "Dilemmas of the Will: Uncertainty, Reproduction and the Rhetoric of Control." *Signs* 27(3): 641–63.

Sanger, Margaret. 1920. *Women and the New Race*. Paris: Brentano's.

Sanger, Margaret. 1922. *The Pivot of Civilization*. Paris: Brentano's.

Smith, Dorothy. 1990. *Texts, Facts and Femininity*. New York: Routledge.

Tone, Andrea. 2001. *Devices and Desires: A History of Contraceptives in America*. New York: Hill and Wang.

Wailoo, K., Livingstone, J., Epstein, S., Aronowitz, R. 2010. *Three Shots at Prevention: The HPV Vaccine and the Politics of Medicine's Solutions.* Baltimore: Johns Hopkins University Press.

Watkins, E. 1998. *On the Pill: A Social History of Oral Contraceptives, 1950–1970.* Baltimore: Johns Hopkins University Press.

Wilkins, Kathryn, Helen Johansen, Marie P. Beaudet, and C. Ineke Neutel. 2000. "Oral Contraceptive Use." *Health Reports* 11(4): 25–37.

Wollstonecraft, Mary. 1792[1975]. *A Vindication of the Rights of Women.* New York: W.W. Norton.

Yasmin. (2009). Accessed 13 July 2009. http://www.yasmin.ca.

11

Promoting Breastfeeding, Solving Social Problems: Exploring State Involvement in Breastfeeding

TASNIM NATHOO AND ALECK OSTRY

The question of what to feed the baby is not a new one. And it is a question that is deeply intertwined with ideas about the family, time, gender roles, science, and technology. Currently, Canadian policy on topics as diverse as early childhood development, nutrition and obesity, and childbirth practices emphasizes the importance of breastfeeding promotion. Historically, since the end of the nineteenth century, breastfeeding practices have received widespread attention in Canada, partly because of the influence of breastfeeding on health outcomes such as infant mortality and morbidity. Over the past century, breastfeeding has often intersected with other areas of the politics of reproduction, including concerns about commodification, medicalization, the moral regulation of mothering, structural determinants of women's "choices," and access to health care services.

In this chapter, we review federal government involvement with breastfeeding since the beginning of the twentieth century and examine the context in which various discourses about breastfeeding have evolved to investigate how these discourses have influenced the promotion of breastfeeding by the state. We suggest that breastfeeding promotion is an important area for government involvement, but requires an approach that focuses on improving the quality of women's breastfeeding experiences rather than one that emphasizes the individual and societal benefits of breastfeeding and places particular importance on increasing overall initiation and duration rates.

INFANT MORTALITY AND GOOD MOTHERING

Public health and medical authorities have long had an interest in infant feeding practices. In Canada, the relationship between breastfeeding and infant mortality was recognized by provincial and municipal governments in the last quarter of the nineteenth century (Comacchio 1993; Bideau, Desjardins, and Brignoli 1997). Mothering practices in general and breastfeeding in particular were seen as key for solving the infant mortality crisis. Public health authorities were beginning to observe shifts away from long periods of exclusive breastfeeding and believed "gastrointestinal problems" could be linked to at least one third of all infant deaths (Nathoo and Ostry 2009).

Reformers and government authorities were accurate in their assessment: the situation was grave. In 1900, approximately one in four infants did not live past their first year. By the 1920s, concerns about the strength of the nation were widespread in both English and French Canada. Fuelled by the loss of life incurred in the First World War and the worldwide flu pandemic of 1918 and 1919, concerns about high infant mortality rates merged with fears about the declining birth rate of English- and French-Canadians. In English Canada, discussions focused on the survival of the British Empire; in French Canada, concerns were about "the survival of the race." All of these debates were supported by the new science of eugenics (Baillargeon 2009; Comacchio 1993).

The development of the first federal department of health in 1919 and the formation of the Division of Child Welfare came from this political desire to strengthen the nation. Charged with the task of "saving and preserving Maternal and Child Life," the new division began its term by developing a series of "Little Blue Books" for mothers. These advice manuals covered a range of topics on childrearing ranging from childbirth to housekeeping in rural outposts (Arnup 1994).

By far the most popular of these publications was *The Canadian Mother's Book* (Lewis and Watson 1991/92). By the end of 1921, over

150,000 copies had been distributed. Between 1921 and 1932, nearly one in four mothers received a copy. Eleven editions of *The Canadian Mother's Book* were published between 1921 and 1991. While it is impossible to know the extent to which mothers valued or followed the advice in these publications, it is clear that they were popular and widely distributed. More important, they chronicle over seventy years of changes in childbirth and child-rearing practices. In every edition, mothers are advised to breastfeed and the benefits of this decision are clearly outlined.

Helen MacMurchy, the author of these early advice manuals for mothers, was concerned about the high rates of infant mortality observed. As a maternal feminist, she wished to show the important, and often vital, national role that mothers could have through their accomplishments in the domestic setting (Buckely 1977; Dodd 1991; McConnachie 1983). A mother was the "First Servant of the State." In this light, motherhood was a natural, sacred right and breastfeeding a national duty. As Cattapan's discussion (chapter 6) of the connection between citizenship and the duties of parents shows, these views were not confined to government health publications. The critical role of breastfeeding and good mothering practices to the health and well-being of the nation was also reflected in popular and political discourse (see figure 11.1).

The intellectual and ideological roots of breastfeeding promotion in the early twentieth century emerged from these broader concerns about citizenship and nation-building as well as from social issues such as the campaign against infant mortality. Ideas about motherhood were at the core of these early efforts. The decline in breastfeeding rates was blamed primarily on women. Mothers failed to breastfeed because they were ignorant ("most mothers think cow's milk is just as good"), because they accepted advice from their family and social networks ("we must give [them] skilled medical advice") or because they needed to work ("[this] should not be allowed to happen") (MacMurchy 1910). The solution was to provide mothers with advice, access to medical professionals, and to elevate and glorify domestic roles for women. Other causes of infant mortality, such as poverty and overcrowded housing, were ignored, as were other factors contributing to the overall decline in breastfeeding, such as the emergence of pediatrics and changing demographics.

11.1 Advertisement for Glaxo the Super-milk, an alternative to breastfeeding. The ad begins: "Mothers of Canada, it is to the Babies you hold in your arms that Canada looks to carry on her great traditions, and upon you and your mother wisdom depends the fitness of those Babies for the mighty destiny that awaits them" (*Globe*, 8 July 1921).

SCIENTIFIC MEDICINE AND THE DESKILLING
OF MOTHERS

Following the First World War, there was growing government support for the use of scientific principles in solving social problems. MacMurchy's advice to seek care from medical professionals reflected the emergence of science into government and the promotion of medical solutions to child and maternal welfare. "Scientific medicine," which involved scientists and physicians in health care issues, gradually became the new authority on breastfeeding (Apple 1987; Nathoo and Ostry 2009). Scientific solutions to national problems, such as high rates of infant and maternal mortality, had implications for breastfeeding – while breastfeeding was promoted for its life-saving properties for infants, scientific principles created barriers to successful breastfeeding for mothers.

Initially, scientists were interested in developing alternatives to breast milk for use in cases where a mother had died or was unable to breastfeed. The medical specialty of pediatrics emerged from these early experiments and pediatricians became known as baby feeders due to their expertise in developing cow's milk formulas for infants. While early pediatricians recognized breast milk as superior to any of their concoctions, infant formula became associated with healthy, "rosy-cheeked" infants and as a modern and efficient way to feed a baby. As well, other aspects of "scientific childrearing" inhibited breastfeeding success. Scientific principles applied to breastfeeding emphasized hygiene (e.g., cleansing nipples before feeding the baby), strict feeding schedules, and monitoring weight gain. This, in addition to a lack of training in practical solutions to common breastfeeding problems, meant that private physicians were creating an ambiguous role for themselves with respect to breastfeeding (Comacchio 1993; Nathoo and Ostry 2009).

A letter written by Mrs R. Payne to the National Council of Family and Child Welfare in 1931 is one example of some of the challenges women experienced in accessing practical support for breastfeeding from physicians:

As stated in the Canadian Mother Book: If the baby has three or four stools per day, do not hesitate and call the doctor. This is what I did as soon as I was aware of the fact. Why did my physician assert that this was not serious? and in whom can one place her confidence? Noticing no improvement, I called a second physician immediately who told me a baby suffering from diarrhea should be placed on a special diet. This was done, but it was too late. If great are the responsibilities of the mothers (I nursed my child) those of the doctor are of the same degree, although some of them seem to ignore this fact. (quoted in Buckley 1979)

Government advice throughout the 1930s, 1940s, and 1950s reflected scientific approaches to infant feeding. By the 1940s, concerns about infant mortality had abated and exhortations to breastfeed had dimmed. Physicians, as the new experts on infant feeding, suggested that formula feeding was just as good as breastfeeding (Nathoo and Ostry 2009).

The shift toward hospital birth solidified public perceptions of physicians and other health professionals as experts in all areas of maternal and child health, from pregnancy to childbirth to childrearing. In 1940, approximately 35 per cent of Canadian women gave birth in hospitals. By 1960, almost every woman birthed in hospital. The shift toward hospital birth resulted in the increasing influence of physicians and nurses in the area of infant feeding. As well, a range of hospital practices, such as delaying an infant's first feeding for six to eight hours after birth and restricting contact between mother and infant to allow the mother to rest both directly and indirectly affected women's breastfeeding success (Strong-Boag and McPherson 1990).

These changes, in conjunction with demographic changes such as urbanization and immigration, life in rural frontiers, and smaller family sizes meant that women who wanted to breastfeed did not have access to their extended families or women in their communities for assistance with breastfeeding. By the 1960s, the practical knowledge and skills required to breastfeed successfully had nearly disappeared and breastfeeding rates were at an all-time low (Nathoo and Ostry 2009). While breastfeeding was supported in theory, the diminished value of breastfeeding in relation to national problems in the 1960s meant that breastfeeding promotion became, in practice, a low priority for government. Concerns over high rates of infant and maternal mortality and their effects on the nation's well-being had abated. The threats associated with potentially unsafe milk and water being used in formula feeding had lessened with the spread of pasteurization and electricity within homes. Furthermore, many women, with support from their health care providers, perceived formula feeding to be "just as good" as breastfeeding while also being socially acceptable and the most readily available "choice."

SCIENTIFIC MEDICINE "REDISCOVERS" BREASTFEEDING

In 1950, Hilary Bourne, a physician in the department of obstetrics and gynaecology at the Royal Victoria Hospital in Montreal, commented: "It is a well-known fact that the worst place in the world as regards breast feeding is the United States; Canada runs a close second. It is also well known that the European, and in particular the Scandinavian, countries are best in this regard. The difference, however, is not due to geographical location, or anatomical development, or even physiological insufficiency. The great difference is one of temperament, education, and so-called modern living" (Bourne 1950).

By the late 1960s, these attitudes toward breastfeeding began to change. Interest in breastfeeding grew within a range of social, cultural, and political movements. The natural childbirth movement emerged strongly in the late 1960s and coincided with feminism's Second Wave, in which women were re-evaluating their roles in society and their relationships with their bodies. The formation of La Leche League, a lay organization supporting breastfeeding, continued a trend away from reliance on experts and toward a valuing of women's experiences (Blum and Vandewater 1993; Dingle 1977). Furthermore, international efforts to counter the marketing practices of infant formula companies in the developing world, in particular the Nestlé boycott of the late 1970s, found widespread support in the Canadian population (Baker 1981; Canadian Press 1979; Hogan 1979; Reuter News Agency 1982; Van Esterik 1989).

The late 1970s marked a renewed period of government interest in and support of breastfeeding. Popular interest in and support for breastfeeding was reinforced by recent scientific findings that documented the immunological, psychological, and nutritional benefits of breastfeeding for both mother and child. These findings also emphasized the potential health care savings that could be incurred through the promotion of breastfeeding. By the late 1970s, health authorities and the scientific community had become outspoken in their support of breastfeeding and efforts to support breastfeeding by government culminated in the national campaign to promote breastfeeding that began in the early 1980s (Canadian Paediatric Society 1978; Canadian Paediatric Society Nutrition Committee and Nutrition 1978; Myres 1988).

This campaign was, by far, the most comprehensive effort in history to promote breastfeeding by government. Under the leadership of the federal government, a task force that included the Department of National Health and Welfare, the Society of Obstetricians and Gynaecologists of Canada, and La Leche League Canada was formed. Recognizing the ambivalence of many health professionals toward breastfeeding and their dearth of practical skills in the area, the first phase of the campaign focused on increasing awareness of the importance of breastfeeding among health care personnel (Myres, Watson, and Harrison 1981). Other initiatives included the development of alliances between mothers' groups and health professionals, the development of an educational booklet for mothers, a collaboration with the National Film Board to develop several films on breastfeeding, the first national survey of Canadian infant feeding practices, and endorsement of the 1981 *WHO Code of Marketing of Breast-Milk Substitutes* (Myres 1983). The national campaign of the 1980s was unique in that it expanded beyond traditional health promotion efforts, which had generally focused on individual behaviour change, and considered other factors that influenced breastfeeding success, such as health professional and hospital practices. Bolstered by a resurgence of interest in breastfeeding and a rapid increase in breastfeeding rates in the late 1970s and early 1980s, scientific and medical support for breastfeeding solidified the "return to breastfeeding." Women, for their own reasons, led the trend back to breastfeeding while government, backed by scientific and medical knowledge and global movements, supported women's interests in and efforts to return to breastfeeding.

THE HEALTH AND WELL-BEING OF CHILDREN

The national campaign to promote breastfeeding drew to a close at the end of the 1980s. During the 1990s, the federal government continued to recognize the value of breastfeeding. In particular, initiatives and activities to support breastfeeding evolved out of international commitments to the well-being and rights of children. These included the ratification of the United Nations Convention on the

Rights of the Child (1991), the announcements of a proposed child benefit in the federal budget (1992), the National Children's Agenda (1997), the National Child Benefit (1998), and the Early Childhood Development Agreement (2000). The focus on early childhood development and healthy families resulted in funds for breastfeeding promotion becoming available.

The most visible federal efforts to support breastfeeding included the development of health promotion materials such as *10 Great Reasons to Breastfeed* and *10 Valuable Tips for Successful Breastfeeding*, the funding of an Expert Working Group on Breastfeeding, the creation of a social marketing campaign entitled *Breastfeeding Anytime, Anywhere* to encourage breastfeeding in public, and the inclusion of breastfeeding in national discussions of child welfare and in the development of national surveys. The government also supported the 1996 launch of the Baby-Friendly Initiative by the Breastfeeding Committee of Canada, a non-profit organization that focuses on the development of practices and policies in health care settings that support breastfeeding (Levitt et al. 1996; Naylor 2001).

While breastfeeding was widely discussed in a variety of policy settings that touched on child health, most government activities continued to focus on providing information to mothers and on addressing the perceived barriers to preventing mothers from breastfeeding successfully as well as the factors contributing to early cessation. As Sokolon (chapter 8) emphasizes, these health promotion materials were criticized for over-emphasizing the benefits of breastfeeding without adequately addressing possible challenges and ambivalence that women might experience (Wall 2001). The federal government did not take any further action to implement the 1981 WHO Code, despite declarations in support of those tenets, nor did it regulate the marketing practices of the formula industry (Sterken 2001). Although it was recognized that there was an increasing demand for human milk banks, there continued to be only one milk bank in Canada (Sibbald 2000). As well, the Breastfeeding Committee of Canada continued to work via committee at the provincial and territorial levels, with minimal financial support, to implement the Baby-Friendly Initiative. By 2000, 132 countries and nearly 15,000 hospitals worldwide had joined the Baby-Friendly Hospital Initiative; at the end of the decade, Canada had only one baby-friendly hospital (Wah 2000; Canadian Institute for Health Information 2004; Canadian Institute of Child Health 1996).

During the 1990s, breastfeeding promotion continued to receive support from government. However, the emphasis remained on child health. Initiatives such as milk banks and hospital birthing practices, which affected women's experiences of their bodies and increased women's choices regarding mothering practices, received less government support. Interestingly, one government policy at the end of the 1990s that had a substantial effect on women's overall mothering experiences, including breastfeeding, had very little to do with breastfeeding itself. In Canada, mothers with children born before 31 December 2000 were entitled to approximately six months of job-protected, compensated maternity leave. For children born after this date, leave was extended to about one year in most provinces. One of the indirect outcomes of this change was significant increases in the duration of breastfeeding. For eligible mothers, breastfeeding duration increased by one month and exclusive breastfeeding increased by half a month (Baker and Milligan 2008). It appears that structural changes providing women with the option of extended breastfeeding could be an effective means of promoting breastfeeding as opposed to public health campaigns that evolved out of individualized concerns with child health.

A REVIEW OF TRENDS IN BREASTFEEDING PRACTICES AND FEDERAL GOVERNMENT INVOLVEMENT WITH BREASTFEEDING

While advice to mothers from scientific and government authorities has always recommended breastfeeding over formula feeding, rates of breastfeeding in Canada have fluctuated enormously. At the turn of the twentieth century, breastfeeding practices began to shift away from near universal rates of breastfeeding for extended periods of time. By the 1920s, rates of breastfeeding initiation and duration were decreasing according to class and education, with women of higher classes leading the trend away from breastfeeding. By the 1960s, only 25 per cent of women initiated breastfeeding, with 2 per cent breastfeeding exclusively. Between 1965 and 2009, breastfeeding initiation rates in Canada increased from 25 per cent to 87.5 per cent, with rates increasing the most quickly in the late 1970s and early 1980s. Since 2005, national rates have held steady at about 87 per cent (Statistics Canada 2010; Nathoo and Ostry 2009).

A review of federal breastfeeding policy over the past hundred years reveals a variety of strategies, initiatives, and programs to promote breastfeeding, ranging from the publication of advice literature for mothers to the ratification of international conventions and codes to supporting provincial efforts to modify hospital birthing practices (see table 11.1) (Nathoo and Ostry 2009). One constant has been an emphasis on educating mothers about the benefits of breastfeeding, so as to increase breastfeeding initiation and duration rates. Less attention has been paid to supporting initiatives that provide women with practical and material supports such as widespread and affordable milk banks, access to maternity benefits for all groups of women, ensuring health professionals have expertise in breastfeeding, and financial support to lay organizations (e.g., mother-to-mother support groups) and non-profit organizations supporting breastfeeding. As well, policies have not been particularly attentive to the diverse needs of women – for example, how the needs of women may vary depending on geographical location, socio-economic status, or type of work. Instead, the infant feeding practices of certain groups of women have received undue attention, for example those of immigrant and Aboriginal women, even in periods when their breastfeeding rates were higher than those of the general population (Nathoo and Ostry 2009).

Since the 1970s, federal, provincial, and territorial relations have had a marked influence on the uptake of various initiatives to support breastfeeding, especially with respect to strategies requiring legislation to be implemented or those that affected structural and material supports to successful breastfeeding. While Canada was a signatory to the 1981 International Code of Marketing of Breast-Milk Substitutes (the WHO Code), the Canadian government, unlike other countries, did not translate the code into legislation. The argument at the federal level was that provincial governments determine the delivery of health care services. The federal government did make immediate changes to hospital policies in the territories, because territorial health care is under federal jurisdiction (Myres 1981). Provincially, only Quebec was willing to use legislation to enforce the code. Other provinces left the decisions up to individual hospital boards ("Timbrell Won't Ban Formula Giveaways" 1981). Over the years, the federal government has developed expert guidelines on birthing practices and breastfeeding support by health professionals. However, as the above example of the WHO Code

Table 11.1
Strategies to promote breastfeeding undertaken by the federal government,
1920–2000.

Strategy	Example
Information for mothers	*The Canadian Mother's Book* (1923, 1928) *A Moveable Feast* (film, 1982) *10 Great Reasons to Breastfeed* (1998)
Information for health professionals	*Feeding Babies: A Counselling Guide on Practical Solutions to Common Infant Feeding Questions* (1986) *Nutrition for Healthy Term Infants* (1998, 2004)
Ratification of international codes	International Code of Marketing of Breast-Milk Substitutes (1981) W H O Innocenti Declaration on the Protection, Promotion and Support of Breastfeeding (1990)
Modification of hospital birthing practices	*Family-Centred Maternity and Newborn Care: A Resource and Self-Evaluation Guide* (1987) Baby-Friendly Initiative (1998)
Social marketing campaigns	*Breastfeeding Anytime, Anywhere* campaign (1994)
National surveys of infant feeding patterns	Nutrition Canada Survey (1970–72) Canadian Community Health Survey (2003)
Demonstration projects and special projects	Mother's Milk Service (collection of breast milk for premature infants) (1949) *Multicultural Perspective of Breastfeeding in Canada* (1997)

demonstrates, the devolution of health care responsibilities to the provincial and local levels means that these guidelines provide direction and support only. Further, the training and education of physicians and other health professionals are often under the jurisdiction of autonomous professional organizations or educational institutions. The Baby-Friendly Initiative, started in 1998 by the non-profit organization The Breastfeeding Committee of Canada, has also had to work at a provincial and territorial level (The Breastfeeding Committee for Canada 2002). While most of their work has occurred on a hospital-by-hospital basis, some provincial governments have provided more tangible support than others. The outcome is a diverse and inconsistent range of practices and support for breastfeeding across the country.

Breastfeeding rates have fluctuated in response to social and cultural trends and do not appear to be affected by traditional health promotion strategies, which rely on the dissemination of information on the benefits of breastfeeding and warnings of the dangers of formula feeding (Nathoo and Ostry 2009). While there is an important role for governments to play in ensuring that accurate information about available infant feeding methods and their consequences, both good and bad, is readily accessible for its citizens, there is clearly a need for breastfeeding promotion policies that do more than provide information and education. As well, popular discussions about infant feeding have tended to pit breastfeeding advocates against naysayers and scientists against women's lived experiences, and reflect an atmosphere of antagonism and controversy over a false dichotomy (formula versus the breast).

Since the 1920s, it has been reasonable to ask: What happens to mothers whose infant feeding decisions clash with the advice of experts or others? When the first edition of *The Canadian Mother's Book* was published, rates of breastfeeding were already beginning to decline. While breastfeeding initiation rates in 2009 hovered around 87 per cent, very few women met current national and W H O recommendations of exclusive breastfeeding for six months: only 24 per cent of Canadian women breastfed their babies exclusively for six months or longer (Statistics Canada 2010). The discrepancies between recommended breastfeeding and women's actual practices clearly indicates that "breast is best" is not always true for individual women. Guilt, shame, coercion, and isolation are words now associated with mothers' decisions about infant feeding – and not just mothers who choose to formula feed. The terrain of infant feeding has become treacherous, and mothers of all backgrounds are constantly on the defensive – defending their right to breastfeed in public, their decision to formula feed, their decision to delay weaning past the age of two years, their decision to breastfeed their first child and then formula feed their second. After nearly one hundred years of promoting breastfeeding for a variety of reasons, how should government and medical authorities proceed?

POLICIES TO IMPROVE THE QUALITY OF WOMEN'S BREASTFEEDING EXPERIENCES

At the turn of the twenty-first century, the context of breastfeeding promotion has changed once again. Critiques of traditional health promotion strategies that focus on the education of mothers remain and broader structural determinants affecting mothers' decisions and ability to succeed at breastfeeding remain unaddressed. The public health imperative to breastfeed remains strong and is often tinged with a moral and judgemental tone, as witnessed in studies of women's experiences and in media (Schmeid, Sheehan, and Barclay 2001; Murphy 1999, 2000). However, unlike the 1920s, when breastfeeding rates were declining, breastfeeding rates have returned to high levels and remained constant. Indeed, in some parts of the country, such as British Columbia, breastfeeding initiation rates are 97 per cent. This suggests a need to explore strategies that emphasize exclusivity and duration over initiation. Yet a historical review of federal breastfeeding policy suggests exploring alternative strategies for the promotion of breastfeeding.

Studies have highlighted the range of factors that influence women's perceptions of successful breastfeeding, including maternal enjoyment, compatibility with family life, physiological and health benefits, the perception of the infant's response, and the mother's feelings of closeness with her infant (Burns et al. 2010). "In general, it appears that women will continue to breastfeed if they are satisfied with the experience and if they believe their babies are satisfied. While some women are able to continue breastfeeding despite dissatisfaction with some aspects of the experience, their perception that their infant is satisfied is crucial to continued breastfeeding" (Ayre-Jaschke 2004, 91).

While breastfeeding is certainly no longer viewed as a national duty, the association of breastfeeding with good mothering continues in various guises. Alternatives to breastfeeding that do not endanger a baby's life now exist and formula feeding no longer verges on traitorous. But the scientific evidence continues to support a myriad of benefits associated with breastfeeding. While these claims may often be overstated and may not have any bearing on women's decisions, they have engendered a culture of controversy in terms of the "breast versus the bottle."

As we have seen, breastfeeding promotion strategies that emphasize exclusivity and duration often create a discrepancy between women's experiences and the perceptions of expert scientific, public health, and government advice. This suggests a need to promote breastfeeding in a way that allows for variation in the emotional and developmental needs of infants and their mothers and the varied contexts in which breastfeeding occurs. As Lee (chapter 12) argues, perhaps it would be wise to find ways of improving the quality of women's breastfeeding experiences, rather than focusing solely on duration and exclusivity. The argument for emphasizing approaches to breastfeeding promotion that address the quality of women's experiences is simple: women who have negative experiences of breastfeeding do not breastfeed for very long, nor do they become advocates for breastfeeding.

Maternal confidence has been considered to be a key component in a mother's perseverance in breastfeeding (Hausman 2004). Practices that support early physical attachment and support in learning about and responding to infant cues are important. Numerous studies have demonstrated the importance of various hospital practices such as rooming-in and encouraging breastfeeding on demand in bolstering breastfeeding success (Saddeh and Akre 1996). Many of these practices are key components in the WHO/UNICEF Baby-Friendly Hospital Initiative or have been part of a movement toward family-centred maternity care since the 1980s. Yet many of these practices are not widespread. For example, the prevalence of rooming-in, the practice of caring for the mother and newborn together in the same room immediately following birth, remains low. On average, 65 per cent of mothers report rooming-in at the hospital where they gave birth; rates range across the country from 16.7 per cent to 78.6 per cent (Chalmers et al. 2009).

The issue of maternal confidence is not limited to addressing the emotional and practical needs of mothers. Historically, formula marketing strategies have exploited mothers' uncertainties, and they continue to do so today. While marketing practices have changed in response to technology (as for example when companies who had only advertised in newspapers expanded to mail-outs and telemarketing), the messages used to promote breast milk alternatives have remained similar. While formula marketing copy agrees that breastfeeding is superior to formula, these messages also suggest that formula should be considered an adequate substitute in the case of insufficient milk, concerns about infant weight gain, or worries about whether the baby is getting enough milk (because formula in a bottle is easier to monitor). Since the mid-1990s, formula marketing practices have intensified, with a shift toward targeting mothers rather than hospitals and health professionals (Sterken 2002; Canadian Press 1994; Kryhul 2000). These practices have remained unmonitored and unchecked by government. Unfortunately, the marketing of formula is not like the promotion of other food or infant products, because the physiological process involved in the production of breast milk is greatly influenced by psychological suggestion and environmental stressors.

Perhaps strategies that are not directly related to breastfeeding will have the most success in improving women's experiences and will have spillover effects that increase the exclusivity and duration of the practice. The significant increase in breastfeeding exclusivity and duration following changes to maternity leave in 2000 is one such example. It appears that if women have the extended opportunity to breastfeed, they will. However, in this particular case, it should be noted that maternity leave is not available to all women in Canada and not all women can afford to take time away from work at a reduced income (Heymann and Kramer 2009). The government of Quebec currently provides women with options for a shorter leave at a higher percentage of pay or a longer leave at a reduced rate. This type of policy can provide mothers with options for how to best meet the needs of their family.

Breastfeeding promotion has a long history in Canada. Successful approaches to breastfeeding should consider the emotional and developmental needs of mothers and their infants as well as the contexts in which they make infant feeding decisions. Decisions about infant feeding have become associated with ideas about good mothering and have engendered discomfort, ambivalence, and resistance in the lives of many. Breastfeeding promotion is linked to broader tensions in a number of other policy areas. Efforts to resolve other dilemmas in the areas of social and health policy, such as the ongoing tension between women's paid and reproductive work or the scrutiny and judgment women experience with respect to other mothering practices, will likely influence women's infant feeding decisions and contribute to improving their experiences of breastfeeding. Regardless, women's needs, perspectives, and choices – not the potential social benefits of increased breastfeeding – must remain central to the development of new policies to promote breastfeeding.

BIBLIOGRAPHY

Apple, R.D. 1987. *Mothers and Medicine: A Social History of Infant Feeding.* Madison: University of Wisconsin Press.

Arnup, Katherine. 1994. *Education for Motherhood: Advice for Mothers in Twentieth-Century Canada.* Toronto: University of Toronto Press.

Baillargeon, Denyse. 2009. *Babies for the Nation: The Medicalization of Motherhood in Quebec, 1910–1970.* Waterloo: Wilfrid Laurier University Press.

Baker, Alden. 1981. "Health Board Abandons Nestle Boycott." *The Globe and Mail,* 29 September, P5.

Baker, Michael, and Kevin Milligan. 2008. "Maternal Employment, Breastfeeding and Health: Evidence from Maternity Leave Mandates." *Journal of Health Economics* 27: 871–87.

Bideau, A., B. Desjardins, and H.P. Brignoli, eds. 1997. *Infant and Child Mortality in the Past.* Oxford: Clarendon Press.

Blum, Linda M., and Elizabeth A. Vandewater. 1993. "'Mother to Mother': A Maternalist Organization in Late Capitalist America." *Social Problems* 40(3): 285–300.

Bourne, Hilary B. 1950. "Breast Feeding." *The Canadian Nurse* 46(12): 969–71.

Breastfeeding Committee for Canada. 2002. *The Implementation and Evaluation of the Baby-Friendly Initiative in Canada: Final Project Report 1999–2002.* Drayton Valley: Breastfeeding Comittee for Canada.

Buckley, Suzann. 1977. "Efforts to Reduce Infant Maternal Mortality in Canada Between the Two World Wars." *Atlantis* 2(Part 2): 76–84.

Buckley, Suzann. 1979. "Ladies or Midwives? Efforts to Reduce Infant and Maternal Mortality." In *A Not Unreasonable Claim: Women and Reform in Canada, 1880s–1920s,* L. Kealey, ed. Toronto: The Women's Press.

Burns, Elaine, Virginia Schmied, Athena Sheehan, and Jennifer Fenwick. 2010. "A Meta-Ethnographic Synthesis of Women's Experience of Breastfeeding." *Maternal and Child Nutrition* 6: 201–19.

Canadian Institute for Health Information. 2004. *Giving Birth in Canada: A Regional Profile.* Ottawa: CIHI.

Canadian Institute of Child Health. 1996. *National Breastfeeding Guidelines for Health Care Providers.* Ottawa: Canadian Institute of Child Health.

Canadian Paediatric Society. 1978. "Breast-Feeding: What is Left besides the Poetry?" *Canadian Journal of Public Health* 69(January/February): 13–19.

Canadian Paediatric Society Nutrition Committee and American Academy of Pediatrics Committee on Nutrition. 1978. "Breast-Feeding: A Commentary in Celebration of the International Year of the Child." *Pediatrics* 62(4).

Canadian Press. 1979. "Anglicans Back Boycotting Nestlé Goods." *The Globe and Mail*, 26 May, 15.

Canadian Press. 1994. Breast-Feeding Moms Furious With Formula Pushers. *Canadian Press Newswire*, 4 August.

Chalmers, Beverley, Cheryl Levitt, Maureen Heaman, Beverley O'Brien, Reg Sauve, and Janusz Kaczorowski. 2009. "Breastfeeding Rates and Hospital Breastfeeding Practices in Canada: A National Survey of Women." *Birth* 36(2):122–32.

Comacchio, Cynthia R. 1993. *"Nations are Built of Babies": Saving Ontario's Mothers and Children 1900–1940*. Montreal & Kingston: McGill-Queen's University Press.

Dingle, Kate. 1977. "La Leche League." *The Globe and Mail*, 30 July, 7.

Dodd, Dianne. 1991. "Advice to Parents: The Blue Books, Helen MacMurchy, MD, and the Federal Department of Health, 1920–34." *Canadian Bulletin of Medical History* 8: 203–30.

Hausman, Bernice L. 2004. "The Feminist Politics of Breastfeeding." *Australian Feminist Studies* 19(45): 273–85.

Heymann, Jody, and Michael S. Kramer. 2009. "Public Policy and Breastfeeding: A Straightforward and Significant Solution." *Canadian Journal of Public Health* 100(5): 381–3.

Hogan, Denys. 1979. "Churches Fight Formula Promotion Nestle Smarting from Boycott." *The Globe and Mail*, 15 December, P15.

Kryhul, Angela. 2000. "Bringing Up Baby: Sampling, Coupons and Baby Clubs are Key Tools for Infant Care Marketers." *Marketing Magazine* 105(28) :13.

Levitt, C.A., J. Kaczorowski, L. Hanvey, D. Avard, and G. Chance. 1996. "Breast-Feeding Policies and Practices in Canadian Hospitals Providing Maternity Care." *CMAJ* 155(2): 181–8.

Lewis, Norah., and Judy Watson. 1991/92. "The Canadian Mother and Child: A Time-Honoured Tradition." *Health Promotion* Winter 91/92: 10–13.

MacMurchy, H. 1910. *Infant Mortality: Special Report*. Toronto: The Legislative Assembly of Ontario.

McConnachie, Kathleen. 1983. "Methodology in the Study of Women in History: A Case Study of Helen MacMurchy, M.D." *Ontario History* 75(1): 61–70.

Murphy, Elizabeth. 1999. "'Breast is Best': Infant Feeding Decisions and Maternal Deviance." *Sociology of Health and Illness* 21(2):187–208.

Murphy, Elizabeth. 2000. "Risk, Responsibility, and Rhetoric in Infant Feeding." *Journal of Contemporary Ethnography* 29(3): 291–325.

Myres, A.W. 1983. "The National Breast-Feeding Promotion Program. Part 2. Public Information Phase – A Note on its Development, Distribution and Impact." *Canadian Journal of Public Health* 74(Nov/Dec): 404–8.

Myres, A.W. 1988. "National Initiatives to Promote Breastfeeding: Canada, 1979–85." In *Programmes to Promote Breastfeeding*, D. Jelliffe and E. Jelliffe, eds. Oxford: Oxford University Press.

Myres, A.W., J. Watson, and C. Harrison. 1981. "The National Breast-Feeding Promotion Program. 1. Professional Phase – A Note on its Development, Distribution and Impact." *Canadian Journal of Public Health* 72(Sept/Oct): 307–11.

Nathoo, Tasnim, and Aleck Ostry. 2009. *The One Best Way? Breastfeeding History, Politics and Policy in Canada*. Waterloo: Wilfrid Laurier University Press.

Naylor, Audrey J. 2001. "Baby Friendly Hospital Initiative: Protecting, Promoting, and Supporting Breastfeeding in the Twenty First Century." *Pediatric Clinics of North America* 48(2): 475–83.

Reuter News Agency. 1982. "Nestle Boycott to Continue." *The Globe and Mail*, 18 October, P12.

Saddeh, Randa, and James Akre. 1996. "Ten Steps to Successful Breastfeeding: A Summary of the Rationale and Scientic Evidence." *Birth* 23(3)154–60.

Schmeid, Virginia, Athena Sheehan, and Lesley Barclay. 2001. "Contemporary Breast-Feeding Policy and Practice: Implications for Midwives." *Midwifery* 17: 44–54.

Sibbald, Barbara. 2000. "Canada's Only Human Milk Bank May Close." *Canadian Medical Association Journal* 163(3): 319.

Statistics Canada. 2010. "Breastfeeding, 2009." In *Health Fact Sheets*. Ottawa: Minister of Industry.

Sterken, Elisabeth. 2001. The WHO International Code in Canada: Twenty Years Later." *INFACT Canada Newsletter*, Spring 2001.

Sterken, Elisabeth. 2002. *Out of the Mouth of Babes: How Canada's Infant Foods Industry Defies World Health Organization Rules and Puts Infant Health at Risk*. Toronto: INFACT Canada.

Strong-Boag, Veronica, and Kathryn McPherson. 1990. "The Confinement of Women: Childbirth and Hospitalization in Vancouver, 1919–1939." In *Delivering Motherhood: Maternal Ideologies and Practices in the 19th and 20th Century*, eds. K. Arnup, A. Levesque, and R. Pierson. London: Routledge.

The Globe and Mail. 1981. "Timbrell Won't Ban Formula Giveaways." 25 May, P5.

Van Esterik, P. 1989. *Beyond the Breast-Bottle Controversy*. New Brunswick, NJ: Rutgers University Press.

Wah, Wong. 2000. "Advanced Breastfeeding: WHO and UNICEF's Existing Ten Steps to Successful Breastfeeding Should be Extended to 12 Steps." *Canadian Nurse* 96(7): 10.

Wall, G. 2001. "Moral Constructions of Motherhood in Breastfeeding Discourse." *Gender & Society* 15(4): 592–610.

12

Care of the Self:
An Alternative Way
to Understand Breastfeeding

ROBYN LEE

Breastfeeding is principally understood in terms of caring for and nourishing babies. Consideration of what women may get out of breastfeeding is often left out of the discussion. Women are subject to discourses of power in carrying out breastfeeding, and in this chapter I discuss these power discourses in terms of both the medical and the maternalist models (Blum 2000). Working to resist these power discourses requires changing one's self-conception to include breastfeeding as an exercise of one's own power and creativity. An overemphasis on the responsibility to care for others can be detrimental to women's sense of self. In this chapter, I aim to put women back into breastfeeding by referring to Foucault's concept of care of the self. Like feminist care ethics, care of the self involves relationality and consideration for others. However, care of the self avoids some of the potential pitfalls of care ethics. Care of the self is a creative endeavour and recognizes that crafting self-identity is an ongoing creative process that requires hard work and the assistance of others. Foucault's care of the self promotes individual agency while still recognizing how selfhood is created and developed through relations with others. I will explore some of the feminist criticisms of care of the self, and finally, I will explore ways in which breastfeeding can be understood as arduous but significant moral work. I conclude the paper by arguing that breastfeeding should be considered moral work and that without adequate social recognition of this work women are poorly prepared for the difficulties that may be involved in reconciling breastfeeding with their sense of self-identity.

BREASTFEEDING AND WOMEN'S AUTONOMY

Breastfeeding advocates often overlook the enormous challenges that breastfeeding poses to women's autonomy: an activity stretching out over many months or even years, it requires time-consuming labour, is inadequately accommodated in the workplace, and is often still viewed as obscene when performed outside the home. For these reasons, breastfeeding can have a huge impact on women's sense of self, an effect that is often overlooked when breastfeeding advocacy focuses solely on infant health and well-being.

Since the 1970s awareness has grown about the risks of infant formula and the benefits of breastfeeding. As a result of the large body of research demonstrating the health, psychological, and developmental advantages of breastfeeding (Lawrence 1995), breastfeeding has been the subject of extensive public health campaigns aimed at improving infant health (Wolf 2007; Kukla 2006). Since awareness of the benefits of breastfeeding is now widespread (Guttman and Zimmerman 2000), formula feeding has become understood as a questionable or risky decision that leaves women open to the charge of being bad mothers (Stearns 1999). Mothers who do not breastfeed are now open to the charge of maternal deviance since they are viewed as knowingly breaking the rules of good mothering (Murphy 1999, 199).

Women are subject to discourses of power that tell them what breastfeeding is (a "natural" and instinctual process) and why they ought to do it (for the good of their infant). Mothers are regarded as passive recipients of expert medical knowledge, while at the same time intense responsibility is imposed upon mothers to make optimal infant feeding decisions. Maternalist breastfeeding advocacy reinforces gender stereotypes in arguing that caring is part of women's "nature." On the one hand, women are treated as less autonomous, less capable, and therefore requiring the advice of experts; on the other hand, the ideology of the "good mother" holds women to increasingly high standards of intensive mothering in isolation from social supports.

Some feminist theorists view breastfeeding as deeply problematic because it requires ongoing responsiveness to an infant and restricts mobility and therefore conflicts with a traditional liberal conception of the autonomous self. For instance, Simone de Beauvoir criticized both pregnancy and breastfeeding because these activities prevent women from realizing their own projects. De Beauvoir describes how, for some women at least, the breastfeeding infant "seems to be sucking out her strength, her life, her happiness. It inflicts a harsh slavery upon her and it is no longer a part of her: it seems a tyrant; she feels hostile to this little stranger, this individual who menaces her flesh, her freedom, her whole ego" (Beauvoir 1989, 508). The dependence of the fetus and infant restricts the free movement of a woman; therefore, de Beauvoir argued that pregnancy, birthing, and breastfeeding are not processes that individuals can engage in without relinquishing their autonomy. Rebecca Kukla similarly argues that breastfeeding necessarily conflicts with women's autonomy, asserting: "A woman who feels that she cannot leave her infant, or even reasonably deny her infant any form of access to her body, cannot do the concrete things that normal humans need to do in order to have a meaningful, distinct identity that is comprehensible to themselves and others" (Kukla 2005, 178).

But the critique of breastfeeding articulated by De Beauvoir and others relies on an individualistic conception of autonomy that is inherently masculinist because it assumes that it is both possible and desirable to live independently of others, an assumption that is inconsistent with many women's experiences of caring for others. Hausman argues against this traditional liberal ideal of autonomous adulthood, pointing out that such an ideal of autonomous adulthood perpetuates sexism because it specifically excludes women from public life (Hausman 2007, 496).

This understanding of autonomy is particularly damaging to women's efforts to breastfeed. Understandings of agency as individualistic and free of physical attachment to others can serve to undermine breastfeeding (Schmied and Lupton 2001) and some mothers turn to formula feeding in an effort to re-establish their identities before motherhood as separate individuals (Earle 2002). Lorraine Code (2000, 181) notes that the ideal of autonomy "paradoxically underpins patterns of oppression and subjection." Despite Code's ambivalence toward autonomy, she nevertheless recognizes its effectiveness and power. Self-determination and independence continue to be worthy goals, which leads some feminists to attempt to reconcile autonomy with caring responsibilities for others through the concept of relational autonomy. Relational autonomy describes selfhood as produced by and continually dependent upon relationships with others. It recognizes that we are the product of our dependencies on others, and that every autonomous action we engage in relies upon a shared social context (Mackenzie and Stoljar 2000).

BREASTFEEDING AND CARE ETHICS

The ethics of care provides one form of understanding relational autonomy that emphasizes the value of relations of nurturance and dependency. Care ethics critiques traditional conceptions of autonomy as devaluing women's experiences. In valuing interpersonal relationships of dependence, Jennifer Nedelsky, for instance, argues for a model of autonomy based on the mother-child relationship (Nedelsky 1989, 12).

The privileging of care and mothering does not always fit into women's autobiographical accounts. Identifying women as natural caregivers can make women feel unnatural when they experience caring as laborious. Conceiving of breastfeeding as natural obscures the social factors that make it difficult or impossible for many women to breastfeed, including the failure of workplaces to accommodate breastfeeding and the social censure that breastfeeding in public places often arouses. When the ideology of natural breastfeeding runs aground on the very real obstacles to successful breastfeeding, the experience can be extremely upsetting. Women who have difficulty breastfeeding often feel like their bodies have failed them, and that they are consequently bad mothers.

As the essays by Sokolon and Nathoo and Ostry in this volume demonstrate, normative discourses of motherhood require breastfeeding to be a "good mother" (Stearns 1999). Being a good mother is considered to be "natural," and as a good mother one is expected to be self-sacrificing and provide intensive caring to one's children. As a good mother, one is also irreplaceably unique: a mother is considered to be able to care for her children in ways that no one else can.

Despite the efforts made in care ethics to valorize caring work done by women, discourses in which mothers are considered to be virtuous or praiseworthy due to their special role as caregivers and nurturers can be problematic. MacGregor argues that an ethics of care limits the possibilities for critiquing how practices of care are gendered and individualized by perpetuating the constructed identity of women as primarily mothers and carers, upholding the stereotype that caregiving experiences are the most powerful or meaningful experiences that women can have, and limiting the potential to overcome gender relations that have oppressed women for centuries (MacGregor 2006, 79). Not all women experience caring as a positive experience and caring for others is often not recognized as "real work" (Lupton 1996). As well, the goal of equally sharing childcare responsibilities is challenged by the gendered activity of breastfeeding (Friedman 2009).

BREASTFEEDING AND DISCOURSES OF POWER

Linda Blum (2000) suggests that both a maternalist and a medical model of breastfeeding have developed in western culture. Both the maternalist and medical models of breastfeeding render the mother as subject with legitimate needs and wants invisible (Wall 2001, 604). Women as breastfeeding subjects disappear as their behaviour becomes subject to public scrutiny and external moral authority. Thus, women's autonomy is severely limited by both the medical and maternalist models. While they may still be able to make decisions regarding whether or not to breastfeed, these choices are circumscribed by discourses of power that categorize women as either "good" mothers or deviants in need of education and assistance.

Maternalist championing of breastfeeding values the process of breastfeeding because it connects infant and mother in a unique bond, while assuming that women will find this physical intimacy fulfilling (La Leche League is a prominent example). Maternalist support for breastfeeding takes for granted that women are naturally well-suited to nourish children. Although maternalism values women's caring roles, like western medicine it has also focused primarily on the benefits breastfeeding provides for infants.

Having assumed authority over infant feeding, western medicine now strongly encourages women to breastfeed because of the nutritional superiority of breast milk over infant formula. Breastfeeding expertise has been transferred away from women as a result of the medicalization of infant feeding. Breastfeeding norms are largely determined by expert medical advice to women. Because breastfeeding is not instinctive, advice and the passing down of knowledge may prove useful for women; nonetheless, these rules, norms, and expert advice represent a form of biopower that is exercised over the identity and behaviour of women (Wells 2006). Medical researchers may assume that their recommendations represent valuable advice that can significantly reduce infant morbidity and mortality. Thus, they may claim to have discovered the optimum biological "norm." They may also assume that they have the right to dispense such advice on the grounds that it represents the sum of a vast quantity of collective experience gained through scientific study. However, Wells provides two criticisms of medical expertise (Wells 2006, 45). The first is that it fails to recognize that breastfeeding is an adaptive process. Since physiology and environment vary between human populations, it is unlikely that the same rules would be optimal for all individuals. Second, strict guidelines do not allow individuals to benefit from their own experiences or those of others. This second criticism is most relevant to Foucault's notion of care of the self, which would make possible an expanded role for women's experiences of breastfeeding in western medicine.

Through medicalization, complex social problems came to be defined individualistically – as the product of a deviant individual – and were treated medically, rather than by attempting to modify the social environment. Likewise, neo-liberal rationality places a greater emphasis on the role of individual choice in self-management and self-responsibility. Current breastfeeding advice is preoccupied with maximizing health and perfecting children. Foucault (2008, 226) argues that *homo œconomicus* is the subject of governmental rationality and the basic assumption of all neo-liberal analysis. Individuals are granted extensive choices, which are understood to be expressions of freedom.

Under neo-liberalism, social risk in the form of health care costs is downshifted to the individual. Mothers are assigned the responsibility for their children's preventive health care, and breastfeeding is required to minimize risk. The same techniques of the self that have been applied to pregnancy have been extended to breastfeeding. Women are discouraged from consuming alcohol, tobacco, and drugs and encouraged to maintain a healthy diet. Despite the common description of breast milk as a pure and healthy food, it is nonetheless dependent on the proper self-management of the maternal body. The female subject is displaced by an emphasis on the health and well-being of the infant, resulting in an expanding list of self-regulatory behaviour for women to abide by.

Benefits to infants are the focus of breastfeeding promotional literature. The content of these materials assumes that women will benefit from what is good for their infants or that they will experience a close and intimate relationship to their infant as rewarding. As Sokolon's discussion in this volume illustrates, when this type of literature discusses the benefits of breastfeeding to women, it normally mentions that breastfeeding will help women lose weight and return to their pre-pregnancy body. This plays into insecurities about the attractiveness of the maternal body and reinforces cultural conceptions of the proper female body shape. However, the reasons women fail to breastfeed are not linked to irrationality or lack of understanding of the benefits of breastfeeding. Nor are they linked to a lack of concern among mothers for their babies' well-being (Carter 1995, 206); (Blum 2000, 120, 161). There are structural and cultural factors that limit the choices women have when it comes to caring for their children. Here, as in other areas of childrearing, the emphasis is on maternal responsibility while taking for granted a cultural model of natural, intensive, self-sacrificing, and isolated motherhood. This model of motherhood is consistent with the dominant neo-liberal pressure to individualize responsibility for health to reduce costs to the state. Rippeyoung (2009) argues that state-sponsored breastfeeding promotion has been used to avoid responsibility for more costly solutions to improving children's and women's health such as affordable housing, employment inequities, and unequal access to early childhood education.

Essential to recognize are the ways in which women's caring work is interpreted with regard to class and race. White middle-class women are seen by the medical profession, children's services, and media as wanting the best for their child, even in rare cases where an infant has starved to death while being breastfed. On the other hand, poor women and women of colour are regarded with suspicion when they breastfeed. Compared with middle-class white mothers they are perceived as being highly sexualized, and suspicion is raised as to whether or not they are "fit" mothers. Bernice Hausman notes that black mothers "are represented publicly as being quite capable, all on their own, of negligently causing the death of their infants, while white women are portrayed as inherently well-meaning and thus needing to be misled by experts in order to inflict the same damage" (Hausman 2007, 485). Not all mothers are under surveillance in the same ways and for the same purposes. While white middle- and upper-class women internalize the demand for "perfecting" children, "women who are more likely to be supervised by the state and who have less social power to enforce their maternal practices publicly may be more circumspect and careful about exposed female bodies in public spaces" (Hausman 2003, 489). Depending on what forces are allied against a woman's breastfeeding, not breastfeeding can be experienced as empowering and as supporting that woman's desired self-identity.

FOUCAULT'S CARE OF THE SELF

Mackenzie and Stoljar (2000, 10) note, "in focusing primarily on intimate dyadic relations, particularly between mother and child, care critiques provide a very circumscribed reconceptualization of autonomy. In particular, they fail to address the complex effects of oppression on agents' capacities for autonomy; and they provide a somewhat limited reconceptualization of the social dimensions of agency and selfhood." Adequately critiquing oppression within interpersonal relationships remains a significant problem for theories of relational autonomy, as we have seen with the assumptions about women that underpin care ethics. I argue that Foucault's understanding of care of the self provides a way of recognizing the value of autonomy without reinscribing the traditional liberal (masculinist) subject.

Fiona Giles suggests self-care as a model for understanding breastfeeding (Shaw and Bartlett 2010). Foucault's notion of care of the self is an alternative to medical discourses that dictate terms of behaviour to women, since care of the self does not deal with universal codes of behaviour, but is self-directed and individualized. As well, care of the self may be a powerful corrective to discourses that privilege the mother on the basis of "natural" virtue and the force of her self-sacrificing care for the child. It provides a way of understanding agency within the context of ubiquitous power relations that we can never step out of. Care of the self recognizes relationality, while also providing a way of challenging relational bonds when they are unjust.

Some feminists object to the general lack of autonomy in Foucault's work that exists due to the ubiquity of power discourses and the extent to which they discipline subjectivity. Lois McNay, for instance, sees Foucault's subject as completely determined and therefore lacking in autonomy. But Margaret McLaren argues that Foucault's subject is not entirely produced through disciplines and practices of power. In the third period of Foucault's later essays and volumes two and three of *The History of Sexuality*, Foucault examines ancient Greek and Roman culture and discovers "the development of an art of existence that revolves around the question of the self, of its dependence and independence, of its universal form and of the connection it can and should establish with others, of the procedures by which it exerts its control over itself, and of the way in which it can establish a complete supremacy over itself" (Foucault 1988, 238–9).

Foucault is interested in ancient formations of the ethical subject, and in the ancient world self-knowledge and self-control are separate from the state apparatus. Volumes two and three of *The History of Sexuality* deal with a period before the rise of governmentality, which Foucault describes as "the way in which the conduct of a set of individuals became involved, in an increasingly pronounced way, in the exercise of sovereign power" (Foucault 2009, 364). Foucault undertakes a historical analysis; he is not promoting a return to these ancient Greek and Roman moral practices, but rather examining earlier ways of approaching the self and others in order to suggest possibilities for the present. In contemporary society, we will certainly establish different moral goals; however, examining ways in which practices of the self have been undertaken in the absence of governmentality makes it apparent how different practices of the self might be possible now.

Foucault's later emphasis on the subject necessarily involves an understanding of how power operates, because for Foucault power and freedom are inextricably connected. Foucault (1983, 221) writes that power includes an essential element: freedom. Power "is exercised only over free subjects, and only insofar as they are free" (Foucault 1983, 222). Freedom is the condition of power; it is what distinguishes power from slavery or physical determination. Power requires that subjects be capable of a variety of possible behaviours and comportments. Foucault therefore characterizes the relationship between power and freedom as agonistic, a relationship of permanent provocation on both sides (Foucault 1983, 222). In his later essays and in volumes two and three of *The History of Sexuality*,

Foucault describes how the self both acts upon itself as well as being acted upon.

Foucault explores how individuals exercise freedom in relation to discourses of power, although they cannot be said to be "autonomous" because the freedom they exercise is always contextual and in response to norms. Karen Vintges argues that in his later work Foucault does not reinscribe the liberal autonomous subject, but that he nevertheless still has a conception of freedom, freedom that is always situated because it "exists within the social discourses and vocabularies that give us the tools for a care of the self. The concept of freedom practices does not reinstall the "original" subject or "deep self" that was deconstructed in his earlier work. Freedom for Foucault is neither absolute nor pure but the effect of discursive self-technologies" (Vintges 2004, 281). Foucault does not reject the subject altogether, but only the formation of the subject as it became constituted through the practices of Christianity and modern European morality.

As Trent Hamann (2009, 48) points out, Foucault's "emphasis on the care of the self and aesthetics of existence ... lends itself quite nicely to neo-liberalism's aim of producing free and autonomous individuals concerned with cultivating themselves in accord with various practices of the self." However, to read Foucault in terms of opposition between power and freedom is a mistake: neo-liberalism both forecloses and opens up possibilities for individual action and self-understanding. Murtagh (2008) notes: "Governmentality is a constraint on freedom only if we insist on understanding freedom in terms of the individual ... Mechanisms of power have both positive and negative effects; they constrain, maintain and produce certain ways of being and living." The process by which subjects are created involves both government rationality *and* individual choices. Freedom and discourses of power are inextricably linked.

CARE OF THE SELF AND RELATIONS WITH OTHERS

Some feminist thinkers believe that Foucault's care of the self is insufficiently relational. For instance, Amy Allen criticizes Foucault's later understanding of the self because she believes the care of the self to be ethically and ontologically prior to care for others, whereas for feminist theorists the opposite is the case: acquiring and maintaining a sense of self is possible only when reciprocal and communicative relations with others are in place (Allen 2004, 246). Allen argues that feminist models of the relational self focus on communication, mutuality, and reciprocity, and that Foucault's linkage between care of the self and mastery over others clearly does not include these elements. However, other interpreters of Foucault see care of the self as necessarily involving relationships with others. Dianna Taylor writes, "from their inception, practices of the self implicate both other people and social institutions" (Taylor 2004, 266–67). She argues that Foucault's care of the self is intrinsically social because it is rooted in the practice of caring and because care of the self is required for participation in the life of the polis and in relations with other people (Taylor 2004, 266–67).

But Foucault argues that it is in fact self-renunciation, not caring for oneself, that leads to tyrannical relations with others. In an interview, Foucault notes that according to the ancient Greeks, "the good ruler is precisely the one who exercises his power correctly, i.e., by exercising at the same time his power on himself. And it is the power over self which will regulate the power over others" (Foucault 1994, 8). Care of the self enables harmonious relationships to others. By being in correct relationship to oneself, one may avoid being enslaved in one's relationships with others. The ancient Greek dictate that it is necessary to master oneself in order to rule over others is inherent in the concept of care of the self. Care of the self implies social relationships with others in at least two ways. It enables one to relate to others in a harmonious manner, and it requires the help of a guide or a close friend (McLaren 2002, 71). Thus, care of the self can combat the social isolation that often accompanies breastfeeding, and promote the reciprocal sharing of advice.

CARE OF THE SELF AND THE ETHICS OF CARE

Fiona Giles suggests the possibility for conceiving of breastfeeding as an act of gifting, and therefore as part of the care of the self: "Lactation is in itself self-caring: it is an act of empowerment that illustrates the strength and resourcefulness of the female body; it is a renewable resource whose supply is stimulated through auto-erotic means, as well as by demand from the other; it is mutually pleasurable; and it literally connects, through suckling and ingestion, two bodies who are otherwise separate. In short, it provides an analogy for the gift of connection which benefits both parties" (Giles 2010, 242).

I support Giles's suggestion to analyze breastfeeding from the perspective of care of the self. However, describing self-care in terms of gifting seems to veer too closely toward an ethics of care. In comparing self-caring with gifting it is essential to recognize that gifting has historically been associated with women carrying an unequal burden of domestic labour (Fischer and Arnold 1990). Not all women experience breastfeeding as mutually pleasurable. For example, Schmied and Lupton (2001, 239) found that only about a third of the women they interviewed experienced a sense of pleasurable connection during breastfeeding. The majority "struggled with the contradictions between their experiences of breastfeeding, pro-breastfeeding discourses and the prominent notions of rational autonomy that are privileged in Western societies" (Schmied and Lupton 2001, 241). Transforming one's sense of self so one can critically engage with breastfeeding norms can be fulfilling, but it is a difficult and sometimes painful process. Gifting is not without cost, as I will explore in the next section when I examine care of the self as moral work.

McLaren argues that Foucault's theory of the self resembles a feminist ethics of care (McLaren 1997, 111–12). Unlike care ethics, however, care of the self does not reinforce gendered inequalities in division of labour because it recognizes the historically situated ways in which caring work has been unequally assigned to women.

In taking up Giles's suggestion to conceive of breastfeeding in terms of self-care and gifting, Stuart Murray's distinction between self-care and care of the self proves useful (Murray 2007). According to Murray, self-care is what we are encouraged to carry out in the modern liberal state; the responsibility to take care of our health becomes a moral imperative. Self-care presupposes the autonomous individual who freely chooses. According to such a conception of the self, giving is freely chosen and does not erode autonomy. Murray contrasts this with Foucault's concept of care of the self, which he describes as "a self-self relation that is inventive and open, as a self that questions the norms and constraints in and by which that self is said to be a self in the first place" (Murray 2007, 7).

Another difference between care ethics and care of the self is that Foucault would not privilege the breastfeeding relationship as a primary example of care of the self. Foucault examines the many types of relationships through which individuals are produced rather than privileging any single type of relationship as central to the formation of identity. Sawicki compares Foucault's conception of the subject with that of mothering theorists, but unlike mothering theorists, Foucault does not privilege the caring relationship between mother and infant (Sawicki 1991, 63).

Foucault insists on examining the *practices* by which the self is created and transformed, de-naturalizing the body. Considering breastfeeding not as a natural function but rather as a practice of the body expands the variety of ways in which it may be expressed. This perspective also recognizes the labour, both physical and mental, that goes into the practice of breastfeeding. Reading breastfeeding as natural, i.e., an unthinking or biologically automatic activity, tends to obscure the extent to which breastfeeding requires hard work. Allison Bartlett applies Judith Butler's notion of performativity to breastfeeding for this reason. She argues that, "a sense of performance enables me to consider women as having agency, including the agency to decide against breastfeeding. Specific acts of breastfeeding can therefore be read as challenging and resisting dominant models and expectations" (Bartlett 2005, 23).

Foucault's notion of the self is not universal and neither is it essentially gendered. Rather, gender is tied to the practices that accompany it. There is a tension in treating feminine disciplinary practices because femininity is *not natural* but rather the result of social and cultural practices. Margaret McLaren suggests that this tension "between recognizing the effect of disciplinary practices and wanting to destabilize the categories produced through them is one of the reasons Foucault himself did not articulate gender-specific disciplinary practices in his work" (McLaren 2002, 99). Ladelle McWhorter notes that Foucault's care of the self can undermine essentialist notions of what it means to be a woman. Although this presents a danger to identity politics, McWhorter notes that it also opens up new possibilities for what it means to be a woman: "Care of the self, therefore, stands opposed to practices that affirm my identity as a woman. Practices of woman-affirmation stand opposed to affirmation of the free play of becoming, differing, and otherness" (McWhorter 2004, 156).

TAKING PLEASURE IN BREASTFEEDING

Care of the self is relational without being radically asymmetrical because it includes as an essential component *pleasure*, which Foucault distinguishes from merely selfish desire. The pleasure that is associated with breastfeeding in both medical and maternalist discourses is derived solely from the attachment between mother and baby. Pleasure is acceptable for breastfeeding mothers only when it is directly associated with their duties as nurturing caregivers; deriving "selfish" or sexual pleasure is viewed as the mark of deviant motherhood.

Although discourses of "good mothering" describe breastfeeding as both natural and pleasurable, this is not always the experience of individual mothers (Wall 2001). Many women experience breastfeeding as arduous and painful, and the closeness derived through breastfeeding may feel stifling when it is perceived as eroding women's independence. May Friedman argues against the automatic association of breastfeeding with pleasure, the assumption that to be a good mother one must enjoy breastfeeding *because* it involves making a sacrifice for one's child (Friedman 2009, 33). She points out that while some women may experience breastfeeding as compatible with a relational self-conception, others experience it as a radical infringement on their bodily integrity and individuality. As Friedman notes, both the child-centred, self-sacrificing model of motherhood and the liberal autonomous self are particular conceptions of subjectivity. However, because these two models of subjectivity conflict with each other so drastically, and because they are both so pervasive in contemporary western society, women often find that their expectations of breastfeeding conflict with reality in unpleasant ways.

Women are explicitly cautioned not to take sexual pleasure in breastfeeding, even though the physiological effects of breastfeeding are extremely similar to those that take place during erotic stimulation of the breasts (Levin 2006). Ignorance about such normal physiological occurrences can sometimes have horrifying consequences. For instance, a mother in Syracuse, New York who called a La Leche League group in 1992 because she was concerned about her feelings of arousal during nursing consequently had her two-year-old child taken away from her, the authorities claiming that she sexually abused the child. Although a judge found there was no case, after eight months in state care the child was returned to the custody not of her mother, but of her grandparents (Yalom 1997, 254).

Mothers who breastfeed children past a certain age are often accused of being indulgent and of putting their personal pleasure ahead of the child's welfare. As well, women are held responsible for negotiating between continued breastfeeding and the pleasure of their partners. Managing the sexual relationship with a male partner is considered to be the responsibility of women, and the radical divide between breasts as sexual objects and as instruments for infant feeding means breastfeeding can make this more difficult (Tyler 2004). Cindy Stearns found in her study that women's major concern when breastfeeding is that their activity be perceived as maternal and not sexual behaviour (Stearns 1999, 321). Murphy notes, "Women have primary responsibility not only for curbing their own possessiveness but also for ensuring that their partners are properly socialised into their paternal roles. Women are made responsible for their partners' 'bonding' with their babies, and the exclusivity of mother–infant breast feeding is seen as threatening this" (Murphy 1999, 201).

Iris Marion Young argues that the separation between maternality and sexuality is what provides the false image of a love that is all giving, without taking any pleasure for itself (Young 2005a, 87). The sublimation of eroticism in mother love reinforces the incest taboo and permits men to refrain from sharing female sexuality with their children. It also keeps women dependent on men for sexual pleasure. Young argues that women's freedom depends on a reintegration of maternality and sexuality.

Although the traditional western division between the sexual and nutritional functions of breasts may make it easier for some women to breastfeed because it allows them to distance themselves from the erotic experience during infant feeding, nevertheless this discomfort originates from the attempt to separate motherhood and sexuality in the first place.

Considering breastfeeding as a *sexual* practice challenges the dominant ideology of motherhood as asexual. This allows us to extend our analysis to the many forms of what has recently been termed "queer breastfeeding" (Giles 2004). Giles argues that although the term "queer" originates in gay and lesbian studies and has been the basis for critiques of heteronormativity, it can also be used to criticize cases of what Adrienne Rich called "compulsory heterosexuality" that have been used to regulate heterosexual behaviour and desire, particularly in women (Giles 2004, 302). Queer breastfeeding encompasses breastfeeding activities beyond what is generally considered acceptable in contemporary western society, which may include men carrying out breastfeeding, the incorporation of breastfeeding into the sex lives of adults, breastfeeding other species, and breast-feeding older children (Longhurst 2008, 114–15). According to Giles, because queer theory centres on performative behaviour rather than identity, the term "queer breastfeeding" can be taken up by anyone who feels marginalized by their breastfeeding practices. In fact, Giles (2004, 303) adds, because breastfeeding as a practice challenges the dominant individualist notion of the Western subject, "breastfeeding, however conventionally practiced, is perhaps already an activity that 'queers' us." The dichotomy of deviant/heteronormative breastfeeding relies on the assumption that breastfeeding practices can be divided between nurturing (child-focused) and sexual (self-satisfying) motivations. To be considered good mothers, women must manage public perceptions of their breastfeeding to avoid being seen as sexual actors (Stearns 1999). However, the distinction between maternal giving and sexual enjoyment is inevitably disturbed in breastfeeding. Breastfeeding is always "queer" because the categories of maternal and sexual can never be adequately separated.

Understanding breastfeeding in terms of Foucault's care of the self is compatible with the project of queering breastfeeding because it re-appropriates pleasure for the breastfeeding woman and opens up new ways of interpreting breastfeeding practice. Taking pleasure in breastfeeding is commonly circumscribed in maternalist and heteronormative ways. Queering breastfeeding creates new possibilities for pleasure by demonstrating how the boundaries between sexuality and motherhood are necessarily porous. Creating alternative ways of understanding breastfeeding is not, however, easy to do because it requires challenging strongly held social norms.

CARE OF THE SELF IS HARD WORK

Considering breastfeeding as moral work means recognizing the time, effort, and energy that goes into it. The self-transformations accompanying this practice may be experienced very differently depending on the circumstances and experiences of individual women. Foucault generally understands transformation of the self to be a positive activity, but depending on the social and cultural context women find themselves in, the moral work of breastfeeding may be pleasurable and empowering or it may painfully disturb one's sense of self. Women's experiences of breastfeeding differ greatly depending on the levels of domination women experience. White middle-class women are likely to receive more social support for breastfeeding and are more likely to internalize the imperative to breastfeed. Women of colour and women of lower socio-economic status, as well as survivors of abuse, are more likely to regard pressure to breastfeed as originating from external authority and as potentially eroding their individual agency. For example, Linda Blum offers an explanation of African-American women's much lower rates of breastfeeding as due, at least in part, to a critique of the racialized discourse of breastfeeding as natural. Having been long stereotyped and identified with nature may lead African-American women to reject an ideology so associated with white women (Blum 2000, 47). The history of black women nursing white babies while their own children were neglected or even sold makes breastfeeding racially charged (Blum 2000, 147).

Elizabeth Murphy draws on the sociology of deviance to explore how mothers justify infant feeding decisions that contravene prevailing breastfeeding norms. She explores how women recognized their decision to formula feed as requiring a defence, and they consequently "engaged in elaborate repair work to legitimise their decision to feed their babies in a way which they recognised was open to condemnation and which they anticipated that others would see in this light. These women can be seen as using their talk to shore up their identities as 'good mothers' in the face of intended actions which, they recognised, could call this into doubt" (Murphy 1999, 200). Women who choose to formula feed must critically engage with breastfeeding norms so they can demonstrate that they are responsible mothers. By contrast, breastfeeding mothers are concerned with reconciling the demands of good motherhood with adequate performance of their other roles (Murphy 1999, 205).

Deborah Payne and David Nicholls explore how women undertake Foucauldian technologies of the self through breastfeeding in the workplace so they can negotiate the competing positions of being a good mother and a good worker (Payne and Nicholls 2010). Women discipline their bodies and their practices of breastfeeding to conform to these two dominant discourses of motherhood and work. Payne and Nicholls describe women who combined breastfeeding and work as undertaking activities that "constituted acts of the self *upon* the self: activities which function served to maximize the possibility of health, happiness, effectiveness and efficiency by defining the woman's subjectivity in terms of being a good mother *and* a good worker" (Payne and Nicholls 2010, 1811). Payne and

Nicholls attempt to distinguish between technologies of power, which involve surveillance in the workplace (both by others and by the women themselves) to ensure that women are not neglecting their roles as good workers, and technologies of the self, which the authors describe as motivating from within: "By the desire to be good mothers with the goal of ensuring the wellbeing of their infant by breastfeeding" (Payne and Nicholls 2010, 1816). However, the dichotomy they draw between the external pressure to be a good worker and the internal pressure to be a good mother is problematic. Their impulse to distinguish between technologies of power and technologies of the self is understandable, but, as they note, this distinction is extremely difficult to draw because ideas about what constitutes a "good mother" come from various (external) sources in society, and the vigilance to prevent breastfeeding from infringing on work duties is internalized by women. Implicit in Payne and Nicholls's paper is recognition of the ambivalence between technologies of power and technologies of the self: individual agency and the influence of social norms are inextricably connected.

Feminist critics of Foucault are not wrong when they argue that the later works of Foucault fail to provide criteria for determining when technologies of the self are imposed on the subject from without and when they are freely chosen by the subject (McNay 2000, 9). But the way this question is posed assumes that these two extremes could ever exist independently. For Foucault there can be no absolute distinction between being subjected to social norms and freely choosing to create oneself. Self-creation necessarily always takes place in relation to norms. Practices of the self are not something the individual invents independently; rather, "they are patterns that he finds in his culture and which are proposed, suggested and imposed on him by his culture, his society and his social group" (Foucault 1994, 11). Care of the self cannot be recognized universally but is instead deeply dependent on individual contexts. Individuals may mobilize different resources of the self when engaging with social norms, developing different capacities, and regarding different influences as external or internal to themselves.

Kath Ryan et al. engage Foucault's notion of care of the self to characterize breastfeeding as moral work in individual actions rather than as adherence to universal norms. They do so in four categories: biographical preservation, biographical repair, altruism, and political action (Ryan, Bissell, and Alexander 2010). Biographical preservation refers to work carried out to maintain an identity as a breastfeeding mother, even when faced with feelings of failure at breastfeeding. Biographical repair refers to the work done by women who move from viewing themselves as a breastfeeding mother to viewing themselves as a bottle-feeding mother, but still consider themselves to be a good mother. This work often includes externalizing the cause for their inability to breastfeed. Moral work as altruism refers to feeling good about oneself through giving, either of breast milk (to one's own child and to milk banks) or of time to breastfeeding advocacy projects. Finally, moral work as political action attempts to change attitudes and improve the environment for breastfeeding, through both policy change and change in views of people in local networks. Ryan et al. conclude that women's embodied experience and sense of self are disciplined within current limited, often punishing, discourses by undertaking painful moral work to maintain or repair their subjective positions. Developing a narrative of one's breastfeeding experiences requires women to maintain and change their self-conceptions, carry out altruistic activities, and perform political activism. Consequently, Ryan et al. suggest the development of new subject positions about infant feeding practices.

Negotiating between the powerful social norms controlling breastfeeding requires women to carry out significant work on themselves, something that is extremely difficult to do without help from others. Helen O'Grady takes up Foucault's notion of care of the self in a therapeutic context (O'Grady 2004, 98–9). She argues that the self-policing that occurs when women internalize oppressive norms can be overcome through therapeutic work. Although Foucault came to be associated with anti-psychiatry, he characterizes his work instead as merely an archeology of psychiatry at the beginning of the nineteenth century (Foucault and Gordon 1980, 192). He does not see psychiatry as good or bad in itself, but asserts that the "problem is to know how one may actually obtain therapeutic results ... without the setting up of a type of medical power, and a type of relationship to the body, and a type of authoritarianism – a system of obedience" (Foucault, Kritzman, and Sheridan 1990, 195). O'Grady argues that certain types of therapeutic work can deconstruct norms that have dominated and oppressed. She sees narrative therapy as an alternative to the traditional expert approach because it relies on collaboration, and the individual seeking help is seen as best situated, through her direct experience of the problem, to be an authority on her intended ways of being (O'Grady 2004, 111–12). This is consistent with Foucault's (1994) argument for the importance of friendship in challenging norms. The hard work of engaging critically with breastfeeding norms requires the assistance of friends or guides, who are not positioned as authorities on breastfeeding but instead explore experiences together with other women.

CONCLUSION

Privileging infant care over women's physical and mental health has so far not been terribly successful; although breastfeeding initiation rates have increased, most women cease breastfeeding long before the one year recommended by current W H O guidelines and do not breastfeed exclusively for the recommended six months. According to the 2009 Canadian Maternity Experiences Survey, 90.3 per cent of mothers initiate breastfeeding, but only 53.9 per cent continue breastfeeding for six months and only a paltry 14.4 per cent report exclusively breastfeeding during this period (Ontario Public Health Association 2010, 3).

In their examination of breastfeeding promotion policy in Canada, Tasnim Nathoo and Aleck Ostry argue that improving rates of breastfeeding requires that women create their own definitions of breastfeeding success. Although duration and exclusivity have been the most common definitions of success in breastfeeding, women perceive success in a range of ways, including "maternal enjoyment, maternal attitudes towards breastfeeding experiences, the compatibility of breastfeeding with family life, the physiological and health benefits of breastfeeding, the perception of the infant's response to breastfeeding, and the mother's feelings of closeness with her infant" (Nathoo and Ostry 2009, 204). Breastfeeding needs to be promoted in a way that improves maternal satisfaction and the quality of women's experiences.

Following Foucault's notion of care of the self is a way to support women's control over their self-understandings. Incorporating the practice of breastfeeding into one's identity requires extensive moral work to negotiate dominant social norms. Considering breastfeeding in the light of care of the self clarifies how breastfeeding can never be carried out in a vacuum, but requires an ongoing, critical engagement with social norms. Care of the self expands our understanding of what constitutes women's health because it requires that women define their health according to their own terms, and in relation to their own life goals. As well, according to Nathoo and Ostry, making women's health a priority will have the effect of improving the situation of infants as well.

Applying care of the self to breastfeeding opens up new possibilities for women and for interpreting the practice of breastfeeding. However, care of the self requires engaging with existing breastfeeding discourses. It is never possible to be or become a self independently of social and historical contexts. Power discourses and freedom can never be separated, according to Foucault. Technologies of domination are resisted by transformative techniques of the self; but techniques of the self are also at points integrated into structures of coercion or domination. Domination and care of the self intersect where individuals are driven by others and is tied to the way they conduct themselves (Foucault 1993, 203).

Care of the self requires that existing discourses of breastfeeding be continually problematized and critiqued to open up new possibilities. Murray describes care of the self as inaugurating a self "that strives to open up a plurality of relations, a multiplicity of possibilities within which that self might relate caringly not only to itself, but to those others in its care" (Murray 2007, 14–15). Foucault's notion of care of the self can be useful in understanding breastfeeding because it offers a view of the self that is inherently relational, and although not autonomous, because care of the self never happens in the absence of power discourses, as nevertheless exercising agency over self-determinations. In caring for oneself, the breastfeeding subject can conceive of how she would like to be, and through moral work can move toward that sense of self.

NOTE

1   In the United States, w I C provides federal grants to states for supplemental food and health referrals for women, infants, and children.

BIBLIOGRAPHY

Allen, Amy. 2004. "Foucault, Feminism, and the Self: The Politics of Personal Transformation." In *Feminism and the Final Foucault*, Dianna Taylor and Karen Vintges, eds., 307. Urbana & Chicago: University of Illinois Press.

Bartlett, Alison. 2005. *Breastwork: Rethinking Breastfeeding*. Kensington: UNSW Press.

Blum, Linda M. 2000. *At the Breast: Ideologies of Breastfeeding and Motherhood in the Contemporary United States*. Boston: Beacon Press.

Carter, Pam. 1995. *Feminism, Breasts and Breastfeeding*. New York: St Martin's Press.

Code, Lorraine. 2000. "The Perversion of Autonomy and the Subjection of Women: Discourses of Social Advocacy at Century's End." In *Relational Autonomy*, Catriona Mackenzie and Natalie Stoljar, eds. New York: Oxford University Press.

de Beauvoir, Simone. *The Second Sex*. 1989. Vintage. Reissue.

Earle, Sarah. 2002. "Factors Affecting the Initiation of Breastfeeding: Implications for Breastfeeding Promotion." *Health Promotion International* 17(3): 205–14.

Fischer, Eileen, and Stephen J. Arnold. 1990. "More Than a Labor of Love: Gender Roles and Christmas Gift Shopping." *The Journal of Consumer Research* 17(3): 333–45.

Foucault, Michel. 1983. "The Subject and Power." In *Beyond Structuralism and Hermeneutics* by Hubert L. Dreyfus, Paul Rabinow, and Michel Foucault. Chicago: University of Chicago Press.

– 1988. *The History of Sexuality: The Care of the Self*. Vintage Books.

– 1993. "About the Beginning of the Hermeneutics of the Self: Two Lectures at Dartmouth." *Political Theory* 21(2): 198–227.

– 1994. "The Ethic of Care of the Self as a Practice of Freedom." In *The Final Foucault*, James Bernauer and David Rasmussen, eds. Cambridge: MIT Press.

– 1994. "Friendship as a Way of Life." In *Ethics: Subjectivity and Truth*. New York: The New Press.

– 2008. *The Birth of Biopolitics: Lectures at the Collège de France, 1978–79*, trans. G. Burchell. New York: Palgrave Macmillan.

– 1980. *Power/Knowledge: Selected Interviews and Other Writings, 1972–1977*. Colin Gordon, ed. Toronto: Random House of Canada.

– 1990. *Politics, Philosophy, Culture: Interviews and Other Writings, 1977–1984*. Lawrence D. Kritzman, ed. New York: Routledge.

– 2009. Security, Territory, Population: Lectures at the Collège de France 1977–1978. Michel Senellart and François Ewald, eds. Picador.

Friedman, May. 2009. "For Whom is Breast Best? Thoughts on Breastfeeding, Feminism and Ambivalence." *Journal of the Association for Research on Mothering* 11(1): 26–35.

Giles, Fiona. 2004. "'Relational, and Strange': A Preliminary Foray into a Project to Queer Breastfeeding." *Australian Feminist Studies* 19(45): 301–14.

– 2010. "From 'Gift of Loss' to Self Care: The Significance of Induced Lactation in Takashi Miike's Visitor Q." In *Giving Breast Milk: Body Ethics and Contemporary Breastfeeding Practice*, Rhonda Shaw and Alison Bartlett, eds. Bradford, ON: Demeter Press.

Guttman, N., and D.R. Zimmerman. 2000. "Low-Income Mothers' Views on Breastfeeding." *Social Science and Medicine* 50(10): 1457–73.

Hamann, T. 2009. "Neoliberalism, Governmentality, and Ethics." *Foucault Studies* 6: 37–59.

Hausman, Bernice. 2007. "Things (Not) to Do with Breasts in Public: Maternal Embodiment and the Biocultural Politics of Infant Feeding." *New Literary History* 38(3): 479–504.

– 2003. *Mother's Milk: Breastfeeding Controversies in American Culture.* New York: Routledge.

Kukla, Rebecca. 2005. *Mass Hysteria: Medicine, Culture, and Mothers' Bodies.* Toronto: Rowman & Littlefield.

– 2006. "Ethics and Ideology in Breastfeeding Advocacy Campaigns." *Hypatia* 21(1) 157–80.

Lawrence, R. 1995. "The Clinician's Role in Teaching Proper Infant Feeding Techniques." *The Journal of Pediatrics* 126(6): 112–17.

Levin, Roy J. 2006. "The Breast/Nipple/Areola Complex and Human Sexuality." *Sexual and Relationship Therapy* 21(2): 237–49.

Longhurst, Robyn. 2008. *Maternities: Gender, Bodies and Space.* Toronto: Routledge.

Lupton, Deborah. 1996. *Food, the Body, and the Self.* New York: Sage.

MacGregor, Sherilyn. 2006. *Beyond Mothering Earth: Ecological Citizenship and the Politics of Care.* Vancouver: UBC Press.

Mackenzie, Catriona. 2001. "On Bodily Autonomy." In *Handbook of Phenomenology and Medicine*, S. Kay Toombs, ed., 417–40. New York: Springer.

Mackenzie, Catriona, and Natalie Stoljar. 2000. *Relational Autonomy: Feminist Perspectives on Automony, Agency, and the Social Self.* New York: Oxford University Press US.

Mara, Miriam. 2010. "Spreading the (Dis)ease: Gardasil and the Gendering of HPV." *Feminist Formations* 22(2): 124–43.

McLaren, Margaret. 1997. "Foucault and the Subject of Feminism." *Social Theory and Practice* 23(1): 109–28.

– 2002. *Feminism, Foucault, and Embodied Subjectivity.* Albany: State University of New York Press.

McNay, Lois. 2000. *Gender and Agency: Reconfiguring the Subject in Feminist and Social Theory.* Hoboken, NJ: Wiley-Blackwell.

McWhorter, Ladelle. 2004. "Practicing Practicing." In *Feminism and the Final Foucault*, Dianna Taylor and Karen Vintges, eds. Urbana & Chicago: University of Illinois Press.

Murphy, Elizabeth. 1999. "'Breast is Best': Infant Feeding Decisions and Maternal Deviance." *Sociology of Health and Illness* 21(2): 187–208.

Murray, Stuart. 2007. "Care and the Self: Biotechnology, Reproduction, and the Good Life." *Philosophy, Ethics, and Humanities in Medicine* 2(1): 6.

Murtagh, Madeleine J. 2008. "A Funny Thing Happened on the Way to the Journal: A Commentary on Foucault's Ethics and Stuart Murray's 'Care of the Self.'" *Philosophy, Ethics, and Humanities in Medicine* 3(1): 2.

Nathoo, Tasnim, and Aleck Ostry. 2009. *The One Best Way?: Breastfeeding History, Politics, and Policy in Canada*. Waterloo: Wilfrid Laurier University Press.

Nedelsky, J. 1989. "Reconceiving Autonomy: Sources, Thoughts and Possibilities." *Yale Journal of Law and Feminism* 1(1): 7–36.

O'Grady, Helen. 2004. "An Ethics of the Self." In *Feminism and the Final Foucault*, Dianna Taylor and Karen Vintges, eds. Chicago: University of Illinois Press.

Ontario Public Health Association. 2010. *OPHA Position Paper: The WHO Code and the Ethical Marketing of Breastmilk Substitutes*. Toronto: Ontario Public Health Association.

Payne, Deborah, and David A. Nicholls. 2010. "Managing Breastfeeding and Work: A Foucauldian Secondary Analysis." *Journal of Advanced Nursing* 66(8): 1810–18.

Rippeyoung, Phyllis. 2009. "Feeding the State: Breastfeeding and Women's Well-Being in Context." *Journal of the Motherhood Initiative for Research and Community Involvement* 11(1): 36–48.

Ryan, Kath, Paul Bissell, and Jo Alexander. 2010. "Moral Work in Women's Narratives of Breastfeeding." *Social Science & Medicine* 70(6): 951–8.

Sawicki, Jana. 1991. *Disciplining Foucault: Feminism, Power, and the Body*. New York: Routledge.

Schmied, Virginia, and Deborah Lupton. 2001. "Blurring the Boundaries: Breastfeeding and Maternal Subjectivity." *Sociology of Health and Illness* 23(2): 234–50.

Shaw, Rhonda, and Alison Bartlett. 2010. *Giving Breastmilk: Body Ethics and Contemporary Breastfeeding Practice*. Bradford, ON: Demeter Press.

Sherwin, Susan, and Feminist Health Care Ethics Research Network. 1998. *The Politics of Women's Health: Exploring Agency and Autonomy*. Philadelphia: Temple University Press.

Stearns, Cindy A. 1999. "Breastfeeding and the Good Maternal Body." *Gender and Society* 13(3): 308–25.

Taylor, Dianna. 2004. "Foucault's Ethos: Guide(post) for Change." In *Feminism and the Final Foucault,* Dianna Taylor and Karen Vintges, eds. Chicago: University of Illinois Press.

Tyler, Melissa. 2004. "Managing between the Sheets: Lifestyle Magazines and the Management of Sexuality in Everyday Life." *Sexualities* 7(1): 81–106.

Vintges, Karen. 2004. "Endorsing Practices of Freedom: Feminism in a Global Perspective." In *Feminism and the Final Foucault,* Dianna Taylor and Karen Vintges, eds. Chicago: University of Illinois Press.

Wall, Glenda. 2001. "Moral Constructions of Motherhood in Breastfeeding Discourse." *Gender and Society* 15(4): 592–610.

Wells, Jonathan. 2006. "The Role of Cultural Factors in Human Breastfeeding: Adaptive Behaviour or Biopower?" *Journal of Human Ecology* special issue 14: 39–47.

Wolf, Joan. 2007. "Is Breast Really Best? Risk and Total Motherhood in the National Breastfeeding Awareness Campaign." *Journal of Health Politics, Policy and Law* 32(4): 595–636.

Yalom, M. 1997. *A History of the Breast.* London: Harper Collins.

Young, Iris Marion. 2005a. *On Female Body Experience: "Throwing Like a Girl" and Other Essays.* New York: Oxford University Press US.

– 2005b. "Breasted Experience: The Look and the Feeling." In *On Female Body Experience: "Throwing Like a Girl" and Other Essays.* Cambridge: Oxford University Press.

13

Indigenous Body as Contaminated Site? Examining Struggles for Reproductive Justice in Aamjiwnaang

SARAH MARIE WIEBE AND ERIN MARIE KONSMO

Recognizing my privileged place as a West Coaster and academic "tourist," I am mindful of the relationships and responsibilities I have to the people and territory discussed here. I ventured from British Columbia to Ontario to examine concerns about reproductive and environmental justice within this particular First Nation community; as such, I draw from the principles of relationship building and reciprocity articulated by the Native Women's Association of Canada. The discussion presented here builds from two years of engaged immersion and fieldwork with citizens of the Aamjiwnaang First Nation, preceded by two years of PhD coursework at the University of Ottawa. Each stage of learning enhanced my understanding about the interconnected relationships between bodies, environments, and health. I wish to acknowledge all those who have shared their knowledge with me. This shared knowledge informs the pages to follow.

Sarah Marie Wiebe

As a Métis, Indigenous woman, I am embedded within all the relationships that make up my life. While co-authoring this piece with another person, I acknowledge all the knowledge that comes from my family (both blood and chosen), community, land, ancestors, and future generations who inform my work each day. The thoughts that I share come from my life experience, but are built up within a web of relationships with my own body, all my social relations, and also

13.1 Artwork by Erin Marie Konsmo

with the land. I feel honoured to have been able to share and learn from the Aamjiwnaang youth and Green Teens who share similar experiences in their fight for environmental justice.

Erin Marie Konsmo

Reproductive politics takes place as communities struggle to achieve recognition and redress for corporeal concerns.[1] In 2005, *Environmental Health Perspectives* published an article on a perceived male "birth dearth" in Aamjiwnaang, which left civil servants dumbfounded and spawned a flurry of media attention worldwide (Mackenzie, Keith, and Lockridge 2005). Scientists and members of the Aamjiwnaang community argued that hormone-mimicking endocrine disruptors could be to blame for the skewed birth patterns, due to the interference of synthetic organic chemicals with natural hormones. According to the Canadian Broadcasting Corporation (CBC) documentary *The Disappearing Male*, pollutants known as endocrine-disruptors can interfere with hormones that determine the sex of a baby (CBC 2008). Many individuals living in Aamjiwnaang voiced concern about the future viability of their community. Consequently, according to Aamjiwnaang environmental community activist Ron Plain, the community began to worry about every child who was born (Crenson 2005). Moreover, the maternal body in this scenario, as a carrier for their children, is deemed particularly vulnerable to toxins. Unlike adults, children cannot excrete or store contaminants as easily and are more susceptible to toxins. Toxins are generally stored in fat and during pregnancy and lactation; women's fat is metabolized and exposes fetuses and newborns to these chemicals at early stages of development (Smith 2005). These endocrine-disrupting toxins mimic natural hormone production, consequently disrupting reproduction and fetal development. In these ways, the maternal body becomes symbolized as a vulnerable potential site of contamination.

Notions of gender intersect with race and place. Bodies at this juncture are affected physically by contamination, pollution exposures, and by language casting the body as vulnerable. The ways in which the maternal body in particular is hailed in the media as "vulnerable to environmental contaminants" reveals how reproductive health is gendered; however, we wish to be clear that reproduction itself is not inherently a "women's issue." Despite this obvious fact, popular and media reports suggest that the maternal body, specifically, is susceptible to hormone-mimicking, endocrine-disrupting chemicals nicknamed "gender-benders," which infiltrate the body and affect reproduction for future generations (CBC 2008; Cohen 2007). Expectant mothers are commonly hailed as the first line of defence against toxins in the environment that have the potential to harm future generations. Expectant mothers become gatekeepers, demarcating the boundary between some environment "out there" and some "body" inside.[2] Consequently, the maternal – or to this we add *reproductive* – body is discursively constructed as a "site of contamination" for both material and discursive practices (Scott 2009). This vulnerability discourse shifts the burden of responsibility of managing health toward reproductive bodies to assume individual responsibility for their well-being. This is an incomplete picture of the broader structural factors that shape and constrain access to reproductive health and justice.

With all the media that have concentrated on the "lost boys," Indigenous perspectives are largely missing from the analysis.[3] We contend that an Indigenous perspective of gender must also be taken into consideration when looking at the media surrounding the Aamjiwnaang First Nation's reproductive health concerns. Smith identifies that to understand the reproductive body colonialism must be recognized as a key to Indigenous feminism (1999). As we discuss, words and seemingly inclusive and deliberative processes alike have the potential to reproduce colonial power relations by the act of discrediting or delegitimizing certain bodily corporeal or experiential claims. Thus, we argue that a reproductive justice framework cannot ignore or cast aside lived experience. To situate our analysis of these political processes, this chapter draws from the ongoing struggle for reproductive justice in Aamjiwnaang and illuminates how practices shape and constrain avenues to address this community's environmental and health concerns.

Our consideration of reproductive justice is grounded by a respect for Indigenous rights. For Indigenous peoples to have their rights fully recognized, including the right to health, self-determination is key.[4] The United Nations Declaration on the Rights of Indigenous Peoples is a key document for engaging Indigenous peoples in any political process. Although Canada has actively engaged in consultation processes, a gendered lens of the political atmosphere in which these discussions have occurred and continue to occur is lacking. Following Andrea Carmen, principles of free, prior, and informed consent (FPIC) connect lands and bodies relating to Indigenous peoples by situating this concept in the experiences of Indigenous women and historical sterilization policies (Yee 2011). As we discuss, these principles also apply to a Canadian context. Indigenous peoples in Canada are frequently left out of negotiations regarding the continued involvement of F P I C as it relates to both their lands and bodies. Reproductive justice seeks to respond to this lack in the negotiations.

Using a reproductive justice framework, in this chapter we bring in an analysis of the body to political science debates. We situate the analysis within a case study of the Aamjiwnaang First Nation's experience seeking recognition for its reproductive health concerns. We discuss some of the ways post-colonial and intersectional theory provide a lens through which we can look at how this community's struggles for reproductive justice take shape. This includes a discussion of the reproductive body as a "site" for political analysis and the correlative implications for knowledge-claims and experiential corporeality. By bringing in a post-colonial and intersectional analysis to the relationship between the body, race, and location in this context, our analysis examines how the reproductive body is embedded in *place*.

An intersectional lens to the study of politics draws attention to the interactions of social locations, systems, and processes in addition to the situated circumstances and voices of those affected by policies. As will be demonstrated throughout this chapter, an intersectional approach to examining struggles for reproductive justice presents a multilevel analysis of intersecting categories – i.e., race, class, and gender – to reflexively assess how power relations affect diverse communities and to situate individuals within a broader social, economic, and geographic context. In pursuit of social justice and equity, this lens seeks to make visible some of the invisible violences affecting communities and to generate knowledge about those experiencing oppression. By drawing attention to the diversity of Indigenous peoples' experiences, and how they are positioned in public policy processes, an intersectional lens can assist scholars and policymakers in placing Indigenous peoples at the centre, leading to better decolonial public policy to address health in/equity.

In this chapter we refer to struggles for reproductive justice, which can be understood through the political configurations shaping and informing public health processes in Aamjiwnaang and Lambton County. A reproductive justice framework builds from social and environmental justice literature to elaborate on the multifaceted ways in which reproductive health is affected by conditions affecting people's lives. By integrating race, class, gender, and place, the intersectional approach to reproductive health we present here connects individuals within a broader socio-economic context and structural inequalities, in contrast to focusing on an "individual choice" model of public health.

What does a reproductive justice framework add to the study of reproductive politics? Our response is anchored in the experiences of citizens fighting for reproductive justice in Aamjiwnaang. We discuss some of the ways a reproductive justice framework can inform and strengthen western and Indigenous perspectives of environmental justice and bodies. This chapter contends that the reproductive body in Aamjiwnaang is at the frontlines for toxic exposures and consequently experiences pollution harm in different ways than the wider population of Lambton County and Canadian citizens at large; this includes exposure to state colonialism. Such struggles for reproductive recognition and justice come to the fore through institutional and discursive responses. We anchor this within the ongoing Lambton Community Health Study, a deliberative process designed to better understand citizens' health concerns at the county level, thus widening the scale from Aamjiwnaang. By drawing from the past, present, and future directions of the health study, this chapter explores the context informing Aamjiwnaang citizens' struggles, whose experiential, corporeal knowledge is disregarded or discredited by members of the broader community and government officials (Fiske and Browne 2008). The conclusion gestures toward a politics of reproductive justice that posits the reproductive body as central to resistance, regeneration, and renewal.

In this chapter, we explore some of the subtle yet pervasive ways in which environmental violence[5] affects the reproductive body in Aamjiwnaang, making it a focal point in the struggle for justice. First, drawing from intersectional and post-colonial scholarship, we clarify our approach to reproductive justice. We bring theory to practice by highlighting the construction of the reproductive body as a site of contamination and its implications. Second, we introduce the background and context for the struggles for reproductive justice in Aamjiwnaang by drawing from popular media accounts and policy responses to date. Third, we situate the struggle for reproductive justice within ongoing deliberative public health processes in Lambton County. In conclusion we draw into focus that Indigenous self-determination is inherently connected to the body: "Sovereignty and autonomy in relation to our lands, territories and resources are intricately connected to sovereignty and autonomy in relation to our bodies, minds and spirits" (IIWS 2010). By bringing forward the body as an essential site, or *place* to understand politics, we problematize the manner in which the body comes into being at the frontlines of reproductive harm.

THEORIZING THE INTERSECTIONS OF REPRODUCTIVE JUSTICE

In addition to studying the macro practices of power, such as the impact of state authority on groups and individuals, we study the micro practices, or manifestation of the effects of power and control, which are of central importance to political analysis. Locating colonization at the micro level of the body brings forward the reproductive body as a core axiom. Furthermore, uneven political processes mark women's bodies in distinct ways. Several scholars contend that the subjection of women, and women's bodies, has been and continues to be a key feature of both micro and macro practices of the persistence of colonization today (Kelm 1998; La Duke 1999, 2002, 2005; Maracle 1996; Monture-Angus 1995; Smith 2005; Yazzie 2000). Our chapter draws from intersectionality and post-colonial theory to situate the reproductive body within a framework of reproductive justice.

Post-colonial approaches to the study of politics can be broadly understood as an interdisciplinary group of theories that share a common political and social concern about the legacy of colonialism and how this legacy continues to shape lives and opportunities. A key component to post-colonial study is the notion of emancipation or social justice (Young 1999). In general, post-colonial scholarship suggests that we must examine the genesis of racialized, classed, and gendered inequities in the past and perpetuated in the present (see Bhabha 1994, 1995; Fanon 1965, 1967; Gandhi 1998; Gilroy 2000; Hall 1995, 1996; Said 1978; Spivak 1994). These approaches extend to the realm of reproductive justice.

Reproductive justice connects bodies to place. This formulation is in stark contrast to biomedical public health models that emphasize individual responsibility for personal wellness. It refers to a shift away from a traditional second wave feminist model that encompasses women advocating for control over their bodies, away from a narrow focus on legal access and individual choices, toward a broader analysis of racial, economic, cultural, and structural constraints to power. While already well-known in many Indigenous communities, reproductive justice framing emerged prominently within the women of colour movement and the term formally appeared in the 1994 American Black Women's Caucus to connect themes of reproductive rights and social justice (SisterSong 2011). Reproductive justice is an intersectional framework that addresses the lived experiences and social realities of inequality, in particular the inequality of opportunities that communities have to control reproductive destinies. Moreover, this framework analyzes how the ability of individuals to determine reproductive destiny is directly linked to the conditions in one's community, which are not merely a matter of individual choice and access. We next discuss the relationship between reproductive justice and the long history and legacy of colonization within many Indigenous communities.

Connecting individuals to place in this way resonates in a contemporary Indigenous context. Following Jessica Yee (2010), executive director for the Native Youth Sexual Health Network:

> Today our work at the Native Youth Sexual Health Network INCLUDES everything from comprehensive, culturally based sex education to reproductive rights to environmental justice to violence prevention and awareness, sex work outreach, prison in-reach, and so much more. We are honored to work with an incredible network of youth, elders, and communities all across the United States and Canada who tell us exactly why we shouldn't back down from working on all these issues together, or if separate at least related. Of course we experience so many of them at the same time – *because since when isn't land connected to bodies connected to spirit?* (emphasis ours)

Interconnectivity is a central tenet of reproductive justice. In addition to connecting individuals to socio-economic and structural inequalities embedded within political processes, bodies and reproductive systems must be considered as connected to land and the environment. As Erin Konsmo (2010) articulates:

> Reproductive justice to me means having my cycles as a woman being connected with the cycles of nature, it means having that connection be strong and healthy. It means being able to make

decisions over that health including when and if I have children, the ability to make decisions to not follow full term with a pregnancy ... It also means having the ability to sit and listen to my kookum (grandmother) tell me in her own indigenous language (which she lost) with my feet in the dirt and hands planting seeds how my reproductive system is interconnected with the earth.

Thinking about reproductive justice in this way illuminates some of the micro practices of colonial power.

As a result, there is a need for critical analyses of peoples' experiences of colonialism and continuing manifestations in both macro and micro practices. This includes both the formal realm of legislative and policy formation (or the lack thereof) and also the informal, subtle, and difficult to document processes. The objective of an inquiry that aims to contribute to a decolonial society requires a deliberate decentring of dominant or mainstream culture, structures, and discourses. This aims to enable the perspectives of those who have been marginalized to become a linchpin for knowledge development to expand our understanding of how conceptualizations of race, racialization, and culture are constructed within particular historical and current neocolonial contexts (Morrow et al. 2007). Specifically, post-colonial scholarship seeks to assess and address the impacts of historical colonial practices on the colonial present.

The link between colonization and the body has a long history. Throughout Canada's colonial relationship with Indigenous peoples, including the process of segregation and discipline through residential schools, doctors – as "experts" – displaced women's confidence in their bodies. Consequently, this led to a climate where women became "discredited medical subjects" (Fiske and Browne 2008). For example, midwives, aunties, and grandmothers were not allowed in delivery rooms, nor were medicines, singing drumming, or birth knowledge (Simpson 2006). Wombs have been colonized through displacement as well as medical technology. Consequently, the way we think about and treat the womb and, moreover, the reproductive body, is political.

Race, place, gender, and the reproductive body are inextricably linked. Intersecting gender-based analyses with post-colonial scholarship seeks to move away from singular conceptual and organizational categories, such as class or gender. In many respects aligned with the reproductive justice movement, discursive and intersectional feminist literature critiques first and second wave feminism for assuming coherence among these categories, specifically of "gender" or "women's issues" themselves (Brown 2003, 1995; Butler 1993, 1990, 1997; McCall 2005). In response to frustration with second wave feminism, which privileged gender as a coherent identity category, post-colonial feminist thinkers began to develop the concept of intersectionality (Hankivsky and Christofferson 2008; Morrow et al. 2007). As Candace Johnson discusses in chapter 4, the term *intersectionality* became popularized by bell hooks, Kimberlé Crenshaw, and Patricia Collins, with a specific emphasis on providing a theory of knowledge that strives to elucidate and interpret multiple intersecting systems of oppression and privilege (Hankivsky and Christofferson 2008). These scholars brought gender issues to the fore of various social analyses (Collins 2003; Crenshaw 1991). Intersectional analyses then seek to discuss, illuminate, and uncover a multiplicity of social formations as part of a "matrix of domination" (Collins 2000). In particular, intersectional theories highlight the importance of multi-sectoral forms of power relations in health that contextualize women in their diverse social and economic circumstances and understand gender as inseparable from other forms of social difference such as race, ethnicity, culture, class, sexual orientation, gender identity, and ability.[6] Intersectional theory seeks to disrupt traditional, rational, linear thought that prioritizes one category of social identity. This is essential to a study of bodies in harmful environments in a colonial Canadian context.

Analyses of the body have not been prominent in Canadian political science and public policy literature, or western philosophy, except to brush such analysis aside as a women's issue. Intersectional and post-colonial literature contest this by making gender and the body central to their analyses. Scholars at the forefront of this scholarship intersect gender with a discussion of colonization (i.e., Pat Collins, bell hooks, Sherene Razack, Gaytri Spivak, and Shiva Vanadana, among others). Much of this discussion begins with the position that gender is inherently tied to the state, neo-liberalism, and structural inequality (Brown 2003; Porter 2003; Razack 2002). Going further, *gender* can be understood as connected to the state, but also beyond the state in a transnational and interstitial context. It takes its form on the body, in the family, in the workplace, by the state, and so on. This could be, but is not, limited to the role of the state (Mahler and Pessar 2001; Razack 2002). Moreover, some post-colonial feminist thinkers argue that the feminine has been and continues to be tied to the unruly construct of nature. Vandana argues that modern science is part and parcel of the patriarchal project, as it suggested and enables a role for the "mastery" over nature (Shiva 1997). The attachment of the feminine body to nature is a significant form of discrimination and inequality perpetuated by contemporary science, knowledge, and practice. Some bodies – Indigenous female bodies – have been greatly harmed by this association of the feminine body as "close to nature," under the gaze and confines of western patriarchal assumptions.

A discussion of race, place, and the reproductive body in a colonial context cannot escape a gendered conversation. Following Linda Tuhiwai Smith (1999): western concepts of race intersect in complex ways with concepts of gender. This refers not just to the roles of women but also of men, and how men relate to women. These concepts replicate fragmented artifacts of knowledge, which have very distinct implications in a colonial context. Both institutions and language reinscribe these knowledges. As a result, it is impossible to separate questions of gender from race. Indigenous scholar Patricia Monture-Angus (1995) describes being unable to describe or name her pain, due to confusion as to whether she was supposed to call it a question of "gender" or "race." These concerns raise awareness that forms of oppression are overlapping and interrelated: they are intersectional.

A common concern in feminist discourse of the body is "corporeality." The tension between the body as corporeality – knowledge of the body – and western science is of central importance to this approach. Broadly speaking, this work is inspired by theorists such as Michel Foucault and Gilles Deleuze, with a focus on bodily phenomenological experience. At the forefront of feminist scholarship on the body and gender, several authors discuss the discursive and material forms of oppression that have persisted over time (Balbus 1985; Butler 1990, 1993, 1997; Brown 1995; Grosz 1994, 2005). In particular, Indigenous bodies have been formed through words, such as the Indian Act, and through subsequent material health policies and practices (Kelm 1998). As we will discuss in the conclusion, some expressions of feminist scholarship seek to take back or reclaim the discourse of the body (Grosz 1995; Haraway 1991; Morrow et al. 2007). However, the ability to reclaim the body itself is a challenge. Not everyone is easily in a position to reclaim the discourse of the body. Some bodies on the fringe of mainstream societies are marginalized in "exceptional" or "abnormal spaces" (Pratt 2005).

The bodies of Indigenous people have been and continue to be a focal point for the persistent processes of Canadian colonization. Consequently, women's bodies and reproductive health function within a site of seemingly invisible violence. This violence is inherently linked to a kind of corporeal violence. As Kelm (1998) outlines, historically epidemics of smallpox, measles, and tuberculosis were "harbingers" of devastation. This health destruction has an eminent legacy today. Quoting a Nisga'a man, Kelm (1998, xv) states: "When we talk about the poor health of our people, remember it all began with the White man." Furthermore, non-Indigenous commentators, politicians, scientists, bureaucrats, and epidemiologists repeatedly point to harmful statistics – obesity, diabetes, suicide, sexual abuse – as the indicators of a community's wellness; there is a moral assumption being made that these data sets indicate the essence of Indigenous health. This presents an incomplete picture. Such accounts rarely go a step further to look at the underlying socio-economic, geographic, and environmental factors that may be related to such harmful health patterns. They misunderstand Indigenous health, which reproductive justice analysis helps to explain. This reveals the importance of bringing in a reproductive justice framework to enhance public health policy, by situating concerns in community experience, taking place on the ground.

When it comes to Canada's treatment of Indigenous peoples, the past and present legislative and policy context has revealed, and continues to reveal the ways in which the body is a marked site of political harm and oppression. As the Royal Commission on Aboriginal Peoples (RCAP) outlined, before colonization, women played a central role in their societies. Women were revered as life givers and their place and role as bearers of children was a celebrated part of Indigenous life. Many women had leadership roles in clans, villages, nations, and confederacies. Of course women's lives before contact were not free of social ills; however, the advance of colonial power, policies, and laws, imposed from the outside, ruptured cultural traditions and introduced discrimination against women. Colonization shook up communities, culminating in a legacy of violence against women. RCAP outlines at length the policies, laws, and practices that directly affected women, their bodies, families, identities, and social positions.

Women in general, and Indigenous women in particular, have been discursively attached to the "wildness of land" and nature in both western science and philosophy. While this has had detrimental effects on White women, the effects of colonization and the conception of "savage" Indian women on Indigenous women's bodies is greatly amplified. In particular, Indigenous women are seen as embodying wild and unruly frontiers. This connection to the savage, natural realm has political, social, and sexual consequences. Attacks on nature are simultaneously attacks on women's bodies. Putting this in perspective, Smith argues that the sexual somatic connection to wildness culminates in the simultaneous rape of land through dispossession and rape of women's bodies in the spirit of taming or mastering nature (Smith 2005). The attack on nature affects bodies in multifaceted ways, as several Indigenous scholars discuss the interconnectedness of women, bodies, and land (Kelm 1998; LaDuke 2005; Maracle 1996; Monture-Angus 2002; Ralstin-Lewis 2005; Smith 2005). This intersection has, and continues to operate at the node, or fulcrum, for systematic physical and discursive oppression. Imperialist state policies of colonization, domination, and expansion have been tied to control over reproductive capacity; some scholars have even referred to this in a context of "reproducing empire" (Briggs 2002). Reproductive capacity is a key area where women's bodies have been colonized through macro and micro practices of domination.

In this chapter we further shed light on some of the ways in which micro practices of colonization appear in Aamjiwnaang. The manifestation of reproductive harm in light of decades of industrial pollution is but one example of the systemic social injustices women in particular and the community, broadly speaking, face in this context. Some bodies are literally "gendering" as a result of their harmful environments (Scott 2009). It becomes clear that mothers face both tangible and intangible, visible and invisible harm. As the next section discusses, while bodies are *becoming* gendered through the advance of chemical reactions with the endocrine system, the language about the body as a potential threat, or site of contamination, is equally powerful and potentially harmful.[7] An example of this language and the perpetuation of colonizing gender is the discourse of intersex animals as a response to endocrine disruptors in and around Aamjiwnaang First Nation. Qwo-Li Driskill (2004, 52) points out that this resulting homophobia and transphobia can be understood in relation to what is happening with language and understanding of endocrine disruptors: "As Native people, our erotic lives and identities have been colonized along with our homelands." Women, and mothers, in this context are faced with simultaneously trying to mitigate the "real and material" consequences of environmental harm alongside the discursive constructions of "naturalness" and "normalcy" of future generations (Scott 2009). The next section situates some of the material and discursive means in which power, colonialism, and state authority perpetuate and legitimate pollution on the landscape and the reproductive body in Aamjiwnaang.

SEEKING REPRODUCTIVE JUSTICE IN AAMJIWNAANG

The Aamjiwnaang First Nation Reserve, home to about 850 Anishinabek, lies across the Canada-US border from Port Huron, Michigan, approximately 7 km south of Sarnia, Ontario, with about 253 private dwellings. For nearly half a century, the land has been surrounded on all sides by one of Canada's largest concentrations of polymer and petrochemical manufacturing centres. Much of the original reserve, founded by the 1827 Huron Tract Treaty, had been sold to industry by the 1960s and is now occupied by pipelines, factories, and dozens of petroleum storage tanks. The location of this community – in what is commonly referred to as Canada's "Chemical Valley" by residents and local media, due to the high concentration of petrochemical plants and the production of 40 per cent of Canada's chemicals – profoundly affects its neighbours.

A series of industrial spills, leaks, and accidents led to the formation of the Aamjiwnaang First Nation Health and Environment committee in 2002. As mentioned in the introduction to this chapter, by 2005, following the release of the EHP sex ratio study, a wave of local, national, and international media attention began to pour over the community. Of particular interest to reporters was the "male birth dearth" and the realization that this is a place "where the boys aren't" (Mittelstaedt 2004, 2005, 2007, 2008a; 2008b; CBC 2008; Hall 2006). Several media accounts demonstrated concern that males were an "endangered species" and that it would only be a matter of time before what was happening in Aamjiwnaang would happen in other communities across the world (Mittelstaedt 2008a, 2008b; Puzic 2008). A 2009 feature in *Men's Health* outlined a sustained concern about the "lost boys" of this community

(Petersen 2009). Although these stories express concern about the loss of male babies, limited attention was paid to the members of the community facing pregnancy and birth in this environment. While women's bodies, experiences, and stories played a pivotal role in the ongoing struggles for justice in the community, it is significant to note some of the ways in which reproductive harm or health becomes gendered, while some voices speak louder than others, eclipsing the subtle socio-structural violences affecting this community's future generations.

As a 2008 *Chatelaine* article highlighted, women played a key role at the forefront of activism to seek recognition of their health concerns from the Chemical Valley (Giese 2008). This movement can be understood through a reproductive justice framework. While the *Chatelaine* story placed women at the forefront, media accounts and scholarly research to date did not explore the link between broader processes of colonization and the reproductive experiences of women, men, and youth who live on the frontlines of this pollution hotspot. Thus, it bears repeating here that reproductive justice is not simply a women's issue, though women often appear, discursively and structurally, at the frontlines of these struggles. A central objective of this chapter is to bring in a discussion of the body, broadly speaking, and the reproductive body in particular into contemporary political science analyses through an intersectional reproductive justice framework, by anchoring the body and lived experience within concrete policy processes in a specific locale.

We situate reproductive justice struggles in Lambton County in southwestern Ontario, home to the Aamjiwnaang First Nation, downstream from Canada's Chemical Valley. The aforementioned 2005 study used a community-based participatory research model, and a team of researchers assessed the live-birth-sex ratios for the Aamjiwnaang First Nation in response to concerns voiced by members of the community regarding the perception of a decreasing male birthrate. This birth-sex ratio assessment was part of a broader community-based investigation undertaken by the Aamjiwnaang in collaboration with the Occupational Health Clinics for Ontario Workers – Sarnia (O H C O W) along with scientific consultants, professionals, and students from a wide range of disciplines (Mackenzie Keith and Lockridge 2005). The exploration included quantitative measurements such as soil, sediment, wildlife, fish, and air sampling, along with a door-to-door health survey and interviews. Moreover, the community provided informed consent and assistance to collect live-birth-sex ratio data from the Department of Indian and Northern Affairs database (Indian and Northern Affairs Canada, Ottawa, Ontario, Canada) for 1984 to 2003, representing the full length of record (see figure 13.2 and table 13.1). The Aamjiwnaang Lands and Memberships clerk reports births and deaths of the Aamjiwnaang First Nation on a monthly basis to the Aboriginal Affairs and Northern Development Canada.

The findings of this study were hotly contested. Community members engaged in this process expressed concern about present and future community health. Results documented an array of health concerns, most notably a skewed birth ratio (Mackenzie, Keith, and Lockridge 2005). While the number of reported live male births remained relatively stable between 1984 and 1992, the period from 1993 to 2003 revealed a declining trend of live male births (see figure 13.2). Worldwide, the human live-birth-sex ratio is remarkably constant, ranging between 102 and 108 male to 100 female live births; in Canada, the sex ratio is generally reported to be 105:100 (M:F) (m=0.512) (Mackenzie, Keith, and Lockridge 2005) (see figure 13.2). In Aamjiwnaang, the most recent interval period analyzed (1999 to 2003) revealed that nearly two females were being born for each male (m=0.348) (see table 13.1). This study, published in *Environmental Health Perspectives,* garnered local, national, and international media attention, as well as piquing the interest of scientists and researchers worldwide. A decrease in the proportion of male births has been attributed to environmental, occupational, and chemical exposures in the community. Although the link between the sex ratio and chemical exposure remains inconclusive, members of the First Nation began to look at their environment with much concern.

Despite widespread media attention, the popular language of concern about the community's "lost boys," "feminization trends," "gender-bending," and the "male predicament," which appear in various media sources, only scratch the surface of the embodied pollution harm (Giese 2008; Petersen 2009). Aamjiwnaang's reproductive struggles demonstrate how bodies become the surfaces upon which pollution stories are inscribed. By analyzing the ongoing politics of reproduction apparent in the neighbouring municipalities of Lambton County and prevalent in the ongoing Lambton Community

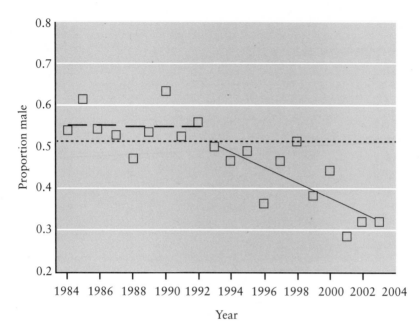

13.2 Proportion of live male births (male live births/total live births) for
Aamjiwnaang First Nation 1984–2003. The dotted line is the expected male
proportion for Canada (0.512). The dashed line is the linear regression line for
the period 1984–1992; r^2 = 0.000; slope not significantly different from zero
(p = 0.990). The solid line is the linear regression line for the period 1993–
2003; r^2 = 0.547; statistically significant deviation of slope from zero (= 0.009)
(Mackenzie, Keith, and Lockridge 2005). Reproduced with permission from
Environmental Health Perspectives.

Health Study, we contend that pollution exposures perpetuate the
legacy of colonization in material and discursive ways. This becomes
apparent both structurally and discursively in struggles for reproductive justice in Aamjiwnaang.

The language of "gender-bending" toxins remains prominent
in scientific analyses of endocrine-disruption. Though the human
health effects of environmental contamination due to toxins in the
environment are largely unknown, scientists looking at local wildlife populations in the Great Lakes have documented the problem of
gender-bending chemicals, as a result of an unknown mixture of
toxic chemicals in the air, soil, and water (Kavanagh et al. 2004;

Table 13.1
Total live births, proportion of live male births (male live births/total births), χ_2, and p-value for Aamjiwnaang First Nation 1984–2003 arranged in 5- and 10-year periods. Reproduced with permission from *Environmental Health Perspectives*.

Period	Total Live Births	Proportion Male Births	χ_{2a}	p-Value
5-Year				
1984–88	173	0.538	0.185	0.667
1989–93	185	0.551	0.532	0.466
1994–98	215	0.451	1.574	0.210
1999–03	132	0.348	7.472	0.006*
10-Year				
1984–93	358	0.545	0.807	0.369
1994–03	347	0.412	7.100	0.008*

*Chi-square was performed using an expected male proportion equal to 0.512; df=1.
*Highly significant statistical deviation ($p < 0.01$) from the expected proportion of males using Chi-square analysis.

Weisskopf 2003). Scientists use the sex ratio as a sensitive indicator demonstrating the effects as a result of exposure to chemicals disrupting the endocrine-system and reproductive health. Because hormones are so important to the development and healthy performance of the body's organs, endocrine-disruptors have the potential to cause a wide range of effects, from damage to the brain and sex organs to decreased sperm production and immune suppression in adults (CBC 2008; Cohen 2007). They may also be responsible for rising cancer rates, reproductive abnormalities, and declining sperm counts.

Research is less clear on the effects of low-level chemical exposures, the effects of which are subtle and harder to document. According to Weisskopf, a research associate at the Harvard School of Public Health, there are a lot of unknowns. In a 2003 study, he and several colleagues found that mothers who consumed large amounts of PCB-contaminated fish from the Great Lakes were more likely to have girls (Weisskopf 2003). It is difficult to say exactly how the effects of endocrine-disruptors affect the general population; however, there is little doubt that endocrine-disrupting pollutants affect the sexual development of wildlife near Aamjiwnaang.

In Lake St Clair, about 50 km from the reserve, fish with both male and female gonads have been discovered. The condition, known as intersex, is caused when a young fish that is genetically male is exposed to chemicals such as the fertilizer atrazine, which causes female gonads to develop by acting like the hormone estrogen (Kavanagh et al. 2004).[8] The research also identified increased reproductive abnormalities for women who consume the fish. Weisskopf's findings suggest that maternal exposure to polychlorinated biphenyls may decrease the sex ratio of offspring (Mackenzie, Keith, and Lockridge 2005). The phenomenon has been documented all over the southern Great Lakes, not just in fish, but in birds and amphibians as well (Mackenzie, Keith, and Lockridge 2005). It is important to note that, according to many traditional Indigenous beliefs, animal health is connected to human health, and, although the science is revealing about the effect of toxins in the wildlife, the human effects remain unknown. The citizens of Aamjiwnaang live with these unknowns on a daily basis, waiting for the security of the known.

The body comes to the fore at the frontlines of environmental harm. Members of Aamjiwnaang are increasingly worried about the pollution of their reserve. In addition to the notion that the environment has a physical effect on the body, there are also cultural, spiritual, and emotional effects. In particular, community members express a growing sense of fear – of the sirens, the outdoors, air, water – and so on. As an Ecojustice report articulates (2007): "These chemicals and related incidents have significant effects on their cultural life, including hunting, fishing, medicine, gathering and ceremonial activities. Health effects include asthma, reproductive effects, learning disabilities and cancer. The most common reported impact was fear. People on the reserve feared the outdoors, the warning sirens and unreported incidences.

When toxins are found in food and wildlife, avoidance becomes impossible, exposure an everyday reality."

As mentioned, before publication of the 2005 sex ratio study, the Aamjiwnaang First Nation conducted a door-to-door community health study with the assistance of the Occupational Health Clinic for Ontario Workers, in Sarnia. This included a survey and body-mapping exercises in which anatomical drawings with colour-coded stickers adorned the community's gymnasium walls to show and visualize the number of health concerns experienced in the community (see figure 13.3).

Statistics collected by Aamjiwnaang Band member and community activist Ada Lockridge and her team showed widespread issues of behavioural and learning disabilities, and asthma at nearly three times the national rate. A body mapping study of 411 individuals

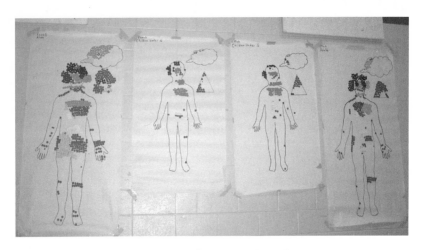

13.3 A body map. Image used with permission from the Aamjiwnaang
Environment Department.

between 2004 and 2005 revealed that 26 per cent of adults experienced high blood pressure, 26 per cent of adults and 9 per cent of
children experienced chronic headaches, 23 per cent of children aged
five to sixteen had learning and behavioural problems, 27 per cent
of children experienced skin rashes, and 39 per cent of women experienced a miscarriage or stillbirth (Ecojustice 2007). Results further
indicated that 40 per cent of band members require an inhaler, about
17 per cent of adults and 22 per cent of children surveyed have
asthma, whereas the Lambton County asthma rate sits at approximately 8.2 per cent (Ecojustice 2007). These results were published
in an Ecojustice report, *Exposing Canada's Chemical Valley* (2007).
They were not published elsewhere.

   Policy-makers at all levels of government disputed whether the
data collected made generalizable and statistically significant findings; even members of the Band Council shied away from verifying
the results. Requests by then-Aamjiwnaang Health and Environment
Committee members for a local epidemiological study from the community fell on deaf ears, as decision-makers – the federal government
and in particular Health Canada, which maintains a fiduciary responsibility for on-reserve health – ignored them.[9] Not only has the federal government maintained an ambivalent position on what action
to take with respect to this community's reproductive health concerns, so too have the local health authorities. In response to the 2005

sex ratio study, the Lambton County Health Unit produced its own reproductive health report. The report concluded that sex ratios in Lambton County do not differ from Ontario rates (Community Health Services Department 2007). The small number of births recorded on-reserve during the same timeframe were considered unrepresentative and too small for any conclusive findings of abnormal health harms and patterns, which is revealing about the limitations of large-scale epidemiological health studies for smaller communities.[10] Due to the overall low number of reported births, Aaamjiwnaang's data were thus considered statistically insignificant.

Following the release of the 2005 sex ratio study, stakeholders and community leaders began to meet and decided that a study of health effects associated with exposure to environmental contaminants was a public health priority for Lambton County (CCI Research 2010). Official representatives of the Aamjiwnaang First Nation entered into conversation with officials from Lambton County about the formation of a county-wide health study, what came to be the Lambton Community Health Study. In 2008, the Lambton Community Health Study emerged with its board membership and a mandate to look at the relationship between industrial activity and human health through three phases: the establishment of a board of directors; a literature review and community engagement (including phone surveys, town hall meetings, and an online survey); and a phase of results communication. The study drew funds from the Province of Ontario ($50,000) a voluntary industry-led association, the Sarnia-Lambton Environmental Association (SLEA) ($15,000), as well as the Chamber of Commerce ($10,000). The federal government committed to offering $100,000 in-kind service (Modern 2010). As a result, questions emerged about whether the Aamjiwnaang First Nation's unique reproductive health concerns were well-represented by the ongoing public health processes.

DELIBERATIVE HEALTH POLICY: AN AVENUE
FOR REPRODUCTIVE JUSTICE?

A central feature of any so-called healthy democratic political community is to bring the people into conversation with decision-makers.[11] Canada has a tradition of calling upon its citizens to consult on a range of deliberative policy processes, exemplified through practices such as royal commissions, the BC Conversation on Health, and the Citizens' Assembly on Electoral Reform, and the use of technologies such as referenda and recall. By engaging in these participatory democratic processes, individuals acquire an identity as engaged agents in the process of becoming a citizen. When governments invite members of the public to participate in consultations in key policy areas, such as health care, they "generally represent themselves as calling upon citizens to engage in a social, but apolitical process" (Fiske and Browne 2008, 1). In our view, the notion that any such process is apolitical is an inaccurate reflection of the political processes taking shape. In fact, these processes are highly charged by competing interests, discursive constraints, and available resources. Thus, we reiterate the importance of connecting reproductive justice to contemporary political struggles.

Encounters with the health care system operate in politically charged environments. The context for health policy development takes place within the rubric of government decisions, or nondecisions. By examining the meanings embedded within health policy discourse – the language, spoken and unspoken, in various documents; terms of reference; technologies and media statements among others – we catch a glimpse into the ways in which social power and disparities are produced, contested, and resisted in a particular domain. An intersectional and interpretive investigation of such text, language, and communication seeks to question the underlying assumptions taken at face value. By bringing citizens into a conversation about health care, and in this case, on reproductive recognition, a paradox of engagement becomes apparent: citizens are expected to adopt the terms for dialogue or debate, which may or may not provide a context for empowerment or recognition for particular claims. It is in this paradoxical context that some citizens' claims may become marginalized.

The process of bringing citizens into dialogue about public health issues shapes, conceptualizes, and even constrains behaviour and action, embedding individuals in a very political process. An intersectional, interpretive approach to policy does not solely examine the raw data of a particular domain; rather, it examines how the language contains, carries, and transmits subtle messages that shape social and political meaning (Fiske and Browne 2008, 4). A critical, interpretive, and discursive approach will examine public conversations, or political dialogue between parties to examine who has the power to define the domain by setting out the terms of engagement, which may reinforce privilege and marginalize some narratives over others. By examining the casual, normalized everyday encounters between citizens and policymakers, political analysts can uncover the implicit meanings that form the context for power relations in particular processes, centred upon the management, care, and regulation of life itself.

We can think of policy as both a process and a product. Specifically, following Fiske and Browne, health policy can be understood as a technology of power (Fiske and Browne 2008, 7). Thus, a critical and interpretive approach to examining health policy as a technology of power focuses on some of the ways in which power stretches beyond the strict parameters of institutions or texts upon individuals, and affects attitudes, beliefs, and everyday practices. By examining the Lambton Community Health Study as a technology of power, we examine the ways in which power relations inform, shape, and constrain the Aamjiwnaang First Nation's claims for reproductive justice.

Early in 2006, community leaders and stakeholders in Lambton County met and agreed to study the health effects associated with exposure to environmental emissions, determining this to be a public health priority for Lambton County. In 2008, the health study board of directors was formalized, comprising a diverse group of stakeholders, including municipalities, First Nations, business, labour, industry, occupational health, victims of occupational illness, and county public health officials (Lambton Community Health Study 2011). Both the local Lambton County health unit and the federal government (Health Canada) pledged to offer in-kind support for the ongoing health study. As mentioned, the board determined that their health study would contain three distinct phases: Phase 1, to establish a community-based governance structure,[12] which would identify a board of directors to oversee the project; Phase 2, including a comprehensive literature review, community engagement, development of research questions, and a call for proposals for Phase 3; and Phase 3, undertaking identified studies, communicating results to Lambton County residents, and identifying the next steps (Lambton Community Health Study 2011). Phase 2 was completed early in 2011. At the time of writing, Phase 3 – actually carrying out a systematic and scientific health study – remains subject to funding.

We suggest several reasons why this process may have eclipsed Aamjiwnaang's struggles for reproductive justice. These reasons focus on the issues associated with the representation of Aamjiwnaang's concerns vis-à-vis the interests of Lambton County constituents at large. First, the Lambton Community Health Study broadens the scale of health concerns from the community to the county as a whole, which encompasses eleven municipalities. This is in stark contrast to the Aamjiwnaang First Nation health study, which began in 2005. The fear here is that the unique concerns facing this community, due to the impact of long-term cumulative effects as well as its distinct geographical location, encircled by industry, will be eclipsed by competing interests at the stakeholder or county level.

Second, the biomedical power and authority embedded within the language of science, epidemiology, and statistical significance discredits Aamjiwnaang's experiential claims. There appears to be a presumption at the county level that the 2005 birth ratio study was not statistically sound and thus was unrepresentative of the county's concerns at large. As mentioned, Lambton County's Health Services Department analyzed sex ratios for the entire county and individual townships "in order to determine if sex ratios differed from provincial ratios and if communities adjacent to the reserve and local industry were differentially affected" (Community Health Services Department 2007, 17). The results of the study revealed "no trends towards a declining sex ratio, i.e., fewer male births, in Lambton County or its individual townships between 1981 and 2001" (Community Health Services Department 2007, 17). The report concluded that sex ratios in Lambton County did not differ greatly from Ontario values as a whole. This study did not look at the data for Aamjiwnaang in particular.

Third, public discourse at the board and county level continues to raise the issue of "lifestyle choices." This language was apparent both in conversations about risk factors during pregnancy and throughout the reproductive process, and was also evident in public statements. For example, in response to the launch of a Charter challenge by two individuals from the Aamjiwnaang First Nation, Dean Edwardson, Lambton Community Health Study board member and director of the industry-led Sarnia-Lambton Environmental Association, told the *Sarnia Observer*: "The cumulative effects of pollution are hard to establish, given local weather patterns, *resident lifestyles* and other factors. It's hard to predict the effect the legal challenge will have on local industry" (Jeffords 2010, emphasis ours). Furthermore, residents expressed concern during the Lambton County town-hall meetings that they were tired of hearing the discourse of lifestyle blaming for reproductive harm, alluding to smoking and drinking habits among residents (Phil Brown and Associates 2011). As participant observation at these town-hall meetings revealed, which took place over five days during the month of November 2010, the discourse of lifestyle blaming and individual responsibility for health outcomes emerged as a recurring theme.

Fourth, the process issues of funding, resource distribution, and fiduciary responsibility for on-reserve health lead to a power imbalance within the structure of representation for Aamjiwnaang's reproductive health concerns. Funding for the health study is provided by a combination of the provincial government and industry (Phil Brown and Associates 2011). The Province of Ontario pledged funding early in 2010, specifically for the completion of a literature review. Before that time, business interests, via the Chamber of Commerce and the Sarnia-Lambton Environmental Association, provided the only real dollars, though both Lambton County and Health Canada contributed in-kind services, in staff time and technical and scientific expertise, to the health study (Morden 2010). According to Ben Martin, assistant to local Member of Parliament Pat Davidson, Health Canada's in-kind service for the study is valued at $100,000, which, she went on to state, is higher in value than the $50,000 awarded by the province. This is pertinent, as, according to formal government fiduciary responsibilities for Aboriginal health, in the Canadian federal system, whereas Health Canada provides funding to provinces that provide direct services through a range of regional authorities, the federal government maintains a direct responsibility for First Nations and Inuit health. In the case of the Lambton Community Health Study, Aamjiwnaang had to vie for its reproductive health concerns to be recognized, yet the legal and administrative authorities responsible for this policy domain remain absent. These four reasons contextualize Aamjiwnaang's struggle for reproductive justice, embedded within structural power relations of inequality, which appear upon the landscape of the reproductive body.

CONCLUSION: FROM CONTAMINATED TO REGENERATIVE BODIES

The body offers fertile ground for political analysis. This analysis takes us beyond the macro level of politics – states, institutions, or political parties – to the body, a site that reveals political struggles that cut across micro, meso, and macro scales. Examining the body as a site for political analysis exposes some of the ways in which power, governance, and authority manifest at the micro level. We have introduced the Aamjiwnaang First Nation's struggle for reproductive justice by examining the experience of this community's claims about their health concerns when living within a polluted hotspot and sought to explain these within the context of ongoing public health processes in the surrounding area. We discussed some of the ways in which such processes obstruct or eclipse marginalized corporeal concerns apparent in Aamjiwnaang's struggle for reproductive justice. Because the Lambton Community Health Study is still underway at the time of writing, awaiting the commencement of Phase 3, it remains to be seen whether the community's interests will be represented and its claims substantively addressed. Situating this struggle for reproductive justice within a broader framework of intersectional theory, which connects race, gender, and the reproductive body with place in Aamjiwnaang, provides some foreground into thinking about how the body can operate as a regenerative force and site of resistance.

Furthermore, we contend that the body is not a passive site for political analysis; it is a site of regeneration. Katsi Cook (cited in LaDuke 1999), a Mohawk midwife, talks about the womb as the first environment and directly links reproductive health to Aamjiwnaang's struggle for environmental justice. Her work draws attention to the impacts of exploration, exploitation, and the extinguishing of land and life on women and future generations. At the same time, while the maternal or reproductive body has been hailed in discourse, media, and research as a "site of contamination," the birth process itself may be a site of resurgence against colonialism. Several Indigenous scholars argue that self-determination begins with the female body (Anderson 2006; Fiske and Browne 2008; Maracle 1996; Simpson 2006; Cook, cited in LaDuke 1999). We further suggest that innovative policy geared toward decolonization and social equity must move away from the singularity of the female body involved in birth and reproduction to think more broadly about the contextually embedded reproductive body. Moreover, we have argued that the production and reproduction of human beings is an inherently political process: it is integral to self-determination and tied to struggles for reproductive justice.

Reproductive justice links issues of health and reproduction to the broader context of social justice. We have discussed the various ways in which claims about the reproductive body are embedded within political struggles. By linking reproductive justice to an intersectionality framework, political analysts gain insight into the challenges individuals and communities face when trying to make claims within processes that systematically disadvantage marginalized communities. At the same time, locating the politics of the body within a broader conversation about politics presents an opportunity to think differently and critically about the execution of power and authority. Though discriminatory colonial processes may write themselves upon bodies, they are also sites of regeneration, forces "to be reckoned with" (Grosz 1994). As communities like the Aamjiwnaang First Nation continue to make their voices heard, it will be imperative for decision-makers to recognize the context for these struggles and begin to investigate both the place where these struggles occur and also pay attention to the experiential knowledge and narratives coming from the individuals within these communities.

Indigenous knowledge and world views present themselves in many different forms that are too often not included within larger political debates. Thinking critically about the ways in which reproductive bodies are discursively and physically constituted opens up space for the regeneration of knowledge. *How* we think about bodies presents an opportunity for resistance. Following O'Neil, Elias, and Yassi (1998), local discourse has the potential to speak out and resist dominant discursive frames. Situating narratives within "fields of resistance" refers to the importance of resisting language as well as formal institutional processes, which in a health care field have a tendency to overemphasize scientific and epidemiological modelling without considering often marginalized voices (O'Neil, Elias, and Yassi 1998, 260). By taking into account experiential, corporeal knowledge in political processes and policies, more equitable public-policy making will emerge, with hitherto silent voices coming to the fore.

Some of the ways in which these voices manifest is through artistic means. For example, through artistic expressions such as paint, film, photography, music, rap, and multimedia, the experiences, concerns, and views of those most directly affected by the past and present practices of colonization can be heard. Thus, by including images into this text, we seek to raise awareness about reproductive health and injustice through creative means, calling attention to the merits of arts-based approaches to study intersectional struggles for reproductive justice. This innovative thinking and form of expression is crucial to how we better understand the relationship between bodies, health, pollution, and power, and has the potential to lead to alternative avenues for decolonial public health policy-making.

Art is an incredibly powerful vehicle for resistance, which is particularly salient with youth as they resist the seemingly all-encompassing forms of oppression. This becomes clear in ongoing work within the Aamjiwnaang First Nation youth through the Green Teens and Kiijig Collective, groups that use creative voices to express concerns about their land and environment. Bearing the responsibility for future generations, youth face the weight of concerns about a viable future on their lands. Thus, going forward, resistance to power relations begins with bringing alternative voices to the fore, including those of women, Elders, and youth, through creative and artistic avenues.

NOTES

1   We would like to acknowledge the citizens of the Aamjiwnaang First Nation, and in particular the Aamjiwnaang Green Teens, for sharing their perspectives. We thank Dr Dayna Scott for supporting this research through her ongoing engagement with the community. This chapter benefitted greatly from the opportunity to present these findings in Montreal during the Politics of Reproduction conference held in September 2010. The approach put forward in this paper also benefitted from author participation in the Policy at the Intersections: Reconceiving Policy Problems and Advancing Equity workshop, led by Olena Hankivsky and her team of researchers at the University of Ottawa in October 2012. We welcome and appreciate the excellent feedback from the chapter reviewers. Thanks also to Jennifer Bagelman for comments on an early version of the manuscript. Erin would like to offer special thanks to Jessica Yee of the Native Youth Sexual Health Network for the guidance and teachings that have helped to build the reproductive justice framework informing this paper. We are grateful for the funding from the Social Sciences and Humanities Research Council of Canada that supported this research.

2   We note that Indigenous women are life givers, life sustainers, and culture holders whose bodies are sacred places that must be protected, honoured,

and kept free of harmful contaminants in order for future generations to be born strong and healthy.

3   Historically, many Indigenous communities and First Nations had places for community members whose gender represented both masculine and feminine roles. Whenever gender is discussed as it relates to Indigenous peoples it is crucial to note: "In Native North America, there were and still are cultures in which more than two gender categories are marked" (Jacob 1997, 2).

4   Thus, the right to free, prior, and informed consent (FPIC) as it relates to Indigenous lands and bodies is crucial to the following discussion. Given the history of FPIC, the Indigenous body is already connected to political science debates around environmental justice in general and to the Aamjiwnaang First Nation's struggle for reproductive justice in particular.

5   We use the term *violence* to refer to environmental contaminants causing disease, birth defects, and death that are deliberately released into the environment *because* they are toxic to living things (i.e., pesticides), or as a result of industrial or military processes that are judged by states and corporations to pose an "acceptable risk" and "allowable harm." States and corporations frequently contest the "provability" of their impacts despite clear evidence that they may cause a range of serious health and reproductive impacts that disproportionately affect Indigenous women and children. Such environmental violence infringes human rights.

6   Despite divergence about agency and emancipation, post-colonial and intersectional feminist scholars align to celebrate a process of decentring dominant culture and coherent singular categories of oppression. By decentring, this approach also aims to think critically about new ways of thinking and being in the world. According to Homi Bhabha (1994), the move away from these singularities led to awareness that race, gender, institutional location, sexual orientation, and geopolitical locale inhabit any claim to identity in the modern world. Bhabha contends that what is theoretically innovative and politically crucial is the need to think beyond narratives of originary and initial subjectivities and to focus on those moments or processes that are produced in the articulation of cultural differences

7   As Linda Smith indicates, colonization is central to how gender is represented when it comes to Indigenous peoples. Understanding how western frameworks construct gender in relation to environmental debates is part of understanding how to address the changes and effects on Indigenous bodies.

8 While science tends to construct gender changes in animals that result from environmental changes as simply defective, we want to challenge this notion and its dominance in environmental discourse. Indigenous communities differently construct gender; western research all too often re-colonizes the language used. While a history of the effects colonization has had on gender is beyond the scope of this paper, we contend that it is significant to acknowledge the ways in which discourse and deliberative processes are gendering. As such, the creation of changes to gender in the environment as they are represented in many health studies often does not take into account how gender is viewed within an Indigenous world view.

9 Indigenous land continues to be governed as Crown land under the authority and control of the federal colonial government. In addition, while on-reserve health and environment programming operate in a seemingly vacuous policy zone, it is also relevant to address that Indigenous health policy overall exists within a climate of reduction: the Conservative federal government recently cut Indigenous health policy and programming, in particular to the First Nations and Inuit Health Branch of Health Canada, the National Aboriginal Health Organization (Picard 2012).

10 While Aboriginal communities have special roles for members such as Elders, youth, and women, science and risk assessment continue to provide averages that do not recognize impacts on these community members and those identified in the aforementioned roles.

11 It is the discursive construction of a healthy deliberative study and healthy political community that we deconstruct and examine in this chapter. Looking at how these authorities are constructed and sustained is often an indicator of what that participation looks like, and how the results are represented and acted upon. Article 3 of the United Nations Declaration on the Rights of Indigenous Peoples explains: "Indigenous Peoples have the right to self-determination. By virtue of that right they freely determine their political status and freely pursue their economic, social and cultural development." Moreover, we are mindful of the fact that the process of consultation in Canada continues to be based predominately on a state-based relationship that does not always recognize Indigenous sovereignty. This is further illustrated by the fact that Canada was one of the last four countries to sign the United Nations Declaration on the Rights of Indigenous Peoples.

12 Traditional governance structures existed and still exist within many Indigenous communities to address issues that arise. The Lambton Community Health Study Board structure was not developed from an Indigenous model.

BIBLIOGRAPHY

Anderson, J. 2002. "Toward a Post-Colonial Feminist Methodology in Nursing Research: Exploring the Convergence of Post-Colonial and Black Feminist Scholarship," *Nurse Researcher* 9(3): 7–27.

– 2006. "Reflections on the Social Determinants of Women's Health Exploring Intersections: Does Racialization Matter"? *Canadian Journal of Nursing Research* 38(1): 7–14.

Anderson, K. 2006. "New Life Stirring: Mothering, Transformation and Aboriginal Womanhood." In *Until Our Hearts are on the Ground: Aboriginal Mothering, Oppression, Resistance and Rebirth*, D. Memee Lavell-Harvard and Jeannette Corbiere, eds., 13–24. Toronto: Demeter Press.

Briggs, L. 2002. *Reproducing Empire: Race, Sex, Science and U.S. Imperialism in Puerto Rico*. Berkeley: University of California Press.

CBC. 2008. *The Disappearing Male*. Written and directed by Marc de Guerre. Canada: CBC and Red Apple Entertainment.

CCI Research. 2010. *Summary Report: Lambton Community Health Study Telephone Survey*. Sarnia: CCI Research.

Cohen, B. 2007. *Toxic Trespass*. Directed by Barri Cohen. Canada: Women's Healthy Environments Network and the National Film Board of Canada.

Community Health Services Department. 2007. *Reproductive Health: Lambton County 2007 Health Status Report*. Sarnia: Community Health Services Department.

Crenson, M. 2005. "Canadian Natives Blame Toxins for Fewer Sons." NBC News, 19 December. http://www.msnbc.msn.com/id/10531498/from/rs.1.

Driskill, Q. 2004. "Stolen from Our Bodies: First Nations Two-Spirits/Queers and the Journey to a Sovereign Erotic," *Studies in American Indian Literatures* 16(2): 50–64.

Ecojustice. 2007. *Exposing Canada's Chemical Valley*. Toronto: Ecojustice.

Fiske, J. 1996. "The Womb is to the Nation as the Heart is to the Body: Ethnopolitical Discourses of the Canadian Indigenous Women's Movement," *Studies in Political Economy* 51: 65–95.

Fiske, J., and A. Browne. 2008. *Paradoxes and Contradictions in Health Policy Reform: Implications for First Nations Women*. Vancouver: BC Centre of Excellence for Women's Health.

Giese, R. 2008. "How to Fix a Toxic Town." *Chatelaine*, June.

Grosz, E. 1994. *Volatile Bodies: Toward a Corporeal Feminism*. Bloomington: Indiana University Press.

356 The Discursive Politics of Reproduction

Gunn Allen, P. 1986. *The Sacred Hoop: Recovering the Feminine in American Indian Traditions.* Boston: Beacon Press.

Hall, J. 2006. "Where Have All The Boys Gone?" *Toronto Star,* 22 April.

Harvey, N., and J. Wessman, J. 2000. "An Interview With Katsi Cook." *Talking Leaves: A Journal of Our Evolving Ecological Culture* 10(1). http://www.lostvalley.org/talkingleaves/node/61.

International Indigenous Women's Symposium (2010). *Declaration for Health, Life and Defense of Our Lands, Rights and Future Generations.* Accessed 1 November 2010. http://indigenouspeoplesissues.com/index. php?option=com_content&view=article&id=6271:declaration-for-health-life-and-defense-of-our-lands-rights-and-future-generations-international-indigenous-womens-symposium&catid=65: indigenous-peoples-general&itemid=92.

Jacob, S.E., W. Thomas, and S. Lang, eds. 1997. *Two-Spirit People: Native American Gender Identity, Sexuality and Spirituality.* University of Illinois: Illinois.

Jeffords, S. 2010. "Valley Targeted in Lawsuit," *Sarnia Observer,* 2 November. http://www.theobserver.ca/2010/11/02/valley-targetted-in-lawsuit.

Kavanagh, R. et al. 2004. "Endocrine Disruption and Altered Gonadal Development in White Perch (Morone americana) from the Lower Great Lakes Region." *Environmental Health Perspectives* 112(8): 898–902.

Kelm, M.E. 1998. *Colonizing Bodies: Aboriginal Health and Healing in British Columbia 1900–1950.* Vancouver: UBC Press.

LaDuke, W. 1999. *All Our Relations: Native Struggles for Land and Life.* Cambridge, MA: South End Press.

– 2005. *Recovering the Sacred: The Power of Naming and Claiming.* Cambridge, MA: South End Press.

Lambton Community Health Study. 2011. Accessed 27 March 2011. http://www.lambtonhealthstudy.ca.

Mackenzie, C., M. Keith, and A. Lockridge. 2005. "Declining Sex Ration in a First Nations Community." *Environmental Health Perspectives* 113(10): 1295–8.

Maracle, L. 1996. *I am Woman: A Native Perspective on Sociology and Feminism.* Vancouver: Press Gang Publishers.

Mittlestaedt, M. 2004. "Where the Boys Aren't." *The Globe and Mail,* 31 July.

– 2005. "Pollution Debate Born of Chemical Valley's Girl-Baby Boom." *The Globe and Mail,* 15 November.

– 2007. "The Mystery of the Missing Boys." *The Globe and Mail*, 11 April.

– 2008a. "Humanity at Risk: Are the Males Going First?" *The Globe and Mail*, 20 September.

– 2008b. "Male Birth Dearth Persists on Ontario Reserve." *The Globe and Mail*, 27 March.

Monture-Angus, P. 2002. *Thunder in My Soul: A Mohawk Woman Speaks*. Halifax: Fernwood Publishing.

Morden, P. 2010. "Health Study Inching Along." *Observer*, 16 September. http://www.theobserver.ca/2010/09/16/health-study-inching-along.

O'Neil, John, B.D. Elias, and A. Yassi. 1998. "Situating Resistance in Fields of Resistance: Aboriginal Women and Environmentalism." In *Pragmatic Woman and Body Politics*, M. Lock and P.A. Kaufert, eds., 260–86. Cambridge, M A : Cambridge University Press.

Petersen, M. 2009. "The Lost Boys of Aamjiwnaang." *Men's Health Magazine*, 5 November. http://www.menshealth.com/men/health/other-diseases-ailments/industrial-pollution-health-hazards/article/442a7febcb6c4210vgnvcm1000003028\u200b1eac.

Phil Brown and Associates. 2011. *Open Houses Summary Report*. Sarnia: Phil Brown and Associates.

Picard, A. 2012. "Harper's Disregard for Aboriginal Health," *The Globe and Mail*, 9 April. http://www.theglobeandmail.com/life/health-and-fitness/harpers-disregard-for-aboriginal-health/article4223490.

Puzic, S. 2008. "The Disappearing Male: Studies Show Rise in Birth Defects, Infertility Among Men." *Windsor Star*, 6 November.

Ralstin-Lewis, M.D. 2005. "The Continuing Struggle Against Genocide: Indigenous Women's Reproductive Rights," *Wicazo SA Review* (Spring): 71–85.

Scott, D. 2009. "'Gender-Benders': Sex and Law in the Constitution of Polluted Bodies." *Feminist Legal Studies* 17(3): 241–64.

Shiva, V. 1997. *Biopiracy: The Plunder of Nature and Knowledge*. M A : South End Press.

Simpson, L. 2006. "Birthing as an Indigenous Resurgence: Decolonizing our Pregnancy and Birthing Ceremonies." In *Until Our Hearts are on the Ground: Aboriginal Mothering, Oppression, Resistance and Rebirth*, M. Lavell-Harvard and J. Corbiere-Lavell, eds., 25–33. Toronto: Demeter Press.

– 2009. "The Responsibilities of Women: Confronting Environmental Contamination in the Traditional Territories of Asubpeechoseewagong

Netum Anishinabek (Grassy Narrows) and Wabauskang First Nation." *Journal of Aboriginal Health* (December): 6–13.

SisterSong. 2011. "What is RJ." Accessed 16 August 2011. http://www.sistersong.net/index.php?option=com_content&view=article&id=141& itemid=81.

Smith, A. 2005. *Conquest: Sexual Violence and the American Indian Genocide*. Cambridge: South End Press.

Smith, L. 1999. *Decolonizing Methodologies: Research and Indigenous Peoples*. New York: University of Otago Press.

United Nations. 2007. *United Nations Declaration on the Rights of Indigenous Peoples*. New York: United Nations.

Weisskopf et al. 2003. "Decreased Sex Ration following Maternal Exposure to Polychlorinated Biphenyls from Contaminated Great Lakes Sport-Caught Fish: A Retrospective Cohort Study." *Environmental Health: A Global Access Source* 2(2).

Yee, J. 2010. "Reproductive Justice – For Real, For Me, For You, For Now," *Doula Right Thing: Reproductive Justice*. Accessed 6 November 2010. http://doularightthing.blogspot.com/2010/11/o6/reproductive-justice.html. Also available here: http://gudumit.net46.net/reproductive_justice.html. Accessed September 25 2013.

– 2011. *Feminism FOR REAL: Deconstructing the Academic Industrial Complex of Feminism*, Ottawa: Canadian Centre for Policy Alternatives.

Conclusion

STEPHANIE PATERSON, FRANCESCA SCALA,
AND MARLENE K. SOKOLON

The chapters in this volume offer important insights on reproduction as a human experience and as an area of scholarly research. As an area of research, the study of reproduction offers a fertile site for multidisciplinary and interdisciplinary collaboration among feminist scholars and social scientists. Drawing from the theoretical and methodological knowledge of their own disciplines, sociologists, political scientists, legal analysts, and public health researchers can all shed light on the relationship between state and societal forces and women's reproductive experiences. While focusing on the Canadian context, the authors in this volume have all interpreted reproduction from a variety of social and political sites and from multiple perspectives. In doing so, *Fertile Ground* contributes to growing social scientific research that places reproduction at the centre of political and social analysis.

The diversity of theoretical frameworks and methodological approaches represented in this volume also mirrors the diversity of women's experience with reproduction. While recognizing the centrality of reproduction in women's lives and identities, the research represented in this collection does not view it in monolithic terms. Rather, the starting point of many of the chapters is a recognition that reproduction, as a biological and psychosocial phenomenon, is situated within a web of interlocking social identities. Within Canada, women's reproductive experiences are mediated by class, race, sexual orientation, disability, and age, and differ across space and time. A number of the chapters on reproduction and maternal health bring to the fore the variability of meanings attached to birth control, conception, childbearing, motherhood, and breastfeeding. Social location significantly affects women's reproductive choices and how they view and negotiate the medicalization of reproduction. For example, Johnson reveals how preference for medical care during delivery among immigrant women often expressed markers of privilege and status; whereas, among Canadian-born women, the preference for midwifery care was expressed in terms of solidarity, women-centredness, empowerment, and autonomy from spouses. Johnson's study revealed how the intersection of gender and immigrant status produce distinct patterns of reproductive preferences that are not made visible in maternal health analyses that conceptualize pregnancy and childbirth as universal experiences. The variability of women's reproductive experiences is also underscored in Gustafson and Porter's discussion of women's "reproductive lives" in Newfoundland and Labrador. Rather than conceptualizing reproduction as a discrete biological event, the authors demonstrate how women's reproductive expectations and desires, which are shaped by societal and familial forces, change over the course of a woman's life and across generations. Commercial discourses also shape meanings attached to reproductive choices, as evidenced by Smith's examination of birth control use among young women. Although the "pill" was first introduced as a woman-centred solution for the control of reproduction, Smith argues that the neo-liberal discourse inculcated in the present-day marketing of the birth control pill has helped shift the discourse away from reproductive autonomy and contraception to a lifestyle choice targeting young women. No longer is contraception solely about controlling reproduction; instead, it is also about controlling unruly young bodies by providing blemish-free skin and painless periods.

The effects of state institutions, policies, and discourses on women's reproductive experiences and choices are also amply displayed in many of the chapters in this volume. As policy venues, courts, Parliament, and federalism directly and indirectly shape reproductive choices and rights in Canada. The Supreme Court takes centre stage in Thomson-Philbrook's examination of abortion policy in Canada. The author discusses how the Supreme Court in Canada, unlike its American counterpart, did not establish a constitutional right to abortion or make abortions legal but rather shifted the debate back to the parliamentary system. As of yet, no government has enacted abortion law, but considering the variation and decline in

provincial and regional services, access to abortion is more fragile in
Canada than most people think. Gruben and Cameron's analysis of
Canada's Assisted Human Reproduction Act uncovers how federalism and disputes over jurisdictional boundaries often affect wom-
en's reproductive rights and health. They argue that the struggle
between levels of government in the Canadian federal system will
almost certainly have a negative effect on women's reproductive
autonomy.

The pivotal role of biomedical agents and discourses in reproduction and reproductive health figures prominently in the work presented in this volume. The medicalization of reproduction and
related practices such as breastfeeding obscures the social, cultural,
and political realities in which reproduction takes place, to the detri-
ment of many women who do not conform to conventional notions
of motherhood. Both Walks and Scala explore how the underlying
medical model of ART policy stratifies reproduction by ignoring the
social, economic, and political contexts that inform issues of reproduction and infertility. In their chapters on breastfeeding, Nathoo
and Ostry, Lee, and Sokolon explore how Canada's policy on breastfeeding, which emphasized infant nutrition and medical goals of initiation and duration, ignores women's experiences of this bio-cultural
practice. These contributions provide further evidence that the medical model devalues women's experiential knowledge and ignore the
agency of women in their reproductive moments. The biomedical
discourse also detaches the various moments of reproduction from
the larger socio-economic context in which women experience their
reproductive lives. For example, Sokolon's analysis highlights the
reductionism at work in the Canadian breastfeeding policy that focused a universal goal of six months of exclusive breastfeeding. This
policy was found to not only ignore the diversity of women's personal experiences with breastfeeding, but by focusing on breastfeeding as primarily infant nutrition the policy neglected the practice's
connection to a woman's reproductive life in its larger political, cultural, and economic contexts.

Neo-liberalism, and its embedded assumptions of autonomy and
individualism, also imbues Canadian policy on reproduction and
reproductive health. Several contributions examine how the neo-
liberal notion of choice ignores the social and economic reality that
affects choices. Cattapan, for example, explores how neo-liberal
discourses gave rise to an infertility policy that supports a notion of

choice for the economically privileged but not equal access to these technologies for all. Smith comes to similar conclusion in her analysis of birth control marketing websites, which depict young women as neo-liberal subjects taking charge of their own destiny while ignoring social forces and the varying degrees of constraint and control on an individual's choice. In breastfeeding policy, Lee exposes the link between the neo-liberal logic of individualized responsibility and risk in health care and initiatives that encourage the proper self-management of the maternal body. In addition, Paterson contributes to these analyses by pointing out that, coupled with declining health care funding and shortages of obstetricians in Ontario, the influence of neo-liberal policy ironically provides a discursive space in which to discuss the alternative health care services of midwifery. These contributions reveal the tension between neo-liberal discourse, which assumes autonomous individualism, and the medical model, which works to displace the knowledge and agency of women. The discourse of neo-liberalism underlying policy and governance arrangements, however, tends to coincide with the medical model, since both privilege social arrangements that ignore the larger personal, familial, cultural, and socio-economic context in which experiences and choices concerning reproduction take place.

Dominant discourses and practices, however, do not remain unchallenged. Several chapters highlight the various ways in which strategies are or could be used to challenge the dominant discourses that perpetuate gender marginalization. Paterson's analysis of midwifery policy in Ontario highlights how the advocates of alternative birth problematized the biomedical multiscalar arrangements of the body and the institution by illuminating women's agency and challenging the idea that pregnancy is something to be treated. This challenge, Paterson stresses, disrupted the biomedical scalar fix to include the home, but did not transform it; the hierarchical ordering of scales remains intact as midwives defer to physicians and biomedical discourse and the provincial scale remains key in the politics of reproduction. Other contributions focus on providing alternative discourses that challenge or disrupt current policy. Gruben and Cameron, for example, offer a response to the Court's ruling that struck down portions of the A H R A as unconstitutional violations of federal/provincial powers. Although this ruling perpetuated the dominant medical-centred discourse, Gruben and Cameron offer an alternative discourse that understands the regulation of reproductive technologies in terms of protecting women's physical and psychological health and preventing the potential exploitation of women in the use of these technologies. Lee's contribution on breastfeeding offers another strategy to disrupt the dominant discourses of maternalism and medicalization in reproductive policy. In the case of breastfeeding, these discourses, which focus on infant nutrition, render women's behaviour subject to public scrutiny and external moral authority. To problematize these discourses, Lee turns to Foucault's notion of care of the self as a way for the breastfeeding subject to conceive of, and through moral work, achieve her sense of self. These chapters and others in the volume identify opportunities for resistance and change in the politics of reproduction at the individual and policy levels.

Together, the chapters in *Fertile Ground* provide insights into the linkages between the politics of reproduction, the state, society, and unequal gender relations in Canada. Issues of reproductive health, fertility, pregnancy, and motherhood can no longer be "stove-piped," without recognizing how reproduction and reproductive health are connected in the wider experience of a woman's life and the political cultural, social, and economic structures that inform and are informed by this experience. As evident in the scholarship brought together in this volume, these linkages speak to the continued importance of reproduction as a fertile site for women's activism, feminist scholarship, and interdisciplinary research. Indeed, many research areas related to reproduction and reproductive health call for further exploration. One important avenue for further research that this contribution raises includes other moments of a woman's reproductive life. Considering that Canada is experiencing an aging population, issues related to menopause, such as hormone replacement therapy and hysterectomies, call for a wider understanding of reproductive health that moves beyond the narrow view of having babies. The implications of advances in medical technology as well as trends in maternal care and health care funding for women's reproductive autonomy and rights provide another area of research for scholars. Finally, this volume's emphasis on reproductive justice also urges researchers to examine how social, economic, and labour market policies contribute to or ameliorate power inequalities in society, which, in turn, shape women's reproductive desires, choices, and expectations throughout their lives. These and other under-explored areas of research will continue to provide fertile ground for the study of reproduction in Canada.

BIBLIOGRAPHY

Apple, R. 1987. *Mothers and Medicine*. Madison: University of Wisconsin Press.

Arneil, Barbara. 2000. "The Politics of the Breast." *Canadian Journal of Women and the Law/Revue Femmes et Droit* 12: 346–70.

Arnup, K., A. Levesque, and R. Roach Pierson. 1990. *Delivering Motherhood: Maternal Ideologies and Practices in the 19th and 20th Centuries*. New York: Routledge.

Bacchi, C. 1999/2005. *Women, Policy and Politics: The Construction of Policy Problems*. Thousand Oaks: Sage Publications.

Basen, G., M. Eichler, and A. Lippman. 1993. *Misconceptions: The Social Construction of Choice and the New Reproductive and Genetic Technologies*. Hull, QC: Voyageur Publishing.

Bezanson, K., and M. Luxton, eds. 2006. *Social Reproduction: Feminist Political Economy Challenges Neo-liberalism*. Montreal & Kingston: McGill-Queen's University Press.

Bourgeault, I.L. 2006. *Push! The Struggle for Midwifery in Ontario*. Montreal & Kingston: McGill-Queen's University Press.

Bourgeault, I.L., C. Benoit, R. and Davis-Floyd, eds. 2004. *Reconceiving Midwifery*. Montreal & Kingston: McGill-Queen's University Press.

Brodie, J., J. Jenson, and S. Gavigan, S. 1992. *The Politics of Abortion*. Don Mills: Oxford University Press Canada.

Cawthorne, J.. 2010. "Maternal Health Initiative is the Mother of Bad Policy." *The Globe and Mail*, 27 April.

Code, L. 1991. *What Can She Know? Feminist Theory and the Construction of Knowledge*. Ithaca: Cornell University Press.

Colen, S. 1986. "With Respect to Feelings." In *All American Women: Lines that Divide, Lines that Bind*, Johnnetta B. Cole, ed. 46–70. New York: Free Press.

Cossman, B. 2002. "Family Feuds: Neo-Liberal and Neo-Conservative Visions of the Reprivatization Project." In *Privatization, Law, and the Challenge to Feminism*, B. Cossman and J. Fudge, eds. 169–217. Toronto: University of Toronto Press.

Davis, Dana-Ain. 2009. "The Politics of Reproduction: The Troubling Case of Nadya Suleman and Assisted Reproductive Technology." *Transforming Anthropology*, 17(2): 105–16.

Ginsberg, F., and R. Rapp, eds. 1995. *Conceiving the New World Order: The Global Politics of Reproduction*. Berkeley: University of California Press.

Hajer, M. 2006. "Discourse Analysis and Discourse Coalitions." In *Words Matter in Policy and Planning: Discourse Theory and Method in the Social Sciences*, M. Van den Brink and T. Metze, eds., 65–74. Utrecht: Koninklijk Nederlands Aardrijkskundig Genootschap.

Harrison, L. 2010. "Brown Bodies, White Eggs: The Politics of Cross-Racial Gestational Surrogacy." In *21st Century Motherhood: Experience, Identity, Policy, Agency*, A. O'Reilly, ed. 261–75. New York: Columbia University Press.

Haussman, M. 2001. "Of Rights and Power: Canada's Federal Abortion Policy 1969–1991." In *Abortion Politics, Women's Movements, and the Democratic State: A Comparative Study of State Feminism*, D. McBride Stetson, ed., 63–86. Oxford: Oxford University Press.

– 2005. *Abortion Politics in North America*. Boulder, CO: Rienner Publishers, Inc.

– 2013. *Reproductive Rights and the State: Getting the Birth Control, RU-486, and Morning-after Pills and the Gardasil Vaccine to the US Market*. Santa Barbara, CA; Praeger.

Johnson, C. 2009. "The Political 'Nature' of Pregnancy and Childbirth." *Canadian Journal of Political Science* 41(4): 889–913.

Kallianes, V., and P. Rubenfeld. 1997. "Disabled Women and Reproductive Rights." *Disability & Society* 12(2): 203–22.

Knaak, Stephanie J. 2006. "The Problem with Breastfeeding Discourse." *Canadian Journal of Public Health* 97(5): 412–14.

Lippman, A. 1999. "Choice is a Risk to Women's Health." *Health, Risk & Society* 1(3): 281–91.

Little, M. 1998. *No Car, No Radio, No Liquor Permit: The Moral Regulation of Single Mothers in Ontario, 1920–1997*. Don Mills: Oxford University Press Canada.

Malterud, K., L. Candib, and L. Code. 2004. "Responsible and Responsive Knowing in Medical Diagnosis: The Medical Gaze Revisited." *Nora: Nordic Journal of Women's Studies* 12(1): 8–19.

Mitchinson, W. 1991. *The Nature of Their Bodies: Women and Their Doctors in Victorian Canada*. Toronto: University of Toronto Press.

– 2002. *Giving Birth in Canada, 1900–1950*. Toronto: University of Toronto Press.

Nathoo, T., and A. Ostry. 2009. *The One Best Way? Breastfeeding History, Politics, and Policy in Canada.* Waterloo: Wilfred Laurier Press.

Nossiff, R. 1998. "Discourse, Party, and Policy: The Case of Abortion, 1965–1972." *Policy Studies Journal* 26(2), 244–56.

O'Brien, M. 1981. *The Politics of Reproduction.* Boston: Routledge and Kegan Paul.

Paterson, S. 2010. "Feminizing Obstetrics or Medicalizing Midwifery? The Discursive Constitution of Midwifery in Ontario." *Critical Policy Studies* 4(2): 127–45.

– 2011. "Midwives, Women, and the State: (De)Constructing Midwives and Pregnant Women in Ontario, Canada." *Canadian Journal of Political Science* 44(3): 483–505.

Ross, L. 1998. "African-American Women and Abortion." In *Abortion Wars: A Half Century of Struggle, 1950–2000*, R. Solinger, ed. 161–207. Berkeley: University of California Press.

Rothman, B. Katz. 1989. *Recreating Motherhood.* New Jersey: Rutgers University Press.

– 2004. "Motherhood under Capitalism." In *Consuming Motherhood*, J.S. Taylor, L.L. Layne, and D.F. Wozniak, eds. 19–30. New Jersey: Rutgers University Press.

Scala, F., E. Montpetit, and J. Fortier. 2005. "Organizational Practices, Policy Influence and the NAC: The Case of Assisted Reproductive Technologies in Canada." *Canadian Journal of Political Science* 38(3): 581–604.

Sethna, C. 2006. "The Evolution of the Birth Control Handbook: From Student Peer Education Manual to Feminist Self-Empowerment Text, 1968–1975." *Canadian Bulletin of Medical History / Bulletin canadien d'histoire de la médecine* 23(1): 89–118.

Shroff, F. 1997. *The New Midwifery: Reflections on Renaissance and Regulation.* Toronto: Women's Press.

Silliman, J., M.G. Fried, L. Ross, and E. Gutierrez. 2004. *Undivided Rights: Women of Color Organizing for Reproductive Justice.* Cambridge, MA: South End Press.

Simonds, W., B. Katz Rothman, and B. Norman. 2007. *Laboring On: Birth in Transition in the United States.* New York: Routledge.

Smith, A. 2005. "Beyond Pro-Choice versus Pro-Life: Women of Color and Reproductive Justice." *NWSA Journal* 17(1): 119–40.

Solinger, R. 1998. *Abortion Wars: A Half Century of Struggle, 1950–2000.* Berkeley: University of California Press.

Thachuk, A. "Midwifery, Informed Choice, and Reproductive Autonomy: A Relational Approach." *Feminism & Psychology* 17(1): 39–56.

Twine, F.W. 2012. *Outsourcing the Womb: Race, Class and Gestational Surrogacy in a Global Market.* New York: Routledge.

Valverde, M. 1992. "'When the Mother of the Race is Free': Race, Reproduction, and Sexuality in First Wave Feminism." In *Gender Conflicts: New Essays in Women's History*, M. Valverde, ed. 3–26. Toronto: University of Toronto Press.

Vosko, L. 2000. *Temporary Work: The Gendered Rise of a Precarious Employment Relationship.* Toronto: University of Toronto Press.

Wajcman, J. 1991. *Feminism Confronts Technology.* University Park: Pennsylvania State University Press.

Weir, L. 2006. *Pregnancy, Risk and Biopolitics: On the Threshold of the Living Subject.* New York: Routledge.

Williams, C. 2004. "Race (and Gender and Class) and Child Custody: Theorizing Intersections in Two Canadian Court Cases." *N W S A Journal* 16(2): 46–69.

Contributors

ANGELA CAMERON is associate professor in the Faculty of Law, University of Ottawa. Her research is generally in the area of social justice, with a particular focus on the equality interests of women. She is the administrator of bloggingforequality.ca.

ALANA CATTAPAN is a PhD candidate in political science at York University, and an incoming postdoctoral fellow in the Faculty of Medicine at Dalhousie University. Her work examines the intersections of women's health, biotechnology, and citizenship theory.

VANESSA GRUBEN is an associate professor in the Faculty of Common Law at the University of Ottawa. She has recently published articles in the *Canadian Journal of Women and the Law* and the *Canadian Journal of Family Law*.

DIANA L. GUSTAFSON is an associate professor of social science and health in the Faculty of Medicine at Memorial University. She has recently published articles in *Women's Studies International Forum*, *Qualitative Health Research*, *Atlantis*, and *Maternal and Child Health*. She and Marilyn Porter co-authored *Reproducing Women: Family and Health Work Across Three Generations* (Fernwood Publishing, 2012).

CANDACE JOHNSON is an associate professor in the Department of Political Science at the University of Guelph. Her latest book, *Maternal Transition: A North-South Politics of Pregnancy and Childbirth* (Routledge, 2014), examines reproductive preferences in Canada, the United States, Cuba, and Honduras.

ERIN MARIE KONSMO is Michif/Cree from Onoway/Lac St. Anne, Alberta and holds a Masters in Environmental Studies from York University. She is the Media Arts Justice & Projects Coordinator for the Native Youth Sexual Health Network and works at the community level to provide visual and multi-media art that creatively resists terra nullius (empty land/empty bodies) over Indigenous spaces.

ROBYN LEE is a postdoctoral fellow in environmental ethics and health at York University.

TASNIM NATHOO has a clinical background in mental health and addiction. Her current research relates to women, trauma, pregnancy, and addiction. She lives in Vancouver.

ALECK OSTRY is professor in the Faculty of Social Sciences at the University of Victoria. He holds a Canada Research Chair in the Social Determinants of Community Health and is also a senior scholar with the Michael Smith Foundation for Health Research in British Columbia. He conducts an extensive program on the social determinants of health with a focus on rural health, food security, and nutrition policy.

STEPHANIE PATERSON is an associate professor in the Department of Political Science at Concordia University. Her areas of expertise include feminist policy analysis, state feminism, and reproductive politics.

JULIA THOMSON-PHILBROOK is a PhD candidate in the Department of Political Science at the University of Connecticut. Her dissertation, "What's Culture Got to Do With It? Explaining Abortion Policy in Modern Democracies," analyzes abortion policy change in fifty states.

MARILYN PORTER is professor emerita in the Department of Sociology at Memorial University. She publishes mostly in the areas of women's economic lives, especially in maritime contexts and is the editor (with Linda Cullum) of *Creating This Place: Women, Family, and Class in St John's, 1900-1950* (MQUP, 2014).

FRANCESCA SCALA is an associate professor in the Department of Political Science at Concordia University. Her research areas include health policy, human biotechnology, and gender and public policy.

MARLENE K. SOKOLON is an associate professor in the Department of Political Science at Concordia University. She specializes in political theory, especially in political emotions, politics and literature, ethics, and the interconnection between sociocultural and physiological processes.

MICHELLE WALKS is a post-doctoral fellow at the University of Ottawa researching "Transmasculine Individuals' Experiences with Pregnancy, Birthing, and Feeding Their Newborns: A Qualitative Study." She co-edited *An Anthropology of Mothering* (Demeter Press, 2011), and served as the guest editor of "Queer Anthropology," a special issue of *Anthropologica* (May 2014).

SARAH MARIE WIEBE holds a post-doctoral fellowship with the Institute for Studies and Innovation in Community-University Engagement at the University of Victoria. Her work focuses on struggles for environmental and reproductive justice, biopolitics, and feminist visual media.

LISA YOUNG is an academic, yoga teacher, activist, musician, and mother of two young boys. She recently completed a PhD in sociology at Carleton University, Ottawa, Canada. Her research focuses on moral and social regulation of youth and reproductive technologies. Her work has appeared in *Social Compass*.

Index

Page numbers in italics refer to figures and tables. See the front of the book for a list of abbreviations used in the index (and the text).

Aamjiwnaang community: body mapping study, 343–4, *344f*; community-based health investigation, 339, 343–4, 347–9, 354n11; lifestyle discourse and reproductive harm, 348–9; live-birth-sex ratios, 339–40, *341f*, *342t*, 348; micro practices of colonialization, 337–8; perceived male "birth dearth," 327, 338–9; seeking reproductive justice, 338–45, 349–52, 352n2; technologies of power and reproductive justice, 347–9. *See also* Aboriginal and Indigenous communities

Aamjiwnaang First Nation Health and Environment committee, 338

Abbott, Deborah, 217

Aboriginal and Indigenous communities: in A B M literature, 190; access to reproduction services, 62, 95; birth experience, 114; breastfeeding rates, 207, 290; and colonialism, 16, 114, 336–7; and federal health policy, 354n9; and gender, 353n3, 353nn7–8; maternal mortality, 102, 118n7; reproductive body embedded in place, 332–8. *See also* Aamjiwnaang community

abortion and abortion rights: and access, 146, 185, 233, 248, 249; Canadian illusion of freedoms, 248–9; constitutionalization in US, 239–42; criminalization, 233–4, 249, 251n13; and liberal governance of ARTs, 167–8; from medical to rights-based models, 13, 243–4, 246–8; mothers and daughters information sharing, 38, 42–3; prominence of debate, 22; public opinion and practice, 230–1, 250nn1–2; and socio-economic factors, 116–17n1; US and Canada compared, 233

Abortion Law Reform Association, 235

Abortion Rights Coalition of Canada, 230–1, 248

Abu-Duhou, Jamileh, 76

access to reproduction services: and Aboriginal and Indigenous communities, 62, 95; abortion and abortion rights, 146, 185, 233, 248, 249; childbirth preferences and health care systems, 114; excluded individuals and groups, 74–5, 82–4, 86n1, 136, 149n31, 171; policy versus practice, 170–2; pressure to increase access to ARTS, 152–3; rights discourses versus access, 12, 14, 362; and social policy as agent of change, 68–70, 167–72

activism. See feminist movements and scholarship

adoption, 31, 53, 55, 74

agency: and autonomy conceptions, 302–3; to express values in reproductive life, 42; feminism and the pill, 258; meaningful choice and, 37–9. See also choice/choice-based model of reproduction; reproductive autonomy

Agnew, J., 181–2

Alberta: midwifery, 184

Alesse (Wyeth), 14, 257–9, 268–76. See also web-based marketing of the pill

Allen, Amy, 309–10

allopathism in childbirth, 187–8, 191

Allowance for Newborn Children (Quebec), 67

alternative birth movement (ABM)/ home births: and biomedical history of birth, 183–7; challenge to medical model, 187–92; as classist, heteronormative, and racialized, 189–91, 199n9; and licensing midwifery, 178–80, 193–7; literature on (list), 186; preferences compared with medicalized childbirth, 99–100, 103–12; spatial politics of reproduction, 12, 179–80 (see also scalar politics); as "traditional," 108–9. See also midwifery

Ambrose, Rona, 3

American Law Institute (ALI), 237

American Medical Association (AMA), 237

Arms, S., 187, 188–90, 191–2, 199n9

Arneil, Barbara, 221

Arthur, Joyce, 249

arts-based approaches, 351–2. See also intersectionality

Assisted Human Reproduction Act (AHRA) (Canada): and consent, 148n18 (see also consent); effect on women's reproductive autonomy, 130–7, 362–3; and evolving public policy, 52, 173–4; history of, 128–30, 164–5; policy versus practice (and access), 9, 58, 68–9, 166–72, 170–2; Quebec's challenge to, 11, 125–6, 129–30, 147n7. See also assisted reproductive technologies (ARTS)

Assisted Human Reproduction Agency of Canada, 136, 143, 165

assisted insemination (AI): history of, 49–50; terminology, 70n2. *See also* new reproductive technologies

assisted reproductive technologies (ARTs): in chapter overviews, 11–12; citizenship and regulation of, 154–5; criminal regulation of, 149n29, 149nn25–6; and feminist scholarship, 50; governing of, 166–72; and government health care funding, 61–2; history of public policy and, 162–6; politics of provision of, 48–52; pressure to increase access, 152–3; regulation of, 140–5, 146–7. *See also* Assisted Human Reproduction Act (AHRA); funding; in vitro fertilization (IVF); new reproductive technologies

Attorney General of Quebec v. Attorney General of Canada, 125, 129–32

autonomy. *See* reproductive autonomy

Baby-Friendly Initiative/Baby-Friendly Hospital Initiative, 209, 212, 220, 288, 291, 291t, 294

Backhouse, Constance, 234

Baird, Patricia, 129, 139

Baker, David, 61

Ball, C.A., 22–3

Barrington, Eleanor, 179, 188, 199n8; *Midwifery is Catching,* 186, 189–90

Bartlett, Allison, 215, 312

Bashevkin, Sylvia, 251n13

Beatie, Thomas, 75, 88n6

Bertaux, D., 33

Bezanson, Kate, 21

Bhabha, Faisal, 61

Bhabha, Homi, 353n6

Bill C-13. *See* Assisted Human Reproduction Act (AHRA)

Bill C-43, 230, 247

Bill C-47, 164

Bill C-389, 83, 84, 90n11

Bill M-207, 83, 84, 90n11

biomedical model. *See* medicalization of reproduction

birth. *See* alternative birth movement (ABM)/home births; medicalization of reproduction; pregnancy

birth certificates, 74–5

Black Women's Caucus (US), 332

Bloc Québécois, 129. *See also* Quebec

Blum, Linda, 304, 316

body and reproductive politics: body mapping study (Aamjiwnaang community), 343–4, 344f; from contaminated to regenerative, 349–52; and home (scalar politics), 183; reproductive body embedded in place, 329, 332–8, 352n2, 353n7

Bolduc, Yves, 67

Borowski v. Canada, 246–7

Bourne, Aleck, 235

Bourne, Hilary, 286

Bradley method of childbirth, 186

breastfeeding and breastfeeding guidelines: advocacy groups, 213–14, 219; baby-friendly and/or woman-friendly, 15–16, 212, 214–15, 220, 222–4, 288–9, 292, 293–4, 319–20, 363; breastfeeding as "natural" (essentialism),

215–18, 303; breastfeeding rates, 206–7, 285, 289, 291–2, 293, 319; breastfeeding substitutes, 207, 216, 283f, 284, 286, 287, 290–1, 294–5, 316; and ethics of care, 303–4, 310–12; exclusive breastfeeding, benefits, 209–11, 214; exclusive breastfeeding, definition, 208; exclusive breastfeeding, duration guidelines, 208–9, 222, 292; human milk banks, 288; infant mortality and mothering, 281–6; and masculine breastfeeding, 80–2; and maternal confidence, 294–5; and maternity leave allowances, 289, 295; medical model of, 12; and mother's weight loss, 208, 210–11, 306; and pleasure, 313–15; policy in Canada, 205–24; policy in Canada, promotion of, 286–7; policy in Canada, suggestions for, 220–3, 292–5; and power discourses, 304–7; queering breastfeeding, 314–15; romanticization of motherhood, 218–20; and sexual pleasure, 313–14; trends in practices, 289–92; women's autonomy, 301–3; and the workplace, 221, 223, 224, 316–17
Breastfeeding Anytime, Anywhere campaign, 288, 291t
Breastfeeding Committee of Canada (BCC), 216, 219, 288, 288, 291
British Columbia: access to ARTS, 57; breastfeeding in the workplace, 221; breastfeeding rates, 206–7, 293; history of reproductive social policy, 158; legislation

addressing non-normative gender identities, 83, 90n11; and queer reproduction, 74–6; study locations for butch lesbians, transmen, and genderqueer individuals reproduction study, 79–80, 90n10
British Fertility Society, 60
Brodie, Janine, 154, 161, 246
Browne, A., 347
Burger, Jack, 178
butch lesbians, transmen, and genderqueer individuals and reproduction, 74–86; parenting and accessing reproduction services, 82–4, 86n1; and a politics of transgender reproduction, 84–6; research methodologies, 78–80, 88–90n9; terminology, 87nn2–4, 88n7. *See also* lesbians
Butler, Judith, 183, 263, 312

Cameron, Angela, 68, 125–47, 274, 361, 362–3; chapter overview, 11; "Regulating the Queer Family," 170–1
Campbell, Angela, 143, 149n25
Canada Assistance Plan (1966), 184, 199n6
Canada Health Act (CHA) (1984), 52, 60–1, 62, 68, 184, 247–8
Canadian Association for the Repeal of the Abortion Law (CARAL), 236, 248, 250n8
Canadian Bar Association (CBA), 237–8, 243
Canadian Environmental Protection Act, 145
Canadian Fertility and Andrology Society, 60

Canadian government. *See* federal government (Canada)

Canadian Human Rights Act, 83

Canadian Maternity Experiences Survey, 319

Canadian Medical Association (CMA), 63–4, 237–8, 243, 247, 248

The Canadian Mother's Book (MacMurchy), 281–2, 284–5, 291t, 292

Canadians for Choice, 248

care of the self (Foucault): and breastfeeding as gifting, 310–11; and discourses of power, 307–9, 317; and ethics of care, 310–12; oppressive norms and therapeutic work, 318–19, 363; and pleasure, 312–15; relational theory, 309–12

Carmen, Andrea, 328

Casey v. Pennsylvania, 241, 251n12

Cattapan, Alana, 152–75, 274, 282, 361–2; chapter overview, 11–12

Chang, Virginia, 54

Charest, Jean, 152

Charter of Rights and Freedoms (Canada), 57, 232, 245

Chatelaine, 339

Chemical Valley (Canada), 339, 344

childbirth: preferences for delivery, 102–12. *See also* alternative birth movement (ABM)/home births

childcare policies. *See* social policy (reproduction)

Child-Tax Benefit (1992) (Canada), 161, 288

choice/choice-based model of reproduction: compared through

generations, 19–20; and "good mother"/"good parent," 8; meaningful choice, concept of, 24; meaningful choice, possibility of, xiv, 26–32, 44; and medical community, 62–3; and non-normative gender identities, 75 (*see also* butch lesbians, transmen, and genderqueer individuals and reproduction); relational model of choice, 20, 22–5, 32; and transmission of values, 39–43. *See also* agency; neo-liberalism; reproductive autonomy

Chrétien, Jean, 247, 251n13

Christakis, Nicholas, 54

church values: role in reproductive decisions, 38–9, 43; and social institution of family, 27

citizenship: in reproductive discourses, 14, 282; and reproductive rights, 153–5; and social citizenship, 98

class and education: and ABM, 189–90, 199n9; and breastfeeding, 218–20, 315–16; breastfeeding rates, 207; in state monitoring of mothers, 306–7; in web-based marketing of the pill, 273. *See also* discrimination; stratified reproduction

Code, Lorraine, 302

Code of Marketing of Breast-Milk Substitutes (WHO), 287, 288, 290–1, 291t

Colen, Shellee, 50, 77–8

College of Nurses of Ontario (CNO), 178

College of Physicians and Surgeons of British Columbia (CPSBC), 57

College of Physicians and Surgeons of Ontario (CPSO), 178, 179, 194–5

Collins, Patricia, 334

colonialism/colonial experience: and decentring of dominant culture, 353n6; and Indigenous feminism, 328; intersectionality and the body, 334–8; and reclaiming birth experience, 114; reproductive body embedded in place, 16, 329, 331–8

commodification/decommodification of IVF, 60–8, 139

Conrad, Peter, 53

consent: free, prior, and informed consent (FPIC), 328–9, 353n4; and reproductive autonomy, 133–5, 137, 143, 148n18 (see also reproductive autonomy)

Constitution Act (Canada): and abortion, 230–2; Quebec's challenge to AHRA, 125, 129–32, 145, 147n3

contraception: changing choices through, 27–8; mothers and daughters information sharing, 38–9, 40; the pill, changing conceptions of, 262–4; the pill and reproductive freedom, 259–62; the pill as a lifestyle drug, 258, 263–4; and reproductive rights, 94. See also web-based marketing of the pill

Cook, Katsi, 350

Cossman, Brenda, 156

courts. See criminal law power (of Parliament); Quebec Court of Appeal; Supreme Court (BC); Supreme Court of Canada

Cream, J., 263

Crenshaw, Kimberlé, 334

Criminal Code of Canada, 83, 140, 149n28, 236–7, 245–6. See also federal government (Canada)

criminal law power (of parliament), 126, 138, 140–5, 149nn27–8

Cromwell, Justice, 132, 137

Cruikshank, Barbara, 264–5

Cuba, 96, 117n4

Currie, Dawn, 267, 268

Davidson, Pat, 349

Daviss, B.A., 192

de Beauvoir, Simone, 260, 274, 302

Delcroix, C., 33

Deleuze, Gilles, 335

Deschamps, Justice, 132, 137, 139–40, 143

Dingwall, David, 164, 164

The Disappearing Male (CBC), 327

discourse, constitutional/rights-based, 230–3, 239–49. See also reproductive rights/freedom

discourse analysis: terminology, 13, 268–9

discourses of power (Foucault), 304–9, 317. See also care of the self

discrimination, 9, 55–8, 60, 69, 74, 83–4, 98, 136, 157, 170–5, 221, 335–6, 351. See also butch lesbians, transmen, and genderqueer individuals and reproduction; class and education; lesbians; race/ethnicity

Division of Child Welfare (Canada): advice manuals, 281

doctors. See physicians

donors and donations. See surrogacy and donors (embryos, gametes, and sperm)

Downie, Jocelyn, 22
Driscoll, C., 265, 273
Driskill, Qwo-Li, 337–8

Eberts, Mary, 193
Ecojustice report, 343, 344
Edney, Rachel, 193
education. *See* class and education
Edwardson, Dean, 348
Elias, B.D., 351
embryos. *See* surrogacy and donors
(embryos, gametes, and sperm)
endocrine disruptors (toxic pollution): environmental violence,
353n5; "gender-bending" language, 341; intersex animals,
337–8, 342–3
Environmental Health Perspectives,
327, 340
environmental politics/violence, 16,
330, 353n5
equality. *See* inequality/equality
essentialism (nature/natural discourses): and breastfeeding,
215–18, 301; and Foucault's
care of the self, 312; motherhood and caring, 303–4; and
natural childbirth terminology,
109–10; and reproductive freedom, 260–1
Established Programs Financing
(1977), 184
Estey, Justice, 140
ethics of care, 300, 303–4, 310–12.
See also morality
ethnicity. *See* race/ethnicity
evidence-based medicine (E B M):
and commodification of I V F,
60–5; terminology, 61. *See also*
medicalization of reproduction

Exclusive Breastfeeding Duration
(2004) (Health Canada), 206,
207–11, 221–2, 223. *See also*
breastfeeding and breastfeeding
guidelines; Health Canada
experience, politics of. *See* politics
of experience
Expert Advisory Panel on Exclusive
Breastfeeding, 213
Expert Working Group on
Breastfeeding, 288
Exposing Canada's Chemical Valley
(Ecojustice), 344

Fallon Jr, Richard, 231
family: children and social institution of, 27; in immigration status
and birth preferences study, 114–
15, 116; and meaning of "family
values," 57, 82–3; official recognition of queer families, 57,
74–5; Quebec as family-friendly,
66–7; as represented in A B M,
190; romanticization of (heterosexual), 41–3, 218–20; social and
ideological institution, 19–20,
43–4. *See also* generational case
study of reproductive lives
Family Allowance/Mothers'
Allowance, 156, 159–60. *See
also* welfare state
Family and Medical Leave Act
(F M L A) (US), 98
Farmer, Paul, 113
federal government (Canada): 1995
budget and reproductive funding,
160; abortion, parliament as
gatekeeper, 246–7, 249; abortion
law and medical discourse, 230,
232–3, 242–8, 250n6, 360–1;

and AHRA debates, 129; breast-feeding, cost of, 218–19; breast-feeding, promotion/education, 207–11, 288, 291t; breastfeed-ing, re-orienting, 220–3; breast-feeding, romanticized/"natural," 215–20; breastfeeding and wom-en's experience, 292–5; breast-feeding assumptions, 212; breastfeeding involvement (review of), 289–92; breastfeed-ing medicalization, 212–15; child benefit, 161, 288; criminal law power and legislative authority, 125–6, 137–45, 149nn27–8; health, response to Aamjiwnaang study, 344–5; health depart-ments, development of, 281; health policy, Indigenous, 354n9; and infant nutrition, 206, 213–14, 221–4, 291t; infertility, initia-tives to decrease, 169; and infertility treatment policy, 52; reproductive policies since Confederation, 3–5. See also Criminal Code of Canada; feder-alism; Health Canada; social pol-icy (reproduction)

federalism: abortion, parliament as gatekeeper, 246–7, 249; and abortion law, 236–8, 242; effect on birth and breastfeeding initia-tives, 290–1; effect on women's reproductive autonomy, 11; and funding of health care services, 184; and lawmaking authority, 147n3; a particular scalar fix, 182; and Quebec's challenge to AHRA, 129–32, 138, 146–7; and stratification of reproduction,

67–8, 69–70, 75–6. See also federal government (Canada)

femininity/masculinity, 75, 80–2, 263, 264–6, 274

feminism, maternal. See maternalist discourses/feminisms

feminist movements and scholar-ship: and abortion, 232, 235–8, 239–41, 242, 244–8, 250n9; breastfeeding debates, 205–6, 220–1, 302; feminist citizenship, 157 (see also reproductive citi-zenship); and infertility treat-ments, 50; and the pill, 258, 259–62, 275; reproduction, sca-lar politics of, 183, 186, 189; and reproductive choice, 22; and reproductive justice movement, 333–4; and reproductive rights, history of, 4–7

fertility services. See assisted repro-ductive technologies (ARTS); in vitro fertilization (IVF)

Firearms Act (Canada), 145

Firestone, Shulamith, 260

Fiske, J., 347

Foucault, Michel, 335; Archeology of Knowledge, 268; The History of Sexuality, 308–9. See also care of the self (Foucault)

Fountain, Robin, 217

Fox, Bonnie, 35

Fox, Nick, 265

France: funding IVF treatments, 50; reproductive social policy, 158

Friedman, May, 304, 313

Fry, Hedy, 90n11

funding: for abortion, 241, 247–8, 251n10, 251n14; for ARTS, 153, 165–6, 169–70; for ARTS and state policy, 166–72, 173–5; commodification of medicalized infertility, 60–5; costs of breast-feeding, 219, 221; eligibility requirements, 50; health care services (Canada), history of, 184–5; in history of reproductive social policy, 156, 159–62; for IVF treatments, 48–9, 50–2, 65–6, 70n6; for Lambton Community Health Study, 345, 349; and medicalization, 53; for midwifery care, 108; neo-liberalism, breastfeeding, and infant care, 306

gametes, human. See surrogacy and donors (embryos, gametes, and sperm)
Gaskin, I., 190, 199n9
gay, queer, and lesbian: and ABM, 189–90, 199n9; citizenship and access to ARTs, 170–2, 173–4. À See also butch lesbians, transmen, and genderqueer individuals and reproduction; lesbians
gender identity: "gender-bending" language of endocrine-disruption, 341, 353n3; and gender politics, 6, 84–6; and human rights legislation, 83; and masculine pregnancy, 81–2; race and place in colonial context, 335, 353nn7–8. See also identity
gender inequality. See class and education; inequality/equality; lesbians; race/ethnicity; stratified reproduction
genderqueer individuals. See butch lesbians, transmen, and

genderqueer individuals and reproduction
generational case study of reproductive lives: H family, 32–9, 39–40; methodology, 19–20, 25–6; operation of choice insights, 43–4; P family, 26–32
Germany: funding IVF treatments, 50
Gerodetti, N., 84
Gibbons v. Ogden (1824) (US), 236
Giles, Fiona, 307, 310–11, 314–15
Ginsburg, Faye, 51
girl power/culture: "girl" and "girl power" terminology, 265–6; and "Reviving Ophelia" girls, 267. See also web-based marketing of the pill
Glaxo the Super-milk advertisement, 283f
Glennon, Theresa, 127
global reproduction preferences: studies comparing local and, 99–102
Globe: "Mothers of Canada," 283f
Gonick, Marnina, 259, 266, 271
"good mother"/"good parent," 8, 12, 15, 50, 281–3. See also breastfeeding and breastfeeding guidelines
government funding. See funding
government policy. See social policy (reproduction)
Granzow, Kara, 262, 271
Green Teens (Aamjiwnaang), 352
Griswold v. Connecticut (US), 239
Grossman, Joanna, 98
Gruben, Vanessa, 125–47, 274, 361, 362–3; chapter overview, 11
Guenther, K., 182

Gustafson, Diana, 19–47, 127, 223, 360; chapter overview, 9; *Women's Experience of Their Reproductive Lives*, 25

Halifax Lesbian Committee on Reproductive Technologies, 57
Hall, Stuart, 268
Hamann, Trent, 309
Hancock, Ange-Marie, 95
Harper, Stephen, 82, 230, 247, 247, 249, 249
Harris, Anita, 259, 264, 265–6, 267, 271
Harris v. McRae (1980) (US), 251n10
Hausman, Bernice, 218, 302, 306
Hazell, L., 189–90, 199n9; "Maternity Motel Complex," 191
Health Canada: baby-friendly and/ or woman-friendly, 214–15, 220, 222–4, 288–9; breastfeeding and advocacy conflicts, 12, 213–14, 219; *Exclusive Breastfeeding Duration* (2004), 206, 207–11, 221–2, 223; and Indigenous health policy, 354n9; *Reproductive and Genetic Technologies Overview Paper* (1999), 164; response to Aamjiwnaang health study, 344, 349. *See also* federal government (Canada)
health care systems: access and childbirth preferences, 114; compared, 199n7; effect on abortion law, 236; and evidence-based medicine (E B M), 60–5; funding for A R T s, 60–2, 169–70, 173;

funding for I V F treatments, 48–9, 50–2, 65–6, 70n6; and gender equality, 83; governing infertility treatments, 52; politics of, 346. *See also* funding; Health Canada; medicalization of reproduction; Quebec
healthism, 265
Health Professions Legislative Review (H P L R), 193
Heitman, Elizabeth, 54–5
Herbert, Spencer Chandra, 90n11
Holland, J., 274
home births. *See* alternative birth movement (A B M)/home births
Honduras, 96, 117n4
hooks, bell, 334
hospitals and health care institutions: and A B M's rescaling of birth, 191–2, 194–7, 199n13; and abortion, 243–4; baby-friendly initiatives, 209, 212, 216, 220, 288, 291, 291t, 294; births, rates in hospitals, 285; and marketing of breastmilk substitutes, 290, 294–5. *See also* scalar politics
human papillomavirus (H P V) vaccine, 6, 22, 262
Human Reproductive and Genetic Technologies Act (Canada), 164
Human Rights Commission (Quebec), 58
Human Rights Council (B C), 57
Human Rights Tribunal (B C), 74

identity: and biological capacity to procreate, 29; and body and home, 183; effect on health of inequality and, 113–16; gender,

6, 81–2, 83, 84–6, 335, 341,
353n3, 353nn7–8; and generational narratives, 35; and girl-
power, 265–6, 267–8, 270; and
moral work of breastfeeding,
317–18; and the pill, 263; of
women and motherhood, 76–7
Ignatieff, Michael, 231
immigrant mothers: "healthy immigrant effect," 113; and maternal
mortality, 102; post–Second
World War, 34–5; undue attention paid to, 290. See also immigration status and birth
preferences study
Immigrant Services of Guelph-
Wellington, 96
immigration status and birth
preferences study: childbirth
preferences compared, 10,
99–100, 103–12, 360; and global
maternal health, 112–16; methodology, 96–7, 97–102, 117n4;
"preferences" terminology,
117n3
inequality/equality: ARTs and
structural inequity, 50–2, 64–5,
68–70; and health care access,
83; and health outcomes, 97–8,
112–16; and maternal health
preferences, 102–12; protections
under AHRA, 125–6, 132–7; sex/
gender primary vector of, 99.
See also class and education;
lesbians; race/ethnicity; stratified
reproduction
Infant Feeding Expert Advisory
Group, 213–14, 219–20
infant mortality, 118n7, 281–6.
See also maternal mortality

infertility: as biomedical condition,
51–2, 53–4, 62–3. See also medicalization of reproduction
infertility treatments: and health status, 60; politics of public provision of, 48–9; and terminology of
"infertility," 54. See also assisted
reproductive technologies (ARTs);
in vitro fertilization (IVF)
intersectionality: and Aamjiwnaang
reproductive justice struggle,
329, 331–3, 351–2; and arts-
based approaches, 351–2; and
empirical testing, 95, 115–16,
117n2; in immigration status
and birth preferences study, 102–
3, 114–16; and politics of health
policy, 346–9; of reproductive
health and justice studies, 363–4;
terminology, 7, 94, 334
interviews. See studies, research
methodologies
in vitro fertilization (IVF): and age-
related infertility, 59; funding as
reducing costs of, 170; non-medical
state requirements for, 55–9;
social policy and reproduction,
162–3, 167–8; studies of effectiveness and cost, 64–5, 70nn4–
5; terminology, 70n3. See also
Assisted Human Reproduction
Act (AHRA); assisted reproductive
technologies (ARTs); funding;
new reproductive technologies
"involuntary childlessness," 54
Iran, 104–5
IVF. See in vitro fertilization (IVF)

Jackson, Emily, 127
Jenson, Jane, 235, 240, 243

Johnson, Candace, 21, 235, 334, 360; chapter overview, 10

Johnstone, Rachael, 22

judicial system. *See* criminal law power (of parliament); Quebec Court of Appeal; Supreme Court (BC); Supreme Court of Canada

Kaposy, Chris, 22

Kauffman, Karen, 193

Kiijig Collective (Aamjiwnaang), 352

King, Leslie, 52

Kitchin, R., 182

Kitzinger, S., 187–8, 189, 192, 199n9; *The Experience of Childbirth*, 188, 190

Knaak, Stephanie, 214, 217

Konsmo, Erin Marie, 325–6, 325–52, 332–3; chapter overview, 16; *Our Bodies Are Not Terra Nullius*, 326f

Korn v. Potter, 57–8

Kukla, Rebecca, 302

labour policy. *See* maternity leave

Lake St Clair, 342

La Leche League, 213, 215, 286, 287, 304, 313

Lamaze method of childbirth, 186

Lambton Community Health Study, 330, 339–41, 345, 347–9, 350, 354n12

Lang, R., 188, 190, 191, 199n9

Law, Jules, 211

LeBel, Justice Louis, 132, 137–40, 143

Lee, Jeeyeun, 97, 98

Lee, Robyn, 21, 217, 222, 293–4, 361–2, 363; chapter overview, 15

legislation. *See* Assisted Human Reproduction Act (AHRA) (Canada); British Columbia; federal government (Canada); Ontario; Quebec

lesbians: access to fertility services, 74–5, 136, 149n31, 170–2; terminology, 87n2. *See also* butch lesbians, transmen, and genderqueer individuals and reproduction; gay, queer, and lesbian; gender identity

liberal market policies. *See* neo-liberalism

liberal personhood. *See* agency

life stories. *See* generational case study of reproductive lives

Lockridge, Ada, 343

Luce, Jacquelyne, 85

Lupton, Deborah, 258, 311

Luxton, Meg, 21

MacDonald, Margaret, 179, 196

MacGregor, Sherilyn, 304

Mackenzie, Catriona, 307

McLachlin, Chief Justice, 137–9

McLaren, Angus, 259, 262

McLaren, Margaret, 308, 311

McLeod, Carolyn, 147n4

MacMurchy, Helen, 282, 284

McNay, Lois, 308

McTeer, Maureen, 144

McWhorter, Ladelle, 312

Mahon, R., 181

male consent in in vitro fertilization, 55–6

Manitoba: abortion access, 249; funding of IVF, 70n6, 166, 174

Marbury v. Madison (1803), 232, 239

Marleau, Diane, 164
marriage and marital status: and
    accessing ARTs treatment, 50,
    55–8, 68–9, 149n31, 170–2; and
    adoption, 74; choice and preg-
    nancy outside, 40; and social
    institution of family, 27
Marshall, T.H., 98, 118n5, 156
Marston, S., 181
Martin, Ben, 349
Martin, Paul, 247
masculinity. See femininity/
    masculinity
Massey, D., 181
Masson, D., 183
maternal health preferences.
    See mother/motherhood
maternalist discourses/feminisms,
    13–14, 15–16, 282, 304
maternal mortality, 101–2, 113,
    118n7
maternity leave, 98, 159, 295;
    and breastfeeding, 289, 295.
    See also pregnancy
May, Elaine Tyler, 262
meaningful choice. See choice/
    choice-based model of
    reproduction
Medical Care Act (1966) (Canada),
    184
medicalization of reproduction,
    5–6; and abortion law, 13, 234–
    5, 240, 242–8; allopathism and
    passivity in childbirth, 187–91,
    198n2, 199n10; and breastfeed-
    ing policy, 12, 212–15, 286–7,
    361; breastfeeding success mea-
    sures, 206; and butch lesbians,
    transmen, and genderqueer indi-
    viduals, 76; care of the self as

alternative model, 307; challenge
    of ABM, history of, 183–7; and
    Church control, 29; discourse,
    limits set by, 235, 361; infertility
    and physician gatekeepers, 49,
    51–2, 52–60, 61, 69; and insuf-
    ficient health information, 29–31;
    in midwifery legislation and prac-
    tice, 193–7; and preferences for
    childbirth, 99–100, 103–12; rela-
    tional moments alternative, 21–2;
    social policy and accessibility,
    167–72, 174; terminology, 16n1,
    52–3. See also evidence-based
    medicine (EBM); physicians
menarche: mothers and daughters
    information sharing, 35, 36–7,
    39–40
menopause, 21, 59
Men's Health, 338–9
methodologies. See studies, research
    methodologies
Meyer, David, 238, 242
Meyer, Madonna Harrington, 52
Michelle, Carolyn, 48
midwifery: and biomedical scalar
    discourses, 193–7, 197–8, 198n2;
    in history of abortion law, 233–
    4; and home birth debate, 179;
    licensing in Ontario, 178–80,
    193–7, 198n3; preferences com-
    pared to medicalized childbirth,
    99–100, 103–12, 118n9; and the
    Ritz Inquest (Ontario), 178–80;
    statistics on, 196
Midwifery Act (1991) (Ontario),
    195
Midwifery is Catching (Barrington),
    186, 189–90. See also
    Barrington, Eleanor

Midwives' Coalition, 194, 200n14
Millennium Development Goals,
   114
Monture-Angus, Patricia, 335
morality: breastfeeding as moral
   work, 315–20; in breastfeeding
   choices, 217–18, 220, 293;
   breastfeeding pressures, 301;
   in reproductive choices, 23–4.
   See also ethics of care
Morgentaler, Henry, 230, 244,
   250n2. See also *R. v. Morgentaler*
Morgentaler v. the Queen. See R. v.
   Morgentaler
mother/motherhood: breastfeeding
   and romanticization of, 218–20;
   and breastfeeding decisions,
   15–16, 293–4; breastfeeding
   pressures, 301; caring as "natural," 303–4; concept and operation of choice in, 22–3, 28–9,
   43–4, 261; evolving generational choices of, 9, 28–9; held
   responsible for infant mortality,
   282; loss of knowledge/auton-
   omy/control, 35–7, 41–2, 43–4,
   284–6, 304–7, 333; maternal
   confidence and breastfeeding,
   294–5; maternal health preferences, 10, 96, 99–100, 101–2,
   102–12, 112–16, 117, 118;
   mother-child dyad, 219–20,
   307; in popular/political discourse, 282, 283f; relational
   decision-making, 31–2; and
   sexual pleasure, 313–14; state
   and construction of, 11; and
   women's identity, 76–7. *See*
   also generational case study of
   reproductive lives; pregnancy

Mothers' Allowance. *See* Family
   Allowance/Mothers' Allowance
"Mothers of Canada" *(Globe), 283f*
Mottier, V., 84
Mullin, Amy, 22
Mulroney, Brian, 251n13
Murphy, Elizabeth, 314, 316
Murray, Stuart, 311, 320
Murtagh, Madeleine, 309
Muskoka Initiative on Maternal,
   Newborn, and Child Health, 3

Nathoo, Tasnim, 213, 222, 234,
   280–95, 303, 319–20, 361;
   chapter overview, 15
National Action League for the
   Repeal of the Abortion Law
   (NARAL) (US), 235–6, 250n7
National Child Benefit (1998)
   (Canada), 288
National Children's Agenda (1997)
   (Canada), 288
National Council of Family and
   Child Welfare (Canada), 284–5
nationalism: in reproductive dis-
   courses, 14
National Organization of Women
   (NOW), 235
National Right to Life committee
   (US), 240–1
Native Youth Sexual Health
   Network, 332
natural childbirth: terminology,
   109–10 (*see also* alternative birth
   movement (ABM)/home births)
nature/natural discourses. *See*
   essentialism (nature/natural
   discourses)
Nedelsky, Jennifer, 303–4
Nelson, Erin, 22

neo-liberalism: and alternative
health care services, 189, 193–4;
and gender, 334; and marketing
of the pill, 258, 273, 360; and
notions of choice, privilege, and
responsibility, 273, 305–6, 309,
360–2; power constructions and
girl power, 267; private and public distinction, 23; privileging of
the individual in policy, 5, 167,
172–3, 174; rights discourses
versus access, 12, 14, 362; and
scalar influences, 181, 194; and
state support for parenting/
reproduction, 161–2, 173, 306;
terminology, 16n1. See also
social policy (reproduction)
Nestel, Sheryl, 110
Nestlé boycott, 286
New Brunswick, 249
New Democratic Party (NDP), 238,
247
Newfoundland and Labrador, 9,
25–43; breastfeeding rates, 206–7
New Midwifery Movement (NMM),
192–3, 197, 198n4, 199n13
new reproductive technologies,
49–52, 94–5, 262; terminology,
49. See also assisted reproductive
technologies (ARTs); in vitro fertilization (IVF)
Nicholls, David, 316
North-South comparisons, 101,
102–3, 112–13

obesity, 60
O'Brien, Mary, 20–1, 260
Occupational Health Clinics for
Ontario Workers (OHCOW),
339, 343

O'Grady, Helen, 318
O'Neil, John, 351
Ontario: abortion criminalization,
234; biomedical scalar fix and
ABM, 183–7, 197–8; demand
for funding of IVF, 152, 173;
funding of Aamjiwnaang and
Lambton community health studies, 349; funding of IVF/ART
treatments, 61, 65–6, 166, 173;
licensing midwifery, 178–80,
193–7, 198n3; and midwifery
care, 108, 118n9; midwifery statistics, 196; Morgentaler case,
245. See also Aamjiwnaang community; R. v. Morgentaler
Ontario Health Insurance Plan
(OHIP), 184
Ontario Law Reform Commission,
55–6
Ostry, Aleck, 213, 222, 234, 280–
95, 303, 319–20, 361; chapter
overview, 15

Palmer, Gabrielle, 211, 218
parenthood, governing, 173. See
also reproductive citizenship
Parks, Jennifer, 59
passivity in childbirth, 187–8,
191
Paterson, Stephanie, 178–98, 215,
235, 362; chapter overview, 12
Payne, Deborah, 316
Payne, Mrs R., 284–5
Peddlesden, Jennifer, 219
pharmaceutical industry/drugs:
individualism, empowerment,
and healthism, 264–5. See also
contraception; web-based marketing of the pill

physicians: as abortion gatekeepers, 238, 243; and abortion reform, 235–7, 244–8; as birthing expert, 187; as breastfeeding experts, 213–14, 304–5; and criminalization of abortion, 233–4; infertility and E B M, 49, 51–2, 52–60, 61, 69; and licensing midwifery, 179; pediatricians as "baby feeders," 284–5

Picard, Pauline, 129

Plain, Ron, 327

Poirier v. British Columbia, 221, 223

politics of experience: overview, 7–10

politics of reproduction. *See* reproductive politics

Porter, Marilyn, 19–47, 127, 223, 360; chapter overview, 9; *Women's Experience of their Reproductive Lives*, 25

pregnancy, 6; allopathism and passivity in childbirth, 187–8, 191; and legal equality, 98; masculine, 80–2; and meaningful choice, 24–5; mothers and daughters sharing information, 35–9; outside marriage and choice, 40. *See also* childbirth; generational case study of reproductive lives; maternity leave; mother/ motherhood

Pregnancy Discrimination Act (P D A) (US), 98

private and public: arbitrary distinction of, 23; effect of privileging privacy, 127; varying experiences of, 114–15

pro-choice, 235–8, 239–41, 243–8, 249, 250n9, 250nn1–2. *See also*

feminist movements and scholarship; reproductive politics

pro-life groups, 240–1, 247, 250n1, 251n13

pronatalism, 51, 67

public health. *See* health care systems

Public Health Agency of Canada: *10 Great Reasons to Breastfeed*, 215, 218, 219, 288, 291*t*

public policy. *See* social policy (reproduction)

Quebec: challenge to A H R A, 11, 125–6, 129–32; funding of A R T s, 48–9, 65–8, 69, 152, 173–4; marketing of breastmilk substitutes laws, 290; maternity leave, 295; Morgentaler case, 244–5; regulation of reproductive technologies, 146–7, 149n31, 165–6; right to in vitro fertilization treatments, 58

Quebec Court of Appeal, 125, 129–32, 244–5

Quebec Human Rights Commission, 58

queer. *See* butch lesbians, transmen, and genderqueer individuals and reproduction

race/ethnicity: and A B M, 189–90, 199n9; and experience of breastfeeding, 315–16; and maternal mortality, 102; reproductive body embedded in place, 331–8; reproductive rights struggles, 94–5, 116–17n1; and romanticization of breastfeeding, 218–20; in state monitoring of mothers,

306–7; in web-based marketing
of the pill, 273. *See also*
Aboriginal and Indigenous communities; discrimination; stratified reproduction
Rapp, Rayna, 51
regional disparity, 5–6, 11, 49,
50–1, 65–8, 101–2, 118, 146–7
Registration of Live Birth (B C), 74,
86n1
relational autonomy. *See under*
reproductive autonomy
relational choice-based model. *See
under* choice/choice-based model
of reproduction
religion. *See* church values
remuneration for reproductive services: and commercial surrogacy,
148n17 (*see also* surrogacy and
donors (embryos, gametes, and
sperm)); and criminal law, 142–3
*Reproductive and Genetic
Technologies Overview Paper*
(1999) (Health Canada), 164.
See also Health Canada
reproductive autonomy: complicated by social location, 23–4;
criminal regulation of, 141–5,
149nn25–6, 149nn28–9; effect
of A H R A and consent, 133–5,
137, 143, 148n18; effect of
A H R A on, 11, 130–7, 146–7,
169–70; effect of A H R A on
health and well-being, 135–7;
effect of A H R A on services, 133;
and meaningful choice, 26–43;
and neo-liberal governance, 167;
protections under A H R A, 125–6;
relational autonomy, 128, 303;
in reproductive politics, 8; and

social norms, 317–19, 319–20;
terminology, 126–8, 147n4, 302–
3. *See also* agency; reproductive
rights/freedom
reproductive choice. *See* choice/
choice-based model of
reproduction
reproductive citizenship, 152–75;
and A R T s in Canada, 166–72;
concept of, 155–8; emergence of,
154–5; and evolving public policy, 173–5; and gay, queer and
lesbian access to A R T s, 170–2;
and medical model, 11–12; social
policy and the individual,
158–62
reproductive health: and environmental justice, 350; and funding
of A R T s, 170; place of breastfeeding in, 206; protections
under A H R A, 135–7, 139–40,
143, 146–7; relationship to
women's health, 3; wider linkages of, 363–4; and women's
health, 11, 135–7, 139, 148, 149,
210–11, 258, 271–2. *See also*
reproductive lives
reproductive justice: intersectional
analysis, 331–8, 363–4; and lived
experience, 113, 328, 338–45;
neo-liberalism and medicalization, 5; political processes and
Aamjiwnaang, 345–9; and social
justice, xii–xv, 8, 85, 351–2. *See
also* reproductive politics
reproductive knowledge, 35–7,
41–2, 43–4, 284–6, 304–7, 333
reproductive lives, 4; and breastfeeding, 223–4; extend beyond
menarche and menopause, 21;

integrated into life narratives, 19,
360; intersecting discrete policy
areas, 6–7, 8; negotiating oppressions and hierarchies, 8; and
relational moments, 20–2; terminology, 4, 21–2
reproductive moments: terminology,
4. *See also* reproductive health
reproductive politics: choice,
changing conceptions of, 262–4;
choice, responsibility of, 261–2;
and constitutionalization of
abortion (US), 239–42; in
Lambton County Chemical
Valley, 340–1; and medicalization of abortion (Canada), 242–
8, 249; policy and practice gap,
82–4; politics of transgender
reproduction, 84–6; and public
provision of infertility treatments, 48–9; scalar politics of
reproduction (*see* scalar politics);
shifting dialogue, 3–7; subjectivity, discourse, and power, 13–16,
304–7. *See also* reproductive
justice
reproductive rights/freedom:
Canadian illusion of, 248–9; and
citizenship, 153–5; constitutional
challenge to abortion laws (US),
239–42, 251n12; overview, 11,
13; and the pill, 259–62; and
queer reproduction, 74–6; social
or human rights, 63–4, 94–5,
118n5. *See also* choice/choice-
based model of reproduction;
reproductive autonomy
reproductive services: and AHRA,
133; and gender equality, 83–4;
and remuneration, 142–3

reproductive technologies. *See*
assisted reproductive technolo-
gies (ARTS)
reproductive tourism, 68
Restell, Madame, 233–4
Rich, Adrienne, 118n9, 314
rights-based framework. *See* repro-
ductive rights/freedom
Riot Grrrl bands, 266
Rippeyoung, Phyllis, 306
Ritz Inquest, 178–80
Roberts, Dorothy, 51, 94–5
Rock, Allan, 164
Rodgers, Sandra, 132
Rodwin, Marc, 61
Roe v. Wade (1973) (US), 231–2,
238, 239–42, 246, 248, 250n3,
251n11
Rose, Nicolas, 264
Royal Commission on Aboriginal
Peoples (RCAP), 336
Royal Commission on New
Reproductive Technologies
(RCNRT) and *Proceed with Care*
(report), 56–7, 59, 62, 64–5, 129,
134, 148n17, 163, 166–72
Royal Victoria Hospital (Montreal),
286
Rubin, Eva, 238
Ruby, Clayton, 178
Ruhl, Leslie, 259, 261, 273–4
rural. *See* urban/rural context
R. v. Morgentaler, 149n28, 231–2,
238, 242, 245, 247, 248–9
Ryan, Kath, 317
Ryan, Marua, 65

Sanger, Margaret, 274, 275;
Women and the New Race, 261
Sawicki, Jana, 169, 311–12

Scala, Francesca, 48–70, 274, 361; chapter overview, 9; "Experts, Non-experts, and Policy Discourse," 167–8

scalar politics: and A B M's challenge, 186–7; the body and the household, 183; homes and hospitals and A B M, 187–92, 194–7, 199n13, 362; and hospitals in medicalization of birth, 185; in identity formation, 12; terminology, 179, 180–2, 198n5

Schlachtenhaufen, Mary, 54–5

Schmied, Virginia, 311

Schwartz, Alan, 193

science: solving social problems, 284–5. See also medicalization of reproduction

Sclater, Shelly Day, 127

Scowby v. Glendinnning, 140

Second World War, 34–5

self-insemination (s i), 70n2, 171. See also assisted insemination (a i)

sexual citizenship, 156–7. See also reproductive citizenship

sexuality: and accessing infertility treatments, 50, 54, 55–8, 68–9; motherhood and, 313–14; and queer reproduction rights, 74–6; and right to a r t s, 63–4. See also gender identity; stratified reproduction

Sherwin, Susan, 24, 44

Shiva, Vandana, 335

Siksay, Bill, 90n11

Simonton, Ann, 205, 216

Smith, Dorothy, 268

Smith, Linda Tuhiwai, 328, 335, 337, 353n7

Smith, Lisa, 257–76, 360, 362; chapter overview, 14–15

Smith, N., 181

social citizenship. See under citizenship

social location, 7–9, 14, 23–4, 27, 50–1, 114. See also class and education; inequality/equality; race/ethnicity

social policy (reproduction): breastfeeding, Canadian policy, 206–11, 220–3, 280–1, 282; breastfeeding as cultural norm, 215–16; breastfeeding assumptions, 212; breastfeeding goals, 207–8; and citizenship, 158–62, 166–72; as family-friendly, 66–7; health policy and reproductive justice, 345–9; history of, 158–62; Indigenous people and reproductive justice, 329–31; and medicalization, 53; national role of mothers, 282; overview of, 10–13; and politics of scale, 180–3; and popular and political discourse, 282, 283f; privileging of the individual in, 5, 172 (see also neo-liberalism); provincial legislation, 83, 90n11; reforms and new initiatives and a r t s, 172–5; and stratified reproduction, 8, 50–2. See also British Columbia; federal government (Canada); Ontario; Quebec; United Kingdom; United States

social reproduction: terminology, 21

Society of Obstetricians and Gynaecologists of Canada, 287

socio-economic factors, 55–8, 99–100, 103–4, 113–14. *See also* funding

Sokolon, Marlene, 21, 205–24, 288, 303, 306, 361; chapter overview, 12

Staggenborg, Suzanne, 238, 242

state policy. *See* social policy (reproduction)

Stearns, Cindy, 314

Steinberg, Deborah Lynn, 54

Stoljar, Natalie, 307

Stowe, Dr Emily, 234

stratified reproduction: in analysis of reproductive technologies, 9–10; and distribution of reproductive benefits, 49–52, 64–5, 68–70; and health status, 59; and masculine pregnancy and breastfeeding, 80–2; and sexuality, 76–8; and socio-economic status, 54–8, 94–5; terminology, 50, 77

studies, research methodologies: Aamjiwnaang First Nation and reproductive justice, 329–31, 339–40, 341*f*, 342*t*, 348; of breastfeeding, 208, 210–11; of butch lesbians, transmen, and genderqueer individuals and reproduction, 78–80, 88–90n9 (*see also* butch lesbians, transmen, and genderqueer individuals and reproduction); discourse analysis of web-based marketing of the pill, 268–9 (*see also* web-based marketing of the pill); of effectiveness and cost of IVF, 64–5, 70nn4–5; generational case study of reproductive lives, 25–6 (*see also* generational case

study of reproductive lives); intersectional analysis of maternal health preferences, 96–7, 97–102, 103, 117nn3–4 (*see also* immigration status and birth preferences study); scalar theory and methodological nationalism, 181 (*see also* scalar politics)

sudden infant death syndrome (SIDS), 209, 214

Supreme Court (BC), 57–8

Supreme Court of Canada: on abortion, 230–1, 243–6, 360–1 (*see also* abortion and abortion rights); Quebec's challenge to AHRA, 11, 68, 125–6, 129–32, 137–45, 146–7; on regulation of fertility clinics, 68

surrogacy and donors (embryos, gametes, and sperm): challenging norms, 51; commercial, 52, 133, 138, 142, 148n17, 163, 165, 171–2; and feminist research, 49–50; reproductive technologies and autonomy, 132; risks, 148–9nn20–21; and social policy, 65, 129–30, 133–4, 138, 141–2, 145, 163, 165, 171–2

Sweden, 52

Swiss Chalet Restaurant, 221

Switzerland, 50

Swyngedouw, E., 180, 182

Task Force for the Implementation of Midwifery in Ontario (TFIMO), 193–5

Tatalovich, Raymond, 234, 235

Taylor, Dianna, 310

10 Great Reasons to Breastfeed, 215, 218, 219, 288, 291*t*

10 Valuable Tips for Successful Breastfeeding, 288
"test-tube" babies. *See* in vitro fertilization (IVF)
therapeutic abortion committee (TAC) system, 238, 243, 246
Thomson-Philbrook, Julia, 230–49, 360; chapter overview, 13
Tone, Andrea, 260, 262, 275
traditional childbirth: terminology, 108–9 (*see also* alternative birth movement (ABM)/home births)
transmen and transgender reproduction. *See* butch lesbians, transmen, and genderqueer individuals and reproduction
transversal politics, 10, 100–3, 113
Tremblay v. Daigle, 246–7
Turner, Bryan: "The Erosion of Citizenship," 155–8, 161–2, 170, 173

United Kingdom: abortion criminalization, 234, 250n6; access and policy versus practice, 170–2; infertility treatments and health status, 60; reproductive rights and citizenship, 155
United Nations: Convention on the Rights of the Child, 287–8; Declaration on the Rights of Indigenous People, 328, 354n11; UNICEF/WHO and Baby-Friendly Hospital Initiative, 209, 220, 288, 291, 291t, 294
United States: abortion and constitutionalization, 231–3, 239–42, 250n3, 251n12; abortion criminalization, 233–4, 250n5; abortion law, federal and state, 236–8, 248; access to infertility treatments, 50, 51, 94–5; breast-feeding, 210–11; breastfeeding rates, 206; economics of infertility treatments, 65; governing ARTS compared with Canada, 167; health care system compared to Canada, 199n7; intersectionality studies in, 98–100; pregnancy and discrimination, 98
Universal Declaration of Human Rights (UN), 153
University of Guelph, 96
urban/rural context: and operation of choice, 38

values: choice and transmission of, 19–20, 39–43; and family, 19–20, 42–3, 57, 82–3, 219; social values and criminal law, 142. *See also* family
Vintges, Karen, 309
violence: colonial legacy against women, 336–7; environmental violence, 330, 353n5

Walks, Michelle, 58, 113, 361; chapter overview, 9–10
Ward, Katie, 265
Watkins, E., 260, 275
web-based marketing of the pill: conflicting representations, 14–15, 274–5, 360; "girl power" campaigns, 257–9; girl-power environment of websites, 269–71; "girl power"/"Reviving Ophelia"/"girls-at-risk," 271–3, 275–6; methodology of study of, 268–9; the pill and girls'

self-control, 258–9; responsibility and control, 273–4
*Webster v. Reproductive Health
Services* (1989) (US), 251n10
Weisskopf, M.G., 342
Weldon, Laurel, 94, 113–14
welfare of the child principle: and
age-related infertility, 59
welfare state: and ARTS services,
166; and history of reproductive
social policy, 159–62; and maternalist discourses, 14; Quebec and
rest of Canada, 66–7; rights and
obligations, 156; and stratified
reproduction, 50–2
Wells, Jonathan, 305
Wiebe, Sarah Marie, 113, 325–52;
chapter overview, 16
Wilton, R., 182
Women, Infant, and Children program (WIC) (US), 210–11, 320n1

women's health: and care of the
self (Foucault), 319–20; and
well-being and AHRA, 135–7.
See also reproductive health
World Health Organization
(WHO), 97; breastfeeding guidelines, 207, 209, 213, 220, 291,
291t, 294; on marketing of
breastmilk substitutes, 287, 288,
290–1, 291t

Yalom, Marilyn, 216
Yasmin (Bayer), 14, 257–9, 268–76.
See also web-based marketing
of the pill
Yassi, A., 351
Yee, Jessica, 332
Young, Alison Harvison, 167
Young, Iris Marion, 113–14,
314
Yuval-Davis, Nira, 100–1